THE
CRAFT

THE
CRAFT

HOW FREEMASONS
MADE THE
MODERN WORLD

JOHN DICKIE

PUBLICAFFAIRS

New York

For Iris, Charlotte and Elliot

PublicAffairs
Hachette Book Group
1290 Avenue of the Americas, New York, NY 10104
www.publicaffairsbooks.com
@Public_Affairs

Printed in the United States of America

Originally published in Great Britain in 2020 by Hodder & Stoughton, a
Hachette UK company

First US Edition: August 2020

Published by PublicAffairs, an imprint of Perseus Books, LLC, a subsidiary
of Hachette Book Group, Inc. The PublicAffairs name and logo is a
trademark of the Hachette Book Group.

The Hachette Speakers Bureau provides a wide range of authors for
speaking events. To find out more, go to www.hachettespeakersbureau
.com or call (866) 376-6591.

The publisher is not responsible for websites (or their content) that are not
owned by the publisher.

Typeset in Sabon MT by Palimpsest Book Production Ltd, Falkirk,
Stirlingshire

Library of Congress Control Number: 2020934569

ISBNs: 978-1-61039-867-1 (hardcover) 978-1-5417-2467-9 (ebook)

LSC-C

10 9 8 7 6 5 4 3 2 1

Contents

Lisbon: **John Coustos's Secrets**

On 14 March 1743, as he was leaving a Lisbon coffee house, John Coustos, a forty-year-old jeweller from London, was grabbed, handcuffed and bundled into a chaise. A short time later, he found himself in one of the most feared buildings in Europe. Looming at the northern end of Rossio Square, the Estaus Palace housed the Portuguese headquarters of the Holy Office of the Inquisition.

Just like hundreds of witches, heretics and Jews who had been brought there before him, Coustos had his scalp shaved, and was stripped naked save for his linen undergarments. Confined in a dungeon, he was subjected to a meticulous regime. Isolation and silence were rigidly enforced: a fellow prisoner with a persistent cough was cudgelled into unconsciousness. No communication with friends and relatives was permitted. No possessions. No books – not even a Bible. Nothing that would interrupt the voice of divine conscience. Nothing to block out the prisoner's all too vivid imagining of the horrors that awaited him in the Inquisition's *auto-da-fé*. This grand spectacle of religious justice was a procession culminating in prayers, incantations and public execution by one of two methods: the mercy of strangling, for those who embraced the Catholic faith at the last minute; and for the obstinate, the unutterable torment of the flames.

Coustos tells us that the Inquisitors initially questioned him in a spiritually nurturing tone. Nonetheless, he had the clear sense that his replies were futile. Eventually he was summoned from his cell and brought before the President of the Holy Office, who read out the charges as if talking to a wall:

> That he has infring'd the Pope's Orders, by his belonging to the Sect of the Free-Masons; this Sect being a horrid Compound of Sacrilege, Sodomy, and many other abominable Crimes; of which the inviolable Secrecy observ'd therein, and the Exclusion of Women, were but too manifest Indications; a Circumstance that gave the highest Offence to the whole Kingdom: And the said Coustos having refused to discover, to the Inquisitors, the true Tendency and Design of the Meetings of Free-Masons; and persisting, on the contrary, in asserting, that Free-Masonry was good in itself: Wherefore the Proctor of the Inquisition requires, that the said Prisoner may be prosecuted with the utmost Rigour; and, for this Purpose, desires the Court would exert its whole Authority, and even proceed to Tortures.

Coustos was taken to a square, windowless room in a tower. Quilted padding lined the door, to deaden the sound of screaming from within. A doctor and a surgeon looked back at him from the shadows. The only light came from two candles on the desk at which the Tribunal's secretary sat waiting to record his confession.

Four burly men seized him and clamped him to a horizontal rack by closing an iron collar around his neck. They fitted rings, with ropes attached, to his feet, and yanked his limbs to their fullest extent. Then eight loops of cord, two over each arm and two over each leg, were passed through the frame and fed out into the torturers' hands. Coustos felt the cords tighten, and tighten, and finally start to saw through his flesh. Blood spattered the floor beneath him. If he died in this torment, he was told, only his own obstinacy would be to blame. Between his own cries, he heard the Inquisitor pose the questions he had already heard many times. *What is Freemasonry? What are its constitutions? What goes on in the Lodge meetings?* Eventually, he fainted and was carried back to the dungeons.

Six weeks later, the Inquisitors tried again, with a different method: the dreaded *strappado*. Upright this time, Coustos had his arms gradually stretched back behind him, palms facing outwards, until the backs of his hands met. Then his arms were pulled slowly upwards until his shoulders were levered from their sockets, and blood poured from his mouth. As he beseeched heaven for patience, the Inquisitors persisted with their questions. *Is Freemasonry a religion? Why do you not admit women? Is it because you are sodomites?*

When the doctors had reset his bones, and he had spent two months recovering, the torture resumed. This time, a chain was wound around his torso and attached to his wrists. Pulleys drew the chain ever tighter, squeezing his insides, and dislocating his wrists as well as his shoulders. *Why all the secrecy in Freemasonry? What do you have to hide?*

3

Coustos tells us that he spent sixteen months in total in the dungeons of the Estaus Palace, and endured nine bouts of torture, before the time finally came for him to be paraded through the streets in the *auto-da-fè* of 21 June 1744. But he was lucky. While eight of his fellow prisoners were burned alive at the climax of the procession, he was condemned to four years as a galley slave. The relative freedom this sentence afforded gave him the chance to contact friends, who mobilised the British government to obtain his release.

JOHN COUSTOS Aged 43 Years,
(a Sufferer during 16 Months in ye Inquisition
at Lisbon for Being a Free Mason.

When he reached London on 15 December 1744, he set to writing his story. But he had barely begun when the Jacobite rebellion of 1745 broke out. 'Bonnie Prince Charlie' Stuart raised his standard in the Highlands of Scotland, intent on enforcing his Catholic claim to the throne that had once been his grandfather's. The Jacobite army descended as far as Derby, in the heart of England, sowing panic in the capital. Although it was eventually crushed, the rebellion revived the public appetite for books documenting the barbarities of the Roman Church. *The Sufferings of John Coustos for Free-Masonry*, complete with engravings of all the tortures its author had endured, was published at the perfect moment. Coustos became a celebrity. The book was widely translated, and remained in print well into the nineteenth century. Here was a martyr for Freemasonry and its 'inviolable Secrecy'.

Except that things did not quite go in the way Coustos said.

Over two centuries later, the Inquisition's transcription of his interrogation surfaced from the Lisbon archives to reveal that he *did* give away the mysteries of Freemasonry that he had vowed to die to protect. Very sensibly, faced with the prospect of the torture chamber and the *auto-da-fé*, he told all. Indeed, he barely waited for the Inquisitors to open their mouths before answering all their questions.

Not that his confession saved him from being tortured. Portuguese Inquisitors rarely needed much of an excuse to break out the instruments of pain. They racked Coustos twice. For a little over fifteen minutes each time. Just to make sure. But he was never subjected to the *strappado* or the nameless torture with the chain wound round his torso.

Something else that Coustos neglected to tell his readers is that, had the Lisbon Inquisitors looked hard enough, they could have found published sources that would have taught them what they wanted to know: like Sam Prichard's pamphlet *Masonry Dissected* of 1730. Exposés of Freemasonry are nearly as old as Freemasonry itself. Masonic secrets have never really been all that secret.

Coustos evidently found the temptation to pass himself off as a hero just too strong. So once back at liberty he doctored his story to perpetuate a beguiling myth: the idea that Freemasons are the bearers of some momentous or dangerous truth, to which only the chosen few can have access, and which they are bound by oath to safeguard at any cost.

Freemasonry's 'inviolable Secrecy' is elusive and powerful. It is the engine of the fascination and suspicion that have always surrounded the Freemasons. It inspires loyalty and attracts trouble. Secrecy is a game, and both Coustos and the Inquisitors were caught up in it. Yet, as I think John Coustos appreciated, secrets are not as important to Freemasonry as *stories* about secrecy. Secrecy is the key to Masonic history in that, if we can grasp it, we can unlock a rich store of narratives about how the world we live in was made.

What Coustos actually confessed were the strange rituals at the heart of Masonic life, and the philosophy that is embedded in them. To understand the Freemasons, we need to appreciate those rituals and that philosophy – both of which are formally secret. However, there is a great deal more to Masonic history than rituals. Drawing on Coustos's confession, in Chapter Two of this book I will rapidly equip readers with all the secrets about ritual they need to know. However, as the Coustos story shows, before we learn those core mysteries, it is important to have more preparation in what to expect from Masonic history, and from the secrecy that has such an important role in it.

When John Coustos encountered the Portuguese Inquisition, the history of the Brotherhood that Masons sometimes call 'the Craft' was already in full flow. In Coustos's day, Freemasonry's mythology placed its origins with the builders of King Solomon's Temple. Now, thanks to a deal of academic detective work, the beginning of its documented history has been located nearly a hundred and fifty years before Coustos. Chapter Three will describe its genesis.

Freemasonry was also, in some important respects, a novelty when Coustos was arrested. Amid a great deal of intrigue, in London in 1717, it adopted both a new organisational shape and a new rulebook. Soon afterwards, Freemasonry became a raging success, and spread round the world with astonishing rapidity. It is one of Britain's most successful cultural exports, comparable in that respect to sports like tennis, soccer and golf. From London, John Coustos himself helped transplant it to France as well as Portugal. Chapter Four will bring my narrative back up to Coustos's day by describing the London roots of what, for the rest of the book, becomes a global story.

In its essence, Freemasonry has not changed since Coustos's time: it is a fellowship of men, and men alone, who are bound by oaths to a method of self-betterment. The method centres on rituals, performed in isolation from the outside world, in which symbols stand for moral qualities. The most important of those symbols derive from the work of stonemasons. Hence the name 'Freemasons'; hence the square and compass, the apron and gloves, that we all associate with the Craft.

If that were the beginning and end of Masonry, its history would be dull. Secrecy is the catalyst that makes it eventful and compelling. For one thing, secrecy has an allure that has attracted many millions of men towards the Craft. Under interrogation in 1743, Coustos explained that secrecy was partly just bait for new recruits: 'as Secrecy naturally excited Curiosity, this prompted great Numbers of Persons to enter into this Society'. The great and the good were among those Persons. All Freemasons are proud of the gallery of outstanding figures who have been their Brothers. Coustos declared himself 'not a little honoured in belonging to a Society, which boasted several Christian Kings, Princes and Persons of the highest Quality among its Members'. Part of the attraction of being a Freemason is the cachet that comes with belonging to such an exclusive band. Secrecy guarantees that exclusivity: possession of the Masonic secrets, whatever they are, is what distinguishes a Craftsman from a Cowan (a non-Mason).

Since Coustos's time, the list of famous Freemasons has grown longer and longer. The Craft likes to point to the makers of nations who have come from among its ranks: Giuseppe Garibaldi, Simón Bolívar, Motilal Nehru and George Washington, who was

7

initiated six years after *The Sufferings of John Coustos* was published. Five Kings of England and, including Washington, no fewer than fourteen Presidents of the United States of America have been Masons. Freemasonry can boast a long list of writers, such as: Scotland's national poet, Robert Burns; the author of *Dangerous Liaisons* (1782), Pierre Choderlos de Laclos; Sherlock Holmes's creator, Arthur Conan Doyle; and the towering figure of German letters, Johann Wolfgang von Goethe. Numerous composers, including Wolfgang Amadeus Mozart, Joseph Haydn and Jean Sibelius, have been 'on the Square'. There are sportsmen in the list, like golfer Arnold Palmer, Caribbean cricket giant Clive Lloyd, boxer Sugar Ray Robinson and basketball player Shaquille O'Neal. There are also many entertainers, ranging from Harry Houdini and Peter Sellers to Nat King Cole and Oliver Hardy. Mason entrepreneurs include such titans as Henry Ford of automobile fame, William Lever the detergent pioneer and mining magnate Cecil Rhodes. Freemasons have excelled at the most disparate spheres of achievement: Davy Crockett and Oscar Wilde; Walt Disney and Winston Churchill; Buzz Aldrin and 'Buffalo Bill' Cody; Paul Revere and Roy Rogers; Duke Ellington and the Duke of Wellington.

Today, there are 400,000 Masons in Britain, 1.1 million in the USA and around six million across the planet. In the past, their numbers have been much greater.

Such names, such numbers, testify to the magnetic power of secrecy, and to the Craft's vast and enduring influence. Plenty of famous Masons will people the pages of this book. Their stories, and the individual style in which each has lived out his Masonry, are fascinating. But more fascinating still is the overarching narrative of Freemasonry itself – a way of binding males in fellowship that has been propelled across the globe and through hundreds of years of history by the force of its mystique.

Wherever the Craft was transplanted, its influence leaked into society. Just one example: the activities that go on in *private*, behind the doors of Lodges, have helped spread the values we associate with modern *public* life. Freemasons have long aspired to live by a code of religious and racial tolerance, democracy, cosmopolitanism and equality before the law.

However, the story I will tell in this book has much more to it than the kind of Enlightenment values I have just alluded to. There is plenty of dark to go with the light. Our modernity, which the Masons have helped shape, comprises things like imperialism and global war, the building and breaking of states and nations, dictatorship and religious fanaticism.

Which prompts me to say a word about the Inquisitors who tortured Coustos. Understanding how the Freemasons and their secrecy were perceived by their enemies helps us grasp just what made them such a novelty to most of the eighteenth-century world, what distinguishes them even today and what makes their history worth telling.

In 1738 Pope Clement XII, who is better known for building the Trevi Fountain, issued the Bull *In eminenti apostolatus specula*: it prohibited Freemasonry, excommunicated all members and charged the Inquisition with probing its inner workings. John Coustos was not the only victim of the inquiry.

The Pope and his Inquisitors had good and urgent reasons for their suspicions. Freemasonry was obviously religious, in some dark sense. It soon emerged that the Craft had its own name for the deity: the Great Architect of the Universe. Its members prayed, took religious oaths and performed rites. Yet they claimed that the Craft was *not* a religion. Freemasonry, the Masons said, did not try to arbitrate between visions of the divine; it held no particular theological line. Indeed, as Coustos protested to the Portuguese Inquisitors, 'in [our] Fraternity, it is not permitted to speak of religious matters': this prohibition was imposed to prevent conflict between Brothers, and to avoid attracting trouble. Hardly surprisingly, however, the freedom of conscience championed by the Craft gave off the sulphurous reek of heresy to a Church dedicated to guarding its monopoly on truth.

Freemasonry's British origins also made it suspect. Coming

9

from such a strange country, with its overmighty parliament, its elections and its daily newspapers, the Freemasons were bound to seem like an alien threat. Perhaps they were spies.

Or even a global network of subversives. Just as Freemasonry's Britishness made it shady, so too did its internationalism. Masons were citizens of nowhere, and subjects of no one.

Freemasonry also attracted a freakishly diverse range of members: tradesmen, merchants, lawyers, actors, Jews, and even the odd African. A social menagerie. Nor was this the usual train of hangers-on, dependent on the patronage of a powerful lord. While many noblemen were involved, they did not always seem to be in command. In fact, it was not at all clear whether *anyone* was in command. To those who believed that society's hierarchies were fixed by Almighty God, this was alarming.

Of course, the Masons always said that they were not political. But then no plotter with any sense would say anything else. In an era when absolute monarchy was the norm, few countries had anything like an open political life as we might know it. Bringing an association of men together for any reason constituted a potential threat to the established order. It mattered little to Freemasonry's enemies that, like religion and for the same reasons, politics was prohibited as a topic of conversation within the Lodge.

So in the eyes of the Catholic Church, Freemasonry was manifestly dangerous. The Brotherhood's furtive manner electrified those misgivings. John Coustos claimed that his Brotherhood had no clandestine agenda, and that instead, 'Charity and Brotherly Love' were 'the Foundation and the Soul of this Society'. Masons still say very similar things. The Lisbon Inquisitors' reply to Coustos feels just as contemporary: 'if this Society of Free-Masons was so virtuous, there was no Occasion of their concealing, so very industriously, the Secrets of it'. Freemasons today bridle when they hear their Brotherhood referred to as a secret society. 'We are *not* a secret society,' they protest. 'We are a society with secrets.' It is hardly a conclusive retort. Once you

say you have secrets, no amount of calibrated honesty and openness will put minds to rest: anyone with even a moderately
suspicious attitude will assume you are still concealing something
vital. So perhaps it is no surprise that the Vatican has never
forsaken its original hostility to the Craft, and remains convinced
that the Lodges are pernicious dens of atheism.

Masonry's enemies have often shared one particular style of
thinking: the conspiracy theory, whose very invention we owe to
the fear of Freemasonry. Since the early nineteenth century,
Masonic conspiracies have never been out of fashion, and they
range from the eerily plausible to the outlandish. The Masons
poisoned Mozart. Jack the Ripper was a Mason, and Masons
covered his tracks. Masons masterminded the French Revolution,
the unification of Italy, the break-up of the Ottoman Empire
and the Russian Revolution. The Internet pullulates with sites
dedicated to the Illuminati, a branch of Freemasonry whose
members, including Bono, Bill Gates and Jay Z, have signed an
occult covenant that binds them to a nefarious plan to rule the
world.

Some of these myths are harmless: they are rather like the
'I-don't-believe-it-but-it's-true' ghost stories that teenagers tell
one another, to share a frisson. Some of them are very dangerous.
Mussolini, Hitler and Franco suspected the Freemasons of
conspiracy, and murdered thousands of them as a result. The
Craft has always been viewed as a devious bourgeois caucus by
communists and it is still banned in the People's Republic of
China. The Muslim world also has a strong tradition of anti-
Masonic paranoia.

The oath of silence that Freemasons take during their initiation is all that is required to give the conspiratorial imagination
free play. Freemasonry's secrecy is like a well. The men who built
it know how deep it is. The rest of us can only peer over the
wall that surrounds it and wonder. While we gaze downwards at
the water, speculating on what might lurk below, the black surface
reflects back our anxieties. That, in essence, is why the Craft has

generated misunderstanding, suspicion and hostility at every step. No history of Freemasonry is complete unless it also includes Freemasonry's foes.

Craftsmen are the inheritors of a venerable tradition. Ask any one of them, and he will tell you something about Masonic history. Many regard historical research as an integral part of deepening their understanding of Craft mysteries.

Yet, until recently, Freemasons insisted on treating their history as confidential – a matter for Masons alone. Cowans were refused access to the archives and libraries of Grand Lodges. Then, a generation ago, the wisest Brothers realised that Masonic history is too important to be the exclusive property of the initiated. Because Freemasonry has had a role in shaping our world, its history belongs to us all. These days, professional historians who are not Freemasons are a familiar sight in the archives of Grand Lodges. Their work, supplementing and challenging the efforts of the best Masonic historians, has mapped out an exciting and ever-growing field of investigation. One of the aims of this book is to bring some of that research to a much bigger audience.

Freemasons' pride in their own history tends to produce many studies that are really identity narratives: their aim is less to discover the truth than to boost the Craft's *esprit de corps*. *The Sufferings of John Coustos for Free-Masonry* is a model for many Masonic narratives in the way it paints a black-and-white picture that pits the Craft's tradition of tolerance, wisdom and brotherly love against the angry, uncomprehending forces of anti-Masonry.

Freemasonry is supposed to be – and often is – about philanthropy, fellowship, ethics and spirituality. There is a rule in Masonry that Brothers are not allowed to join because they want to get a boost to their career chances or some other personal advantage. Such rules have their weight. It is too cynical to dismiss them as just a cover story for grubby aims. Any historian who cannot see the power of the nobler motive forces in the Craft is telling a very one-eyed tale.

However, for their part, Freemasons are too reserved about one undeniably important theme of their history: networking. Like the rest of the human race, Masons network. In the right circumstances, Lodges can be a great place to build a network, for all kinds of good and bad reasons. There is a word to be said in defence of the Masons here. In Britain, for example, male networks tend to unite people from a similar background: the right private school, or the right group of pub mates. Just like these other circles, Masonry tends to exclude women. But it is different in that it can cut *across* between the social classes – or at least a more representative sample of social classes. Masons will point out that the reason they wear gloves in their ceremonies is so that no Brother can tell the difference between the hands of a Duke and the hands of a dustman. That said, Lodges *have* sometimes become nests of nepotism and even shadowy plotting. Not all the conspiracy theories and suspicions of Masonic foul play are hooey. Moreover, the Masonic idea – a template for male fellowship forged by myth, ritual and secrecy – proved contagious from the outset, and impossible for the Masons to control: it has been adopted and adapted, used and abused, in innumerable different ways. Both the Sicilian mafia and the Ku Klux Klan share important strands of the Craft's DNA.

One of my motivations for writing this book is to reflect many more varied textures of human experience than are included in Freemasonry's identity narratives, or in the cynics' obsession with mutual Masonic back-scratching. Rather than flatten out those textures by surveying the vast landscape of the Craft's story from high above, I have chosen to dive down into times and places around the world that are particularly significant. The principle I follow is that Freemasonry has never been able to cloister itself away from society. Just as the Craft was forged in the peculiar circumstances of seventeenth- and eighteenth-century Britain, so – while remaining recognisably itself – it has

13

adapted to whichever circumstances it subsequently encountered. It is the interaction between Freemasonry and society that interests me. Masonry has helped make modern men, in all their idealism and clubbiness. As for women, I will have more to say about them later. (The same goes for the people the Inquisitors labelled 'sodomites'.)

Our curiosity persists. *What goes on in the Lodge meetings? What exactly do you have to hide?* When it comes to Freemasonry, most of us have something in common with the Lisbon Inquisitors. Give or take an obsession with sodomy, their questions remain our questions. The Internet has now made the Masons' secrets less secret than ever. Nevertheless, we non-Masons never seem to learn. There is always one more TV documentary in the pipeline, promising unprecedented access to the inner sanctum. The Masonic exposé genre never seems to die.

Freemasonry's secrecy is richer than anything that can be laid bare by any exposé. It is more complicated, more subtle and, I happen to think, much more enjoyable to investigate. It has many strands, and is so entwined with myths and misconceptions that they have become part of its very fabric. But at its heart, as John Coustos confessed, lies a sacred drama that begins at the door of a temple, set outside time and space . . .

Nowhere: **The Strange Death of Hiram Abiff**

A man in an apron wielding a drawn sword makes you surrender your money, keys, phone – all the metalwork that anchors your person to the world outside. He blindfolds you. You feel your right sleeve being rolled up, and the left leg of your trousers, so as to expose the knee. Your arm is taken from the left sleeve of your shirt, thus leaving your breast naked. A slipknot loop of rope is placed over your head.

You step forward. Your life as a Freemason has begun.

What follows is a sketch of what an aspiring Mason is put through once he has been prepared in this way to cross the threshold of a Lodge for the first time. The ceremonies I describe here are very close to what John Coustos underwent in the Rainbow Coffee House in Fleet Street. Successive rites mark a man's initiation, and his passage from one status within the Craft to the next. These marks of status are called Degrees. Secrets are central to the drama of Masonic Degree rituals.

The Lisbon Inquisitors called the rituals 'ridiculous'. Over the centuries, many satirists have agreed. So, while it would be very easy to laugh at Masonic ritual, it would not be at all original. The more I have learned about Freemasonry, the more uncomfortable some of the laughter makes me, because it quashes our desire to hear Masons' stories by stopping us seeing how like us they are.

When we laugh at the rituals of others, we forget how much of our own lives is invisibly ritualised. Habits like beating our palms together to show appreciation, or clasping hands when we meet, or saying 'cheers' when we raise a drink. However materialistic or computerised we may get, however confidently we may believe in Natural Selection and the Big Bang, we are never going to shake off our need for the structuring influence of ritual. Births, marriages and deaths: none of us feels properly hatched, matched or dispatched without some ceremonials.

The average Mason understands, better than most of us, the magic in a well-performed rite. Initiation rituals tell us, more suggestively than any other experience, that we have become someone new. Familiar rituals unite people because they are a shared experience, within a shared frame of reference. Yet ceremonies also have a tendency to make us suspicious of those who ritualise in different ways. Although I am not at all religious, I grew up in a culture of Anglicanism. So when faced with the Muslim Hajj (pilgrimage to Mecca), or a Jewish Brit Milah (circumcision rite), or a Hindu Vedic sacrifice, people like me tend initially to find them bizarre. Anyone new to Masonic ritual, and the terminology it uses, is almost certain to find it all opaque, at the very least. Luckily, while Freemasons have to spend inordinate amounts of time memorising all the speeches and movements in what they call their 'workings', we only have to know a little bit about them to enjoy Masonic history.

Once the blindfolded candidate has entered the Lodge, he is asked to kneel for a prayer. He is then led three times round the room before being presented to the senior officers of the Lodge, who certify that he is at least twenty-one years old, 'of good report' and 'free-born'.

At the prompting of the Master of the Lodge, the candidate then makes a series of pledges, notably that he believes in a god of some description, and that his desire to become a Mason is not motivated by 'mercenary or other unworthy motives'.

Then comes the walk. The candidate takes three steps forward, each one bigger than the last, with his heel coming to meet his instep at a right angle so that the feet form a square (that is, the right-angled tool). Immediately after the walk the candidate has to make another square with his legs, by kneeling before an altar on his bare left knee, and planting his right foot forward. He is then asked to place his hand on his choice of a Bible, a Qur'an, or whichever 'Volume of Sacred Law' he chooses. At which point he swears never to write down the Masonic secrets he is about to learn. The penalties to be inflicted should he betray the Masons' secrets are blood-curdling: 'under no less a penalty . . . than that of having my throat cut across, my tongue torn out by the root, and my body buried in the sand of the sea at low water mark, a cable's length from the shore, where the tide regularly ebbs and flows twice in twenty-four hours'. Once he has mouthed these words, and sealed his pledge by kissing the Volume of Sacred Law, he has become a 'newly obligated' Mason. Accordingly, his blindfold is whipped off. He is then told that there are three great 'emblematical lights' in Freemasonry. The first lies open on the altar in front of him, and is shared with the major world religions: the Volume of Sacred Law, which is a guide to faith. The second and third are the insignia of Freemasonry, displayed on buildings, aprons and lapel pins across the world: the Square, which stands for rectitude; and the Compass, an image of self-control.

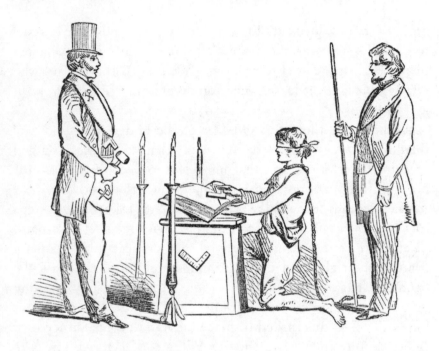

At this point the initiated Brother is helped back to his feet and invited to stand at the right-hand side of the Master, whence he can return the solemnly benevolent gaze of the Brothers seated round the edge of the room. He can also contemplate the rect-angular interior of the Lodge, with its famous chessboard floor. In Coustos's day, the chessboard pattern was usually drawn in chalk – just as he told the Inquisitors.

The furnishings of the Lodge prick the initiate's curiosity. For example, the two free-standing pillars with globes on top, both roughly shoulder height. There are also, around the altar where the Volume of Sacred Law lies open, three candles supported on miniature columns. Each column has a different design. One is topped by the elaborately carved foliage of the Corinthian order of architecture. The other two are an Ionic and a Doric column. Needless to say, this all carries Masonic symbolism. But at this stage, the Master restricts himself to explaining what the candles mean (the 'lesser lights', as they are termed in Masonic parlance): they stand for the three guides that will accompany the initiate in his Masonic life: the sun, the moon and the Master of the Lodge. This is because, as Coustos divulged, 'as the Sun gives light to the day, and the Moon to the night, so must the Master rule and direct his officers and apprentices'.

The Master continues the lesson. Freemasonry has several Degrees, of which this one, known as the Entered Apprentice Degree, is only the first. So the newly initiated Brother can expect to go through further ceremonies. For now, he is allowed to learn the secret *Sign*, *Token* and *Word*, as Masons call them.

The *Sign*, a reminder of the penalties that face anyone who betrays Masonic mysteries, is (as Coustos confessed) 'the putting of the right hand in front of the throat in the manner of seeking to cut it'.

The *Token*, which Masons also call their *Grip*, is known to the rest of us as the Masonic handshake. Its purpose, according to Coustos, is for a Mason 'to be recognised in any part of the World by the other Brethren, and to be able to warn himself against those who are not'. The Master demonstrates the grip by placing his thumb on the first knuckle-joint of the initiate's index finger.

The *Word*, finally, is BOAZ, which is the name of one of the two pillars at the entrance to Solomon's Temple, as described in the Book of Kings. Freemasonry draws many of its symbols from Solomon's Temple and its builders. This Word is so secret that Masons are only ever allowed to spell it out to one another, and never to pronounce it whole. Coustos, of course, told his captors all about it. BOAZ too has a symbolic meaning: it stands for strength.

The new Mason then has to do another round of presentations to the officers of the Lodge, each time exchanging with them the Sign, the Token and the Word. All of which entitles him to be presented with a Masonic sheepskin apron.

Once he has promised to make a contribution to the welfare of distressed Masons and their families, the initiate could be forgiven for thinking that the procedure is nearly at an end. But he still has to learn about the symbolic tools appropriate to the Entered Apprentice Degree: they are a 24-inch gauge (or ruler), a gavel (or mallet) and a chisel, and they metaphorically remind a Mason about the importance of using his time well, working hard and persevering. He also has to learn more symbols and abstract nouns. There is lots about Truth, Honour and Virtue. And Prudence, Temperance and Fortitude. Benevolence. Charity. As well as Fidelity, Obedience and – of course – Secrecy. He is also told some more rules, such as the duty not to 'subvert the peace and good order of society'.

Then, finally, comes a long rite that marks the closing of the Lodge, which involves more signs, prayers, knocks, solemn utterances and dignified movements. At which point, after a good hour of ceremonials, the Brethren go off for a celebratory meal.

While the newly initiated Brother is eating and drinking his fill, he may ask himself what all the fuss was about. The grave undertakings and ghastly warnings were supposed to grant him a place in a band of Brothers chosen to stand guard over life-changing secrets. He has joined the band, but where are the secrets? All he has learned are secrets *about* secrets. He knows the sign, the handshake, the password and so on. Yet all it points to is the proposition that he needs to try to be a decent fellow.

Perhaps, he reflects, he has to wait for the next Degrees for enlightenment to arrive. Yet, when they come around some time later, the initiation ceremonies that mark his admission to the Second and Third Degrees of Freemasonry – known as the Fellow Craft and Master Mason Degrees – consist of more of the same, with tweaks.

In the Second (or Fellow Craft) Degree ceremony, the candidate is prepared by having his *right* knee and *right* breast bared – the opposite of the First Degree. The second grip or Masonic handshake involves pressing with the thumb on the knuckle of the *middle* finger rather than the index. The moral messages are just as simple as in the First Degree, albeit slightly different: the candidate is told that, as well as being a decent fellow, he ought to try to find out about the world. The initiate takes the oath on pain of having his breast torn open and his heart plucked out and eaten by vultures. The Word is JACHIN – the name of the other pillar of Solomon's Temple.

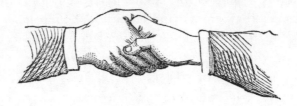

A candidate for the Third (Master Mason) Degree is readied by having his shirt completely removed, and *both* knees bared. The Master Mason handshake involves a Spock-like parting of the fingers between the middle and ring. The penalty for oath-breaking involves being cut in two and having your bowels burned to ashes, which are then scattered over the face of the earth. The Word is MAHABONE; its meaning is uncertain, but some say it means 'The Lodge door is open' in some unspecified language.

The Master Mason Degree ceremony is the most important of the three, the climax of the process of becoming a Freemason. It is much longer than the previous two, and its thematic subject matter is death. However, it does seem rather a lot of fun. The Brethren get to perform a miniature play, re-enacting the murder of Hiram Abiff, the architect of Solomon's Temple. The story goes that, when he refused to give up the secrets of a master mason, Hiram was killed with a series of blows to the head. The candidate plays the part of Hiram: he is shouted at, gently roughed up, and then 'buried' in a canvas body bag, which is carried in procession around the Lodge. In the end, Hiram Abiff is resurrected by the magic of the Master Mason handshake, and a special life-giving Masonic hug.

A candidate for the Master Mason Degree is ritually roughed up
in an attempt to force him to divulge Masonic secrets.

Secrecy is triple-locked into the Degrees that mark a man's
admission into a Masonic Lodge: the existence of the rituals is
secret; several terrifying oaths of secrecy are taken during them;
and the secrets themselves are concealed behind symbols. The
ceremony of the Master Mason Degree culminates when the
deepest and most terrible mystery is laid bare. And the ultimate
secret of Freemasonry is . . . that death is a serious business, and
it puts a perspective on things.

That really is all there is to it. For all the layers and folds of mystery,
Freemasonry's promise to reveal hidden verities turns out to be the
wrapping for a few home truths. The Craft, as the ritual for
the Second Degree explains, is nothing more or less than 'a peculiar
system of morality, veiled in allegory, and illustrated by symbols'.

Whatever talk you may have heard about Thirty-third Degree
Masons and the like, there are no higher Degrees in Masonry

than Master Mason, the Third Degree. But over time, enthusiastic Brothers have developed lots of what they call 'side Degrees', of which the Scottish Rite, with its thirty extra Degrees, is the most Byzantine. The point to remember for now is that these side Degrees are just extra variations that branch off from the three core Degrees that I have just described. When I asked one Mason why he had so enthusiastically embarked on joining lots of side Degrees, he simply said, 'it's addictive'. There is no great novelty in any of them: they are all based on the same mixture of allegory, run-of-the-mill moral rules and a ceremonial sense of togetherness. But there is enormous scope for imaginative use of symbols and splendid costumes.

Just as we should not dismiss how captivating Craft ceremonies can be, so we should not regard the morals and philosophy that Masons express through their rituals as just trite. The meanings behind all the symbolism may seem singularly unimpressive: be a good person, try to be well informed, embrace religious tolerance. But then, compared to the dangerously ludicrous notions peddled by many an orthodox religion – burn witches, kill infidels, stigmatise sinners – the nostrums that Freemasons are called to obey are heart-warming.

Freemasons will stress that their Brotherhood is *not* a religion. Others might counter that if it has ceremonies and symbols like a religion, and covers the same moral and spiritual territory as a religion, then it is splitting hairs to claim that it isn't a religion. Perhaps it will suffice to describe Freemasonry as a kind of second-order religion: it grants freedom of conscience, allowing the individual male to make his own decisions on intricacies of theology, while at the same time providing a framework for living together in a spiritually constructive peace. It might be easy to laugh at it, but it is harder to knock. Many Masons do a great deal for charity too.

When John Coustos confessed all this to the Portuguese Inquisition, they repeatedly affirmed that they found him 'worthy of credit'. Worthy of credit, that is, until it came to his answer to the question of what the point of all the rituals was. Here is what the Inquisitors noted down:

> [Coustos] said: that the only purpose [the rituals] have is to maintain the secrecy which all the members are to keep.

> Asked: if the only motive to which the said Rules and other ceremonies are destined is for the enforcing of secrecy, as he says, what is therefore the end and final purpose aimed at by this secrecy in view of the heavy and unusual penalties they undertake [. . .]?

> [Coustos] said: that the final purpose of such procedure was such secrecy.

The purpose of Masonic secrecy is secrecy. The elaborate cult of secrecy within Freemasonry is a ritual fiction. All the terrifying penalties for oath-breaking are just theatre – never to be implemented. Unsurprisingly, the Inquisitors found this part of Coustos's confession 'abbreviated, evasive and deceitful'. That is why they tortured him: because the truth about Masonry was so completely underwhelming.

Even though Coustos was not the hero he claimed to be, it is to his eternal credit that he did not make something up to meet the Inquisitors' expectations. He could easily have invented some ghastly sacrilege that would have made the torturers feel they had not been wasting their time. When an Italian Freemason, Tommaso Crudeli, was arrested by the Inquisition in Florence at around the same time, the case against him was based on an insider's claims that recruits were masturbated by a senior Brother, and then made to sign a blood-curdling oath in their own semen: they supposedly undertook to commit any crime – with the sole exception of sodomy. Thus, in a way, Coustos *was* a martyr: to anticlimax. Yet ever since then, Masons like him, and enemies of Masonry like the Inquisitors, have surrendered to the urge to see much more in Masonic secrecy than is really there. That is the irony threading through many of the stories that follow. In the end, while Masonic secrecy has very little to it in the pure sense, it is also all the many things that, throughout history and across the world, both the Brothers and their enemies have made of it.

Edinburgh: **The Art of Memorie**

G is for . . .

The most significant symbols that Masons use in their rituals – the aprons and columns, the squares and trowels – derive from the work of stonemasons. Freemasons believe that, as well as having a moral meaning, these things also tell a story about how Masonry originated from the lives of medieval craftsmen. The story expounded in countless guides to Masonry is that the Brotherhood grew out of medieval stonemasons' guilds. The name 'the Craft' encapsulates this belief: 'craft' is a synonym for 'guild'. Freemasons find the notion that they are the direct descendants of medieval stonemasons appealing: it links them back to the builders of the great cathedrals like Salisbury, Lincoln and York Minster; it is very 'merrie England'.

Yet, when it comes to trying to demonstrate how guilds developed into Masonic Lodges, Masonic historians have faced insurmountable difficulties, because medieval stonemasons were particularly bad at forming guilds. In fourteenth- and fifteenth-century England, pretty much every respectable trade in every town had a guild of its own. Butchers had a guild. Bakers had a guild. Candlestick makers had a guild. Every curious trade from days gone by had a well-established guild: cordwainers and lorimers, fellmongers and tawyers . . . Every trade, that is, except stonemasons.

The reason was that there was not enough work. Most buildings in medieval England were not made of stone, but of wattle and daub, which was an ignoble combination of twigs, straw, clay and dung. There was not remotely as much demand for the services of masons as there was for, say, carpenters and thatchers. As a result, in most places, there were not enough masons to make a decent game of dice, let alone a guild. On those occasions when stonemasons *were* organised in guilds, they were usually mixed in with other men from the building trade, especially wrights (i.e. joiners).

Stonemasons led a wandering life, drawn hither and thither across the land, and congregating in those rare places and times when there was a stone bridge or house to be built. In many cases, there was a fine line between a stonemason and a common labourer. When it came to big projects – a castle, an abbey, a cathedral – stonemasons were recruited in large numbers from far afield. Quite often recruitment was compulsory – *empressment*, it was called. They were commanded by a master mason, who was contracted to the king or bishop. These élite master masons were also peripatetic, but individually very powerful. So it often proved impossible for a conventional guild to represent both them and the mass of the labour force.

The stubborn fact is that, of all the many artisans of the English Middle Ages, the stonemasons were the *least* likely to have their trade organisation survive over the centuries and transform itself into a fraternity like the Freemasons. Over the generations, Masonic historians failed to demonstrate a link between what they call *operative stonemasons* – men with chisels and plumb-lines, muscles and calluses – and today's *speculative Freemasons* – men whose tools have a philosophical meaning rather than a practical use.

If the guilds of the Middle Ages are not the link between operative masonry and speculative Freemasonry, what is? We can only inch closer to an answer when we look, not at the reality of the working lives of medieval stonemasons, but at their culture and stories, elements of which were later integrated into Freemasonry.

The collective life of all medieval trades was rich in regulation, ritual and myth. There were rites of passage to undergo. There were solemn and frightening oaths, so as to protect trade secrets and reinforce solidarity. There were laws and passwords to memorise, some of them intended to smoke out imposters who might present themselves at the city gates looking for work. There were celebratory holy-day feasts. There were fables too: the cordwainers, who made luxury footwear, believed that, after his martyrdom, their patron St Hugh had his bones transformed into shoemakers' tools.

Stonemasons across Britain made up for the weakness of their guild organisation by having an especially rich store of rules, symbols and myths. Known as the 'Old Charges', this masons' lore was memorised and handed down by word of mouth. Human memory being the fallible thing that it is, the content of the Old Charges varied widely, as bits were added and subtracted, garbled and forgotten. Now and again, a version of the Old Charges would be written down. The first written text to have survived this haphazard process is in verse, making its 826 lines rather easier to memorise; it is famous to Freemasons the world over as the Regius Poem. Its provenance and date are uncertain: probably Shropshire, maybe 1430.

The regulations the Old Charges enumerate are standard stuff for medieval artisans. They range from general advice on good manners (don't swear in church, don't blow your nose on your napkin) to rules specifically aimed at regulating the working lives of masons. Thus a master has to pay his men fairly, and safeguard the quality of the work. But what is really distinctive about the stonemasons' Old Charges, and what sets us on the trail of what would become Freemasonry, is stonemasons' mythology – a story of how stonemasonry was born at the very dawn of time, and how it was handed down by great masons through the ages.

The story's *dramatis personae* are plucked from a lucky dip of sources: ancient Greek intellectuals rub shoulders with some of the big beards from Genesis and the Book of Kings. There are a few personalities who really count here because they would later be integrated into the legends of Freemasonry. One is Hermes Trismegistus, a learned man who, after Noah's Flood, rediscovered the geometrical rules of masonry, which pre-Flood masons had thoughtfully chiselled into two stone pillars. Euclid, the Greek mathematician, is the next great mason in line, because he taught the ancient Egyptians all they knew about stonework: hence the pyramids. Then comes Solomon, who employed forty thousand stonemasons to build his Temple, that great summation of masonic skill and learning. His chief mason was from Tyre; he would be given the name Hiram Abiff in later versions of the tale – the same Hiram Abiff destined to have a starring role in the Freemasons' Third Degree ritual.

There is grandeur in the stonemasons' mythology: a motley group of tradesmen was giving itself a lineage as ancient and mighty as any royal dynasty. They had very serious intellectual pretensions too. The Old Charges associate the stonemasons' craft with the science of geometry: that is why the ancient Greek mathematician Euclid, known as the 'father of geometry', was important. Masons thought masonry and geometry amounted to the same thing; and geometry was a very serious pursuit. Along with grammar and logic, rhetoric and arithmetic, music and astronomy, geometry went to form the core curriculum of medieval universities. Indeed, the Old Charges argued that geometry-masonry was the most prestigious of all the fields of human knowledge. Freemasons still revere geometry as a metaphor for the fundamental order of the universe. The capital G that often appears with the square and compass as Masonic insignia stands for both Geometry and God.

All this considered, we are still a long way from making a real historical connection between the Old Charges and Freemasonry. (This is as far as Masonic historians got in trying to link medieval English stoneworkers and today's Freemasons.)

After centuries of mystification (for which eighteenth-century

Masons are the main culprits, as we shall see), a convincing account of Freemasonry's origins has only emerged in recent years: the breakthrough came with academic research published in 1988. What we now appreciate is that the roots of Freemasonry are not medieval. Rather they lie in the time when the medieval world was being torn apart and modernity being born. Moreover, the Craft's creation was sparked, not in the medieval England of guilds and Gothic cathedrals, but in the Renaissance court of Scotland's capital, Edinburgh.

Scotland's Solomon

The Reformation split Europe asunder. Until 1517, the Holy Roman Church had been the only pathway to God, and the only guarantor of the authority of kings. Rome sat firmly at the centre of Christendom. Across the continent, the great Gothic cathedrals, in all their soaring permanence, proclaimed a heaven-inspired order in human affairs.

Then came Luther's attack, and the birth of Protestantism. Christendom was irreparably fissured. Monarchs broke with Rome. An era of religious war began. A hunger for new ideas, and for the printed paper that communicated them, raged across the continent. In half of Europe, hitherto unquestioned aspects of the faith, like the doctrine of Purgatory and the veneration of relics and icons, were now seen as the work of the Antichrist.

In Scotland, the Reformation hit late and hard. From 1560, religious buildings felt the full impact of the new zeal. Scots Protestants were notable for the fury with which they smashed the devil's idolatrous statues, stained-glass windows and stone ornaments. The Cathedral of St Andrews, which was the largest ecclesiastical building in the country, the exquisite result of a century and a half of devout labour, was vandalised and abandoned. In Edinburgh, a mob looted and wrecked Holyrood Abbey, the burial place of kings. The faithful of the new Protestant kirk believed that God liked his places of worship to be brutally austere – a mere rectangular box with walls of rubble would suffice. Thus Scottish stonemasons had more reason than most to be dismayed by the Reformation. No more cathedrals, monasteries or elaborate churches to build and maintain. The loss of a client like the Church was a calamity.

To make matters worse, the collapse of the Crown's authority put a halt to major royal building projects. King James VI of Scotland was in every sense a child of the Reformation, and had a tumultuous upbringing even by the standards of the age. His mother was Mary Queen of Scots, a Catholic, who was forced into exile when she married the man who probably orchestrated the gunpowder assassination plot that ended in the death of James's father. Six years of civil war ensued, and the thirteen-month-old James was kidnapped and hastily crowned at a parish church in Stirling. The boy-king was brought up a Protestant by bullying tutors who told him his mother was a witch. Meanwhile, rapacious court factions fought it out around him. With their feuding and raiding, Scots noblemen behaved like blue-blooded bandits.

James was still only nineteen when, in 1585, he shook off the last of his aristocratic co-rulers and took the reins of government himself. Patiently and cleverly, over the coming decade and a half, he tamed the religious extremists and practised a measure of toleration. He won the support of the nobility, so that aristocratic violence went into decline. Wisely, he lodged only a formal protest when Elizabeth I of England had his mother beheaded in 1587. With every year that passed, it became more likely that James would succeed the childless Elizabeth I and unite the crowns of Scotland and England.

Apart from his political successes, James was also an intellectual: a poet and theologian, and the author of works on the theory and practice of kingship. *Daemonologie*, a book on witchcraft he wrote in 1597, would become Shakespeare's main source for the witches in *Macbeth* (1606). The scholar-king James revived the Scottish court, and further opened it to the influence of the European Renaissance. Noblemen travelled to France and Italy, and returned with an interest in the full range of international intellectual fashions: everything from poetic theory, medicine and military technology, to alchemy, astrology and magic.

Suspected witches brought before King James VI of Scotland (1566–1625). From James's own study, *Daemonologie*.

James built an administration, loyal only to him, from among the ranks of the gentry and intellectuals. One of those new men was William Schaw, who was a well-travelled and cultivated minor nobleman. Schaw was appointed to the post of *Maister o' Wark* (Master of Works). His job entailed responsibility for the construction, repair and maintenance of all the King of Scotland's buildings. He was also in charge of arranging royal ceremonials.

Like other northern European intellectuals, Schaw was fascinated with the way the Renaissance was returning to classical examples for inspiration. The key text for him was *De architectura*, written in the first century BCE by Vitruvius, a military engineer and builder who served under Julius Caesar. Vitruvius argued that the men who designed buildings needed to be intellectuals and not just builders. Under his influence, the prestige of the old master builders waned, and a new hero emerged on Renaissance Europe's cultural landscape: the architect. William Schaw would become the first man in Scotland ever to be referred to as an architect.

In February 1594, the court rejoiced at the news that a royal heir had been born in Stirling Castle. King James was determined to turn the baby boy's baptism into a show of sophistication and piety. For this purpose, he ordered the rapid construction of a new chapel at the castle. Schaw was responsible for the design, and top stonemasons were drawn in from across the country to work on the project. With its Florentine-style arched windows, the Chapel Royal at Stirling is the earliest Renaissance building of its kind in Britain. Like the Sistine Chapel in the Vatican, built in the 1470s, the Chapel Royal's dimensions and design were modelled on the Temple of Solomon as described in the Book of Kings. One English emissary at the Scottish court referred to it as 'the great temple of Solomon'. As the Old Testament incarnation of regal wisdom, King Solomon made a flattering *alter ego* for a scholar-monarch like James, and Scottish court poets did not hesitate to draw the comparison. Several royal processions also saw James VI being likened to Solomon.

Four years later, Schaw sat down in Holyrood Palace in Edinburgh to begin confidential negotiations on behalf of his Solomon. Across the table from him was a group of master masons, some of whom had been involved in the construction of the Chapel

Royal in Stirling. This meeting would inject some of the most exciting ideas circulating in the Renaissance culture of James VI's court into the medieval lore of working stonemasons as embodied in the Old Charges. The result would be Freemasonry.

Just as in England, Scottish stonemasons lacked organisational strength: their guilds included wrights as well. They had been further weakened by the Reformation. But once King James VI was firmly in charge, there was an upswing in the number of prestige building projects. The climate was right for a revival in the stonemasons' fortunes. Here and there in the years leading up to the meeting with Schaw, masons began to form local mason-only groups separate from, and unknown to, the guilds. They called these groups Lodges – the name being borrowed from the temporary shacks set up at building sites. For the first time, 'Lodge' was ceasing to be the name of a shack, and starting to be the name of an organisation.

The meeting with the *Maister o' Wark* in 1598 had an ambitious agenda. Schaw saw the nascent masons' organisations as a chance to bring an important train of followers into the royal fold. He wanted to set himself up as a nationwide patron, a 'General Warden', of the stonemasons. In the process, the stonemasons' Lodges would become part of a permanent national structure, holding regular meetings and keeping written records. This was a system that would exist in parallel to the town guilds at local level, but which would, in contrast to the guilds, be exclusively for stonemasons, and linked directly to the king.

Schaw's Lodges were secret, hidden from the eyes of the guilds and local authorities. Although the minutes of Lodge meetings were to be written down, they were to be concealed from outsiders; and even then, only the practical affairs of the building trade were to be recorded. But there was much, much more to Schaw's Lodges than practicalities. As one document from a seventeenth-century Scottish Lodge put it, there were 'secrets which must never be written'. But we can identify clues to those unwritten secrets – and the first of them is to be found in the agreement drawn up between Schaw and the stonemasons.

As a habitué of court life, Schaw understood how important flattery was. So he cosseted the stonemasons' collective pride by convening the meeting for 27 December, St John the Evangelist's day, a feast that the stonemasons, for reasons unknown, regarded as their trade's own holy day. (St John the Evangelist's day is still sacred to Freemasons, as is St John the Baptist's day in June.) Schaw also quoted the Old Charges at length in the agreement he drew up: his promise to the stonemasons was that the new Lodge system would allow them to enforce those long-cherished rules. Schaw could also reassure the stonemasons that a king who styled himself as Scotland's Solomon could only be sympathetic to their needs.

It was a powerful pitch. But Schaw went even further, drawing on Renaissance culture to find things that appealed to the stonemasons. He stipulated that all masons and apprentices should be subjected to a 'tryall of the art of memorie and science thairof' (a trial of the art and science of memory). Here was Schaw's most innovative move. Being a stonemason certainly entailed memorising a great deal, not least the Old Charges. Schaw now told the masons gathered about him that they were not just remembering, but practising the Art and Science of Memory.

It takes a little detour into the outer edges of Renaissance thought to understand the lavish scale of Schaw's flattery here. The Art of Memory was one of European culture's favourite borrowings from the classical past. The ancient Roman orator Cicero was the Art's most famous exponent, using it in every speech he ever made. King James VI is known to have taken lessons in it from one of his court poets. The trick is to picture yourself walking a set route through a large building. Each room represents a paragraph of your speech. Each feature in the room (like a column, an altar, a pattern of tiles in the floor) represents a particular point you want to make. Experienced practitioners of the Art of Memory could store and recall every word of a long discourse.

During the Renaissance, a few philosophers came to associate the Art of Memory with the search for wisdom. The idea was that God himself practised the Art of Memory, encoding the ultimate secrets of the universe in the world he created.

The small scholarly élite who practised the Art of Memory were the theoretical physicists of their day. The prospect they opened up was exhilarating, but potentially dangerous. Could mankind handle the enormity of what, at any moment, they might reveal? What if the newly rediscovered truth contradicted the Bible? For these reasons, some Renaissance intellectuals pursued their research in exclusive academies and secret societies. They hid their findings from profane eyes by using yet more codes and symbols. In their search for occult knowledge, the men in such groups were particularly drawn to a series of writings attributed to the semi-mythical ancient wise man Hermes Trismegistus. Indeed, because of him, they were often called Hermeticists. Britain's leading Hermeticist, the enigmatic Alexander Dicsone, was a regular presence at the Scottish court in the 1590s; James VI used him frequently as an emissary and propagandist.

Schaw was effectively telling the Scots stonemasons that they too were Hermeticists. Though they had not realised it, they were right at the forefront of humanity's most exalted philosophical endeavour. Just as Vitruvius had recommended in *De architectura*, they were intellectuals as well as builders. Hermeticism chimed powerfully with many of the bits and pieces of folklore that were already there in the stonemasons' Old Charges. Geometry. Arcane wisdom handed down since time immemorial. Hermes Trismegistus: the same wise man who, according to the Old Charges, had found masonic wisdom engraved on a pillar after the Flood. Secret societies devoted to the pursuit of occult truth. Great buildings as stores of sacred knowledge. The Art of Memory. And then, of course, symbols, symbols everywhere. The energy released by this confluence of the oral, craft culture of the medieval stonemasons, and the scholarly, Hermetic strand of Renaissance court culture was electrifying. The possibilities it opened up were endless. One consequence was that the stonemasons' Lodge was soon transformed from just an organisation to a place that was as much imaginary as real, where masons could exercise the Art of Memory together. The truths memorialised in the Lodge's allegorical layout and furnishings – columns, a patterned floor, and so on – helped convert the performance of craftsmen's rituals into something altogether momentous, and indeed almost magical. The Masonic Lodges of today are theatres where the Art of Memory is performed.

Under Schaw's influence, the Lodges remained full of *operative* stonemasons, but they also became *speculative* in the sense that they engaged in rituals with a philosophical aim – to use the terms employed by Masonic historians.

Schaw's negotiations with the stonemasons never reached a satisfactory conclusion. He drew up Statutes for the Lodges, but died in 1602. The new office of Warden General, as he envisaged it, did not outlive him. Thereafter, political change put paid to any stable deal between the stonemasons and the centre of power in Edinburgh. In 1603, Elizabeth I died. James VI of Scotland became James I of England, and the two crowns were united.

Nevertheless, Schaw's network of territorially based Lodges did survive and spread. By 1710, there were around thirty of them across Scotland. There is no English Masonic Lodge that can boast a documented date of birth earlier than 1716. Yet 80 per cent of the Scottish Lodges we know about from Schaw's time still exist today. Kilwinning, Edinburgh, Stirling: these are the oldest Masonic Lodges in the world, and have now been around for more than four centuries. Scottish Masons are very proud of this continuity over time.

In retrospect, we can see that through Schaw, the Renaissance court culture of James VI's day triggered a chain reaction within the stonemasons' Lodges. Over the coming decades, the kudos Schaw bestowed slowly began to draw in gentlemen.

Money was one important reason for this broadening of membership. If the new joiners were gentlemen rather than workers by hand, their generous contributions to the Lodge's shared feast or funeral fund would be very much welcome. They might bring the odd building commission too.

The ferocious religious and political tensions unleashed by the Reformation also played a part in making the Lodges attractive to outsiders. The stonemasons of Scotland were united by their trade, and not by their faith; there were both Protestants and Catholics among them. The Reformation had taught them to put career before credo. Schaw himself was a Catholic who had learned the discretion and deference needed to survive and prosper at a Protestant court. The Lodge was a haven, and it still is today. If Freemasonry has helped make the modern world, it is in part because it offers a refuge from the turmoil outside.

William Schaw's meeting with the stonemasons back in 1598 had created a system of Lodges, each based in a particular terri-tory. Within them, the members enacted secret rituals based on the Art of Memory, and cultivated a mixture of medieval artisan lore and some pickings from Renaissance scholarship. They prac-tised mutual assistance, brotherhood and a non-denominational form of piety. But the members of those Lodges were not quite Freemasons in the form we understand it: first, because they would not have recognised the label 'Freemason', which was almost unknown in Scotland; second, because their organisation was not centralised; and third, because the Lodges were still tied closely to the needs of the working stonemasons.

The transformation of the Schaw Lodges on the Scottish model into modern Freemasonry would begin as they spread southwards into England, where they became known collectively as the Acception.

Free and Accepted Masons

Freemasons often refer to themselves more formally as 'Free and Accepted Masons'. Few of them realise what the 'Accepted' part of the title actually refers to. Yet of the two adjectives 'Free' and 'Accepted', it is the second that is far more helpful in tracing the English stages in the early development of the Craft.

'Freemason' originally meant a mason who worked in 'free stone', which was a fine-grained sandstone or limestone. *Free-stone masons* or *free-masons* were the craftsmen who cut the stone to shape, as opposed to the less skilled *setters*, who merely put the dressed blocks into a wall. Over time, 'free mason' came to mean any superior craftsman working in stone. People kept using the word in this same way even after Freemasonry as we know it had emerged – a terminological slippage that creates great difficulties for historians.

In England, it is only when the historical documents start mentioning 'Accepted Masons', or a secret organisation known as the Acception, that we can identify the immediate predecessors of today's Brethren, because of the strong similarities between their rituals and those practised both by the Schaw Lodges and by modern Craftsmen. As the Acception spread, more evidence of the 'secrets which must never be written' leaked out. It was *Accepted* Masons of England who, over time, would make the name of Freemasons their own.

The appalling events during the reign of King James's son, Charles I, were crucial to the spread of the Schaw Lodges into England. The Civil Wars were triggered in Scotland in 1638 by a dispute over a prayer book, and only reached a definitive end in 1651. The whole of the British Isles was pitched into the very pit of hell. An estimated 800,000 were killed out of a total of 7.5 million inhabitants. Perhaps 40 per cent of the pre-war population of Ireland died. All this made the stonemasons' version of the Hermetic quest for enlightenment through symbols even more of a spiritual shelter.

Elias Ashmole, who was originally from Staffordshire in the West Midlands, became an Accepted Mason in October 1646 – the diary entry recounting his initiation is one of the earliest references to such a ceremony in England. Both the place of the initiation, and what Ashmole was doing at the time, are significant: he was initiated in Warrington, Lancashire, near where he was staying with his in-laws in order to recuperate from the ordeal of serving in the defeated Royalist army. For much of the Civil War, Lancashire was occupied by a Scots army. That army is thought to have been one of the main conduits for spreading the beliefs and practices of the Scottish Lodges. (The records of the Schaw Lodge in Edinburgh indicate that in May 1641, masons serving with the Scots army in northern England initiated other Civil War officers.)

Ashmole's military role made him a particularly good candidate: he was an artillery officer. Knowing their Vitruvius as they did, the Lodge members would have recalled that the revered author of *De architectura* had himself been a heavy weapons specialist in Julius Caesar's legions, constructing and operating all manner of missile-throwing engines. Artillerymen, with their understanding of trajectories and other aspects of the great science of geometry, were pretty much honorary stonemasons.

Ashmole developed into a man of wide and (to our eyes) very peculiar interests. He was an antiquarian who studied, catalogued and collected everything from ancient coins to unusual zoological specimens; he is best known today because his artefacts formed the basis of Oxford's Ashmolean Museum. He was passionately devoted to the study of heraldry, and his insights as an astrologer were valued by King Charles II. He researched magical sigils and alchemy, and thought that he was endowed with intellectual powers deriving from the movements of the planet Mercury.

These were just the kind of esoteric pursuits that drew gentlemen towards the Lodges. One example was Ashmole's

Elias Ashmole (1617-1692).

interest in Rosicrucianism, which was part of a fashion for secret societies and occult wisdom. In the mid-1610s, European culture had been transfixed by reports from Germany that a mysterious and sacred brotherhood, centuries old, had been discovered. Known as the Order of the Rose Cross, or the Rosicrucian Order, it owed its name to its founder, a mystic and doctor called Christian Rosenkreuz, who had learned great secrets during his travels to the Orient. Rosicrucian texts expounded a new mélange of Hermeticism and Christianity, and proclaimed the imminent dawning of a new spiritual age.

Alas, like its founder, the Rosicrucian Order did not exist: it was an allegory, and possibly even an outright hoax. But that did not stop people wanting to join it, or being galvanised by its ideas. Some of the gentlemen drawn to the Lodges in Scotland

and England may have thought they were joining the Rosicrucian Order, or something like it. And even if they did not, the Rosicrucian myth helped them add more layers of symbolism to Masonry. For example, the ritual of Hiram Abiff's death and resurrection is thought to derive from Rosicrucian necromancy.

Ashmole remained a member of the Acception throughout his life. He attended a meeting of Accepted Masons in London in 1682. His diary tells us that 'I was the Senior Fellow among them (it being 35 yeares since I was admitted)', and that afterwards, 'We all dyned at the halfe Moone Taverne in Cheapeside, at a Noble Dinner prepaired at the charge of the New-accepted Masons.'

The most detailed account of the Acception's workings, one that bears marked similarities to the rituals of Freemasonry, comes from the county of Ashmole's birth, Staffordshire. In 1686 Robert Plot, Professor of Chemistry at Oxford University, published an account of the county that devotes several pages to the Accepted Masons. Professor Plot was not a member himself. However, as well as being an Oxford don, Plot was also the keeper of the university's newly established Ashmolean Museum, so Ashmole may well have been his inside source.

Plot was deeply suspicious of the Brothers' secretiveness, and concluded that they were liable to commit 'mischeif' [sic]. Nevertheless, he had heard enough about them to offer important evidence. Accepted Masons were initiated 'at a meeting (or *Lodg* as they term it in some places) which must consist at lest of 5 or 6 of the *Ancients* of the *Order*, whom the *candidats* present with *gloves* . . .' The initiation ritual, he explained, 'cheifly consists in the communication of certain *secret signes* whereby they are known to one another all over the *Nation*'. There were two routes to joining the Acception: either you could be a stone-mason; or you could be a non-mason of high standing who was 'adopted' or 'accepted' – hence the name Acception.

Apart from the Civil War, other social changes were increasing the appeal of the Lodges across Britain. The Renaissance had begun in Italy in the fifteenth century as a drive to rediscover classical learning. By the middle of the seventeenth century, the ancients had been surpassed. Could Aristotle disseminate his findings in printed books? Did the Phoenicians discover the Americas? Could Caesar's legions deploy cannon? A host of useful novelties, from microscopes to pocket watches, from musket cartridges to air pumps, not only beat anything that the classical world had to offer, but also exalted the skills and knowledge of technical folk. A newly discovered fondness for technology was narrowing the gap between the life of the mind and a hands-on engagement with the world. It no longer seemed distasteful that an intellectually inclined gentleman might have a thing to learn from a craftsman. The idea that Almighty God might be thought of as the Great Architect of the Universe was no longer a demeaning analogy.

As more gentlemen were recruited to the Schaw Lodges and the Acception towards the end of the seventeenth century and the beginning of the eighteenth, more information about their rituals and beliefs surfaced. The Lodges themselves kept more records, and they even wrote down the 'secrets which must never be written' to provide handy guides for gentlemen joiners. Both the Schaw Lodges and the Accepted Masons had the same mixed bag of oaths, secret signs and myths that bears all kinds of similarities to the Masonic ritualising described by John Coustos to the Lisbon Inquisition in 1743, and carried out in today's Masonic Lodges. Being initiated involved taking a vow of secrecy on pain of 'being buried within the flood-Mark, where no man shall know'. There were signs to learn, including a throat-cutting gesture, and a handshake: 'som secret signe delivered from hand to hand'. Masons absorbed a mythical story of the organisation's origins in Solomon's Temple; they learned the code-words, BOAZ and JACHIN (the names of the two pillars at the entrance to the Temple).

Thus far, Freemasonry had evolved slowly. At around the year 1700, a century after William Schaw's catalytic meeting with the

Scots master masons, it was widespread, but remained uncentralised, and was still connected to the working lives of stonemasons. Outside Scotland, there were important concentrations of Accepted Masonry in areas like Staffordshire and Cheshire, and in cities like York and London.

It would take more than the passage of time to work the final emergence of Freemasonry. First of all, it would take the regenerative catastrophe that famously began on 2 September 1666 with a spark at Thomas Farriner's bakery on Pudding Lane in London. A Great Fire consumed the City of London in five days. The reconstruction would last fifty years, and require the skills of England's greatest workers in stone.

London: **At the Sign of the Goose and Gridiron**

Topping out

On 26 October 1708, a small party of men reached the uppermost planks of the scaffolding that cradled St Paul's Cathedral's cupola, which was newly clad in the finest Derbyshire lead. As they recovered their breath, they had every reason to relish the view.

Far out beyond the cathedral's twin west towers, Windsor Castle stood proud of the landscape. To the north, the men could gaze on the wooded hills of Hampstead and Highgate. Looking east, as far as the sea, they could follow the meandering of the Thames, its waters crowded with ships and barges bringing the wealth of Boston, Barbados and Bengal. Although, at this height, the surrounding streets were enveloped in quiet, London's characteristic sooty reek still filled the nostrils. Indeed, once the open countryside ended and buildings began – at Piccadilly in the west and at White Chapel in the east – a good part of the view was masked by coal smoke. Nevertheless, among the slanting plumes, church spires and towers revealed themselves. The men knew them like they knew the faces of their children. St Bride's in Fleet Street, with its slender stack of pagodas. The cylindrical steeple of St Michael, Crooked Lane, with its elegantly curved and arched buttresses. There was no mistaking St Benet's in Paul's Wharf, its red brick tower cornered in stone and capped by a neat dome and lantern. Each church was new, each unique, and each a noble testament to the glory of God, to the skills of the men gathered high on the scaffolding, and to the years they had spent resurrecting London after the inferno that consumed it in 1666.

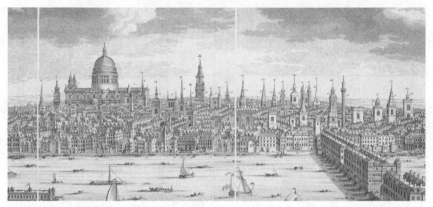

St Paul's Cathedral and the Wren churches seen from the south
at the time modern Freemasonry was born.

Sir Christopher Wren was the directing intelligence of that resurrection: the chief architect of the cathedral, as of the fifty-one new churches that graced the city. Wren was at St Paul's that day. However, burdened by his seventy-six years, he had not attempted the ascent. Instead he waited below while the group led by his son performed the topping-out ceremony: the brief but solemn moment when the last stone was placed in the lantern that crowned the cathedral dome.

Setting the finishing stone brought a justifiable sense of closure. It was not just that Sir Christopher Wren had become the first architect in history to oversee the entire process of constructing a cathedral from beginning to end. Several families, including Wren's own, were integral to the story of the new St Paul's. When the foundation stone had been laid in June 1675, Wren's son Christopher was only four months old. Thirty-three years later, the baby had become his father's right-hand man, worthy of the honour of leading the topping-out ceremony. Also present at the laying of the first stone in 1675 had been Wren's most trusted master mason, Thomas Strong. After Strong's death, his younger brother Edward smoothly replaced him, and now took part in the topping-out ceremony. Alongside Edward Strong was his own son, also called Edward, who was a bosom friend of Christopher Wren junior. Edward Strong junior had constructed the great lantern that they were now completing.

Yet it was more than family, friendship and a generation of shared endeavour that united the men on the scaffolding above the dome that day. A Wren family memoir recorded the moment for posterity, and made it clear that the little group performing the topping out were Brothers: 'The highest or last Stone on the Top of the Lantern was laid by the Hands of the Surveyor's Son, Christopher Wren, deputed by his Father, in the Presence of that excellent Artificer Mr. Strong, his Son, and other Free and Accepted Masons, chiefly employed in the Execution of the Work.' *Free and Accepted Masons*. The Strongs were members of the Acception. When Edward Strong senior died in 1724, a weekly newspaper referred to him as 'one of the ancientest Masons and FREEMASONS in England'. The following year, Strong's son Edward junior was listed as belonging to a Masonic Lodge that met in Greenwich.

Christopher Wren, both father and son, were also Accepted Masons. Sir Christopher was 'adopted a brother' of the Acception on 18 May 1691, at 'a great Convention at St Paul's of the Fraternity of Accepted Masons'. When Wren died, several newspaper tributes would refer to him as a Freemason, which – given that the great man was definitely not a stonemason – can only mean that he was a member of the Acception. Christopher Wren junior was certainly a member: he would serve as Master of his Masonic Lodge in 1729.

We know of other Accepted Masons involved in the rebuilding of London. Thomas Wise (1618–85) was a master mason who took on contracts for some of the early work on St Paul's Cathedral; he is known to have presided over a meeting of the

Acception in 1682. John Thompson (?–1700) was an Accepted Mason who was the contractor for a number of Wren's City of London churches, including St Vedast's, St Mary-le-Bow and All Hallows in Lombard Street.

As architects, the Wrens had an obvious affinity with the master builders who formed the backbone of the Acception. Apart from the Wrens, there were other leading figures in public life with no links to the construction industry who were accepted. In 1708, the year of the topping-out ceremony at St Paul's, one documenter of London life called the Acception a 'Fraternity of many of the Nobility and Gentry'.

The Acception in London had begun life as part of the Company of Masons: there are sparse references to it in the Company archives dating back to 1630. The London Company of Masons was one of the very few stonemasons' guilds, founded in the mid-fourteenth century and granted the right to wear livery in 1481. But unlike the guilds of other trades, it was a club exclusively for the élite of the construction business, with just their favourite artisans. Membership of the London Acception was by invitation only. Joining was also expensive – fees were twice the already costly dues for joining the London Company within which it grew. The Acception has been described by one of the most important historians of early Freemasonry as 'an exclusive cell within the London Company'. Towards the end of the seventeenth century, it became an independent body.

Accepted Masons in London were an élite within the élite, therefore – and the Strongs very much belonged in that category. Edward senior inherited quarries in two counties from his stonemason father. On top of their income from the family quarries, the Strongs earned substantial fees for taking on major contracts for building parts of St Paul's Cathedral and Wren's churches, organising the large teams of stoneworkers that were needed for the job. They undertook many other prestigious projects too – including the Royal Naval Hospital, Greenwich, and Blenheim Palace, the Oxfordshire seat of the Churchill family. The Strongs had very deep pockets: because the government was not very good at paying its contractors promptly, they often had to advance huge sums in wages and materials. At one point they even loaned the government money to help keep the work on St Paul's going. Edward Strong senior also got involved in property speculation on the side; and he would bequeath a number of country houses to his son at his death. The Strongs, in short, are nothing like the humble medieval artisans of Masonic legend. They, and other members of the Acception, became enormously wealthy on the public money that flowed into rebuilding England's capital after the Great Fire.

The topping-out ceremony at St Paul's signalled the beginning of the end of the reconstruction of London – and of the funds. Much of the money came from a tax on coal, which was the very fuel whose smoke masked the view from the dome of St Paul's. The last of the three government levies on coal expired in September 1716, and the reconstruction budget ran out early the following year. London's resurrection was complete.

The London Acception was certainly exclusive and prestigious, but it was relatively unknown. The end of London's rebuilding precipitated events that would turn it into the most famous secret society in the world.

As well as being a genius, Sir Christopher Wren was by all accounts a very nice man. Mild of temperament, he was loyal to his friends, dedicated to his job and utterly untainted by corruption – which in eighteenth-century England was little short of saintly. There would be a good case for portraying him as the embodiment of the ideals of Freemasonry. But he was elderly, his task was finished and he was now a tempting political target. In April 1718, he was sacked as Royal Surveyor, a post that he retained in a largely honorary capacity in recognition of his life's work. He was substituted by a political placeman who proceeded to launch vindictive mismanagement charges against him.

Wren's problem was not just that the coal tax had run out: even more seriously, he found himself on the wrong side of the major political cleavage of the age. British history in the seventeenth and early eighteenth centuries pivoted on the questions of religion and the relationship between parliament and the monarchy, as was clear from the so-called 'Glorious Revolution' of 1688–9. James II, of the Stuart dynasty, produced a male Catholic heir by his Catholic wife; he also dreamed of emulating the absolutism of Catholic Europe, in which the king was invested with unconditional authority directly by God. So, in the Glorious Revolution, those for whom Catholicism and absolutism were abhorrent replaced James with his Protestant daughter Mary, and her Protestant Dutch husband William. The kings and queens who ruled from then on did so on condition that they needed the approval of the Lords and the Commons to make law. Yet even after the Glorious Revolution, the same religious and political issues rumbled on, taking the form of the struggle between Tories and Whigs.

Tories were partisans of monarchical power and the Anglican Church. At its edges, Toryism blurred into pro-Catholicism and Jacobitism, which was the programme to bring a Catholic male descendant of James II, deposed in the Glorious Revolution, back to the throne. The decades after the Glorious Revolution were punctuated by a series of Jacobite uprisings.

Whigs, by contrast, were partisans of a monarchy that ruled subject to parliament's approval, and of a measure of religious toleration within an Anglican state presided over by a Protestant monarch.

In 1714, the struggle between the two parties reached a critical stage when Queen Anne died without an heir. Anne was a member of the Stuart dynasty, a conservative Anglican in religion, and Tory in her political sympathies. The only plausible Protestant successor was George, the Prince-Elector of Hanover in Germany, who was a Lutheran, and very much a Whig. When the Prince-Elector took the throne as George I, thereby founding the Hanover dynasty, the Whigs embarked on a flagrant power-grab. They expelled Tories from every possible position of influence in the civil service, the professions, the armed forces, the universities and the Church. Sir Christopher Wren was attacked because he was a prominent Tory: his family's loyalty to the Stuart dynasty dated back to his father's service to Charles I before the Civil Wars. The placeman who took his position was a Whig. The charges against Wren were thrown out a year later, and his replacement dismissed for incompetence and corruption. But the great architect's vulnerability was clear.

This dramatic change in the balance of power between Tories and Whigs, along with the end to London's reconstruction, severed the Tory patronage networks that had helped the contractors of the London Acception grow so rich over the past half-century. It was time for the Whigs to take control, and transform the Acception into a patronage network of their own.

Dr Desaguliers

The Goose and Gridiron ale house stood in St Paul's Churchyard, a street running along the south side of the great cathedral, whose taverns and booksellers had been a hub of London's cultural life since long before the Great Fire. The Goose and Gridiron had a specific resonance for Free and Accepted Masons. Absolute documentary proof is wanting, but it is likely that it was the very place where Sir Christopher Wren was 'accepted' in 1691.

On St John the Baptist's day, 24 June 1717, men from four different Masonic Lodges assembled at the Goose and Gridiron. Each of the Lodges took its name from the tavern where it met: the Crown in Parker's Lane, near Drury Lane; the Apple Tree in Charles Street, Covent Garden; the Rummer and Grapes in Channel Row, Westminster; and the Goose and Gridiron itself.

The main business of the meeting was to elect an otherwise undistinguished gentleman bookseller called Anthony Sayer to a new post within the Craft: Grand Master. The consequences of the meeting would be immense. A Grand Lodge emerged, claiming the authority to decide and enforce the rules of the entire Brotherhood. Modern Freemasonry dates its beginnings from that day in 1717: in 2017, the three-hundredth anniversary was celebrated by Brothers across the world.

The famous meeting in the Goose and Gridiron was a turning-point in the history of the Craft. Which is why it is so perplexing that we know so little about it. No material traces are left: the Goose and Gridiron and the other three pubs where the founding Lodges met have long since been demolished. More curiously, the Freemasons, who are normally punctilious documenters of their own activities, have no contemporary records of the meeting. As we shall see, there are reasons to suspect a cover-up. The years between 1717 and 1723 were the most important in the whole history of Freemasonry, and yet they are also the most enigmatic: they deserve to be placed under the historical microscope.

The birth of what would become the Grand Lodge took place just as the money to rebuild the City of London ran out, and just as the new Whig regime was establishing itself. The men who created the Grand Lodge were ambitious, formidable networkers, and all Whigs. There is much to be learned from a pen portrait of the most important of them, the real orchestrator of the Goose and Gridiron meeting: Dr John Theophilus Desaguliers.

Dr Desaguliers was a crucial figure in shaping the history, ritual and values of the Craft in ways that still endure. Apart from being one of the main creators of the Grand Lodge, he introduced educational lectures in Lodge meetings, and helped establish the Grand Lodge charity. On his travels, he would also help spread the Craft to Europe.

Like a good number of early Masons, including John Coustos, Desaguliers was from a family of French Protestant refugees – his father was a Huguenot. Like many Huguenots, indeed like many immigrants, Desaguliers was ambitious, hardworking and eager to fit in. Despite the hardship of his early surroundings, he went to Oxford University and embarked on an ecclesiastical career. But religion seems to have been a means to an end for Desaguliers, who became notorious for his tedious sermons.

His real interests lay in his flourishing career as a scientist, public lecturer and showman. As a student at Oxford, he had fallen under the spell of Sir Isaac Newton, and he developed a zeal for demonstrating Newton's theories in striking experiments. In Enlightenment England, especially London, there was an audience prepared to pay well for such entertainment. Thanks to Newton, without disbursing the usual membership fee, Dr Desaguliers was invited to join the Royal Society, where commoners and aristocrats mixed in the shared pursuit of scientific knowledge and the prestige that went with it. Desaguliers was even paid to curate experiments. He would become Newton's principal demonstrator, and the leading public lecturer in a very competitive field. In 1717, the year of the Goose and Gridiron meeting, the 'ingenious Mr Desaguliers' was invited to demonstrate his experiments before King George. It was to be the first of several such royal engagements, which earned him significant financial rewards. Desaguliers also set out his stall as an engineering consultant, and addressed practical challenges such as brewing beer, draining coalmines, orchestrating firework displays and mending the smoking chimneys in the House of Commons.

The multi-talented John Desaguliers would not have achieved half as much without one talent in particular: a gift for making influential Whig friends. In 1716 he became chaplain to James Brydges, soon to become 1st Duke of Chandos, a Whig grandee whose patronage would be crucial in his rise. His network of contacts quickly spread deep into the community of scientists and their aristocratic patrons. One indicator is the list of godparents he managed to secure for his children in the 1720s. Apart from Sir Isaac Newton, they included the Marquis of Carnarvon, who was the eldest surviving son of the Duke of Chandos, and the Earl of Macclesfield – a fabulously wealthy Whig courtier and Lord Chancellor who would later be prosecuted for taking enormous bribes. It was mightily impressive for the son of a refugee like Desaguliers to have such traction in high places.

John Theophilus Desaguliers (1683–1744).
The inscription contains a boast about his
connection to the Duke of Chandos.

Desaguliers *lived* by networking and self-promotion. Freemasonry was all part of this personal strategy. In a society where power and wealth were still overwhelmingly concentrated in the hands of the landed and titled, those who wanted to better themselves had little choice but to make influential friends. So we should not imagine that Desaguliers' hungry networking made him, and many other Masons like him, any less sincere in espousing Masonic values. Indeed, he took Masonry with gouty seriousness, using his power in the Grand Lodge to eliminate the knockabout comedy that had crept in to the way some Lodges performed their rituals: one manuscript from the 1690s talks about the way candidates for membership would be frightened with '1000 ridicolous postures and grimmaces'. After Desaguliers, Masonic workings would become much more solemn.

Nor should it strike us as strange that a man of science like Dr Desaguliers was drawn to a Brotherhood so wedded to pre-scientific beliefs as the Freemasons. Certainly, he performed famous experiments to prove the inanity of myths like the perpetual-motion machine. Yet he lived in an age where the boundaries between science and superstition were still far from clearly demarcated. Sir Isaac Newton himself believed in the alchemical search for the Philosopher's Stone and the Elixir of Life; the great man was no Accepted Mason, but he pored over the design of Solomon's Temple in the search for ancient truths.

For Desaguliers, Freemasonry was all of a piece with his personal ambition, his politics and his intellectual passions. He was nothing like the power-hungry placemen who represented the worst face of the Whig regime. His Freemasonry breathed the most rarefied vapours of Whig philosophy: he even wrote a poem that merged the Newtonian system, Masonic symbols and the Hanoverian monarchy into a single vision of universal harmony. But Desaguliers' politics were nonetheless crucial in the formation of the Grand Lodge. Allied with him behind the scenes in the creation of the Grand Lodge, and in the subsequent rapid expansion of Masonry, were some influential Whig networks concentrated in two places in particular. The first was among the natural philosophers of the Royal Society. All of the Secretaries of the Royal Society from 1714 to 1747 were Freemasons. The second Whig Masonic network dominated the magistrates' bench. The magistracy was responsible for London's law and order as well as a range of other duties, such as licensing taverns. As the historian responsible for the best research into early Masonic networks puts it, 'many London Freemasons represented precisely the type of men the Whig government would have favoured on the bench as conformist and conventional upholders of the status quo'. In Whig London, in return for political loyalty, Freemasonry offered access to prestige and influence that had little to do with the construction industry. The Whig takeover finally broke the link between 'operatives' and 'speculatives', that is between workers in stone and Freemasons.

Whig power is stamped all over Freemasonry as it emerged after the fateful meeting in the Goose and Gridiron in 1717. But the subsequent history of the Craft would also be shaped by a crisis that nearly brought the regime down. The political season that permitted the Whig power-grab following the accession of George I turned out to be short. In 1720, the South Sea Bubble calamitously exposed the state's weakness. Whole swathes of the élite, both Whig and Tory, were implicated in the fraud and corruption that fuelled the boom in the stock price of the South Sea Company, and most made huge losses when the bubble burst. Suddenly, protecting the establishment from the fallout overrode all other political priorities. Sir Robert Walpole emerged with a plan to screen off the worst effects of the scandal at the head of a more conciliatory form of Whiggism. Walpole would also command a system of patronage and corruption on an unheard-of scale. Now generally referred to as the first ever British Prime Minister, he would remain in charge for more than two decades.

One sign of how close the Craft was to these developments is that, although the date of his initiation is uncertain, Walpole had become a Freemason by 1731 at the latest. Among Free and Accepted Masons, as in British politics generally, there was a panicked outbreak of hatchet-burying in the aftermath of the South Sea Bubble. The Whigs remained in charge, but their arrogance was now subdued. Freemasonry sought internal peace at all costs, and needed to bind itself tightly to the Whig regime. Drawing on his contacts, in 1721 Desaguliers recruited the Duke of Montagu, a Whig insider and member of the Royal Society, as Freemasonry's first blue-blooded Grand Master.

On the prompting of Desaguliers, the Duke of Montagu then ordered a Masonic rulebook to be written so as to cement the authority of the Whig Grand Lodge. The rulebook would also comprise the first official history of Freemasonry – one designed to bury anything politically controversial about how the Grand Lodge had come into being, including whatever really happened at the Goose and Gridiron.

Harmony and history

By far the most important book in the history of the Craft is *The Constitutions of the Freemasons. Containing the History, Charges, Regulations &c. of that Most Ancient and Right Worshipful Fraternity*. First published in 1723, it was issued again in a revised edition in 1738 when Freemasonry, and the Grand Lodge's pre-eminent place within it, were well established.

At the book's core are the 'Charges of a Free-Mason': the rulebook that makes Masonry what it is. The *Constitutions* contain new laws about the conduct of Lodge business that are obviously meant to help establish the Grand Lodge's dominance: anyone founding an unauthorised Lodge will be considered a 'rebel', for example. There are also the more traditional ground rules often referred to by Masons as their Landmarks. We know many of the other Landmarks already, having encountered them in John Coustos's confession, and in the precepts that are still explained during initiation rituals today. Masons must be respectful to the powers that be, and keep the Brotherhood's secrets. Craftsmen are all equal: 'brethren upon the same level'. Between them, religious and ethnic tolerance must reign: 'we are of all Nations, Tongues, Kindreds and Languages'. They are not to be 'stupid atheists' or divided by their religious faith, since they are all to believe in the 'Great Architect of the Universe'. Religion is not to be a topic of discussion in the Lodge. Women are not allowed, and neither are 'bondmen' – so strictly no slaves. (This is a prohibition that would cause a good deal of trouble as the story of Masonry unfolded.) Most importantly, and somewhat hypocritically given how the Grand Lodge emerged, Masons were ordered to be single-mindedly averse to all factionalism: 'resolv'd against all *Politicks*'.

In addition to Landmarks, the *Constitutions* also contain a history of Freemasonry that is mostly fantastical – as fantastical as the medieval stonemasons' Old Charges, which are one of its main sources. The book's title page states that it was published in *Anno Domini 1723*, or the *Year of Masonry 5723*. Masons were so confident of their place in the eternal order that they thought themselves custodians of a wisdom that dated back to the start of the world in 4000 BCE. Thus Masonic history starts with the first man: Adam must have had 'Masonry written on his heart' because he taught his son Cain, who built a city – and therefore was a Mason. Adam's direct male descendant Noah was also a Mason because, although his ark was made of wood rather than stone, it 'was certainly fabricated by *Geometry*, and according to the rules of *Masonry*.' The Israelites, who learned the Craft during their captivity in Egypt, 'were a whole Kingdom of *Masons*, well instructed, under the Conduct of their GRAND MASTER MOSES, who often marshall'd them into a regular and *general Lodge*, while in the wilderness'. And so breezily on. There is nothing at all unusual in this style of history-writing in the early eighteenth century. The anachronistic gimmick is simple: anyone in history who built anything vaguely memorable was, by that very fact, a Freemason. The Emperor Augustus, for example, was 'rationally believ'd' to be 'the *Grand-Master* of the Lodge at Rome'. Naturally enough, this invented Masonic tradition found its high point in the building of Solomon's Temple in Jerusalem, and has carried on virtually unbroken until the present day.

The 'history' set out in the *Constitutions* is little more than a procession of Masons that oozes Brotherly Peace and Harmony. Only a few passages betray its partisan Whig intent: notably the ones where the Tory Sir Christopher Wren is given a hard time.

The original 1723 edition of the *Constitutions* does mention Wren a couple of times. But given that early Freemasons were so proud of Britain's neoclassical architecture and its place in the

Masonic tradition, and given that Wren was a neoclassical architect who utterly dominated the British architectural scene, those mentions are pointedly short and grudging. The *Constitutions* do not even do Wren the minimum honour of referring to him as a Freemason: the Whig Craft clearly did not want to claim him as one of its own.

The 1738 edition of the *Constitutions* is more forthcoming about Wren, but also more damning. Admittedly, Wren is now granted his due place in the pantheon of great builders. He is also acknowledged as a Freemason, and referred to as the Deputy Grand Master of Freemasonry in 1666, and Grand Master a few years later. (The dates and titles may well be meaningless, given that the *Constitutions* called everyone from Augustus to King Charles I a Grand Master.) But when it came to the foundation of the Grand Lodge in 1717, the *Constitutions* of 1738 tell us several times that the London Lodges were driven to take the initiative at the Goose and Gridiron because they felt 'neglected' by Wren. It is also claimed that Wren abandoned the duties of Grand Master from the moment in 1708 when his son set the last stone in the lantern of St Paul's Cathedral.

In the world of Masonic Peace and Harmony set out by the *Constitutions*, neglect is about the most severe criticism that can be directed at a Brother. No allowances are made for Wren's age and frailty: he was nearly eighty-five years old when the Goose and Gridiron meeting happened, and he passed away in the year the *Constitutions* were first published. The Grand Lodge was securely established by the time the second edition of the *Constitutions* appeared, and Wren had been dead for fifteen years, yet still his Tory affiliation led to his being traduced.

The sideswipes at Wren are not the only sign that something suspicious was going on behind the scenes. The *Constitutions* mention the destruction of highly significant historical documents that took place at various points in the recent history of Freemasonry. In particular, in 1720, the year of the South Sea

Bubble crisis, 'at some private Lodges, several very valuable Manuscripts (for they had nothing yet in Print) concerning the Fraternity, their Lodges, Regulations, Charges, Secrets, and Usages [. . .] were too hastily burnt by some scrupulous Brothers'. Cryptically, the only explanation offered for this drastic cleansing of the historical record is 'a Fear of making Discoveries' and the need to stop the papers falling 'into strange Hands'. Someone clearly wanted the recent past erased, and the *Constitutions* were not at all keen to explain why.

That was not the end of the editing. Whole chapters of Masonic history as I have summarised it thus far were cut out by the *Constitutions*. The crucial 1717 meeting at the Goose and Gridiron does not even rate a mention in the 1723 edition. In the 1738 edition, we get a brief account of the Goose and Gridiron meeting, and its role in creating the Grand Lodge. But beyond telling us that the meeting happened, and providing a list of the four Lodges in attendance, the book says virtually nothing. As a result, we will never know exactly what went on in that pub on that particular day. The only conclusion we can possibly draw is that Dr John Desaguliers and the other founders of modern Freemasonry broke one of the great Masonic taboos when they set up the Grand Lodge: they indulged in low-down, power-grabbing, partisan *Politicks*.

The Acception is also chopped out of Masonic history by the *Constitutions*. We can only guess that this was because it was so tainted by Toryism.

Going right back, Scotland and the Lodges influenced by *Maister o' Wark* William Schaw are virtually obliterated. The *Constitutions* give us a shamelessly anglicised narrative that contains little more than a few anodyne references to the venerable 'Records and Traditions' of the Scots Lodges.

The omission of the Schaw Lodges is all the more remarkable given that the man who actually wrote the *Constitutions*, under Dr Desaguliers' close supervision, was a scholar called James Anderson. Anderson could hardly have been a better incarnation of Scottish Masonry: a red-headed, nonconformist minister whose own father was a senior member of an Aberdeen Schaw Lodge.

Several things account for the way Scotland was edited out of Masonic history by the *Constitutions*. The first is prejudice. At a time when lots of Scots like Anderson were moving to London, English perceptions of them were stereotypical: a funny accent, red hair, ignorance of the proper way to use a privy, etc. More significantly, Scotland inspired nervousness because of its religious extremism: both Catholic Jacobitism and Protestant nonconformity were strong north of the border. Finally, Scotland was the ancestral home of the Stuart dynasty, to which Tories and Jacobites were attached. Scotland meant controversy, which was the one thing the Whig Masons grouped around the Grand Lodge wanted to avoid. So the crucial role that Scotland had played in the early history of the Craft was excised. Schaw may have taught Craftsmen the Art of Memorie in Edinburgh, but the *Constitutions* taught them the art of forgetting in London. No wonder Freemasons since then have had such a hard time tracing their true lineage.

Yet in 1722, when the evasive, rose-water history of Freemasonry contained in *The Constitutions of the Freemasons* had been written but not yet published, controversy exploded nonetheless, and it nearly proved disastrous.

Duking it out

Two men stand facing one another in graceful three-quarter poses. Crowned, bewigged, and draped in velvet and ermine as they are, there can be no doubt of their noble pedigree. Framing them, a floor of square tiles and a roofless classical colonnade recede geometrically towards an archway. Floating between them, captioned by the word 'Eureka!' in Greek script, is a diagram illustrating Euclid's 47th proposition: the square of the hypotenuse is equal to the sum of the squares of the two sides. In the sky above, the sun-god Apollo ascends to the high noon of wisdom in his chariot. To our left, one man – he looks slightly older than the other – is graciously proffering two things: a Masonic compass and a scroll on which can be read the word CONSTI-TU-TIONS. To our right, with the slightest of bows, the second man gestures his respectful acceptance. The whole scene radiates proportion and harmony, dignity and sagacity: it is one of Freemasonry's many dream visions of itself.

The engraving I have just described was specially executed as the celebratory frontispiece to *The Constitutions of the Freemasons* of 1723. This is the volume represented, at the centre of the engraving, by the scroll bearing the word CONSTI-TU-TIONS. For all that it is highly idealised, the engraving nonetheless depicts a real event. The nobleman at the centre-left of the engraving – the one proffering the compass and scroll – is John Montagu, 2nd Duke of Montagu, Freemasonry's first aristocratic Grand Master, and the man who ordered the *Constitutions* to be written in September 1721. Publication came in 1723, when the Grand Lodge was presided over by its second noble Grand Master, Philip Wharton, the 1st Duke of Wharton, who is the man accepting the compass and scroll.

What the engraving wants us to imagine is a smooth handover of authority in the Grand Lodge, and the serene incorporation of the *Constitutions* into the fabric of Masonic life. What the engraving demands that we forget, by contrast, is the fact that the 1st Duke of Wharton was a libertine, drunkard, political chancer, blasphemer, spendthrift and traitor who nearly wrecked modern Freemasonry before it had taken its first steps.

Wharton had only been initiated into Freemasonry in the summer of 1721, just a few weeks after Montagu became Grand Master. He was a young man, twenty-two at the time, so the Grand Lodge may have hoped that he was impressionable enough to learn the Craft's ways. If so, the hope was soon destroyed: Wharton broke protocol after the ceremony by parading back to his house in Pall Mall in his new apron and gloves. Trouble was on the way.

The illustration on the frontispiece of *The Constitutions of the Freemasons* (1723) shows the two noble Grand Masters who were central to the intrigues behind the foundation of modern Freemasonry.

Whoever proposed Wharton for initiation into Freemasonry probably intended to provoke the Whig faction around Dr John Desaguliers that ran the Grand Lodge. Wharton was a profoundly unstable character. At sixteen, in 1715, he had eloped with a Major-General's daughter. His father's death, a few weeks later, gave him a Dukedom and broke any remaining restraint on his behaviour. The following year he betrayed his family's Whig allegiances by paying a visit in France to James Francis Edward Stuart – the Catholic 'Old Pretender' whom the Jacobites were conspiring to place on the throne. There could be no doubting the treasonous nature of the meeting: Wharton received a noble title from the Old Pretender. The Whig political establishment made patient efforts to bring him back into the fold. But in 1719 he founded the Hellfire Club with the aim of promoting blasphemy and sacrilege. Wharton was also a gambler and drunkard. Worse still, he was by this time hopelessly in hock to Jacobite moneylenders, and invested much of the borrowed cash in the South Sea Bubble. He lost the colossal sum of £120,000 (roughly £14 million today) in the crash of 1720, and lashed out against the Whig government in the House of Lords as a result. Late in 1721, he voted with the government again – but only after pocketing a chunky bribe.

Wharton's volatility was matched by his ambition. In June 1722, only ten months after his initiation into Freemasonry, he seized the Grand Mastership. The day before the annual feast at which the Duke of Montagu was due to be reconfirmed, Wharton gathered a meeting of a Tory faction within the Craft, and had himself hailed as Grand Master. At the feast the following day in Stationers' Hall, the Whigs engineered a last-ditch compromise: Wharton was confirmed as Grand Master, and the trusty Whig Dr Desaguliers became his Deputy. There was nonetheless a drunken stand-off. The Tories sang 'When the King Enjoys his Own Again', a Jacobite marching song that was pretty much guaranteed to spark a fight in any tavern in the land. The Whigs responded with toasts to King George and 'the present Administration'.

After a long delay caused by all the politicking, while the fragile truce within Grand Lodge Masonry held, the *Constitutions* were finally approved for publication in January 1723 – complete with the frontispiece showing a fictionalised version of the transition between the previous Grand Master and the current one. The publication of the *Constitutions* was to be the only achievement of the Duke of Wharton's reign as Grand Master. Hopes that he could be held in check were dashed when he became ever more outspoken in his endorsement of Jacobites – and this at a time when troops were camped in Hyde Park to deter the threat of an insurrection. A terrifying prospect opened up: Freemasonry could become caught up in treason.

The chance to remove Wharton would only come at the St John

the Baptist's day feast of June 1723. Desaguliers identified the Earl of Dalkeith, a politically inert Whig, as a suitably inoffensive replacement. Wharton may have gone along with this plan initially, but when he learned that Dr Desaguliers was to be re-elected as Deputy Grand Master, he demanded a recount and then stormed out.

Wharton never ceased to be an embarrassment. In 1724, he attracted a deal of press attention when he founded the Gormogons, a short-lived secret society intended as a parody of Freemasonry. The following year, fleeing his wife, his creditors and his political enemies, he went into exile, and tried to execute a hare-brained scheme for a Jacobite revolt. He then converted to Roman Catholicism. But his lewd behaviour and his fondness for brandy soon ruined his credibility among Jacobites in Europe. On the grounds of treason, he was also stripped of his titles by the Whig government. Reduced to poverty, he drank himself to death in 1731.

With Wharton out of the way, modern Freemasonry had survived its birth-pangs. The *Constitutions* had smothered almost all trace of political in-fighting and packaged a Peace and Harmony narrative for posterity. The Craft was set to grow rapidly. But to do so it needed liquid fuel.

'Tis wine, ye Masons, makes you Free

Every single English Grand Master since Montagu and Wharton has been a Lord, Viscount, Earl, Marquess, Duke or Prince. Well might Freemasonry term itself 'the Royal Art'. For all the Masons' talk of fraternity, the effect of the patronage bestowed on the Craft from the very top of the social scale was compelling. Just one indicator: Grand Lodge meetings had at first been held in private upstairs rooms in taverns; after the Duke of Montagu became Grand Master, they filled some of the most capacious public meeting halls in London.

Thanks to the sponsorship of the nobility and royalty, when they crossed the threshold of a Lodge for the first time, men from many different walks of life also opened the door on a large store of useful connections. For example, writers and artists found clients and sponsors. The Anglo-Scottish painter Jeremiah Davidson was asked to paint a portrait of James Murray, 2nd Duke of Atholl, after meeting him in a Lodge; a chain of similar commissions ensued. Later in the century, Scots poet Robert Burns was introduced to James Cunningham, the 14th Earl of Glencairn, at a Lodge meeting. The poet would later refer to the Earl as 'my first, my dearest Patron and Benefactor'. In 1786, the Freemasons provided funds to publish the verse collection that launched Burns's career: the Kilmarnock Lodge, and wealthy individual Brothers, signed up in advance to buy copies. A *quid pro quo* was involved: the enthusiasm for Masonic life expressed in Burns's poetry was a PR coup for the Brotherhood.

As well as networking, charity was an important part of Masonry's appeal. In an age before state welfare or health insurance, families were ultimately dependent on the kindness of relatives and friends. Joining the Craft, and paying its dues, meant hedging against hard times.

For all that it strained to present itself in the ceremonial garb of antiquity, Freemasonry was excitingly modern – and modern in a way that distilled some of the peculiarities of London life and bottled them ready for export. Thus, although there is nothing modern about noble patronage, eighteenth-century Freemasonry did endow patronage with a distinctly modern style. In November 1737, at a specially convened Lodge in Kew, the Masons initiated the first affiliate from the royal family: Frederick, the Prince of Wales. Although Frederick did not hold Masonic office, the fact that even the heir to the throne had condescended to undergo the same blindfolding, knee-baring, apron-wearing palaver as every other Brother conferred enormous prestige. It strongly implied that, at least within the symbolic arena of the Lodge, there was a measure of equality between royalty and the common man, a shared subservience to Masonic ideals.

It is difficult to imagine this peculiar form of fellowship between noblemen and their social inferiors being invented anywhere else in Europe. For one thing, Britain had more social mobility than many other countries: new commercial money and old landed wealth were slowly beginning to merge. Foreign observers of eighteenth-century Britain noticed how hard it was to distinguish the different classes in society. Whereas in Europe, a man's clothes advertised his social status and the job he did, the British middle and lower orders tended to emulate the dress style of their betters. In a Masonic Lodge, aprons and regalia differentiated men by their standing within the Brotherhood, and not by their wealth or power outside. A formal egalitarianism is rooted in the Masonic psyche: as the *Constitutions* had it, the Masons were 'all brethren upon the same level'.

The Masons' fondness for the ceremony and fairness of constitutional rules was also a sign of the times. A popular political slogan referred to 'English liberty'. (Then, as now, the English were hazy about the distinction between England and Britain.) The Freemasons took the Whig constitutional ideology that went under the name of English liberty, and elaborated it into a code of fellowship.

The seclusion of Lodge meetings allowed Freemasons to be experimental, to develop regulations and styles of behaviour that pushed the boundaries of what was possible in the world outside. Masonry is democratic: members are elected from among the applicants, as are Lodge officers from among the members. Masonic power rotates: each officer serves only for a year or two before he moves on. In other words, the early Masons tried to transform 'English liberty' from a constitutional slogan into a practical utopia.

Freedom of conscience was central to English liberty. In England, the political settlement put in place by the Whigs was also a religious settlement – one that made Freemasonry's brand of tolerance newly relevant. Of course, this English liberty was always a slogan more than it was a summation of the true state of society. Anglicanism was enshrined as the religion of state. At least 40 per cent of the British population did not belong to the established Churches favoured by the settlement. Jews and more extreme Protestant sects like the Unitarians were excluded. Catholics were treated like an enemy within. But for all these limits, the link between faith and power was looser in much of Britain than it was elsewhere in Europe. A nervy form of toleration centred on the cohabitation between the official Anglican creed and various forms of nonconformist Protestantism, like the Baptists and Quakers. Political loyalty was gently uncoupled from religious conformity.

Religious pluralism also enjoyed philosophical prestige among some intellectuals. As did Deism, a loose term denoting a belief in a creator God whose benevolent will was manifested, not through any specific church, but in the harmony of nature.

Freemasonry was in the perfect position to absorb this new atmosphere, and push it further. Ever since the time of William Schaw in the Edinburgh of James VI, the Lodges had been havens from sectarian conflict. True to this tradition, eighteenth-century Brothers had to be believers, but they could worship the Great Architect of the Universe in any way their conscience dictated. The climate within the Lodges was accepting. There were a number of Deists. Even Jews were becoming Freemasons in London as early as the 1720s; by 1730 one London Lodge had a Jewish Master. Remarkably, in January 1730, Thomas Howard, the 8th Duke of Norfolk, was installed as Freemasonry's first Catholic Grand Master.

The differences of rank and religion within the eighteenth-century Craft were also softened by a good soaking in alcohol. Freemasons loved a drink. Even in an incorrigibly boozy culture like that of London at the time, the Masons stood out for the amount they put away. Already in 1723, the 'illustrious topers' of the Craft were being given particular plaudits in the comic work, *In Praise of Drunkenness*:

> 'Tis wine, ye Masons, makes you Free,
> Bacchus the father is of liberty.

One particularly drunken Mason was immortalised by an engraving in 1736. *Night* depicts a chaotic scene: a well-oiled

Worshipful Master (identified by his apron and set square medallion) is being helped down the Charing Cross Road by his Tyler (another officer of the Lodge); from above, someone is emptying the contents of a chamber pot over their heads. Despite being satirical, the image encapsulates some important truths about early Freemasonry. After all, the artist who created it was himself a Mason: the great William Hogarth. The Worshipful Master at the centre of the picture was Thomas de Veil, a fiercely loyal Whig who was appointed to the magistrate's bench in 1729. De Veil presided over many cases brought under the controversial anti-drink Gin Act of 1736 – hence the mockery. In due course, the government would reward his loyal service with a lucrative sinecure and a knighthood.

Night, from William Hogarth's series, *Four Times of the Day* (1736–8). A drunken Freemason can be seen wearing an apron and a set square pendant.

So male bonding over a drinking session was a crucial part of the Lodge experience: backs were slapped, and arms put around shoulders. The same is often true today. But Freemasonry has never been an alcoholic free-for-all. Masonic feasts (or 'Festive Boards' in Craft jargon) have their own rules and ceremonies. A Freemason, be he ever so exalted in the world outside, is expected to take his turn at serving his Brethren at table. There are Masonic songs to sing, and Masonic toasts to drink. In the eighteenth century, the assembled Brethren would typically drain a glass to the health, in sequence, of the King, the Craft, the Master, the Grand Master, the Officers, the Apprentices . . . The structured indulgence of the Festive Board was a powerful way of forging masculine togetherness.

Clearly it was no coincidence that so many early Masonic Lodges took their name from an inn or tavern like the Goose and Gridiron. But there is more to it than just a taste for ale. In the early eighteenth century, the public house was at the centre of a revolution in social life. By gathering in pubs, Masons were riding one of the fastest currents of modernity.

The late seventeenth century saw a huge increase in the quantity and quality of pubs in England, particularly in English cities. Coffee houses, some of which were rebranded taverns that continued to serve alcohol, were part of the same trend: there were an astonishing two thousand of them in London when the Grand Lodge was founded. These venues, neither private nor wholly public, answered a need for people to interact in new ways. Cities were growing, and their social life acquiring an unprecedented buzz. Metropolitan society was becoming more prosperous, mobile and diverse. Whether you were a journalist or a politician, an architect or a merchant, a tradesman or a lawyer, you went to the tavern or coffee house to network for fun and profit.

Inns generated their own forms of shared entertainment, ranging from cock-fighting and magic-lantern shows, to concerts and scientific lectures. But the most important social trend germinated in

London pubs was a mania for clubs and societies. Visitors could not help but notice that the capital had 'an infinity of CLUBS, or SOCIETIES, for the Improvement of Learning, and keeping up good Humour and Mirth'.

No matter if your interest was in history or horticulture, gambling or debating, medicine or sport, London had a club for you. The eighteenth-century passion for association was an easy target for parody. Ned Ward's 1756 spoof, *A Compleat and Humorous Account of All the Remarkable Clubs and Societies in the Cities of London and Westminster*, explained the practices of such imaginary associations as the No-Nose Club (for people disfigured by syphilis), the Yorkshire Club (where the members carried on as if they were in Monty Python's Four Yorkshiremen sketch) and the Farting Club, which met every week in a public house in Cripplegate in order 'to poison the neighbouring Air with their unsavory *Crepitations*'.

There was a whole swathe of real clubs that were formed as a practical joke, and others with strange names whose purposes were entirely obscure: the Purple Society, the Potentisignittarians, the Brothers of the Wacut . . . At the same time, some clubs commanded enormous prestige. The Royal Society, founded in 1660 as a 'College for the Promoting of Physico-Mathematical Experimental Learning', helped establish modern scientific method. Some of the political clubs housed intense concentrations of influence. Many societies had initiation rituals and some claimed access to esoteric knowledge. The Freemasons were by far the most successful example.

The Craft caught the mood of the age. The galaxy of clubs that operated free of government harassment showed that Britain was a more open society than many on the continent. There was also a noisy press unhindered by official control. Eighteenth-century London's publishers, newspapers, coffee houses and taverns were laboratories of politics. As were its Masonic Lodges. Freemasonry did not necessarily espouse a particular political programme, or even provide a place where different ideologies could be freely aired. As we have already discovered, political debate was frowned upon. What Freemasonry did provide, however, was training in the practicalities of politics. The Craft's highly formalised rituals and protocols gave men from various backgrounds a way to learn the manifold skills they needed to work in modern institutions: being discreet, making speeches, interpreting constitutional rules, advising younger Brethren and judging their character. The aptitudes required by an open society could be learned within the closed space of a Masonic Lodge. Just as importantly, the relatively narrow sample of men who frequented the Lodges came to flatter themselves that they spoke in the name of universal values. For an example, we need only think of John Coustos. The Inquisition's transcripts of his interrogation show how composed and eloquent he was throughout: my bet is that he owed those discursive skills to his Masonic training. His book about his sufferings also showed how clever he had become at playing politics with Masonry's universal values.

The Free-Masons Surpriz'd

What did the early Freemasons have against women?

The exclusion of women is the most obvious hole in the Craft's code of universal inclusiveness. The *Constitutions* of 1723 were the first Masonic document to explicitly ban them: 'The Persons admitted Members of a LODGE must be good and true Men, free-born, and of mature and discreet Age, no Bondmen, *no Women*, no immoral or scandalous men, but of good Report [my emphasis].' No explanation is given. With insouciant sexism, the early Grand Lodge Masons assumed that the *Constitutions* were merely cementing the existing, male-only order of things.

Today, the official Masonic line on the question of early Freemasonry's sexism is that it was a reflection of its time. The women of the eighteenth century were barred from all sites of public power, fenced out of property and politics, government and the law, business and trade. It would have been a surprise if Sisters had joined Brothers in the Craft.

For their part, the women of eighteenth-century Britain were not battering down the doors of the Lodges in their enthusiasm to enrol. The kind of men who made up the backbone of Freemasonry's leadership in England were minor gentry, professionals and the mercantile classes. Their womenfolk had other places they could go to socialise. If it was polite, mixed company a lady was after, she could visit a theatre, pleasure garden, assembly room or spa. What these new and distinctively British theatres of female social life had in common is that they were carefully managed to avoid any threat to a lady's decorum. Masonic Lodges, by contrast, seemed set up to dishonour any woman who dared enter. The secrecy that surrounded Craft proceedings was an incitement to gossip. Boozy Masonic feasts would have seemed vulgar to any lady of polish. Most genteel women would have no more contemplated entering a Lodge than barging into a cock-fight with a rooster under one arm and a flagon of ale under the other.

So Masonic historians are not entirely wrong when they blame the eighteenth century for the lack of women in the Craft. But we can't let them off the hook entirely. For then we would be at a loss to explain why the no-women rule was such a source of awkwardness for many eighteenth-century Brothers.

A significant trend in Enlightenment philosophy put the Masons on the defensive. Women, it was widely believed, exercised a civilising influence on men. Males in segregated groups like Masonic Lodges were liable to degenerate into oafishness unless females tempered their barbaric instincts. In response, the Masons threw up a ramshackle stockade of arguments around their policy of excluding women. In numerous speeches and pamphlets, Masons protested that they revered the fairer sex: it was just that all men, Masons included, were inclined to rivalry and jealousy, and could not be trusted to preserve the Masonic spirit of harmony when in voluptuous company. In any case –

they continued – the Brothers' hands were tied by the traditions they venerated: the exclusion of women had been dictated in medieval times, and there was little Masons could do to change that. There were frequent efforts to reassure Masonic wives, who were invited to open dinners and balls, and made to listen to speeches about how lucky any woman was to have married a Craftsman.

The most widespread justification for the Lodges' gender policy was that women were gossips, and could not be trusted to keep the Brotherhood's secrets. Pushing this line of thinking further, Masons flattered themselves that all women were incurably curious about the Craft – a view encapsulated in a saucy print produced for Masonic consumption in the middle of the eighteenth century: *The Free-Masons Surpriz'd* (1754?).

The FREE-MASONS SURPRIZ'D, or the SECRET DISCOVER'D.
A True Tale from a MASONS LODGE in CANTERBURY.

A Lodge meeting has been disrupted. Brothers run for cover, and Masonic objects are scattered across the table and floor. One Brother even looses off a musket towards the cause of the disturbance: the legs of a woman, naked from the knees up, dangling through the ceiling. The caption tells us that the woman in question, a maid called Moll, had climbed into the garret above the Lodge room in her eagerness to spy on the meeting and learn the Masons' secrets. But, 'by an unlucky Slip', she had crashed through the ceiling. Thus her scheme to discover the Masons' secrets had ended in the 'Secret' hidden under her skirts being exposed to a roomful of men. Indeed, led by the Master and his Wardens in their regalia, most of the Masons are ogling her exposed crotch. The tale was both a warning to 'prying Lasses', and a cue for elbow-digging among the Brothers.

The Masons' defence of the no-women policy set out in the *Constitutions* of 1723 was manifestly flimsy. It makes obvious the fact that creating a male-only environment was integral to Masonry from the outset. Even at the time, outsiders plainly thought Craftsmen were odd because of the rigour with which they excluded women. That is why satirists also made much comic play around the idea of female Freemasons. One of the earliest skits published in London was a magazine article dating from 1724: it parodied the *Constitutions* by reporting the rules and history of a non-existent 'Sisterhood of Free Sempstresses'. Suggestions about homosexuality were also widespread.

The alchemy of international success

Before the meeting at the Goose and Gridiron in 1717, there was little to suggest that Freemasonry would ever amount to anything momentous. After 1717, it blossomed. At the assembly to elect the Grand Master in 1721, twelve London Lodges were represented. By 1725, the Grand Lodge could list sixty-one 'regular' Lodges in London – ones that recognised its authority, that is. The system caught on: Ireland obtained its own Grand Lodge in that same year; many of Scotland's Lodges recognised the authority of a Grand Lodge established in 1736. By 1738, the Grand Lodge in London listed 106 Lodges in the capital, and a further 47 across the country, from Norwich in Norfolk to Chester on the Welsh border, and from Plymouth in the south-west to Newcastle-upon-Tyne in the north-east.

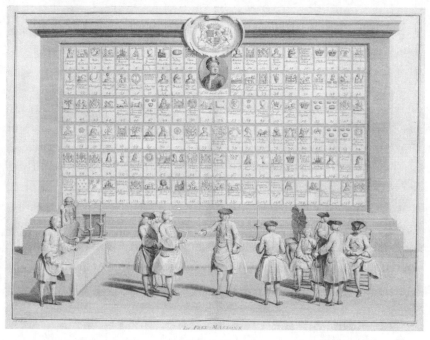

Bernard Picart's engraving, published in 1736, celebrates the rapid national and international spread of Freemasonry. Each panel on the mural represents a Lodge.

The Constitutions of the Freemasons, having successfully sanitised early Masonic history, was a triumph. The book was soon translated into all the major European languages, helping spread the Masonic gospel. In Philadelphia in 1730, an intellectually voracious young printer joined a recently formed Masonic Lodge. Four years later, he became the Lodge's Master, and reissued the *Constitutions* for his Brethren: it was the first Masonic publication in the Americas. The printer's name was Benjamin Franklin, and his edition of the *Constitutions* would help turn North America into Freemasonry's most fertile soil.

In 1738, the year of the confident second edition of the

Constitutions, the Grand Lodge in London could also boast of formally recognised outposts in Bengal, Spain, France, Russia, Germany, Switzerland, Portugal, Italy, South America, the Caribbean and West Africa. The first Masonic Lodge in Istanbul was established in the 1720s; the first in Aleppo in the 1730s. The kind of cosmopolitanism espoused by the Craft was a way of life for men who were following the routes of trade and empire to almost every corner of the globe.

Freemasonry could not be ignored – especially because it became much noisier and more visible. Parades quickly became a staple of the Masonic calendar. On 28 April 1737, the officers of the Grand Lodge and many other Brothers, 'all duly clothed' in their gloves and aprons, processed 'in a very solemn Manner' from their new Grand Master's House in Pall Mall, all the way across town to Fishmonger's Hall near London Bridge where the Grand Lodge meeting was held. They were accompanied on their march by '3 Bands of Musick, Kettle Drums, Trumpets, and *French* Horns'. Eight months later, and more than four thousand miles away in Charleston, South Carolina, a very similar Masonic parade ended with the joyful firing of cannon from ships in the harbour, and 'a ball and entertainment for the ladies'.

In many of Masonry's new homes across the world, the Craft's fondness for laddish high jinks was integral to its appeal. In 1780s Vienna, for example, Wolfgang Amadeus Mozart and his fellow Masons in the True Harmony Lodge held booze-fuelled feasts where lewd songs were sung, and a ceremonial Masonic trowel was used to shovel huge helpings into gaping mouths. It seems that even 'Papa' Joseph Haydn, who was a member of the same Lodge, took part.

Freemasonry was a halfway house along the journey from a world dominated by religious belief, into one that was less pious, more educated and more mobile. The Brothers' way of rubbing along together turned the Craft into an international school of what we now call secularism: the principle that the church should be kept at a sanitary distance from the state. Many foreign

Lodges, such as the ones in Lisbon and Florence that were targeted by the Inquisition in the 1740s, included both Protestants and Catholics. Religious tolerance was the secret of Masonry's success in North America, where the British colonies owed their origins to religious dissent.

Generations and generations of Masons would also find in the Craft a way of fitting in, of networking far and wide, and of making influential friends. Respectable, ambitious, middle-class men have been the key to Freemasonry's success since its inception. Indeed, if we can now be said to live in a male, middle-class world, a good part of the credit, and the blame, lies with the Masons.

In tracing the fate of Freemasonry through subsequent chapters of this book and subsequent eras of history, we will also be tracing some of the twists and turns of the various universal ideals that eighteenth-century British Freemasons extracted from the society around them in concentrated form: brotherly love, secularism and religious tolerance, cosmopolitanism, egalitarianism, and so on. However, the whole Masonic project has been beset by contradictions since the beginning. Although it was egalitarian in theory, in practice the Craft put up financial barriers to entry: subscriptions were expensive. Part of the appeal of membership has always been about the costly collectables: badges, sashes, aprons and jewels. (As a jeweller, John Coustos knew that his Brethren were a ready market for his wares.) Moreover, Masonry's universal values become paradoxical when they are promoted by a self-proclaimed moral élite operating in secret: this is members-only democracy, a clubby form of cosmopolitanism. Most egregiously of all, the Craft's brotherhood of man excludes women, and helps cement that exclusion in every other sphere of life that it touches. The Masonic utopia is open to all. Except when it isn't.

Such internal contradictions have made Freemasonry acutely sensitive to the social, political and religious pressures of the three centuries that followed the meeting in the Goose and

Gridiron ale house in 1717. Indeed, the fascination of Masonic history lies precisely in the interaction between those wider forces and the ethos that the Masons tried to create among themselves.

As if in some unrepeatable alchemical demonstration carried out amid the hubbub of London's taverns, modern Freemasonry was generated from an unstable compound of ingredients. A thirst for wine and ale. An excitement about the new social life of clubs. A hunger for the fruits of preferment. A mixture of snobbery and male fellow-feeling, of ambition and philanthropy. A fascination with ritual and mystery, married to a taste for rational discourse and a shrewd inclination towards political and religious compromise. A willingness to erase history in the interests of harmony. Hammered into shape between 1717 and 1723 by the very peculiar Politicks of the Hanoverian succession and the Whig ascendancy, the Brotherhood became the bearer of values that transcended its origins.

Thus, from improbable beginnings, Freemasonry began to reach every corner of the globe. But it had only crossed the English Channel when it ran into trouble.

Paris: **War on Christ and His Cult; War on Kings and All Their Thrones**

The view from the Edgware Road

In 1796, France was unrecognisable.

Roadside altars and crosses had been smashed. Many churches had been stripped of their icons and statues, or simply abandoned to the elements. Monasteries and nunneries were turned into warehouses, stables or barracks; Rouen Cathedral was a gunpowder factory. In many places, the priests and friars who had mingled with the population just a few years before were all gone. In their place, the forlorn poor who had been left without the shelter of the Church's charity. Sundays were eerily silent, since church bells had been melted down to pay for guns.

Many once-splendid châteaux were now fire-blackened shells. The only men working in the fields were the young and the old. Conscription had carried off most of the rest to the battlefields of Europe; desertion had turned others into bandits who swooped on travellers along the dilapidated highways.

In Paris, the signs of the upheaval were just as manifest. The brooding walls of the Bastille prison had vanished, and a timber yard occupied the site. Most of the Bois de Boulogne had been cut down. Wealthy quarters like the Faubourg Saint-Germain were depopulated, their streets choked with weeds, their largest noble homes bearing signs that proclaimed them 'national property'. Statues in marble and bronze had been uprooted, and wood and plaster replacements now squatted on their plinths. Royal insignia and aristocratic coats of arms had been hacked from above arches and doorways. Instead, many buildings sported slogans: 'The French people recognises the supreme being, and the immortality of the soul'; 'Liberty, Equality, Fraternity, or death'. But even these had been edited or partly erased. The streets felt dangerous; stories of robbery and murder were on everyone's lips. Fear and suspicion had seeped into the collective psyche to the point where anyone who did not have a tricolour cockade in their hat ran the risk of being picked on.

The Revolution that had caused this devastation was not over; indeed, France's huge and increasingly successful armies were hell-bent on exporting it. Nevertheless, in 1796, a comparative calm reigned in France, allowing Europe to turn its shock and bewilderment into reflection, and the search for an explanation. The French Revolution defied understanding. Historians have been arguing over its causes ever since. But one man, a priest, had already found a compelling explanation.

The Abbé Augustin de Barruel contemplated the ravaged landscape of Revolution in the tranquillity of a house at 25 Edgware Road on London's outskirts. From his desk he could hear the mooing of the cows that supplied the city's milk. Our only image of him shows a small, bald man with a long nose suspended between doleful eyes that reflected sorrow at the horrors he had witnessed. Both of the noble châteaux where he served as a children's tutor were left in ruins by rampaging peasants. His spiritual mentor, Father Antoine de Nolhac, was butchered by revolutionaries in an Avignon prison in October 1791. Eleven months later, for fear of being caught up in the massacres, Abbé Barruel had fled to England, and thrown himself into writing.

Abbé Augustin de Barruel (1741–1820).

In 1797, in the first pages of *Memoirs Illustrating the History of Jacobinism*, which was to become an exhaustive five-volume analysis of the Revolution's gestation, Barruel set out his thesis:

> Everything in the French Revolution, everything right down to the most appalling deeds, was foreseen, premeditated, arranged, resolved upon, and decided; everything was caused by the deepest wickedness, because everything was prepared and directed by men who alone held the thread uniting the intrigues that had long been woven within the secret societies.

The French Revolution was the result of a dastardly conspiracy by the Freemasons.

Barruel had a warning for all those who observed the conspiracy unfold from abroad. They must not delude themselves that the danger had ended because the Jacobins, the most radical of the revolutionaries, had fallen from power in 1794. The conspiracy was international, it was only just beginning, and it was coming for your children: 'If Jacobinism triumphs, then that is the end of your Religion, your Laws, your Property – of all forms of Government and Civil Society. Wealth, fields, houses (right down to the humblest cottage), children: nothing will belong to you any more.'

The Abbé Barruel's many readers found his book thrilling. The British Member of Parliament and political theorist Edmund Burke was a fan, writing to Barruel that 'the whole of the wonderful narrative is supported by documents and proofs with the most juridical regularity and exactness'. Even the poet Percy Shelley, whose politics were poles apart from Burke's, enthusiastically devoured the *Memoirs Illustrating the History of Jacobinism*. This was a time when no institution, no tradition, no monument seemed able to withstand the political cataclysm. With Barruel, everything suddenly seemed to fit. There was one cause, one group to blame. His analysis became one of the most widely read books of its era.

Thus was the modern conspiracy theory born.

Memoirs Illustrating the History of Jacobinism was idiotic. It has nothing to contribute to our understanding of the causes of the French Revolution. Yet it does still have much to teach us about how conspiracy-thinking makes complex events seem simple, and makes us feel clever for oversimplifying them.

The most obvious flaw in Barruel's argument is that no authority could win recognition across French Freemasonry, still less harness it to a single political plan. To look back over pre-Revolutionary France, as I will do in this chapter, is to see the Craft adopt an ungovernable variety of forms. Eighteenth-century French Freemasonry was peopled by a highly diverse range of characters, many of whom we will encounter more than once. We will meet them as they really were before, during and after the Revolution. Towards the end of the chapter, we will also see them, barely recognisable, in the conspiratorial role that Barruel imagined for them. As will become clear, one of the remarkable things about *Memoirs Illustrating the History of Jacobinism* is just how much information about Freemasonry's history Barruel had taken on board before he squeezed, twisted and cropped it to fit his monomaniacal vision.

The inextricable Scottish mess
The first Masonic Lodge in France is thought to have been established in Paris in 1725 or 1726 – so just a couple of years after the publication of English Freemasonry's *Constitutions*. A handful of other Lodges followed. Britons were the founders, and they initially struggled to attract French members because they were so divided between Whigs and Tories. Eventually, to keep the peace, an impartial French Duke was appointed as Grand Master. The number of Frenchmen in aprons began to grow.

Geopolitics ensured that the division between British Freemasonry and its French off-shoot would be permanent: after 1744 the two countries were at war for much of the rest of the century. The number of Lodges increased, and their membership became still more French. By the end of the 1780s, there would be some one thousand Lodges and a total of members that is impossible to gauge accurately, but which has been estimated at between fifty and one hundred thousand. Freemasonry became part of French life. The result was, in the words of one historian, an 'inextricable Scottish mess'.

Because the drama and togetherness of ritual is at the heart of the Craft, Masons have often felt the temptation to refine and elaborate their rituals, and to invent new ones. When the *Constitutions* appeared in 1723, there were only two Degrees a Mason had to pass through before achieving full membership: Apprentice and Fellow Craft. By the time the second edition of the *Constitutions* came out in 1738, a third Degree, Master

85

Mason, had been added. These three basic Degrees – sometimes referred to as 'Blue' or 'Craft' Degrees – remain in force today; they are the ones I outlined in Chapter Two. But the creativity of the early Freemasons did not stop there. In the 1740s, a supplementary Degree, known as Royal Arch Mason, began to appear – it was open only to men who had served as the Master of a Lodge. (Being awarded the Degree of Master Mason, it should be made clear, is not the same thing as assuming the office of Master of a Lodge. The latter, referred to in different Masonic traditions as the Worshipful Master or Venerable Master, is the man elected to take charge of the Lodge.) The Royal Arch Degree quickly led to the foundation of a rival Grand Lodge, and this schism in English Freemasonry was to last more than sixty years. Charges of Masonic heresy were hurled by both sides.

Disputes like this are Freemasonry's congenital disease. No ritual, Masonic or otherwise, has much allure unless it has a widely accepted form, a tradition to hallow it and an institution to back it. Participants in a rite that feels newfangled find it hard to give themselves up to enchantment. Any time a new Degree is invented, awkward questions about Masonic authority are raised. Who will codify the freshly minted sacraments, and distinguish legitimate from spurious versions? The emotional temperature frequently runs high because many Masons feel that their very identity is invested in the correct observance of Craft workings. The illness frequently spreads across national borders. Senior Masons spend inordinate amounts of time negotiating over which of the many different strains of Freemasonry in other countries they officially recognise as compatible with their own.

Try as it might, no Grand Lodge is able to control the Masonic 'brand'. Soon after it arrived in France, the brand began to spin out of control.

In December 1736, a well-known Mason and Jacobite thinker called Andrew Michael Ramsay gave a speech to an assembly of the Paris Lodges that was destined to echo around the Masonic world. Some months later, he sent a revised version of the speech to Cardinal Fleury, Louis XV's chief minister, with the intention of convincing him that Freemasonry was compatible with Catholicism. Ramsay's speech was received warily: it was probably what provoked the Cardinal to order police raids on the Paris Lodges. The aged Ramsay withdrew from all Masonic activity for fear of incurring the Cardinal's further displeasure.

If it failed disastrously in its short-term objectives, Ramsay's speech cast a spell over the French Brotherhood once it was published in 1738. Much of it was pretty standard fare: a summary of Craft myth and philosophy as expounded by the *Constitutions*. But Ramsay also deviated from the *Constitutions'* narrative in one highly significant respect: he worked in the crusaders. He claimed that crusading knights rediscovered the secrets of Solomon's Temple and the Craft while they were in the Holy Land, and used them to revive the sense of Christian mission that had first inspired them to capture Jerusalem for Christ. Ramsay explained that the Masonic crusaders had vowed to rebuild the Temple and imitate the Israelites by 'wielding the trowel and mortar in one hand, and the sword and buckler in the other'.

In evoking the crusaders, and with them the culture of medieval chivalry, Ramsay tapped a vast source of imagery and myth that would soon generate a complex of Masonic Degrees known as the Scottish Rites. Why *Scottish*? Although Ramsay was a Scotsman, the reasons are tenuous. Ramsay's new crusader myth attributed a key role to his homeland in preserving and transmitting the Masonic tradition. When the Holy Land was all but lost, he claimed, in 1286 a leading knight brought the Craft's mysteries back to Scotland for safe keeping. The connection is no closer than that. In reality, the origins of the Scottish Rites are entirely French. But invoking Scotland had the undoubted geopolitical advantage of bypassing London and its Grand Lodge. So

Scotland's real role in the development of Freemasonry, having been expunged from the record by the *Constitutions*, made a return in France in an entirely mythical guise.

Ramsay triggered a creative frenzy among French Masons. By 1743, they could progress upwards through three new Scottish Rite Degrees, each with its own elaborate symbols, ceremonials and moral allegories. By 1755, there were five in the hierarchy in Paris, and seven in Lyon and elsewhere. The growth rapidly became exponential, and utterly confused: there were soon rites with dozens of Degrees. The most authoritative history of French Freemasonry has referred to a 'tropical forest' of Degrees that sprouted from the 1750s. Some of them carried the flavour of the original chivalric inspiration of the Scottish Rite, such as 'Knight of King Arthur's Round Table', 'Elect Philosopher Knight', 'Knight of the Argonauts' and 'Knight Kadosh'. French Brothers also relished bearing dozens of such exotic Caledonian titles as 'Scotsman of the Scottish Academy', 'Scotsman of Messina', 'Scotsman of the Celestial Jerusalem', and even 'Scots Englishman'. There were still more obscure Scottish Rite Degrees with an esoteric inspiration: 'Master Theosopher'; 'Master of Esmeralda's Table'; 'Companion of Paracelsus' . . .

Freemasonry arrived in France with its luggage already bulging with symbolism. The Scottish Rites piled on every possible ensemble of signs and codes, mythologies and rituals: chivalry, the Bible, the occult, Rosicrucianism, alchemy, Greek and Egyptian legends, the zodiac, the Kabbalah (an ancient Jewish tradition of mystical interpretation). Manichaeism, a belief system founded by a third-century Iranian prophet who taught that the universe was fought over by good and evil, spirit and matter, light and dark, was a particularly effective source of dramatic rituals. The individual Degrees were combined into myriad superimposed and incompatible ritual systems that varied by locality and faction: the Rite of the Blazing Star; the Illuminated Theosophers; the Architects of Africa.

Unsurprisingly, the spirit of brotherly harmony came under severe strain in the 1760s. In Reims, in June 1764, two factions within a local Lodge shouted insults at one another and battled with canes in the street before the eyes of baffled onlookers. In February 1767, the government suspended the Grand Lodge itself after a meeting descended into a fist-fight.

Under such intense pressures, the Grand Lodge lost control and the higher structures of French Freemasonry fragmented. Only in 1773 was peace made with the setting up of a new national governing body, the Grand Orient of France, presided over by no less a personage than the King's cousin Philippe, who would later inherit the title of Duke of Orléans. Theoretically, the Scottish Rite Degrees fell under the Grand Orient's jurisdiction, but it took a decade and a half of often painful negotiations to bring any kind of unity to the major branches of the French Craft. The Degrees continued to proliferate. Pandora's box was open.

What was driving this hyper-inflation in Masonic Degrees? The simple answer is snobbery. In France, the social classes were more fixed than they were in England, and took the legal form of estates: the first estate of the clergy; the second estate of the nobility; and the third estate of everyone else. There were also deeply embedded distinctions within each estate. The nobility were over-represented in the Lodges compared to their numbers in French society at large. Much of the Craft's success was down to them, as was much of its snobbery. Nobles were keen to find ways to mix with one another away from the heavily controlled environment of the court at Versailles. They also sensed the advantages of socialising with a broader group of people than were to be found in aristocratic academies and salons. To that extent, Freemasonry was a useful way of relaxing some status boundaries among the well-heeled and well-educated. But Masonic values could *never* be taken as a licence to dissolve the whole hierarchy. So all of the gradations of social class had to be re-invented in the Lodge's other-worldly atmosphere. By creating ever higher Degrees, with ever more stringent selection processes, and ever more expensive regalia, the Scottish Rites served to confine the shopkeepers and traders to the lower echelons. Chivalry offered a justification. Whereas, in Britain, the link between Freemasons and medieval stonemasons gave the whole Brotherhood an artisanal feel, Ramsay's fable about Freemasonry's origins in the crusader knights and their code of chivalry was reassuringly aristocratic.

Religious and ethnic prejudice also influenced the multiplication of Scottish Rite Degrees. France did not have the same political impetus towards tolerance as did Britain. Nor did the Pope in Rome have the authority to enforce his 1738 excommunication of the Freemasons in the French king's realm. As a result, many of the new Scottish Rite Degrees gave Masonry a strong Catholic flavour. Many French Freemasons expressed traditional forms of Catholic chauvinism. In 1767, the Perfect Sincerity Lodge of Marseille recorded regulations that were particularly frank: 'all those profanes [i.e. non-Masons] who have the misfortune to be Jews, Mohammadans or negroes may not be proposed for membership'. In many places, the Craft's tolerant ideals were simply ignored.

The Nine Sisters

In France as in Britain, many Brothers joined Masonry for friendship, fun and networking: they had little time to waste staring into the kaleidoscope of Scottish Rite Degrees. One frequent visitor to France in this period, the Venetian adventurer and rake Giacomo Casanova, recommended the Craft heartily to wanderers like him: 'In this day and age, any young man who travels, who wants to get to know the great world, who doesn't want to find himself inferior to others, or excluded from the company of his equals, must get himself initiated into what is called Masonry.' Casanova was as good as his axiom, exploiting his Masonic contacts to inveigle and seduce his way across Europe.

Freemasonry could also lend itself to higher pursuits. Some of the earliest French Brothers were attracted by the philosophical ethos of the Lodges: the brotherly observance of constitutional rules, the religious freedom and the fashionable fondness for science, reason and ancient truths. Later in the century, some Masonic Lodges became part of a growing intellectual arena of salons, cafés, clubs and societies. Britain continued to be a more open and mobile society, but France did begin to catch up from mid-century. Censorship slackened. The multiple volumes of Denis Diderot and Jean le Rond d'Alembert's great audit of human knowledge, the *Encyclopédie*, began to appear in 1751; it offered a platform and rallying point for the *Philosophes* who pushed Enlightenment concerns with rationality and progress to the centre of public awareness. Voltaire's campaigns against religious persecution in the 1760s made him a figurehead of the Enlightenment movement.

One famous Parisian Lodge was explicitly conceived as a vehicle for Enlightenment: the Nine Sisters – named after the ancient Greek muses who inspired literature, science and the arts. The Lodge's founder, and first Master, was the leading astronomer Jérôme Lalande. His aim was to attract the intellectual élite to Masonry, and to provide a Masonic hub for the capital's cultural life.

Founded in 1776, the Nine Sisters scored some successes, particularly in recruiting celebrities. One notable member was Benjamin Franklin, who was in Paris to secure French support for the American fight against Britain; he even succeeded Lalande as Lodge Master. In 1778, leaning heavily on his friend Franklin's arm, the most famous Enlightenment intellectual of them all, Voltaire, was initiated in a ceremony that was abbreviated in consideration of his failing health. Voltaire had previously shown no enthusiasm for Masonry, and indeed viewed its rituals as symptomatic of a human weakness for hocus pocus. But in 1778 he graciously accepted membership as a tribute from his admirers. He died seven weeks later without attending another meeting.

There were other famous Masons in the Nine Sisters Lodge. Dr Joseph Guillotin, the hospital reformer who would later become synonymous with a beheading machine, was one of the orators at Voltaire's initiation. The Montgolfier brothers, Joseph-Michel and Jacques-Étienne, were also members: they created an international sensation when they staged the first demonstrations of their 'aerostatic machine', or hot-air balloon, in 1783.

Yet Freemasonry as a whole did not advance cutting-edge Enlightenment thought. Of the 272 men who contributed to the *Encyclopédie*, only seventeen were Freemasons. Frankly, one would have expected a much higher number if the *Philosophes* had seen the Craft as part of their mission. Nor was the Nine Sisters Lodge representative of French Masonry as a whole. When Lalande set up the Lodge, he had great trouble obtaining authorisation from the Grand Orient, whose more conservative members were nervous about what the authorities would think. The Nine Sisters was also very clubby, and did not seek to broadcast its discussions by publishing a journal. So Lalande's Lodge was no more typical of the Enlightenment than it was of the Craft.

Yet, at least in some of its variations, the rank-and-file French Lodges did provide a way for men to 'live the Enlightenment'. That is, you did not have to have as exalted a mind as an intellectual Freemason like Montesquieu to find that certain Enlightenment assumptions about cosmopolitanism and the formal equality of all men became part of the ground rules of Masonic life.

The Elect Cohens of the Universe

French Freemasonry hosted at least as many mystics as it did scientists. Many men felt a strong inclination to believe that the secrets transmitted through the ages by Masonry, rather than being a worthy set of moral precepts, were actually the most momentous esoteric truths. No one encapsulates the encounter between the Craft and the occult better than Jean-Baptiste

Willermoz. Born in 1730, this affable Lyon silk merchant was known for his devotion to local charities, his irreproachable business ethics and the pleasure he derived from mixing in the Lodge with his social betters. Unbeknownst to the good people of Lyon, Willermoz also voraciously absorbed the most mystical exemplars of Masonic lore, and carried on a constant correspondence with esoteric Masons and philosophers as far afield as Russia, Sweden and Italy. By his mid-thirties, he had already been initiated into over sixty Masonic Degrees, and created his own, highly secretive version of the Craft: the Knights of the Black Eagle aimed to find a stone that brought universal happiness, and transmute base metal into gold – in both solid and drinkable forms.

Willermoz's annual business trips to Paris gave him the chance to get closer and closer to what he believed to be Freemasonry's essence. It was in the capital, in 1767, that he met the Masonic clairvoyant and Kabbalistic visionary, Martinès de Pasqually, who opened his mind to new worlds of wisdom. Pasqually believed that all men were originally demi-gods, and that Masonic ritual could help a chosen few recover this lost state. He founded the Order of the Knight Masons Elect Cohens of the Universe to conjure up manifestations of the divine using enchanted circles, the names of angels, and astrology. The magic was particularly strong at midnight on the spring equinox when, after lengthy spiritual preparation, the most qualified Masons in the order could lie down, barefoot, with their heads resting on closed fists, and receive communication from the Supreme Cause in a form of transcendence known as Reintegration.

Willermoz became a follower of Pasqually's and was soon the leader of the Elect Cohen order in Lyon. As each spring equinox passed, he kept his faith despite the fact that Reintegration failed to arrive. Some of his followers, by contrast, grew restless as Pasqually found endless excuses to avoid coming to Lyon to perform the Masonic séances correctly. Willermoz was undaunted when Pasqually abandoned France in 1772 to take up an inheritance in the Caribbean.

Meanwhile, Willermoz was also absorbing the latest thinking in Germany – a new trend in the Scottish Rite that was destined to be highly influential across the Masonic world. As it turned out, it was not just any old crusaders who had rediscovered Masonry in the Holy Land and brought it to Scotland: it was the Knights Templar. The Knights Templar were a real military-monastic order created in the twelfth century. They became financially powerful during the campaign to capture the Holy Land, and their wealth drew envious eyes when the Crusades were over. In 1307 the Pope ordered the arrest of the order's leaders, accusing them of abominable crimes against God and nature, including sodomy, child murder and worshipping a goat-headed false god called Baphomet. The Templar leader, Jacques de Molay, was burned at the stake in front of Notre-Dame Cathedral in Paris.

The Knights Templar were still controversial figures centuries after they were disbanded. For devout Catholics, they were heretics who had met their comeuppance. For others, they were martyrs to the Church's greed and cruelty. But they had initiation rituals, and their most senior officers were known as Masters and Grand Masters. Such coincidences were more than enough for Willermoz and many other Brothers to regard them as Freemasons. In 1774, Willermoz and a select group of his disciples constituted a Templarist chapter in Lyon. Four years later, he merged the Templars and the Elect Cohens in the Rectified Scottish Rite of the Beneficent Knights of the Holy City.

In the 1780s, Willermoz's restless imagination was captured by yet another novelty. A few years earlier, the Vienna-trained physician Franz Mesmer had made an epoch-making discovery: he claimed that the same gravity that caused the movement of the planets also flowed through living organisms in the form of a fluid he called 'animal magnetism'. In humans, a blockage in animal magnetism caused ill health. Fortunately for those affected, Mesmer had the gift of storing and directing the fluid, and could induce restorative fits or trances by touching patients in magnetic zones of their bodies – he 'mesmerised' them, that is. Mesmer came to Paris in 1778 and gained a huge following by giving ever more spectacular demonstrations of his cures.

Prominent believers in Mesmerism formed themselves into a 'Lodge of Harmony' – a quasi-Masonic body devoted to learning from the great man and protecting his highest secrets. There were soon branches across much of the country. Willermoz incorporated the local Mesmerist cell into the Rectified Scottish Rite of the Beneficent Knights of the Holy City.

Jean-Baptiste Willermoz would continue his quest for spiritual enlightenment through Freemasonry until his death in 1824. He was only the most eclectic and doggedly enthusiastic of the many mystical Masons of the later eighteenth century. Occult Masonry was so popular that charlatans thrived. The most notorious of them was Giuseppe Balsamo – known to everyone by his assumed name of Count Cagliostro. Born into poverty in Palermo in 1743, Cagliostro travelled Europe forging documents and pimping his wife. When, after a spell in a London jail, he was initiated into Freemasonry in a Soho pub in 1777, he acquired a whole new tool-kit of chicanery. He resumed his wandering, this time as the 'Great Cophta' of his own version of Masonry, the Egyptian Rite, whose highest secrets involved the power to regenerate the bodies of the elderly.

It is only too easy to look back on the occultist Freemasonry of the later eighteenth century with little more than bemused curiosity – as if characters like Pasqually, Willermoz, Mesmer and Cagliostro were ludicrous accidents of history. But to do so is to patronise the past. Mesmerism, for example, felt entirely plausible to many educated and rational observers because animal magnetism was just one of many obscure forces identified at the time. Thanks to Newton and Franklin, people knew what gravity and electricity *did*, but it was much harder to say what they *were*.

Revelatory forms of Masonry like those explored by Willermoz also tell us a great deal about the decline in institutional religion in France in the second half of the eighteenth century.

Congregations thinned out, and less money was bequeathed for the saying of Masses. Instead of joining Catholic confraternities, the good burghers of France enlisted *en masse* in Masonic Lodges, where they did very much the same things, only outside the framework of the Church and its top-down theology: they socialised, did philanthropic work and sought shared mystical experiences. As in England, Masonry eased the transition to a more secular world.

Many clergymen belonged to the Craft – despite the Pope's disapproval. According to one survey, an extraordinary 35 per cent of the Brothers in the Angers and Mans area to the southwest of Paris were priests or curates. Like all Brothers, churchmen lived out their Masonry in very varied ways. In 1778, 13 of the 150 members of the prestigious scientific Nine Sisters Lodge were men of the cloth. In 1752, in a Parisian Lodge, Casanova befriended a pudgy *bon viveur* from Bologna who also happened to be a cardinal – the Papal Legate, no less; together they enjoyed 'fine suppers in the company of pretty girls'.

All of which brings us to a straightforward conclusion: French Freemasonry mirrored the diversity of French society at large – or at least the upper, male portion of it. It was diverse enough, indeed, to accommodate one of the most enigmatic and unusual Freemasons of all time.

'If'

Charles de Beaumont, known as the Chevalier d'Éon, was a formidable French lawyer, soldier, diplomat and spy. In 1763, d'Éon arrived in England and created a sensation. The Chevalier was known for wanton spending and duelling, and ran into trouble with both London creditors and a powerful faction back at Versailles. In October 1764, a heavily armed d'Éon took refuge in a barricaded Soho house, and later went on the run after being found guilty of libel and made an outlaw. The French authorities only retrieved the situation when d'Éon blackmailed them with compromising secret documents. Remarkably, this harum-scarum career on the London diplomatic scene continued for another thirteen years.

What really made d'Éon stand out among London's many scandalists was that he – or she – often dressed as a woman, and deliberately cultivated doubts about his/her sex. In private, to a fellow French spy, the Chevalier confessed to being biologically female. In public, when huge bets were accumulating on the issue, s/he indignantly claimed to have all the attributes of a man. And then refused to provide proof.

At the height of the gambling frenzy in 1768, the Chevalier was admitted as a Freemason at the Crown and Anchor on the Strand. Some eighteen months later, s/he served as one of the Lodge's officers. By becoming a Mason, d'Éon furnished enough proof of masculinity to dampen speculation for a while. Presumably, his/her chest betrayed no obvious feminine characteristics when it was bared for the ceremony.

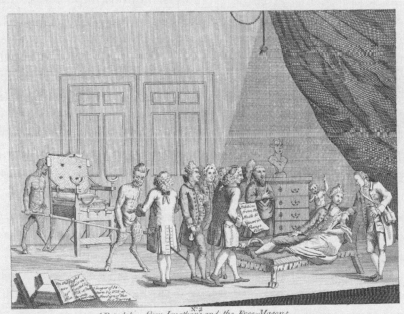

A Deputation from Jonathans and the Free-Masons

Miß Epicane D'Eon is discovered in close consultation with its Wine Merchant & Privy Counsellor. The Free-Masons beg the Secret of its Sex may be kept inviolable; the Committee of Under-writers on the other hand Petition for the Discovery, & propose that Monsr A shall explore the sexual Signature manually after the manner used in the election of a new Pope for which purpose the Doctor is seen introducing his new invented Night-Chair.

There was hilarity across London when the news that d'Éon was a Freemason leaked out. Satirical engravings appeared to capitalise on the Craft's humiliation. One showed the Chevalier (referred to as 'it' in the accompanying text) receiving two deputations. The first, made up of embarrassed Freemasons, pleads with d'Éon to keep 'its' biological identity a secret. The second deputation, from the bookmakers, wants the controversy resolved once and for all, and proposes that d'Éon submit to the kind of manual genital assessment that a Pope allegedly undergoes after being elected. Two devils are seen bringing the chair used in the Vatican for the test (it has a hole in the middle of the seat), and a priest stands ready to fumble under d'Éon's skirts.

The Chevalier was understandably fonder of another, more flattering, print – so much so that s/he bought ten copies. It portrays a figure of indeterminate gender who is both wearing a dress and bearing such masculine accoutrements as a sword, a cane and Masonic insignia. Pictures of famous imposters can be seen in the background.

Gambling about d'Éon's sex picked up again until, in 1777, those who had wagered that the Chevalier was female went to court. They emerged victorious on the say-so of two witnesses: a surgeon who testified that he had administered treatment for a feminine malady to the contested body in question; and a French journalist who swore that he had had sex with the Chevalier. Doubts lingered: the two key witnesses in the London case could have taken bribes. Nevertheless, not long after the verdict, at the age of forty-nine, with her features and frame becoming sturdier, d'Éon finally declared herself a woman, to be known as the Chevalière d'Éon. She then made plans to return to France.

The Chevalière took Freemasonry in earnest, as evinced by the fact that she read many books about the Brotherhood and its history. Her Masonic contacts were also important to her when, after a short period in the Parisian limelight, she was

sent back to the provincial obscurity of Burgundy where she had been born. Her cousin and a number of friends were on the Square, as were most of the craftsmen she employed, such as her wigmaker.

More striking still is the fact that the Lodge in her home town of Tonnerre was willing to accept her as one of its own. In August 1779, when the Grand Orient of France blocked her admission, the members in Tonnerre protested, proffering compassionate reasons why they had felt unable to refuse her: 'Despite her transformation [into a woman], we would have believed that we were betraying not only our patriotic feelings and our ties of blood and friendship, but still more our title of Brothers.' The Chevalière d'Éon may have been a woman, but she was still a Brother.

What explains this display of open-mindedness by the Masons

of Tonnerre? Perhaps they were being deferential to the Chevalière, who was, after all, a local celebrity and a scion of the minor nobility. Loyalty to a relative and old friend may have played a part. There is also a chance that the Brothers just took d'Éon to be a man in a dress. In any case, there were less parochial reasons too. Back in England, female Freemasons were no more than a figment of the satirical imagination, a grotesque send-up of the Craft's men-only stuffiness. In France, by contrast, they were a living, breathing, apron-wearing reality.

Sublime Scotswomen and English Amazons

Any woman presenting herself for initiation must be healthy, not pregnant, and not menstruating. Before entering the Lodge she shall be shown into a darkened room where there will be a single light and a skull. There she meets a Lady, who will ask her if she is ready to undergo terrible trials. She is asked to remove her right sleeve and glove, and then her left garter, which she replaces with a blue ribbon one yard long. Once she has put on a blindfold, she is ready to knock at the door of the Lodge.

Adoption. Or Women's Freemasonry, Paris, 1775

Female Freemasonry was not unique to France, but it was certainly characteristic: nowhere else were there as many Sisters. Once the Craft had crossed the Channel and established its independence from London, the very same chaos that had permitted the profusion of Scottish Rite Degrees also permitted the admission of women. The first *Maçonnes* we know about appeared in the 1740s. Thereafter, their spread across the country was uneven: such major centres of Masonic activity as Montpellier, Marseille, Toulouse and Toulon had no organised female Masonry that we know of. Nevertheless, by 1774, Masonic Sisters were so well established in places like Paris and Bordeaux that the Grand

Orient had little alternative but to recognise them. Thereafter, their number grew even further, as did the range of guide-books to help them in their Masonic self-fashioning. At the peak, there may have been as many as a thousand *Maçonnes*.

Just like its male counterpart, female Freemasonry placed ceremony at the centre of its collective life. For women Masons as for men, rites marked the birth of a better self; they were a passport to a country where friendship was sovereign.

In every locality where women were allowed into Masonry in France, they were governed by the same ritual formula: the Adoption Lodge. Adoption Lodges admitted both women and men, and they explored Old Testament themes in their rites.

The earliest historians of female Masonry, whether sympathetic to the Craft or not, assumed that Adoption Rites were concocted to fob off curious women, while allowing men to get on with the real thing in peace. Feminist historians saw them as misogynistic: the tale of Eve's temptation by Satan, which is used in many Adoption initiation rituals, is about as ancient as male chauvinism gets.

However, recent research has demonstrated that the Adoption Lodges actually had a dignified pedigree based in a minor regional tradition of English Masonic workings that may have been brought over to France by Jacobites. Thus, if initiating women was a novelty created in France, the ritual mechanisms for doing so were not.

The charge of misogyny levelled against the Adoption rituals needs to be qualified too, because they gave the Old Testament stories a twist. For example, in many of these workings, Eve bit the apple, but rejected its pips. Translated out of its ceremonial allegory, this meant that Eve took on the knowledge of Good and Evil, but rejected the wrongdoing that could germinate from it. From being the Old Testament woman whose curiosity brought sin into the world, the Masonic Eve was restyled as someone who, like Christ, shouldered the burden of sin for the good of all.

With time, some *Maçonnes* reached more senior ranks, took charge of Adoption ceremonies, and even invented higher Degrees for themselves. In the process, they came to reflect on what Enlightenment might mean for women. Some found enough freedom of expression to advance emancipatory sentiments that have a very modern ring to them. Here, for example, is the speech delivered by one Mason in Dijon after her initiation: 'Oh my Sisters! How sweet it is for me to pronounce that name! . . . Let us take delight in an honour that avenges our sex for the multiple insults that we have endured for so long.' The historian who has done most to help us discover the world of female Masonry has argued that 'there is no question that an incipient type of feminism had begun to form within the [Adoption] Lodges'.

Nevertheless, the incipient feminists within the Adoption Lodges faced serious obstacles. The primary reason why Masons admitted women into the Craft was to head off the accusation that men-only Lodges were homosexual debauches. The accusation was particularly insistent in France, where it was widely believed that homosexuality was the Craft's notorious secret, and that the rituals were a naked initiation into sodomy. The fact that, in Paris, members of the gay subculture used secret hand gestures and code-words to meet one another in safety from the authorities only increased the suspicion. Homosexuals even started adopting Craft terminology among themselves, calling one another 'Brother', for example. Adoption Lodges were intended to safeguard Freemasonry from this mortifying association.

Adoption Lodges remained constitutionally subordinate, existing only in the form of an annexe to a 'proper' male Lodge. This subordination was set in stone by the Grand Orient in 1774 when it approved Adoption procedures, including the humiliating proviso that women could not be initiated while menstruating. Adoption Lodges, like the many female adjuncts to Masonry created in other times and places, did not challenge the principle that the Craft is a male-only association.

Eighty-two per cent of the women recorded as belonging to Adoption Lodges were aristocrats; the others were all from élite families: that fact alone explains much of what we need to know about female Masonry. These were women born to regard themselves as being above the laws that applied in the rest of society. Over several generations, intellectually inclined French aristocrats of both sexes had become used to the culture of the *salon* – a private literary or artistic circle that was often hosted by a tone-setting female impresario. In the typical salon, the emphasis was placed on witty and polite conversation that included both men and women. To many aristocrats in the middle decades of the eighteenth century it would have been odd to exclude women from a group like the Freemasons that claimed to advance virtue and social intercourse.

In Freemasonry at large, Adoption Lodges remained controversial. Many of the arguments against initiating women that had been put forward in the United Kingdom continued to be heard in France: women couldn't be trusted to keep secrets; and men couldn't be trusted to keep it in their breeches.

Female Masonry was a constant worry for the Masonic authorities. In 1777, some Brothers were found to have used the Adoption formula to invite prostitutes to their celebrations.

It was probably around the same time that the intellectuals of the Nine Sisters Lodge asked the Chevalière d'Éon to attend one of their solemn occasions. The following letter from the Nine Sisters was found among her papers: 'I enclose an invitation to this ceremony, in which you have a prominent place as a Mason, as an author, and as one who is now the glory of your sex, having previously brought such honour to ours.' The letter is flattering, but nonetheless ambiguous. Was she being invited along as a woman? As a former man? As a Mason, irrespective of her sex? Or did the very doubtful nature of her identity make her a unique case? As the letter continued, 'Mademoiselle d'Éon *alone* has the right to cross the barrier which excludes the fairer sex from our labours' [my emphasis]. One suspects that the poor Chevalière may just have been summoned out of amused curiosity. Certainly, some Masons regarded her as a figure of fun rather than an offence to the Masonic *Constitutions*. In some Lodges a ribald song was sung about the Chevalière – it was set to the words of a popular air, 'The Staff of St Barnabas'. The same double-entendre ended every verse:

> We Masons have a zealous Brother
> Who knows our secrets like no other.
> If it's said that he's a lass,
> We'll need to see his St Barnabas staff.

It is not hard to think of modern labels to try out on d'Éon. Yet her story would be a lot less historically interesting if any of them fitted neatly. We simply do not know how far her choice of clothes and gender was an expression of her identity. Voltaire, for one, firmly believed that her metamorphosis was just an expedient – a drastic but effective way of shedding the enemies and responsibilities accumulated during her tumultuous life as a man: 'His – or her – chin is adorned with a very thick and spiky black beard, so I just cannot believe that this d'Éon person is a woman.'

Many other intellectuals who encountered her were as confused as Voltaire about the difference between sex and gender. The Chevalière returned to live in London in the mid-1780s, still trailing confusion in her wake. James Boswell chatted with her at a party one evening, and later commented: 'I was shocked to think of her a kind of monster by metamorphosis. She appeared to me a man in woman's clothes.' Many observers thought of her as a kind of amazon. The puzzle of the Chevalière d'Éon would find no solution. At least in her lifetime.

The Illuminati

Google 'Illuminati' and you get over 54 million hits, most of them exploring a secret plan by a global élite to create a New World Order by strategic use of mind control, assassination and triangles. As the masthead of one such website, *The Vigilant Citizen*, proclaims: 'Symbols Rule the World, Not Words Nor Laws'. Behind the world of appearances in which we live, there are sinister machinations. Once you realise this, it becomes laughably obvious that Lady Gaga is a puppet of the Illuminati. Why else would she stand with her legs in a triangle shape and cover an eye in one of her videos? The Illuminati conspiracy myth was most recently revived after a cluster of rap musicians referred to it in their lyrics in the mid-1990s. However, its notoriety originated two centuries earlier, and we owe much of it to the fact that the Abbé Barruel's *Memoirs Illustrating the History of Jacobinism* made the Illuminati the leading villains of the Masonic plot behind the French Revolution.

All of which is very far removed from the real story of the Illuminati, who originated in Germany, where Freemasonry developed in similar ways to France. Berlin, the Prussian capital, was home to one of the international figureheads of the Craft: King Frederick II the Great of Prussia, a friend of Voltaire's. In the late 1730s, when Freemasonry was suspected of being subversive, the then Prince Frederick had embraced it, and after he became King had helped make it respectable. Yet Frederick's interest waned as Freemasonry became fashionable, and more and more people crowded to join. Just as had happened in France, the advent of the Scottish Rites and the cult of the Knights Templar saw German Masonry descend into a chaos of 'oddities, contradictions and mysteries'. Brothers indulged in fits of jealousy, hatred and intrigue over imaginary Masonic command structures, over ribbons and medals that meant nothing in the world outside. Lodges began to exclude anyone but the upper classes from the higher Degrees, indulged in financial malpractice and spent far more on their feasts than they did on charity. According to one well-informed observer, would-be workers of wonders and outright con-artists submerged German Masonry in 'the follies of Asia and China, universal medicines, the art of making gold or diamonds, immortality beverages, etc. etc.'.

By the 1780s, Freemasonry was widespread in Germany. Just as in France, however, it was also a grave disappointment to those who had hoped that all the Masonic talk of brotherhood, tolerance and reason might actually have a positive impact on the world at large. The political temperature was rising across Europe, and some began to feel that the Lodges had shirked their responsibilities in the Enlightenment struggle against superstition and despotism. In Germany, as in France, it looked as if Freemasonry's best days were behind it. One man who shared that view was Adam Weishaupt, a young university professor from the town of Ingolstadt in Bavaria. In response, he built a secret society whose influence was modest, whose lifespan was short, but which was destined to become the most notorious variety of Freemasonry of all time.

Weishaupt was only a recent convert to the most radical ideas of the French Enlightenment when he began to dream of a secret society devoted to putting an end to despotism and superstition. In 1776 his plans became concrete when he enlisted his favourite students into what soon became the Order of the Illuminati. The new group may have had only five members, but it aimed at nothing less than a reign of freedom, justice and reason for the world. Unfortunately, there were contradictions in Weishaupt's scheme that would encumber the Illuminati throughout their short existence. Their universal aims sat uneasily with the fact that their real message was known only to a select inner coterie. Moreover, Weishaupt's ideal Illuminatus was somehow supposed to combine a fiercely independent critical mind with blind obedience to orders from the Illuminati hierarchy.

Adam Weishaupt (1748–1830),
founder of the notorious Illuminati.

Weishaupt envisaged an organisation with three tiers. At the bottom level, young apprentices were watched over by the leaders as they made their first steps. In the second 'Minerval' tier, affiliates would be put through an intensive and wide-ranging programme of reading. Only the brightest and best would be admitted to the third tier, the Areopagus (named after an ancient Athenian council of elders), where they would learn the true purposes of the Illuminati and formulate strategy.

But this organisational schema remained little more than a plan. The Illuminati grew painfully slowly in the early years. Weishaupt loathed Freemasonry and what he called its 'pure inanities' – its rituals and symbols. Yet he realised that the Illuminati needed precisely such inanities if they were to draw in future members of the élite. After joining a Templarist Lodge in Munich, the Bavarian capital, he lighted upon the tactic that would finally take his secret society beyond Bavaria, and beyond a few dozen members: the Illuminati would infiltrate Masonic Lodges, and twist them to their purposes.

Shortly after the Illuminati took control of their first Masonic Lodge, in January 1780, Adolph Knigge, a gentleman journalist from the Electorate of Hanover, was recruited to the cause. Knigge was a democrat, a prolific writer and a mystic Freemason. But he had been intensely disappointed when his ambitious plans for an entirely new rite devoted to achieving a higher state of being were rebuffed by the Masonic authorities. For Knigge, the Illuminati represented just the radical break he needed; their rationalist, emancipatory programme offered a new way to realise his dream of restoring Freemasonry to an elevated goal. For the Illuminati, Knigge's vast network of Masonic and society contacts opened a gateway into northern Germany. Knigge worked sixteen-hour days in his Bockenheim office, even pawning his silver to pay for postage. It is largely thanks to him that, at their peak, the Illuminati numbered between six hundred and a thousand, at a generous estimate.

Nevertheless, it was the quality of the members that counted rather than their quantity. By that criterion, the movement's achievement was notable. Several princes and dukes joined, as well as a raft of lesser noblemen. The bulk of the membership was made up of government officials, journalists and academics. Businessmen were put off by the extremely demanding curriculum of Enlightenment reading. The most famous Illuminatus of them all had no such aversion to study: the writer and senior advisor to Grand Duke Karl August of Saxe-Weimar-Eisenach, Johann Wolfgang von Goethe. It is possible that Goethe joined simply to keep a governmental eye on the society.

The Illuminati grew despite being in a state of flux. Knigge, who formally only belonged to the second tier of the organisation, wrote desperate letters to Weishaupt asking to know more.

He had been reduced to stringing his members along when they demanded to be rewarded for all their studying with access to higher Degrees and superior knowledge. Weishaupt replied shamefacedly that the Illuminati were still a work-in-progress, and invited Knigge to Bavaria in 1781 to take part in elaborating a proper programme.

The resultant discussions endorsed Weishaupt's ultimate aims. Through Masonic Lodges, the Illuminati were to infiltrate the highest echelons of the various German states, surrounding their rulers with advisors who would steer government in an enlightened direction. Eventually, as the masses awoke to their own potential for self-realisation, Weishaupt prophesied, 'princes and nations shall disappear from the face of the earth peacefully, mankind shall become one family, and the world shall become a haven of reasonable people'. The Illuminati were a non-violent conspiracy. The problem was that neither the precise nature of the society they were conspiring to create, nor the precise methods needed to create it, were ever clear to anyone involved.

It did not last long. Knigge resigned at the end of 1783, worn out by incessant battles with the overbearing Weishaupt. Some conservative members defected in the spring of 1784, and informed the Bavarian authorities. Secret societies were banned in June, and the Illuminati explicitly condemned as 'traitorous and hostile to religion' the following March. Weishaupt fled Bavaria never to return, and his organisation collapsed.

When the scandal broke, most former Illuminati were perplexed by all the fuss. Only a tiny minority of them had been admitted to the Areopagus, the brotherhood's inner sanctum. For the majority, it was a glorified book club. There may have been Illuminati in influential positions in courts across Germany, but they had no perceptible influence in implementing Weishaupt's programme – largely because they had no idea that there even was a programme.

There is an obvious irony in the fact that so hapless a conspirator as Adam Weishaupt should inadvertently give rise to one of the most widespread of all conspiracy myths, and indeed help shape the conspiracy theory as we know it today. The story of the Illuminati fired the imaginations of conservative clergy and academics, who whipped up an Illuminati panic, portraying Weishaupt's followers as atheistic sodomites, murderous enemies of society. Autocratic governments had the cue they needed to crack down on the Freemasons and liberal ideas of all kinds. The initial Illuminati panic matured into a deep-rooted terror of subversive secret societies. Everywhere, an idea that had lain submerged since the 1740s resurfaced: the Freemasons were the guardians of dangerous secrets. Fears of Masonic secrecy became vastly more insidious thanks to the Illuminati. For Masons trying to counter charges that their Brotherhood was subversive and conspiratorial, it was no longer any use to point to the number of good Freemasons, or to their principles of loyalty to established authority. Only dupes took Freemasonry at face value, because it was like a fiendish system of Chinese boxes – a nest of compartments, each more secret and more sinister than the one containing it. Behind the Lodges, secret Lodges. Behind the secret Lodges, the Illuminati. And behind the Illuminati, an evil mastermind exerting a mesmeric control over his followers. The Illuminati panic helped make conspiracy-thinking about the Masons immune to contrary evidence. At the same time, the fragmentation of Freemasonry exemplified by the Scottish Rites left it without a unified voice to respond effectively to even the most outrageous of charges. And this just as a political earthquake back in France made the charges much more outrageous.

The Abbé Barruel

The French Revolution began in 1789 when a wrangle over tax between the king and the nobility exploded unexpectedly into the widespread and euphoric aspiration to create a new era of liberty. Sovereignty was to reside in the nation, and not in the monarchy. Government was to be answerable to public opinion, rather than to cliquish aristocrats and bishops. Rights would triumph over privileges. Never before had a society sought so completely to reinvent itself.

Yet, in the face of truculent opposition at home and abroad, the attempt to realise the dreams of 1789 brought turmoil. Violence accompanied the Revolution's every stage. There was popular retribution against representatives of the Old Regime, and popular resistance against the heavy-handedness of the new one. Radicals who clamoured to push the Revolution further met brutal repression from those trying to stop it spinning out of control. The new France went to war with its foreign enemies, and war pushed the Revolution to the extremes. A Republic was declared, and King Louis XVI was executed. Opponents were increasingly branded as traitors, while spies and plotters seemed to lurk in every shadow. The bloodshed was often ghastly in its theatricality: fusillades and grapeshot fired into crowds; severed heads mounted on pikes and gate-posts; bodies dismembered.

Under the Jacobins, France entered a life-or-death struggle during what soon became known as the 'Terror' of 1793–4. Constitutional government was suspended. Mass conscription provoked rebellion in the west of the country: more than a hundred thousand were killed in savage fighting. In Paris, those labelled 'counter-revolutionaries' were beheaded by the dozen. But even when the military and economic situation improved, the executions gathered pace because of score-settling among the Jacobin leaders.

As the horror mounted, so too did the Revolution's quest for ideological purity. To some, Terror was the doorway to a realm of virtue. The Revolution had already declared freedom of religion, confiscated the Church's property and subordinated the Church to the state. Now it sought to replace religion with some entirely new creed: the Cult of the Supreme Being, or the Cult of Reason.

To the Revolution's enemies, it seemed that a cult of insanity had taken hold. The Terror exposed the true meaning of the optimistic slogans of 1789. And if the Terror defined the Revolution, then one implement defined the Terror: the guillotine. Joseph-Ignace Guillotin, the doctor, Freemason and member of the Nine Sisters Lodge, dreamed up the idea of 'decapitation by mechanism', although he did not design the model that went into operation. Like many of his Brethren, he was inspired by Enlightenment thinking amid the idealism of the Revolution's early days. During the Old Regime, culprits were broken on the wheel, or hung, drawn and quartered. In the new age of Reason, Dr Guillotin argued, execution should be swift and painless. On 25 April 1792, an armed robber became the first man to die under the dropping blade.

Brother Dr Joseph-Ignace Guillotin (1738–1814) demonstrates his idea for a beheading machine. From a later representation.

The following year, during the Terror, the 'national razor' reaped thousands of victims, making a grotesque mockery of Dr Guillotin's humanitarianism. The stories and scenes from Paris's Place de la Révolution, exaggerated as they probably were, would haunt Europe's dreams for decades: the crowds baying as the tumbrils passed; the rows of old women calmly knitting while they watched the blade fall; the gore spurting across the cobbles to form vast pools that were lapped at by dogs.

Eventually, on 10 August 1794, the figurehead of the Terror, the Jacobin leader Maximilien Robespierre, was himself guillotined. A bloody retribution was soon inflicted on the Jacobins.

For the Abbé Barruel, steeping himself in Masonic writings in the safety of his Edgware Road house, the origins of the conspiracy that brought about the French Revolution were ancient: they took us back to the dawn of Satan's campaign against the Church of Christ in third-century Babylonia. Manichaeism, the earliest of many devilish heresies, taught that, in the great battle between good and evil, illumination was to be sought by blending all religions into a comprehensive credo. Christ was no longer the Way, the Truth and the Life: he was just one spiritual example among many. Christianity was to be submerged in a poisonous syncretistic soup, in other words. Following their masters the Manichaeans, the Masons would serve this same soup to their affiliates under the deceptive label of 'religious tolerance'.

Later, the 'monstrous' and 'impious' Templars, worshippers of the goat-headed false god Baphomet, became the bearers of the plot. When the Knights Templar were repressed by the Pope and the King of France, the survivors swore vengeance against all monarchs and Popes, and all manifestations of Christianity. They took refuge in Scotland, where both their mysteries and their thirst for revenge were incorporated into Freemasonry.

Yet, as the Abbé Barruel explained, these terrible secrets at the heart of Masonic lore were fiendishly well cloaked. Freemasonry's centralised system of oaths and degrees served two ends: to hide the Brotherhood's darkest purposes; and to seduce new members into imbibing ever larger doses of the Craft's addictive ideology. Naïve Masons were lured deeper and deeper into the system until they lost all capacity to resist. From the ordinary Lodges they graduated to the Occult Lodges. From the introductory Degrees they passed, stage by stage, towards the ultimate Degree of Knight Kadosh. There then came the blood-curdling final disclosure: the Masonic watchwords of brotherhood and freedom, so cosy and bland when first encountered, actually meant nothing less than a secret declaration of 'war on Christ and his cult; war on kings and all their thrones'. This was the wicked mission that would be fulfilled in the French Revolution.

Yet Freemasonry was not the only conspiracy that fed into the Revolution. Barruel explained that the murderous reign of the Jacobins, the Revolution's most zealous wing, came about when Masonry merged with two other great plots.

The first was that of the *Philosophes*, the thinkers and reformers who schemed to destroy Christianity during the Enlightenment. There were three masterminds: Jean d'Alembert, the mathematician who edited that great compendium of rationalist heresy, the *Encyclopédie*; the Prussian King Frederick II, who ended censorship, implemented religious freedom and surrounded himself with godless intellectuals; and, most sinister of all, the prolific unbeliever Voltaire. By preaching rationality and tolerance, these men instilled atheism and immorality. The *Philosophes* gravitated towards the Masonic Lodges, fusing their conspiracy against Christianity with the Masons' plans to subvert the monarchy. The last *Philosophe* to join the Craft was the most influential. For much of his long life, as Abbé Barruel conceded, Voltaire was a monarchist. But secretly, as he grew older, he became more fanatical, until, in 1778, he took his Masonic oaths with the Nine Sisters Lodge.

Now all that was needed for the French Revolution to explode upon the world was for the third and most deadly branch of the conspiracy to appear. It was a black crusade against all religion, all government, all property, all law – against any social order of whatever kind: the Illuminati. They only *appeared* to have been repressed in Germany in the 1780s. In reality, they had metastasised by sending a deputation to France disguised as devotees of Mesmer's theory of animal magnetism. Once in Paris, they recruited all the most senior Freemasons and *Philosophes* into their ranks and converted the entire Masonic organisation to their programme of anarchy and general dissolution. Thus were the Jacobins born, and France's fate sealed.

Barruel had insider knowledge, he said, because he joined the Freemasons himself. Knowing that the Craft was suspicious all along, he made his excuses when the oaths he was asked to swear became too compromising. He heard of the hidden intentions of the chief conspirators from sources he could not reveal for reasons of security. Regrettably, he had lost the most incriminating of the conspiratorial letters he cited.

To our eyes, this evidence-base is as manifestly flimsy as the theory it supports. Yet just a few months after Barruel's work was released, it was bolstered when John Robison, a leading physicist and mathematician at the University of Edinburgh, published a book denouncing far-reaching subversive manoeuvres by the Masons and Illuminati. Barruel and Robison had worked entirely independently of one another. The striking similarities between their conclusions clad their argument in iron. The United States had an Illuminati panic in 1798. Even Great Britain was gripped by the fear of clandestine brotherhoods. In 1799, Parliament passed the Unlawful Societies Act, which forbade associations that compelled their members to take an oath; the Masons had to lobby hard not to be banned.

The flaws of *Memoirs Illustrating the History of Jacobinism* are hardly worth countering in detail. Many of the men Barruel thought were Brothers were nothing of the sort. The Craft's links to the Manichaeans and Templars that Barruel took as a damning reality were in reality the Scottish Rite Masons' own myth-making. At a stretch, the most that any modern historian of the French Revolution would be prepared to concede to Barruel's analysis is that the formal equality of Lodge procedures was one of the many influences that went into the emergence of the political clubs, including the Jacobins, that were so important to the events of the 1790s. That said, there is no more powerful way to demonstrate the febrile idiocy of any explanation of the French Revolution as a Masonic conspiracy than to follow what happened to many Brothers after 1789.

Citizen Equality

Freemasonry went into rapid decline when the winds of Revolution blew. Some Brothers were sucked into the political tempest, and others blasted into exile. By 1793 the Jacobin regime regarded the Craft with deep suspicion: its secrecy, as ever, seemed a threat to the state, and its aristocratic leaders were, by that very fact, actual or potential counter-Revolutionaries. Soon the Grand Orient, so painstakingly constructed two decades earlier, would cease to function.

There were plenty of Jacobins who were not Masons – Robespierre being the prime example; and plenty of important Masons who did not become Jacobins. Indeed, the aristocratic Brother Auguste-Jean-François Chaillon de Jonville, who was the effective leader of the Paris Grand Lodge in the 1760s, not only – like Barruel – fled the Revolution for the safety of foreign shores, but also wrote a book denouncing the whole revolutionary enterprise.

The most prominent Mason of the period was Philippe Duke of Orléans. Grand Master of the Grand Orient for over twenty years, Philippe threw himself enthusiastically into the Revolution, to the extent of becoming a Jacobin and renaming himself 'Citizen Philippe Equality'. In January 1793 he even voted in the

National Convention to have his cousin, King Louis XVI, sent to the guillotine. Which was all fodder for Barruel, who tells us that the Duke was moulded by the Exterminating Angel himself for the purposes of leading Freemasonry's bloody project. Yet, as ever, Barruel omits facts that do not square with his conspiracy theory. First, Philippe was a figurehead rather than an enthusiastic Mason, and did not bother to attend a meeting of the Grand Orient until four years after he was appointed. Second, he was intimidated into voting for the death penalty against Louis XVI. Third, he repudiated his Masonic connections not long after the King's execution; he said that, compared to the real equality that the Revolution had brought, the Craft was a mere 'phantom'. And fourth, poor Citizen Equality was guillotined by the Jacobins in November 1793. So the vast Masonic conspiracy did not work out particularly well for him.

Many more of Barruel's Freemasons felt the Revolution's wrath. The political scientist Nicolas de Condorcet features high on Barruel's list of conspirators. But he wrote his most famous work in hiding after being branded a traitor by Robespierre and his friends. Captured after nine months, Condorcet died in prison while awaiting execution.

The Marquis de Lafayette, the French Brother who was a hero of the American Revolution, quickly embraced the ideals of 1789; indeed, he was one of the principal authors of the Declaration of the Rights of Man and of the Citizen, the French Revolution's founding statement of values. Yet in August 1792, these credentials did not save him from the arrest warrant that forced him to flee the country.

Dr Joseph-Ignace Guillotin very nearly died at the hands of the execution machine that bore his name. He was imprisoned by the Jacobins, but released following Robespierre's death. Disillusioned with politics, he spent the rest of his life devoted to medicine, and to trying to get the guillotine renamed.

In Lyon, the mystic Jean-Baptiste Willermoz survived the Revolution, although at the height of the trouble in 1793 he was

The MARTYR of EQUALITY
Behold the Progress of our system.

A British satirical take on the beheading of Philippe
Égalité, formerly known as Louis Philippe II,
Duke of Orléans and Grand Master of the
Grand Orient of France (1747–1793).

forced to go into hiding, taking his archive of occultist papers
with him.

Aristocratic Masons fared badly. Female Masons, who were
overwhelmingly from the nobility, therefore suffered dispropor-
tionately. Philippe Equality's wife and sister, both of whom had
been initiated in Adoption Lodges, were imprisoned during the
Terror and only allowed to escape to Spain after Robespierre's
death. One prominent *Maçonne* met a particularly horrible fate.
Marie-Thérèse-Louise de Savoie-Carignan, the Princess of
Lamballe, held the key court post of Superintendent of Queen
Marie Antoinette's Household. She was initiated into an Adoption

Lodge in 1777 and was elected Grand Mistress of the Scottish Mother Lodge in 1781. So determined was the Princess to live by the Masonic code of friendship that she remained close to Marie Antoinette even when the Queen became a figure of loathing after the Revolution. This loyalty would cost her dearly. The historian who has studied the Princess's Masonry most intensively describes what happened to her in September 1792: 'She was imprisoned and summarily executed after a short trial by a kangaroo court. Her headless body, badly mutilated, was dragged through the streets to an area outside Marie Antoinette's prison window where it was dumped to terrorise the Queen. Her head was paraded around separately.'

Then there was the unique case of the Chevalière d'Éon, who spent her last years in England, sheltered from the turmoil. The fall of the monarchy nevertheless put an end to the royal pension that was her only means of support. There began a slow descent into indignity: she was forced to gather money by putting on displays of her sword-fighting skills, and then by selling her possessions. She died in penury in 1810. A post-mortem examination confirmed that she was biologically male. Of course, these anatomical facts do very little to solve the enigma. But they were enough for the British Craft to forget the embarrassment the d'Éon affair had caused, and create a cover story – no matter that it did not fit the facts. The Irish Masonic historian, W.J. Chetwode Crawley, reflected in 1903: 'If we are permitted to conjecture that the Chevalier D'Éon's mind gave way partially under the strain and stress of the disastrous years during which his sex was bandied about from mouth to mouth, and that he laboured under the hallucination that he really was of the female sex, all would be explained.' For Chetwode Crawley, D'Éon was insane and, as such, deserving of fraternal compassion.

Despite being so wrong, the Abbé Barruel's *Memoirs Illustrating the History of Jacobinism* ensured that the myth of a Masonic conspiracy was the major legacy of the history of Freemasonry in the era of the French Revolution. Ironically, moreover, as the swirling smoke and rhetoric of the French Revolution spread to other parts of Europe, many conspirators lighted on Masonry as a pattern for how to organise their schemes. Nowhere more than in Italy did the myth of conspiracy mutate into a reality.

Naples: **A Raving Sickness**

Freemasonry in Napoleon's Empire

We do not know if Napoleon Bonaparte was ever a Freemason. If he was initiated, it was in 1798 or 1799 when he was still General Bonaparte. At that time, Freemasonry was reviving after the end of the Jacobin Terror, albeit under the wary eye of the police, and its future remained uncertain. In November 1799, Napoleon seized power in a coup. In 1804, he would proclaim himself Emperor. He was faced with a choice that many rulers before him had confronted: should he tolerate the Masons, or ban them? He did neither, opting instead to absorb them into the regime. The French Lodges that had once explored the arcana of the Scottish Rites in a spirit of freedom bordering on chaos became instruments of authoritarian government.

Napoleon's Empire was certainly authoritarian, but the Emperor was not a conservative: everywhere Bonaparte conquered, he endeavoured to build a state machine like the one he was creating in France. His aim, first and foremost, was to support the vast armies required for his constant campaigning. The new model administration embraced novelties of all kinds, from codes of law and police forces, to metric measurement and house numbers. It was centralised, standardised, and run by professionals rather than aristocratic placemen. In France as in the lands it subjugated, a class of administrators and army officers evolved to run the state: these were men proud to believe that they, like the Emperor, owed their positions to their own talent rather than to any accident of birth.

Napoleon's bureaucrats and soldiers needed to network, and Freemasonry met that need. In 1803, despite only having been a Brother for two years, Napoleon's brother-in-law Joachim Murat was elected First Senior Warden of the Grand Orient of France. In 1804, the year Napoleon crowned himself Emperor, his elder brother Joseph Bonaparte was made Grand Master of the Grand Orient, and senior state figures like the formidable Minister of Police, Joseph Fouché, were made Grand Officers. Even the Empress Josephine joined in. Indeed, her Masonic credentials were better than those of any other member of the Bonaparte clan: she had been initiated in a Strasbourg Adoption Lodge in 1792. In 1805, as Empress, she returned to Strasbourg to hold court. She visited her Mother Lodge, where she had one of her ladies of honour initiated. This was a public occasion, as one account attested: 'Perhaps never was an Adoption Lodge so brilliant; the entire city took part in these Masonic solemnities.' In its new, domesticated form, the French Craft prospered and grew – especially the military Lodges that were so good for building *esprit de corps*. There were only fourteen Lodges in France in 1802. By 1806 there were 624. At a time when the Revolution had ripped up webs of patronage centred on aristocrats, the Craft offered opportunities to those seeking to make useful contacts. As part of the same process, the Lodges also became temples in which to celebrate the cult of the Emperor, and reservoirs of informers for the police.

Napoleon upgraded statecraft in ways that would influence European societies long after he had departed the scene. Even the language of his British enemies felt the influence of his reforms; French gave English a new meaning for an old word meaning 'path' or 'course': *career*. Freemasons found a ready place among the military and civil career men of nineteenth-century states.

The following pages tell the story of what happened when Napoleon's imperial system, including his tame version of Freemasonry, was imposed on the Kingdom of Naples. The result was anything but tame. The Craft was pitched into a vortex of policemen, spies and double agents; of patriots, conspirators and revolutionaries; of fanatics, bandits and gangsters. In the wake of the French Revolution, quasi-Masonic political brotherhoods appeared in many of Europe's trouble-spots. Examples include the United Irishmen, the Greek Filiki Eteria and the Russian Decembrists. Yet nowhere did the enthusiasm for secret societies take hold as firmly as it did in southern Italy. As one official remarked in despair, it was 'a raving sickness that has consumed the people entirely'.

Grand Master Joachim Murat

Southern Italy was profoundly changed by the French Revolution. Late in 1798, King Ferdinand, of the Bourbon dynasty, fled the capital Naples in the face of a French advance. Early the following year a Republic was established: it was supported by a French army, but led by Neapolitan intellectuals enamoured with Liberty, Equality and Fraternity. Within a few months, when the French forces withdrew, the Republic was overthrown amid scenes of terrible violence that left a legacy of bitterness. King Ferdinand returned to his throne.

In 1806, Ferdinand fled again before French military power. He took refuge in Sicily – the part of his realm protected by the British Royal Navy. Southern Italy became part of the Napoleonic Empire, and was ruled over by two French Kings, who were the same two men who had led the Emperor's domestication of Freemasonry in France. First, his older brother Joseph was sent to wear the crown. Two years later, when Joseph left to become King of Spain, it was the turn of Napoleon's brother-in-law, and his boldest cavalry commander, Joachim Murat.

With a confident smile spread across his handsome face, Joachim rode into Naples for the first time on 6 September 1808. In conformity with Napoleon's wishes, he dressed not as a king, but in a flamboyant version of his cavalry uniform. The

Neapolitans quickly decoded the message in the clothes: their new ruler was an imposing military presence. At the point of a sabre if necessary, southern Italy was to maintain its primary function of funnelling cash, recruits and *matériel* into the Emperor's war machine.

Murat's outfits were to be a signature of his reign, proclaiming an *élan* he thought the locals would admire. In 1811, at the height of his power, he commissioned a portrait that, once contemplated, cannot be unseen. Neither the spectacle of Mount Vesuvius spouting smoke on the horizon, nor the hysterical posture of Murat's rearing charger, manage to wrench the eye away from his clothes. A flayed tiger is spread where a saddle should have been. The King wears pointed red boots, and haunch-hugging apricot nankeen trousers with a double scarlet stripe down the side. A well-nigh bullet-proof assemblage of medals and braid adorns his chest. His silken shako somehow stays balanced atop his abundant dark curls, despite the heavy swing of silver tassels at its side and the extravagant white plumes adorning the front.

Image-making was not the only tool of Murat's government. Just as in France, Freemasonry was to be a pillar of the Bonapartist regime. Before the French Revolution, Masonry had been more-or-less tolerated by Italian governments. After the French Revolution spread the fear of subversion across Europe, the Craft was banned and forced to work in secret. In Napoleonic Italy, by contrast, it became quasi-official. On assuming the southern Italian throne in 1806, Joseph Bonaparte was elected Grand Master of the Neapolitan Grand Orient – a new supreme supervisory body linked to similar bodies in northern Italy, where the French had exercised control for longer. In 1808, Joachim Murat completed the job of building Masonry into the Napoleonic monarchy by taking over Joseph's Masonic high offices and installing senior government men at the head of southern Italian Lodges. Many of Murat's most senior officials were Grand Masters.

Yet all was not as it seemed in Napoleonic Freemasonry in Naples. As early as Murat's first winter there, he wrote to the Emperor to warn that Masonic Lodges were being used as 'correspondence offices' for conspirators. Masonic or quasi-Masonic secret societies opposed to Napoleonic rule in Italy were not new. In the occupied north of the late 1790s, anti-French brotherhoods such as the *Lega Nera* ('Black League') and the *Raggi* (or 'Rays') appeared. After 1800, more secret societies coalesced: the *Adelfi* (from the ancient Greek for 'brothers'); the *Guelfi* (borrowed from the name of a medieval political alliance); the *Spilla Nera* ('Black Pin'); and the *Decisi* ('The Resolute'). Many Masons resented the French state's interference in their cherished rituals. Some who smarted at the foreign occupation of their land found a place to gather and grumble in the seclusion of the Lodges, or they took the Masonic template and used it to form brotherhoods with a political direction. But there was something altogether more remarkable going on here too. The French invasion had subdued and humiliated the peoples of the Italian peninsula. At the same time, it had unified them under a single source of authority and transfused French Revolutionary ideas into their culture. As a result, for the first time in history, a politically unified Italy became thinkable. Murat's agents among the Brothers had stumbled upon signs that an Italian national identity was being born. Freemasons were among the first to feel it make their hearts beat faster. As Murat wrote to Napoleon, 'I tell you again, Sire: their only dream is the unification of the whole of Italy.'

Under Murat, the world of Masonry felt the pull of competing political energies from the start. Over time, the field of force would become even more complicated, as Murat himself grew to resent Napoleon's interference in his realm, and seek greater autonomy.

On 24 June 1811, St John's Day, he presided over a grand Masonic lunch for one and a half thousand Brothers from across the land. Pointedly, the feast was held amid the Baroque magnificence of the Santi Apostoli Monastery, recently cleared of its Theatine monks when Murat abolished many religious orders. Alas, no record survives of any *outré* Masonic regalia he wore.

Among the Freemasons who rounded off their luncheon with coffee, ice-cream and *rosolio* that day were Italians who occupied important offices within the Napoleonic administration and military, and who were a crucial political constituency for Murat. Naturally, the locals working for his government were in an ambiguous position because their power had been handed to them by a foreign invader. Yet many were reformers who liked the way the regime drove the ideas of the Enlightenment deep into southern Italian society, abolishing the feudal privileges of the nobility and clergy, privatising church land, and injecting fresh talent into the administration. French rule gave many Brothers a role in modernising their homeland in line with the rational ideals that they had nurtured in their Lodges. There were even those who hoped that Murat's modern state might pave the way for a united, democratic Italy. Some of Murat's own Italian administrators had belonged to anti-French secret societies in the north before taking up government jobs in the south after the Napoleonic takeover. Such radicals might follow Murat a long way if he were to loosen ties with Paris and become a figurehead for the Kingdom's independence.

The full scale of the trouble being stored up in southern Italy's Masonic Lodges would only become apparent in the fateful year of 1812. That summer, Napoleon's *Grande Armée* of 600,000 men advanced deep into Russia. As ever, Murat rode at the Emperor's side. By December, the vast majority of their troops had died of cold and hunger on the steppe. The Emperor, his authority catastrophically damaged, returned to Paris and left his disintegrating army in Murat's hands.

In Naples, minds began to turn to what would happen if the Empire fell. It was in that moment that a dangerous new mutation of Freemasonry came to notice. In December 1812, while Joachim Murat was still in Poland, his ministers in Naples met to adopt a policy response to a secret society that bore the unmistakable stamp of the Masonic idea: brotherly love, oaths, rituals, symbols and – of course – secrets. Rather than 'Freemasons', its members called themselves *Carbonari* – 'Charcoal-Burners'.

The Charcoal-Burners were a much more serious proposition than any of the earlier secret societies. They addressed one another not as 'Brothers', but as 'Good Cousins', and referred to their Lodges as *Vendite*, after the forest clearings where woodsmen made and sold charcoal. Their rituals emphasised the lowly origins of their members, their commitment to a shared cause and Christian devotion through suffering. Jesus was a central figure in the Good Cousins' lore, allowing them to make their high-flown ideals accessible to Italy's Catholic common people. The movement appealed particularly to monks whose religious foundations had been closed by the Napoleonic author-ities. Masons disaffected by their Brotherhood's subservience to the French regime were also to be found among the first cells. Indeed, many *Vendite* remained attached to Masonic Lodges.

In the early days, the Charcoal-Burners only had two Degrees. Rather like the Illuminati, the Good Cousins revealed their real aims only to holders of the Second Degree. The true purpose of the sect was to 'purge the wolves from the forest' by defeating tyrants and anyone else who stood in the way of the natural rights of man. Jesus was shown to be a martyred enemy of tyranny. There was to be revolution to unite Italy and set up a republic.

Here was the Masonic idea born anew, with fewer pretensions, based on a humbler archetype. It was a winning formula. With Napoleonic authority in Italy now in question, the ranks of the *Carbonari* were burgeoning. Estimates of their numbers in Italy at their peak range from 300,000 to 642,000, with half of them in the south. The Charcoal-Burners were destined to become the most feared secret society of the nineteenth century.

The *Carbonari* were probably a monster of the Napoleonic state's own making. The key man here was Pierre-Joseph Briot, a Freemason and Napoleonic administrator who was put in charge of two Neapolitan provinces that would later turn into hotbeds of *Carbonari* activity. Briot hailed from the forested slopes and plateaux of the Jura mountains in eastern France. The Jura was home to a rudimentary Freemasonry of woodsmen known as the *Charbonniers* – the Charcoal-Burners – who were almost certainly the template for the Italian Charcoal-Burners. Members of both brotherhoods addressed one another as 'Bon Cousin', or 'Good Cousin'. The symbolic furnishings of their meetings were drawn from the day-to-day life of woodsmen. The presiding Good Cousin at a meeting had before him a cross, a bundle of sticks (a metaphor for strength through unity) and a stove (which stood for the light and heat of the creed). For the Italian Charcoal-Burners, as for the original *Charbonniers* of the Jura mountains, turning logs into charcoal was a metaphor of how men could be purified by a deep, transformative fire. Pierre-Joseph Briot was a *Charbonnier*, and the likelihood has to be that he imported the *Charbonnier* idea to take advantage of political divisions within Freemasonry and create a radical secret society in Italy.

In doing so, Briot almost certainly had the approval of his superior, Antonio Maghella, who had run Murat's police and spy network until March 1812. Caroline Bonaparte, Murat's wife and the Emperor's sister, was among those who believed that Maghella was the man behind the creation of the *Carbonari*. Born near Genoa, but now a citizen of the French empire, he was a dapper, balding man whom contemporaries and historians alike have described as 'shadowy'. He was a Freemason who had faithfully served the French in his home city, but many suspected that, like Pierre-Joseph Briot, he retained democratic, republican sympathics. For Maghella and Briot, the *Carbonari* were intended as a political instrument against conservatives in the Kingdom of Naples and within Murat's administration, and

Pierre-Joseph Briot (1771–1827) and Antonio Maghella (1766–1850),
the Freemasons who were probably responsible for establishing
the Charcoal-Burners in the Kingdom of Naples.

a sword to offer to Murat himself in order to tempt him towards
more radical, pro-Italian policies. As a bonus, the Charcoal-
Burners were a useful way to monitor potential subversives by
keeping them in one place and placing spies in their midst. As
would soon become evident, Maghella and Briot had begun a
dangerous game in which the Napoleonic authorities were by
no means guaranteed winners. In an increasingly volatile geopolitical situation after Napoleon's disastrous Russia campaign,
the new secret society, indeed the whole Masonic environment,
was at constant risk of slipping out of control. Particularly in
the provinces, where the growing authority of Naples was
resented, the *Carbonari* were becoming a rallying point for
opponents of all kinds.

Rise of the Charcoal-Burners

On 4 February 1813, King Joachim, his face blasted to bronze by the glare of the Russian snows, made a solemn return to Naples. Even he could not keep up the pretence that this was a triumph to match his first entry five years earlier. As he processed through the streets, everyone noticed the tears trickling either side of his long nose.

Tension in the Kingdom was acute. The economy was tanking. The tax burden imposed on the country to fund the war was far past tolerable levels. Conscription was meeting resistance. Bandits were on the rampage in the provinces.

In early March, the military commander in Cosenza, down among the mountains of Calabria at the 'toe' of the Italian 'boot', raised the alarm that secret Charcoal-Burner meetings were 'cultivating democratic principles'. The commander added that, with the city's garrison committed elsewhere, he could not answer for any trouble that might ensue.

Initially, it seems, Murat contemplated simply killing the leadership of the sect. Yet wiser heads in his government saw that it would be foolish to give it publicity by taking overt or brutal action. While many Charcoal-Burners were recruited from among Freemasons, many also came from the lower ranks of the army and the less educated classes. Perhaps, therefore, the Freemasons could be used quietly to bring the Good Cousins back under control. In April, across the provinces of southern Italy, officials called in the known *Carbonari* leaders and tactfully asked them to disband. Freemasonry was already there for them, it was explained, and it was nurtured and protected by the state, so what need was there for another secret society?

The Charcoal-Burners made a show of being convinced; some even handed over signed declarations that they had closed themselves down. But before the government could relax, reports of continuing *Carbonari* activity reached its ears. In places such as Cosenza, the Good Cousins merely changed the venue for their meetings. Thus, even a delicately handled attempt to ban the sect had only succeeded in making it more secretive, and more resolute in its opposition to the government.

In the heat of August 1813, Joachim Murat again journeyed to join his brother-in-law's forces in Germany, as a new European alliance was assembled to defeat Napoleon once and for all. The King had hardly left Italy before a Charcoal-Burner rebellion broke out in Cosenza. The instigator, and leader of the sect across the whole region, was a bullish, blond property-owner known locally as 'White Head'. His followers attacked the houses of the rich, tried to steal government cash stocks and exchanged gunfire with troops. The Cosenza *Carbonari* revolt was chaotic, but profoundly worrying. The area was a known trouble spot. But White Head had previously been a supporter of the French government, and had joined its recent crackdown on bandits. Evidently the regime's own supporters were now turning against it.

The political context also exacerbated the situation. The previous year, under pressure from the British, the Bourbons granted a Constitution to Sicily. Constitutional government of some form was exactly what many on the French-controlled mainland were hoping for. The Bourbons now looked like a progressive alternative to the Napoleonic monarchy that had deposed them back in 1806. British agents in southern Italy were whispering this message in Masonic Lodges and Charcoal-Burner *Vendite*; British gold probably helped fund the uprising. White Head proclaimed that the prospect of a constitutional version of Bourbon monarchy appealed to the *Carbonari*.

There could no longer be any doubt about the Good Cousins' revolutionary intentions. In the words of one government circular, 'these clandestine unions use brotherly love to provoke popular convulsions'. Yet the hard-pressed government did not have the men it needed to carry off a thorough clampdown. With the Cosenza revolt still underway, senior ministers evolved a new divide-and-rule strategy: the ringleaders of any rebellion would be treated severely; meanwhile, the ranks of ordinary Charcoal-Burners would be warned, investigated and subdued to official Freemasonry.

Shortly afterwards, White Head was betrayed by one of his followers, summarily tried, and beheaded in the central piazza the very same evening. The execution was lit by torches so that the people of Cosenza could draw a lurid lesson about the risks that conspirators ran. The general in charge of repressing the revolt announced that anyone from a 'secret union' who tried to meet without express government approval would be arrested.

The new policy left even the officially approved Freemasons in a tricky position. Were they part of the government's answer to the problem of the Charcoal-Burners? Or were they a 'secret union' to be warned and watched? Days after White Head's execution, the leaders of the Grand Orient in Naples were summoned to police headquarters and given a talking to.

Before the ambiguities of this new policy had time to play out, just over two weeks after White Head's execution, events on the battlefields of northern Europe again brought tumultuous change in southern Italy. After a gigantic four-day slogging match near Leipzig in October 1813, Napoleon's forces were pushed into retreat. In the wake of the battle, the Napoleonic Empire in Germany and the Low Countries began to collapse, and the allies ranged against him advanced to take the war onto French soil.

Murat, whose habitual, reckless cavalry charges at Leipzig had proven futile, slunk back into Naples; this time, he did not even gesture at public ceremony. From now, egged on by his radical ministers, he made ever more unlikely attempts to save his throne by embracing the cause of Italian independence. There was obviously a great deal of cynicism in this move, but that did not stop it resonating in a peninsula utterly weary after nearly twenty years of invasion, war and blockade. He also hinted that he might grant a Constitution. Murat was now the potential king of an independent, united Italy: it looked like the Charcoal-Burners might finally have the Murat they wanted. Accordingly, he turned to Antonio Maghella, the creator of the Charcoal-Burners, and tasked him with building support for his bid to become King of Italy.

In January 1814, Murat made an alliance with Austria, and sent a force northward to join the war – *against France* this time. The resourceful Maghella went on ahead to try to set up Charcoal-Burner units as a fifth column to aid the Neapolitan army's advance through Rome. In Milan, the capital of Napoleonic power in northern Italy, local Charcoal-Burners and Masons were mobilising to support Murat's drive for Italian unification.

Maghella's operation was a partial success at best, and Murat's plans to extend his realm northwards were checked. In any case, he inspired little trust among many Freemasons and Charcoal-Burners. A few weeks after the fighting began, the opposition to Murat within Neapolitan Freemasonry came out into the open. A new Scottish Rite Lodge was established by one Orazio De Attellis, who was just the kind of Italian who had previously been loyal to French government in the peninsula: he had fought in many a campaign in the Napoleonic armies. Yet De Attellis had now become disaffected with Murat's rule. The authorities responded by dissolving his Lodge and sending him into internal exile in the far south.

In April 1814, after months of desperate fighting in France, Napoleon Bonaparte attempted to commit suicide, and when the attempt failed, he abdicated. Soon afterwards he began his demeaning exile as 'Emperor and Sovereign' of the impoverished little Italian island of Elba. French forces in northern Italy conceded to the Austrians and Neapolitans.

Murat had helped defeat his own brother-in-law, and hoped for a share of the spoils. But the Charcoal-Burners in the provinces of southern Italy gave him no respite. There was serious trouble in the Abruzzi, at the northern frontier of the Kingdom of Naples. There, on the night of 26–7 March 1814, the Charcoal-Burners raised their rebellious flag: a tricolour of horizontal black, red and sky-blue bands. The unrest quickly spread through most of the province, and the local institutions of the Napoleonic state melted away.

Murat's hard-pressed government had little alternative but to come down hard this time. The Charcoal-Burners were banned: and the law now treated them like bandits or deserters who could be shot on sight. In preparation, a letter was sent to Masonic Lodges demanding that they break all ties with the rebels.

Halfway through April 1814, three thousand troops and five hundred cavalry filed two abreast through the narrow streets of Città Sant'Angelo, the main centre of the Charcoal-Burner revolt in the Abruzzi; they set up two cannons in the main square. The troops had been sent on a punitive mission by Murat. However, after this intimidating entrance, there was little left for them to do. The Charcoal-Burner revolt had gone underground at the news that the army was coming, having already been undermined by a nervously noncommittal response among the common people. The Italian general commanding the expedition intimated to the local dignitaries who came to meet him that he would have joined the uprising if it had been better supported. He knew very well that there were plenty of Charcoal-Burners in the ranks of the army, and he could sense the discontent in the country. For that reason, he did not subject the area to the kind of fire-and-sword retribution that Murat expected.

Murat's reaction was to replace this Italian general with a French commander who had orders to make an example of the chief Charcoal-Burners. There followed a ruthless manhunt. Female relatives were thrown into the most fetid jails in the hope of extracting information from them. In Basciano, one young woman, the sister of a Charcoal-Burner, had her brains blown out when troops raided her house. When all this effort yielded only two suspects, the authorities embarked on mass arrests aimed not just at the Charcoal-Burners, but at the government servants who had chosen not to stand up against them: men, women and children were led away to the dungeons in

Chieti. Even more Good Cousins went into hiding to avoid the dragnet. Some villages were all but emptied. In the summer, three men condemned to death for their part in the uprising were taken back to their home town to be executed in the piazza; one of them, a priest, had to be publicly defrocked before he faced the firing squad. All three then had their heads cut off and put on display, whereupon their families were forced to look on and applaud.

News of these and other Charcoal-Burner martyrs spread far and wide. What support there had been for Murat's monarchy in the Abruzzi dwindled to almost nothing. All in all, the revolt, and the stupid brutality that followed it, proclaimed the weakness of Murat's reign. By the time that the last of the Abruzzi rebels was publicly decapitated in December 1814, that weakness had entered its terminal phase. In Vienna, the great powers meeting to draw up the political map of a post-Napoleonic Europe had made it abundantly clear that there was no place for Joachim Murat in their plans.

In February 1815, when Napoleon Bonaparte escaped from Elba, Murat swapped sides for the last time. Again, he marched northwards – this time to fight the Austrians on behalf of his brother-in-law in the hope that Napoleon would finally award Italy its independence. Part of this strategy was to create a breakaway branch of the Charcoal-Burners that would support Murat unambiguously. The new sect was to be called 'The Agriculture', its Lodges termed 'Haystacks', and the members known as 'Farmers'. In a last gamble, Murat was planning to start the Charcoal-Burner project all over again.

It was hopeless: undersupplied and insubordinate, Murat's army was already crumbling when it was routed at the Battle of Tolentino in May. Murat fled to Corsica.

However, the decade-long Napoleonic era of southern Italian history was not over. Not quite, at least. On Sunday 8 October 1815, hundreds of kilometres to the south of Naples, the inhabitants of the tiny seaside town of Pizzo in Calabria saw what they first thought was a hallucination. A small group of French soldiers marched into the square and began shouting, 'Long live King Joachim'. Murat himself appeared among them, flawlessly tonsured, and sporting his tight nankeen trousers, a blue jacket with golden epaulettes and a tricorn hat decorated with silk trimmings and a huge, jewel-encrusted cockade. He had set sail from Corsica twelve days earlier with the aim of triggering a rebellion in a Charcoal-Burner stronghold that would return him to his throne.

The result was a disaster. Murat was quickly caught and roughed up by a band of peasants; the golden epaulettes were torn from his shoulders, the cockade stolen. In captivity in the local fortress, he raved to his men that the Charcoal-Burners would rise up and liberate them. After a hastily convened military tribunal, he was taken out onto the fortress's narrow esplanade. It is said that, after refusing a blindfold, he issued a last order to the firing squad: 'Aim at the heart. Spare my face.'

The Charcoal-Burners under Murat became many things to many people. They began as a republican society close to a group at the heart of the Napoleonic state. But as time went by and the political situation fluctuated, the sect became more and more impure, as recruits joined of many different shades of opinion: they ranged from Italian patriots, some of whom chose to bet on Murat's potential as a national leader, to radicals, to constitutional monarchists (whether of a Murattian or a Bourbon variety); there were also Catholics offended by Murat's anti-ecclesiastical policies, and even reactionary Bourbon royalists who just wanted to turn the clock back to a time before anyone had even heard of the French Revolution. Under the authoritarian Napoleonic system, the Charcoal-Burner brotherhood became just about the only place, outside the court, where political activity could happen at all. The

Charcoal-Burners were now deeply embedded in southern Italian society, and the intrigues surrounding them were set to become even more tangled.

A secret meeting of the Charcoal-Burners in southern Italy, in an image from 1821.

Cauldron-Makers

On 17 June 1815, the day before Napoleon suffered his final defeat at the Battle of Waterloo, the stooping figure of King Ferdinand rode back into Naples at the head of his army. Along the route, lined with Austrian and British troops dressed in white and red tunics respectively, the man the people called 'King Big Nose' was greeted with frenzied rejoicing. The sense of relief in the city was palpable. Despite the support that Murat's regime had enjoyed in some circles, the return of the Bourbon dynasty was an entirely bloodless affair – thanks in good measure to the Charcoal-Burners. They had been reassured, by British spies among others, that Ferdinand would grant a Constitution in return for their loyalty.

Now that Ferdinand had been restored to the throne, the offer of a Constitution was a compromise policy on which most of the varied factions among the *Carbonari* could agree. But not for long.

The Bonapartist state machinery Ferdinand inherited provided him with vastly more effective levers of central power: nobody could now conceive of governing without them. But French administration had also sown political discord, and that discord was set to get worse. For example, in Naples, how were King Ferdinand's ministers to reconcile the noblemen who had remained loyal to the Bourbon dynasty during the French decade, and who had often lost their land as a consequence of their loyalty, with the soldiers, bureaucrats and new landowners who had done so well out of the Napoleonic regime? Other problems were legion. A bad harvest in 1816 pushed the mass of the population to the edge of famine. Moreover, because Ferdinand's reign was protected by a large contingent of Austrian troops, it seemed to many former opponents of Murat that Naples had just swapped one foreign overlord for another. The Kingdom of the Two Sicilies, as the Kingdom of Naples was now rebranded, had no money to spend on solutions to these problems, since it was straining under the burden of enormous debts.

Ferdinand quickly made matters much worse. Not only did he fail to bring in a Constitution in the southern Italian mainland; he also abolished the one that the British had pressed on him in Sicily.

The government also moved to exclude Masons and Charcoal-Burners from government jobs. No force was used against them, and members faced no sanctions if they demonstrated their loyalty. The aim – very similar to the tactics of Joachim Murat's government – was to divide the Good Cousins, and isolate trouble-makers.

It did not work. Or, at least, did not work nearly well enough to counteract the furious sense of betrayal that King Ferdinand's failure to grant a Constitution had embedded in the Charcoal-

Burner mind-set. Lawlessness spread across the country, and it was made all the more disturbing because many branches of the state, including the army, were infiltrated by the secret society. In the capital, the police seemed unwilling to do anything about the inflammatory political posters that appeared on the walls every day. By January 1816, one general reported from Calabria that the judiciary was utterly unable to administer justice: 'If the accused are Charcoal-Burners, there is no threat or punishment formidable enough to make any witnesses come forward. And if they aren't, then a thousand Charcoal-Burners will stand ready to give evidence against an innocent man.' The Good Cousins were setting themselves above the law.

Ferdinand's response to the crisis was to put the police in the hands of a fanatical conspiracy theorist: Antonio Capece Minutolo, Prince of Canosa. Influenced by the Abbé Barruel's paranoid epic, *Memoirs Illustrating the History of Jacobinism*, Canosa thought that the French Revolution was a thorough catastrophe brought about 'by the different sects and by perverse philosophy'.

Once placed in charge of Ferdinand's police network in January 1816, Canosa ordered selective arrests of both Masons and Charcoal-Burners. Yet he knew he could not defeat the sects this way. So he came up with the rashest possible scheme: against the menace of the Charcoal-Burners and Freemasons, he would deploy another, reactionary secret society called the *Calderari* – the 'Cauldron-Beaters'.

The Cauldron-Beaters probably grew out of a secret society called the *Trinitari* ('Trinitarians' – because they were devoted to the Father, Son and Holy Ghost). The Trinitarians were themselves the result of a political schism within the Charcoal-Burners in the last stages of Joachim Murat's reign. Hence the rituals and structure of this new brotherhood were a mirror-image of the Charcoal-Burners' rituals and structure. One estimate at the time was that, by the time Murat fell, 23,000 men had taken the

Trinitarians' oath of loyalty to the Church and the Bourbon dynasty. An article of faith for the Trinitarians was a loathing for Freemasons and Charcoal-Burners. Indeed, it was the Trinitarians' enemies among the Masons and *Carbonari* who dubbed them 'Cauldron-Beaters' as a put-down – probably because one of the Trinitarians' early centres of activity, the town of Rivello, had a lot of artisans who made pots and pans. The nickname stuck.

Canosa had big plans for the Cauldron-Beaters. He had studied the history of Freemasonry – after a fashion. He believed that, some five thousand years ago, it was founded to encourage men along the true path of Christianity. With the Cauldron-Beaters, Canosa thought he would return the Craft to the 'divine principles' that had first inspired it all those millennia ago. If the Pope became its leader, and Rome its capital, this new 'Catholic Masonry' had the potential to reach around the world. In southern Italy, Canosa thought, the Cauldron-Beaters could also constitute a kind of political party that would slowly outdo the Masons and Charcoal-Burners in their ability to corner the market in public sector jobs. Accordingly, he sent agents out into the provinces to stiffen the resolve of the Cauldron-Beaters and assure them of the government's support.

The fires of factional conflict were already burning intensely in many localities across southern Italy. More than thirty years of political turmoil, of oscillation between reform and reaction, of successive invasions and restorations, had created a lethal instability that could only be made worse by giving the Cauldron-Beaters government backing.

When Canosa informed the cabinet about his strategy, there was a furious row, and his political enemies took the initiative. The King reluctantly relieved him of his duties at the end of May 1816. The question was whether it was too late.

According to documents uncovered by his successor, Canosa was using the Cauldron-Beaters as a private army: it looked for all the world as if he had been planning to instigate a secret-society civil war. In a few weeks between April and May 1816, he had handed out no fewer than 16,000 firearms licences. In one province, the Cauldron-Beaters were drawing up a list of Masons and Charcoal-Burners to be eliminated, and one report concluded that the reactionary secret society was 'ready to plunge itself into anarchic horrors'. The Cauldron-Beaters had the potential to become even more disruptive than the Charcoal-Burners they were supposed to counteract.

Ministers revoked the firearms licences that Canosa had issued, and had many Cauldron-Beaters arrested. The Prince himself was dispatched into exile in Tuscany. Such a headlong fall from office was a humiliation for the Bourbon loyalists who, like Canosa, had only recently returned from their Sicilian exile. In private, they spat bile about how the Freemasons controlled the government from behind the scenes.

And in one literal sense the Bourbon loyalists were right. A gloomy alley near the Royal Palace, strada Solitaria, was the home of both the Justice Ministry and the Interior Ministry – the nerve centre of a nervous kingdom. Its occupant, Donato Tommasi, was the man tasked with sorting out the Prince of Canosa's mess. He had all the experience necessary to confront the Kingdom's unprecedented secret-society problem. In his youth, before the French Revolution, he had been an Enlightenment thinker and avid Freemason; in 1786, he even became one of the founders of a Neapolitan branch of the Illuminati – two years after the organisation collapsed in its native Bavaria. Yet for Tommasi, as for many Masons, there were things in life more important than the Craft: like his career and loyalty to his King.

In August 1816, Tommasi issued an edict banning all secret societies – Masons, Charcoal-Burners and Cauldron-Beaters alike. But the copious documentation that arrived on his desk from the provinces told him that a mere ban could do little to cool southern Italy's obsession with secret societies. The case of don Ciro Annicchiarico – priest, teacher of Gregorian chant, armed robber, multiple murderer, revolutionary and Charcoal-Burner guru – provides a clamorous example.

Don Ciro Annicchiarico was born in 1775 or 1776 into a poor background in Grottaglie, a town in Puglia, the province that forms the heel of the Italian boot. Although all agreed that he had an admirable physique and a long face, quite what he looked like depends on whether you read accounts by his friends or enemies. For the former, he had 'a physiognomy that was far from unpleasant, and he was a fine talker'; for the latter, 'he had a brooding, reflective disposition, and ferocity emanated from his face'. By 1803, don Ciro had taken holy orders, and also become a Freemason and a political radical. In that year, following a violent romantic dispute, he was tried and convicted for murder. The Napoleonic invasion of the Kingdom of Naples in 1806 came just in time to secure his freedom: he escaped from prison, gathered a band of toughs around him and joined the local police militia. In 1808, following a complaint by the father of the man don Ciro murdered, an arrest order was issued. But by this time don Ciro's reputation was so fearsome that no one dared carry it out. Only in 1813 was an attempt made to ambush him at a dinner party. When the fruit was served (the signal for the shooting to start), don Ciro's brother was killed, but the main target escaped. He took to the countryside and built a crew of draft-dodgers and deserters, all vowing to avenge the wrongs done to their leader. A bloody series of attacks followed. Don Ciro was declared an outlaw, a *bandito*, which meant that anyone could win a reward for killing him.

After Murat's fall in 1815, don Ciro sought to take advantage of the pardon that King Ferdinand offered to anyone who had fought the Napoleonic regime, even if they had committed crimes in the process. But the commission that judged his case decided that he did not qualify. He escaped justice once again, and then offered his services to the Charcoal-Burners.

Under Murat, the Charcoal-Burners had ended up being treated like bandits. Under the restored Bourbon monarchy, they were now enlisting bandits to their ranks. The aim was to use thugs like don Ciro to provide protection from the menace of the reactionary Cauldron-Beaters.

On don Ciro's home turf in Puglia, local factions had quickly assumed the guise of secret brotherhoods: there were thought to have been around six thousand Cauldron-Beaters in 1815. The number of brotherhoods began to multiply: in addition to the *Calderari* and *Carbonari*, there were groups like the Philadelphians, the European Patriots, the Reformed European Patriots and the Solitary Greeks. They called themselves 'Philanthropic Societies', but they were in reality politico-criminal gangs comprising a startlingly diverse range of people: rough-handed artisans combined with dukes and barons; murderers and robbers with soldiers and policemen; starving peasants with canny lawyers. Don Ciro was far from being the only priest drawn in. Such was the tension in some communities that there was no neutral ground: in search of protection, everyone gravitated towards a sect.

Don Ciro joined the most radical of the anti-government secret societies, the Resolute. He soon rose to a leadership position, bringing together an alliance of all the brotherhoods ranged against the Prince of Canosa's Cauldron-Beaters. He set out a personal utopian doctrine for his followers: there would be a Great European Republic in which, thanks to the support of the 'Great Architect of the Universe', Christianity would be restored to its primitive purity. The band wrote out their oaths in blood, decorated them with skulls, crossbones and Masonic symbols, and undertook military training by night. Lethal justice was handed down to affiliates who broke the rules. Don Ciro declared 1817 to be Year One of a new age.

Thanks in good measure to don Ciro, savage acts of violence were committed by all sides in this Puglian civil war. One sect member who contravened the regulations was cut up, and the pieces of his body were fed to dogs. An enemy was butchered, and his body suspended above the front door of his father's house. There were public throat-cuttings and shootings, some of them entirely motiveless. Dozens of women were tied naked to trees and/or raped before the eyes of their menfolk. None of those responsible for the violence faced any consequences, as all the personnel in the police and justice system had joined the secret societies.

The sexual violence perpetrated by the secret societies at this time offers a grim commentary on the fact that, in areas including southern Puglia, there were women among the Charcoal-Burners. The female Lodges attached to male *Vendite* were known as 'Gardens', and their members as 'Gardeners'. But there seems to have been no opportunity for women to assert their independence in the Gardens in the way that French women had sometimes done in the Adoption Lodges. As well as devotion to Freedom and Fatherland, the dutiful Gardener was supposed to resign herself to the role appropriate to her female nature and be faithful to her husband. The Good Cousins, for their part, swore to respect the honour of their 'Sisters'. But if the rapes and assaults of 1817 are anything to go by, some Good Cousins clearly regarded *other* women's honour as fair game.

Meanwhile, the Charcoal-Burners across southern Italy had moved to a position of revolutionary opposition to the Bourbon monarchy. In May 1817, in the picturesque surroundings of the ruins of Pompeii, the brotherhood's leadership held a night-time planning meeting. Austrian troops were being withdrawn from the Kingdom: the time for an uprising was nigh. But lack of coordination meant that the uprising kept being postponed.

In Puglia, the government declared don Ciro an outlaw again. He responded by publishing a *Justification* of his actions, which claimed that he had been forced into a life of crime by unjust persecution, and that he was a kind of Robin Hood. Enough was enough: in November 1817, the Irish general Sir Richard Church was ordered into don Ciro's realm at the head of a small Neapolitan army.

While General Church was still on the march, the chiefs of all the secret societies in the region met in an isolated tower outside Galatina to resolve their differences and plan a response. They chose a number of leaders, mostly aristocrats, to form a Charcoal-Burner *High Vendita* – a steering committee for conspiratorial activity. Don Ciro was put in charge of the military response to the approaching army. With fifty of his men he rode far and wide announcing to the populace that the revolution was imminent.

Once General Church had garrisoned his troops in the city of Lecce, he called in the Charcoal-Burner hierarchy and explained that he would forgive their political misdemeanours and support them against the Cauldron-Beaters – *if* they helped him kill or capture don Ciro. The proposal was eagerly accepted: don Ciro's death certificate was as good as signed.

The bandit ranged frantically across the province, in a futile search for escape. When his gang members were caught, they faced instant justice – thus conveniently depriving them of the chance to give evidence in court of their links to the upper echelons of society. All but the most loyal of don Ciro's followers abandoned him in terror. Exhausted, hungry and ragged, he was eventually cornered in a farmhouse near Francavilla, where he surrendered after a vicious firefight. Local semaphore operators were so afraid of reprisals that they abandoned their posts rather than assume the responsibility of communicating the news that don Ciro had been captured. The following afternoon, after being subjected to a cursory trial, he was shot in the back as a mark of infamy. His head was cut off and displayed in an iron cage.

In Puglia as elsewhere, the threat of the reactionary Cauldron-Beaters receded during 1817, but the revolutionary Charcoal-Burners were now far too deeply rooted for the Minister Tommasi and the rest of the cabinet to do much more than gather intelligence and fret. The secret-society sickness reached everywhere, it seemed. In the summer of 1818, Tommasi was informed that, thanks to confiscated documents, a network of *Carbonari* had been discovered in two Naples prisons, with links much further afield. Many of the members were not political prisoners, but lifers and 'men hardened by the path of crime'. The author of the report proposed scattering the ringleaders among the various prison islands off the coast of Sicily and the mainland. He did not, it seems, consider that this would only spread the sect even further through the carceral system.

In the end, it once more took international developments to precipitate a crisis in Naples. In Spain in 1820, the King was forced to grant a Constitution following a rebellion. Here was a powerful example for the Good Cousins to follow – particularly because, like Ferdinand, the Spanish king was a Bourbon.

When it finally arrived, the long-awaited Charcoal-Burner revolution was a work of improvisation rather than centralised planning. On the night of 1–2 July 1820, some thirty *Carbonari* in Nola, a market town east of Naples, induced soldiers stationed locally to desert. Sporting cockades in the Charcoal-Burner colours of sky-blue, black and red, and shouting slogans like 'Long live liberty and the Constitution', the group then marched the twenty-five kilometres to Avellino, a centre of sect activity, gathering strength as they did so. From there, word of the uprising spread by messenger and mountaintop beacon. The army high command, knowing that their units were heavily infiltrated by Charcoal-Burners, could do little to change the course of events. One general, Guglielmo Pepe, went over to the rebels' side and assumed command of their forces. Within days, King Ferdinand was forced to issue an edict promising a Constitution; Tommasi and the other ministers resigned.

On Sunday 9 July the rebel soldiers entered Naples to be crowned with laurels; they were followed by musical bands and massed ranks of Charcoal-Burners. The sky-blue, black and red flag was hoisted over the city. Shouting 'Long live the Charcoal-Burners!', the procession assembled before the Royal Palace. Although the King pretended to be ill, the rest of the royal family appeared on the balcony. In an unconvincing attempt to stay in tune with the mood of the hour, they were wearing Charcoal-Burner rosettes.

Sects

After the strange twists and turns of the Charcoal-Burners' story, it will not come as a surprise that their revolution failed. They had fallen out with one another even before an Austrian army arrived, in March 1821, to restore King Ferdinand's authority yet again. Charcoal-Burner conspiracy in the rest of Italy – Piedmont, the Papal States – bore even less fruit. In Ravenna, in the Romagna region of the Papal States, the Good Cousins were notable only because Lord Byron joined them soon after the Neapolitan Revolution of July 1820. For all his revolutionary fervour, however, he was unimpressed, writing in January 1821 that, 'the C[*arbonari*] seem to have no plan – nothing fixed among themselves, how, when, or what to do'.

Many *Carbonari* fled abroad. One of them was the academic Gabriele Rossetti; his children, including the poet Christina Rossetti and her painter brother Dante Gabriel, would be born in London. Another Charcoal-Burner exile in England was Antonio Panizzi, a northerner. He would go on to be Britain's first Professor of Italian, with an institutional home at University College London, where I have the good fortune to hold a profes sorship. Lord Byron's Charcoal-Burner secretary, Antonio Lega Zambelli, also ended up in London, where he started up a pasta business.

The failure of the 1820 uprising was not the end of the story. The *Carbonari* had already been exported to France by then. Sicily, hitherto largely immune to the secret-society fever, caught it badly thereafter. In some provinces of the southern Italian mainland, the *Carbonari* remained operational for over a decade. There were occasional, localised revolts. In 1828, following a constitutional uprising, the mountain village of Bosco was razed to the ground by cannon-fire, and its inhabitants scattered. Charcoal-Burner activity continued in other Italian states too. They took an active role in many of the revolutions that flared up in 1830. But their influence faded rapidly thereafter. Their contradictory mixture of ritualised secrecy and openness to members with widely varying political philosophies had been shown to be a failure. Naples in 1820–1 proved to be the peak of their influence. Neither the *Carbonari* nor any of the other Italian secret societies that followed them would play much of a role in the events that led, forty years later, to the unification of Italy.

Yet the pages of history that the Good Cousins had scrawled in charcoal would not be entirely erased by subsequent events. The *Carbonari* were the first secret brotherhood to lead a major European revolution, thus setting a powerful precedent. In several notable ways, the vast and peculiar conspiracies of the Napoleonic and Restoration years left a profound impression.

The first was to influence a coming global age of revolutionary movements in Europe and beyond. Indeed, the typically modern role of the revolutionary, conspiring in secret to forge a better world by violence, was first created as a by-product of Freemasonry in the age of Romanticism. As one historian has argued: 'The modern revolutionary tradition as it came to be internationalized under Napoleon and the Restoration grew out of occult Freemasonry.'

The second legacy, now that *real* conspirators had come to people the reactionary dreams of the Abbé Augustin de Barruel, was to fuel a holy terror of secret societies. One thing that the Charcoal-Burners definitely were *not* was a disciplined subversive conspiracy, although that would be how they would often be recalled.

A third influence was local to Italy: despite the Masonic laws against meddling in *Politicks* set out in the Craft's *Constitutions*, thanks to Napoleon and the *Carbonari* Italy developed the most politicised Masonic tradition on the continent.

The fourth, still more local, was to turn secret-society fever into an endemic disease in the Kingdom of Naples. To understand this peculiar legacy of the different secret societies of the Charcoal-Burner period, it is helpful to review the sheer range of their activities. They colonised local politics, helping to reduce it to a grasping and sometimes violent factional competition. They lifted themselves above the law, to the point that in places they formed a state within a state. They were mixed up in insurrectionary conspiracy and violence, yet were also used by the state to fight political opposition. Their networks controlled state jobs and resources. Within their ranks, extortionists and murderers rubbed shoulders with the élite. They controlled the prison system from within.

In the years after the south became part of a unified Italy in 1860, in Naples and especially in the Sicilian capital Palermo, the police came across secret societies of criminals who specialised in extortion. Most of their members had been involved in the political violence that culminated in the foundation of the united Italian state. Many had been spies for the Bourbon police, and had made ties to elements within the Italian police. They used their networks to muscle in on the economy and local government. They had powerful friends among the élite, who sheltered them from prosecution. They were deeply rooted in prisons. When evidence about just such a secret society in western Sicily was included in a government report in the 1870s, the London *Times* correspondent described it as 'an intangible sect whose organization is as perfect as that of the Jesuits or Freemasons, and whose secrets are more impenetrable'. 'Sect', following a well-established practice, was indeed the term the first Italian investigators often used to describe this sinister phenomenon. They also used another word, and still do to this day: mafia.

The most representative men of eighteenth-century Freemasonry had been internationally minded intellectuals. During the Napoleonic Empire and the Restoration, Masonry's ideological centre of gravity shifted. Whether they were Bonaparte's bureaucrats and officers, or the conspirators that the French Empire spawned, the most representative Brothers were now patriots and nation-builders. This would be the pattern for the rest of the nineteenth century — and nowhere more so than in the United States of America, where the Craft became something akin to a religion of state.

Washington: **A Lodge for the Virtues**

During the American War of Independence, George Washington gathered the shoeless forces of thirteen disparate and mutually suspicious colonies and, after nearly eight years of fighting, led them to victory over the world's most formidable military machine. In December 1783, shunning the temptation to seize power in the new Republic, he resigned his commission, retired from public life and went back to his Virginia plantation. Three years later, with apparent reluctance, he was drawn into politics when he was asked to chair the Convention that would draw up the Constitution of the United States. In 1789, he was the unanimous choice to be the first President – an office whose powers and responsibilities he was allowed to shape around his person. But rather than accumulating power, he recruited talented ministers, delegated, and bore the burdens of office with self-sacrificing dignity. In 1792, against his fondest wishes, he was elected to a second term unanimously once more.

Triumph in war made George Washington an untouchable hero. Humility in its aftermath gave him the luminosity of a lay saint. His political career, rather than diminishing his stature, only seemed to enhance his reputation for integrity, sagacity and dutiful strength. Throughout his career, shrewd image-management and an understated *élan* prevented his commanding reputation from tipping over into perceived arrogance or entitlement. Washington was transformed into the great American patriarch, the embodiment of republican virtue. Without ever seeming ambitious, he became the most famous man in the world. Early in his first term, his birthday became a national holiday across the country. His legend, celebrated in paint, marble and print, helped make a nation.

Such was the reverential trust that Washington inspired that, in 1790, he was given all but unchecked authority to design and build what was initially referred to as the 'Federal City' – a seat of government for the new nation that would rise by the Potomac River, just a few miles from his Mount Vernon estate. In 1791, the commissioners supervising the project decided that the American capital would be called Washington. It could hardly be called anything else. Plans included a prominent equestrian statue of the great man, and a monumental tomb before which an awestruck posterity would contemplate his memory.

Washington DC's outlines were only just emerging from the Potomac's muddy banks when, on the late morning of 18 September 1793, the city witnessed what the press called 'one of the grandest MASONIC processions, which was perhaps ever exhibited on the like important occasion'.

The civic authorities led the way, in the form of the Surveying Department and the City Commissioners, all marching two abreast. In line behind them came a company of artillerymen, colours flying. Next, a band played music of 'the greatest solemn dignity'. The band was followed by a squadron of stonecutters and engineers; these were the men responsible for the scaffolding and earthworks that the procession was heading towards. Then came the Masons from the Lodges of Virginia and Maryland, in spotless gloves and aprons. They were preceded by their sword-bearers, and divided neatly into orders: Brethren of the First, Second and Third Degrees were accompanied by their officers in full regalia, from the Wardens with their truncheons to the Treasurers with their Jewels. Just behind them came the Masons chosen for the special honour of carrying the array of ceremonial kit that would be required: a Masonic Bible on a velvet cushion; an engraved silver plate; a silver trowel with an ivory handle; a walnut set square and level; a marble gavel; and finally golden cups containing the sacred wine, oil and grain.

The event had been well advertised – not least because it was supposed to revive flagging interest in buying plots of land in the area marked out for construction. The large crowd, indifferent to the boosterist ulterior motive for the show, waved flags and cheered enthusiastically.

The procession reached its destination on Jenkins Heights (or Capitol Hill, as it would become known) and parted into two lines, each snaking around the outside of a shallow pit. At the pit's centre, hanging in mid-air beneath a tripod of tree trunks, gleamed a flawless stone cube.

A thunderous artillery salute startled the air clear of birdsong and the spectators' chatter. In the respectful silence, the tall man in Masonic regalia who had been at the very back of the procession stepped down into the pit: Worshipful Master George Washington, then six months into his second term as President of the United States.

Washington nodded gravely and three workmen lowered the stone into position. As the accoutrements were handed to him, one by one, he applied them to the stone. The square, symbolising virtue, to make certain each angle was perfectly cut. The level, a symbol of equality, to check that its placement was true. He then sprinkled the wheat, wine and oil to augur plenty, friendship and peace. The silver plate came next: its inscription proclaimed that the cornerstone of the Capitol had been laid in the thirteenth year of American Independence, and the year of Masonry 5793. Washington set it on the stone, before using the silver trowel to administer a few slops of cement, and then the marble gavel to give a short succession of taps.

As he looked up and smiled, cheering and applause broke out. The Capitol, which Thomas Jefferson called 'the first temple dedicated to the sovereignty of the people', had its unshakeable foundation in Masonic ritual.

It is easy to see why Washington made such a good symbol of

what the new nation wanted itself to be: to his contemporaries, even his statuesque physique seemed to mark him out for exalted status. What is less obvious is why Freemasonry, on highly charged occasions such as the cornerstone ceremony at the Capitol, should have been picked to provide the Republic's ceremonial language. An international secret society that had never been too far from suspicion and controversy during its short history now had a public role in bringing credibility to the institutions of the United States.

Freemasonry accompanied George Washington throughout his adult life. He was initiated when he was not yet twenty-one, at Fredericksburg Lodge, Virginia, on 4 November 1752. The young Washington was ambitious to assert himself among the planter élite. In Virginia, as in the other American colonies, joining the Royal Art was a way of acquiring and advertising gentry status. But changes were already afoot in Freemasonry that would reshape it in ways attuned to Washington's destiny, and America's, making it both more democratic and more martial.

It is no coincidence that the same century that saw the astonishingly rapid international dissemination of Masonry also saw war become a global affair. Freemasonry attracted many recruits in the army, and was particularly successful in setting up military Lodges, whose members were authorised to carry on Masonic workings wherever they happened to be posted. A long and profound bond between Freemasonry and military life was thereby cemented. Ever since then, soldiers and veterans of all nations have found in the Craft a stylised camaraderie able to soothe the dislocation and trauma of war. After 1753, for example, the French and Indian War drew large numbers of British troops to the American colonies, where the regimental Lodges spread Masonic practice to local militiamen.

Twenty years later, the War of Independence brought the upheaval of divided loyalties to Freemasonry in America. Many

Lodges simply ceased to meet. The contending armies became the focus of Masonic culture for the duration of the conflict: there were regimental Lodges on both sides. But in Washington's Continental Army, Freemasonry proved particularly important to morale. Masters spoke with a sureness that army chaplains, inhibited as they were by America's diverse religious denominations, could not match. Patriot officers were initiated in large numbers: there were ten military Lodges, the largest of them with several hundred members, and 42 per cent of the generals Washington led were Masons. Military Lodges toasted both fallen Brethren and their Commander-in-Chief, Brother George Washington.

For his part Washington, who had gained his first military experience in brutal frontier conflict during the French and Indian War, encouraged Masonry among his troops. The military Lodge environment allowed him to fraternise with his officers without undermining his authority. He was given to attending meetings as if he were just another Brother, 'on the Level' with his comrades in arms.

American Freemasonry caught the reflected light of Washington's glory during the War of Independence. In December 1778, the General visited Philadelphia, where the Continental Congress was in session. The Grand Lodge of Pennsylvania awarded him the place of honour beside the Grand Master in its procession to celebrate the feast of St John the Evangelist. A Masonic poem was published to mark the occasion:

> See WASHINGTON, he leads the train,
> 'Tis he commands the grateful strain;
> See, every crafted son obeys
> And to the godlike brother homage pays.

By the time the British surrendered at Yorktown in 1781, Freemasonry's association with the Continental Army had given it lustrous patriotic credentials. Washington was happy to link his presidency to the Craft: in April 1789, he swore his oath of office on a Bible borrowed for the occasion from St John's Lodge, the oldest in New York. Thereafter, he led a campaign to deck American public life in Masonic trappings.

The America that emerged victorious from the Revolutionary War was a laboratory of political communication. By shaking off monarchical rule, the Republic had also forsaken all the rituals and emblems that created the aura surrounding the European thrones. No more sceptres and crowns; no more cathedral coronations and *Te deums*. To fill that vacuum, the United States created the cult of George Washington; and George Washington, in his turn, made Freemasonry into a patriotic liturgy.

The War of Independence had unleashed turmoil: civil conflict raged; working men in the north embraced their own radical versions of Liberty and Equality; slaves in the south threw down their tools and fled; women took to the streets; crowds moved as one to tear down symbols of royal authority. Irreversibly, politics had become a mass participation sport. The explosion of newspapers in the 1780s and 1790s only spread the enthusiasm for politics deeper and wider, and gave every local parade or demonstration a national audience. Rapid economic growth followed the war too, and unmanaged westward expansion: America was quickly becoming a more go-getting, rumbustious society than the Founders had imagined only a few short years previously.

Freemasonry provided a composed response to such disorder. Nobody did processions like the Masons: ranks of Brothers, organised according to their status and flanked by their Lodge officers, projected a serenely hierarchical image that suited the political instincts of men like Washington who regarded themselves as society's natural leaders.

Part of the reason why the Craft performed its new role so well is that America was a religious mosaic. Puritans escaping discrimination had established the New England colonies in the 1630s. Successive immigrants all brought their own beliefs to the

New World: not just Anglicans, Catholics and Jews, but a panoply of Protestant sects like the Quakers, Baptists and Presbyterians, or the different German denominations, such as the Moravians, Mennonites, Dunkers and Schwenkfelders. Colonial society bred its own forms of piety, particularly the evangelical creeds that took hold during the so-called First Great Awakening of the 1730s and 1740s. With the Revolution, even those states where the Church of England had been the established colonial religion cut the ties between the government institutions and faith of whatever stripe. During Washington's first term as President, the Bill of Rights enshrined freedom of worship and the separation of Church and state in the Constitution.

Freemasonry opened its doors to men of all faiths; it embraced only 'that Religion in which all Men agree' – in the usefully vague formulation set out by the *Constitutions*. Washington's own religious beliefs put him at Freemasonry's spiritual centre of gravity. He has been described as a 'lukewarm Episcopalian' who never went to communion, and generally invoked 'Providence' and 'Destiny' rather than God; he was less concerned about personal piety than he was about religion's role as a guarantor of public morality.

The meeting of minds between Freemasons and the founders of the American Republic went deeper even than religion. Freemasonry's principles were universal: self-betterment, and the brotherhood of all men regardless of birth or status. Such ideals harmonised with the United States of America's inborn sense that it stood for something bigger than its own particular national identity, that it was the bearer of universal truths like the ones proclaimed to be self-evident in the Declaration of Independence.

The fledgling United States also needed something else that Freemasonry could supply: virtue. Republicanism, the ideology to which Washington and the other Founders subscribed, had a history full of stern lessons. Everywhere, from ancient Athens and Rome, to Renaissance Italy and Oliver Cromwell's British Commonwealth, the attempt to set up a system of government without monarchy had collapsed. The only hope for a modern republic like the United States was that the population, and in particular the governing class, could learn enough virtue to resist the slide into tyranny.

Since its inception, Freemasonry had presented itself to the world as a builder of virtuous men. While he was in office, Washington received a stream of high-flown salutations and dedications from Masonic Lodges, all of them hailing him as a model of Masonic and civic rectitude. In 1790, the King David Lodge in Newport, Rhode Island, wrote to the President in these stumbling terms:

> With unspeakable pleasure we gratulate you as filling the presidential chair, with the applause of a numerous and enlightened people; whilst at the same time, we felicitate ourselves on the honor done the brotherhood by your many exemplary virtues, and emanations of goodness proceeding from a heart worthy of possessing the ancient mysteries of our Craft.

To such praise, Washington would always offer gracious replies that merged the language of Republican civic virtue and the jargon of the Craft. In 1791, he wrote to a Grand Lodge in Charleston, South Carolina, as follows: 'The fabric of our freedom is placed on the enduring basis of public virtue, and will, I fondly hope, long continue to protect the prosperity of the architects who raised it. I shall be happy, on every occasion, to evince my regard for the Fraternity.'

When, in 1796, Washington announced his intention to retire, he received a letter of thanks and best wishes from the Grand Lodge of Pennsylvania. His response included the hope that the United States would continue to be 'a sanctuary for brothers, and a lodge for the virtues'. Many such Masonic exchanges with the President were published soon after they were written. Taking up the President's cue, a whole new literature appeared, proclaiming Freemasonry to be the school of virtue and knowledge that would ensure the Republic lived up to its promise.

For Washington, managing his own image was a constant and delicate task in which Masonry became an important resource. By embracing the Craft's cult of brotherly love, a formal egalitarianism that harked back to its historical roots as an artisans' organisation, Washington endeavoured to ward off any fears that he might turn into a king.

Washington was not just the leader of the campaign to turn Freemasonry into a civic religion; he was also that campaign's most arresting symbol. Soon after laying the foundation stone of the Capitol, he sat in his sash and Past Master's medal for a portrait by William J. Williams. Uncountable images of Washington-as-Craftsman would be reproduced over the coming century.

President George Washington (1732–1799). A drawing based on
the only portrait of him in Masonic regalia painted
during his life.

The ceremony on Capitol Hill, which had been reported with great enthusiasm across the land, was only one of many Masonic dedications. On 4 July 1795, two Masonic heroes of the Revolution, Grand Master Paul Revere and Governor Samuel Adams, together laid the cornerstone of the Massachusetts State House. Buried with it was a copper time capsule that would be unearthed during repair work in 2014: it was found to contain, among other things, a George Washington medal. Freemasons in important positions also performed cornerstone ceremonies at buildings such as Virginia State Capitol (1785) and the University of North Carolina-Chapel Hill (1798), not to mention at the dedication of numerous bridges, boundary stones and the like.

Washington died from a throat infection in December 1799. His funeral on his Mount Vernon estate was arranged by Lodge 22 at Alexandria, where the Episcopalian minister chosen to preside over the burial rites was also a Brother. A Masonic apron and two crossed swords were placed on the casket. There were six pallbearers – all of them former officers in the Revolutionary Army, and at least five of them Masons. Craft rites were performed at the crypt and, just before entombment, Brothers cast evergreen acacia sprigs onto the coffin – a Masonic symbol of the soul's immortality.

Freemasons were prominent in the weeks of national mourning that followed: it has been estimated that they participated in an official capacity in around two-thirds of the commemorative parades held across the country. The Massachusetts Grand Lodge organised an elaborate procession in February 1800 at which over 1,600 Brothers marched through the streets of Boston. Six pallbearers, among them Paul Revere, carried a lock of Washington's hair in a golden urn on a pedestal, with a statue of the 'Genius of Masonry' weeping over it.

Over the coming years, as the Revolution began to pass from the recollections of one generation to the commemorations of the next, Masonry maintained its ceremonial prestige. Indeed, the Freemasons worked regularly in tandem with local authorities to organise cornerstone-laying rites and other ceremonies. One example, dating from 4 July 1815, was Baltimore's monument to Washington. With the citizens and dignitaries gathered around the pit where the foundation stone was suspended, the Worshipful Grand Master of Maryland announced:

> Honourable sir, on behalf of the free and accepted masons of this state, I accept, with pleasure, your invitation, and it will afford us peculiar satisfaction to render all the assistance within our power, so that the stone may be laid agreeably to the ancient usages of the order, especially, as the object of the building to be erected is to hand down to the latest posterity the virtues and patriotism of the greatest of men; who, during his valuable life, honored our order by becoming a zealous and faithful member of the fraternity.

Clearly no one begrudged the Craft its right to take advantage of these ceremonial duties to issue a reminder of its place in George Washington's life, and claim a prominent part for itself in the story of how the United States came to be.

Similar rites were performed up and down the country. There was a wave of them in 1824–5 during the Marquis de Lafayette's triumphal national tour. Lafayette was a French aristocrat who, aged only nineteen, had volunteered to fight in the cause of American liberty. He was probably initiated into Masonry at a military Lodge soon after joining the Continental Army. His exploits during the war, and his later sufferings during the French Revolution, cemented his reputation as a paladin of freedom. By the time he was invited to return to the United States by President James Monroe (also a Mason), he was the most celebrated living link to the Revolutionary War, and particularly to the person of George Washington, who had treated him as a son. During a thirteen-month stagecoach and steamboat progress around all twenty-four states, Lafayette was greeted everywhere he went with laurels, fireworks, dinners, orations – and invitations to administer the Masonic wine, oil and grain to the cornerstones of numerous monuments.

The Freemasons had become America's impresarios of solemnity, specialist technicians of national memory. When early nineteenth-century America wanted to speak to posterity, it did so through the good offices of the Brotherhood.

Freemasonry's high public profile, and the endorsement of illustrious personages like Washington and Lafayette, sent a clear message to ambitious and/or patriotic American men: if you want to get ahead, get an apron. An accelerating social change played in Freemasonry's favour too. The frontier was being pushed further and further west; business was booming; cities and towns were mushrooming; family ties were loosening. American men from humble backgrounds wandered in search of opportunity, and grew wealthier and more self-assertive when they found it. Joining the Craft gave them a nationwide network of trusted contacts, and a safety net of mutual assistance.

Freemasonry spread further and faster in the United States than it had ever yet done, anywhere else. In the first quarter of the nineteenth century, membership more than tripled, from twenty-five to eighty thousand – perhaps one adult white male in every twenty. By the time of Lafayette's tour, there were more Lodges in America than there had been in the whole of the rest of the world half a century earlier. In New York City, there were forty-four Lodges by 1825, which was double the number recorded in 1812. In the state of New York, the expansion was even more rapid: seventy Lodges were approved between 1806 and 1810 alone. By 1825 there were nearly five hundred Lodges statewide. The numbers reflect just how well Masonry harmonised with the life of the Republic. They also give the measure of the catastrophe that was soon to follow.

There is blood upon the order of Masonry

The feast of St John, 1825: another momentous day for the United States, and yet another display of ritual *savoir faire* by the Freemasons.

The township of Lockport, situated some twenty miles from Niagara Falls, had sprouted from the forests only three years ago; its Masonic Lodge had only been warranted the previous February. But on 24 June 1825, a crowd of four or five thousand gathered to watch the assembled Masons of Lockport and nearby counties open the gateway to a new future. Their ceremony celebrated the placing of the capstone on the flight of five double combined locks to which the town owed its existence, and that carried the Erie Canal down sixty feet from the level of the Niagara River. The locks removed the last major obstacle in the way of a direct waterway from the Atlantic at New York, via the Hudson River, to the Great Lakes. What one excited local called 'the American Mediterranea' was open for business.

Watching the proceedings that day was the recently elected constable of Niagara County, Hiram B. Hopkins. His interest in the Brotherhood had first been stimulated by the suggestion, made by the local sheriff, that the Lodge's support would help with his political career. At the capstone ceremony Hopkins was impressed by the sight of some of his young associates, clad in aprons and sashes, mingling with men of influence. He found the main speech, made by a Presbyterian minister, intriguing: Freemasonry had been 'supported by all the wisest and best of men in every age, from the building of Solomon's Temple to the present time'. Straight after the ceremony, Hopkins applied to the Lockport Lodge. Within a short time, he had undergone the first three Degrees and was hungry to acquire more. In the middle of August 1826, he endured a four-hour initiation to become a Royal Arch Mason, a Degree that Masons regarded as 'indescribably more august, sublime, and important, than all which precede it . . . the summit and perfection of Ancient Masonry'. Hopkins had been assured, in addition, that becoming a Royal Arch Mason would put him on a par with any of his peers when it came to political traction.

Before he left the Chapter on the evening of what Masons call his Royal Arch 'exaltation', Hopkins was told in confidence that trouble was afoot. A disaffected Brother by the name of William Morgan, from nearby Batavia, was soon to publish an exposé betraying everything about Masonry, right up to the Royal Arch Degree. Hopkins would later state that he heard his Brother Masons were contemplating 'proper measures to put Morgan out of the way'. He shared the anger at Morgan's outrage, and confessed that, 'I thought he deserved to die.'

What Hopkins had stumbled upon were the beginnings of the most notorious Masonic conspiracy in American history.

William Morgan, born around the time of the Declaration of Independence, was a journeyman stonemason, and a finagling drunkard. His main reason for being in the Craft seems to have been to scrounge charitable donations from his Brethren. In 1825, he managed to have himself exalted as a Royal Arch Mason in Le Roy, ten miles east of his home. However, his companions in Batavia were loath to count him as one of their own, and when they constituted a new Chapter of the Royal Arch early in 1826, they engineered his exclusion. An indignant Morgan swore revenge aloud. Together with his drinking partner, a cash-strapped printer called David C. Miller, Morgan resolved to publish all the Craft's secrets. In the early summer of 1826, the two men announced their plan to the world.

The Masons immediately made their anger known. Warnings to other Brothers were also printed in the local newspapers: 'Morgan is considered a swindler, and a dangerous man.' They approached the defector directly, and thought they had brow-beaten him into surrendering his manuscript. But it soon became apparent that he had only handed over a rough copy, and that publication was still on course.

The campaign to stop publication escalated. Masons in law enforcement had both Morgan and Miller prosecuted for small debts. Morgan's home was illegally searched while he was in custody. A crowd, comprising Masons from as far away as Buffalo and even Canada, gathered to mount a raid on Miller's print shop; they dispersed when they learned that Miller, a former soldier, had assembled 'two swivels, fifteen or twenty guns, and several pistols' to defend himself. Soon afterwards, there was a night-time arson attack on the shop using turpentine-laced rags; Miller's cries of alarm attracted enough help to put out the flames.

Early the next day, Monday 11 September 1826, it was Morgan's turn to be targeted: on a warrant from a neighbouring county, he was arrested for stealing a shirt and cravat. Confident that he could prove that he had only borrowed the clothes, Morgan went with his captors to Canandaigua, some fifty miles east of his home in Batavia. When he arrived, the charges against him were changed, and he was jailed for a debt of two dollars.

The following evening two men arrived to release him, claiming that they had paid off his debt. Morgan was suspicious, but agreed to go with them. Minutes later, just outside the jail, he was heard screaming 'Murder! Murder! Murder!' as he was bundled into a carriage.

In places like the outer reaches of New York State, where the government's authority was patchy, the citizenry could channel their fears into 'vigilance committees', appointed by public meetings. Our word *vigilante* comes from this practice. On 25 September, the first such committee to look into Morgan's disappearance sprang up in Batavia; its members conducted many of the first interviews with suspects and witnesses. They concluded that, once taken from jail in Canandaigua, Morgan was driven thirty miles north-west to Handford's Landing on the banks of the Genesee River. Then his path followed the Ridge Road westwards another eighty-five miles to the Niagara. At various points along this route, the horses, driver and even the carriage were changed, which meant that a large number of people were involved. Reports of Morgan's movements thereafter were hazy and contradictory.

Soon there would be five county vigilance committees looking into the Morgan case. It was inevitable that Freemasonry would come under scrutiny. Everyone knew who had carried out the harassment of the printer David Miller. A number of Masons had made no secret of their loathing for Morgan: some were happy to be quoted in the press as saying that he had got what he deserved. With each day that passed, and with Morgan still missing, the conviction grew that the Masons' loathing had driven them to murder. The population at large grew angrier. The Brothers closed ranks in response, accusing the vigilance committees of anti-Masonic prejudice. Wasn't it obvious that Morgan and Miller had orchestrated the disappearance themselves to crank up publicity for their book? Opinions polarised, inexorably, between Masons and anti-Masons. As autumn turned into winter, Morgan's disappearance escalated into the 'Morgan affair'.

Morgan's book was published a few weeks after he vanished. In the end, it contained only the first three Degrees – and a promise that the higher Degrees would follow in another volume. The polemic surrounding the case created a market for further revelations, both true and spurious. Yet, as ever, the suspicion surrounding the Craft proved resistant to any exposé, and continued to give apparent legitimacy to the most sinister theories about what might have happened to William Morgan. Amid the tensions of that time and place, it was hard for anyone to argue that the blood-chilling oaths taken by initiates were just part of an innocuous moral playlet. Many observers concluded that Masonic oaths robbed men of their sense of right and wrong.

Rumours about what had happened to Morgan quickly entered circulation. Some witnesses claimed that he had been taken to a Canadian port to be press-ganged into the British navy. Some maintained he had been tortured to death at Fort Niagara. Others that he had been paid hush-money to go overseas for good. No evidence other than a sense of melodrama seems to have inspired a few of the theories about Morgan's demise. It was said that he had been handed over to a Mohawk chief 'to be executed with savage cruelty'. Inevitably, there were also those who insisted that the poor man had been lashed to a canoe and sent down the Niagara to meet his doom over the mighty Horseshoe Falls. Many anti-Masons suggested that Morgan had met the very end depicted in the Craft's initiation ritual: *his throat cut across, his tongue torn out by the root, and his body buried in the sand of the sea at low water mark, a cable's length from the shore, where the tide regularly ebbs and flows twice in twenty-four hours.* Masons responded by claiming that Morgan had merely fled his many creditors.

While the vigilance committees continued their probing, there began a long sequence of county grand jury investigations and criminal trials. At the first trial, in January 1827, large crowds braved the aftermath of the biggest snowstorm in living memory to follow events at the Ontario County Assizes, in a courtroom decorated with busts of Franklin, Washington and Lafayette. What the public heard there ramped up tensions even further, and put Freemasons across the state on the defensive. Three of the four men indicted entered a guilty plea. Among them was Nicholas G. Cheseboro, Master of the Canandaigua Lodge. Cheseboro was the coroner who obtained the warrant to arrest Morgan for stealing a shirt and cravat; he then led the posse of Masons who apprehended Morgan in Batavia and took him to Canandaigua jail. The arrest was legally dubious to say the least. Despite the fact that the alleged theft had taken place nearly five months previously, the warrant was obtained in an unseemly rush – on a Sunday. According to the prosecution, it was Cheseboro who persuaded the jailer's wife to release Morgan into the hands of the men who claimed to have paid off his two-dollar debt. He then stood by while Morgan was muscled into a carriage.

Like the other defendants, Cheseboro was convicted. He was found by a later court to have stuffed a handkerchief into Morgan's mouth to stifle his cries.

The only possible conclusion was that Morgan's abduction was carried out by a team of Freemasons, for Masonic reasons. In his concluding remarks, Judge Enos T. Throop praised the people of Ontario County for their 'virtuous indignation'. Such sentiments could only fuel the anti-Masonic fury.

Judge Throop went on to pinpoint a legal problem that would muddle many subsequent proceedings. There could clearly be no murder trial without Morgan's corpse, or other firm evidence that he was dead. So kidnapping would be the charge. At the time, kidnapping was classified in the state of New York as a minor 'misdemeanor', rather than as a grave 'felony'. Suspects who confessed to the misdemeanour were given short sentences – a year in Cheseboro's case. They could not now be retried. Nor could there be any way of knowing whether they had tailored their confessions to fit the lesser crime, rather than risk a murder charge if Morgan's body ever surfaced.

The range of perfectly plausible scenarios made it well-nigh impossible to verify who was guilty of what. Perhaps most of the conspirators did not know that the ultimate aim was to murder the captive – if indeed that had been his fate. Perhaps his death had been an accident.

Mired in such difficulties from the outset, the Morgan affair placed the judicial system itself on trial. The friction between Masons and anti-Masons obviously cast doubt on how impartial the vigilance committees were. Yet they could not easily be dismissed as gangs of anti-Masonic vigilantes. Many of the committees' findings were accepted as valid from the outset by the widely respected governor of New York, DeWitt Clinton, who was a former Masonic Grand Master of New York and one of the most senior Brothers in the country. Clinton issued a statement urging all citizens to collaborate with the investigations, and offered a reward for information leading to the discovery of either Morgan or his kidnappers. He was one of many Masons in important institutional offices who handled the Morgan affair with impeccable impartiality.

The behaviour of witnesses and suspects brought yet more legal difficulties. Several fled the state, some of them after receiving tip-offs from fellow Masons. Many refused to testify on the grounds that they would incriminate themselves. Some were prosecuted for giving blatantly reticent statements. Others gave different versions of events to different courts. One witness, who had testified that Morgan's captors had drawn lots to decide who would have the duty of performing the murder, went insane soon afterwards. Some courts struggled for days to form a jury: when the defence pointed out that there were Masons among the jurors, there followed tortuous debates on whether Masonic oaths disqualified Craftsmen from reaching an impartial verdict. In several instances, by contrast, jurors were removed because they had expressed the view that all Masons were guilty, whatever the evidence.

In the confusion, many of the accused were acquitted. As a result, the public believed what they wanted to believe. Where Masons viewed the misfired trials as evidence of prejudice against them, anti-Masons saw clear signs of a double conspiracy to both silence Morgan and shield his assassins from justice. The middle ground was shrinking ever faster.

Unwisely, the Freemasons of William Morgan's home town of Batavia chose to celebrate St John's Day, 25 June 1827, with a parade. It was bound to be taken as a display of power. A counter-demonstration was organised by the anti-Masonic newspaper run by William Morgan's partner, the printer David Miller. His editorial invited the public to come and express their feelings at the sight of 'the masons arrayed in robes of royalty, with sceptres in their hands, and crowns upon their heads, marching through the streets of a republican country'. There was a stand-off between three hundred Brothers and several thousand protestors. Stones were thrown, and a wagon driven into the Masonic ranks. Thankfully there were no serious injuries, the Brothers refused to be provoked and a major outbreak of violence was averted.

Nonetheless, the Batavia incident exposed the social tensions that underlay the increasingly angry divide between Masons and anti-Masons. The statistics explain why it was that, when Miller accused the Masons of regal arrogance, his words resonated so widely in Batavia and the county of Genesee. Ninety per cent of the workforce in the county was employed in agriculture, yet 80 per cent of Masons in Batavia and nearby towns worked in the professions. Moreover Masons, who were at most 5 per cent of the population, held 60 per cent of the county's public offices. The Craft was an invaluable networking hub for the merchants, attorneys and doctors who were the county's natural political class: in a rural society, they were the only people with the time, money and education to engage in the contest for office. But to anti-Masonic protestors, it looked as if a shadowy clique had control of their world.

Social divisions were exacerbated by religious differences. Eighty-four per cent of the members in Batavia Lodge no. 433 belonged to the more establishment Episcopalian Church, which derived from the Church of England, with its undogmatic approach to belief. Yet evangelical Christian sects thrived in the western counties of New York. For many evangelicals, far from being the 'handmaid of religion' as Masons claimed, Masonry aimed to subvert faith: it was the snake in America's Garden of Eden, 'a profanation and a mockery of sacred and holy ordinances'. Baptists were particularly prominent in the nascent anti-Masonic movement. Baptist ministers, Elder John G. Stearns and Elder David Bernard, published two of the bestselling anti-Masonic tracts. They spoke with the spiritual intensity of repentant sinners, for both had been Brothers. Bernard's book, *Light on Masonry*, which combined detailed revelations of the full range of Craft Degrees along with a narrative of the Morgan affair, would become known as the 'Bible of anti-Masonry'. The campaign against the Craft had a missionary fervour. The cry went up that 'There is blood upon the order of Masonry.'

Late on the morning of Sunday 7 October 1827, nearly thirteen months after the kidnapping, three men walking on the shores of Lake Ontario came across a corpse lying face down in the mud. The alarm went up only when the coroner's report was published: the dead man had an unusual double row of front teeth, just like Morgan; and, at five foot eight inches and an estimated forty-five to fifty years old, he was the right size and age too. Friends recognised the blackened, swollen body as Morgan by a lump on his balding forehead, and by the abundant grey hair in his ears. Morgan's wife Lucinda confirmed the identification. The coroners concluded that only 'the hand of an overruling Providence' could be responsible for such an unhoped-for breakthrough. Crowds gathered from surrounding towns and villages to pay homage at the burial in Batavia: the anti-Masonic movement now had a proper focus for its rage, and made William Morgan into a martyr.

The body was not his. A few days later it was dug up again when news came of a Canadian who had recently been lost in the Niagara River. The new autopsy was categorical: the Canadian man was known to have the same double teeth, and his clothes matched those on the corpse perfectly.

There would never be a resolution to the Morgan mystery; many more sightings were reported, but none were confirmed. The trials for kidnapping and other minor crimes resumed, and would drag on until 1831. Eventually, there would be eighteen of them, along with two special investigations ordered by the governor's office. Only the most conscientious of journalists, or the most obsessed of campaigners, could follow the various fragments of the case as they traced their erratic trajectory through the legal and political system. Preconceptions formed early in the affair could not be shaken by further news. Meanwhile, the country became infested with what one journalist called 'mountebank Anti-masonic professors of Masonry' who tried to scrape a few dollars by putting on scurrilous shows of what they claimed were Craft workings.

One trial did rise above the din to shed fresh light on Masonic influence over the legal process, and renew the public indignation. Much suspicion surrounded the sheriffs in the counties directly concerned with the Morgan affair, all of whom were Masons. One of a sheriff's responsibilities was to select the grand jurors who made preliminary investigations into potential criminal conduct. There is strong evidence that the Morgan grand juries were packed with Masonic Brethren. The most prominent case was the trial of the Sheriff of Niagara County, Eli Bruce. The main witness was Hiram B. Hopkins, the ambitious young constable who was so enthralled by the capstone ceremony at Lockport in 1825. Before the Ontario County Court of Sessions in June 1827, Hopkins confessed that, on Bruce's instruction, he had picked Freemasons for the grand jury.

Sheriff Bruce, who had been feted as an innocent victim by the many Masons who visited him during the trial, was eventually sentenced to two years and four months in jail. The governor sacked him.

All of the men either convicted in relation to the Morgan abduction, or most heavily suspected of involvement, were Freemasons. Yet the Masonic authorities refused to admit the problem, thereby boosting the worst suspicions. In June 1827, the New York Grand Lodge granted the controversial Sheriff Bruce $100 in view of his 'persecution' by anti-Masons. The following June, the Grand Lodge met again amid expectations that it would finally say something to distance Masonry from the Morgan case, and share in the public concern about subversion of the legal process. It did no such thing. Nor were any of the Masons found guilty during the Morgan affair expelled or censured.

Former Masons numbered among the most avid anti-Masons. Many Masons chose to make a big deal of resigning their membership in protest at the Morgan scandal, and dissolving their Lodges. In February 1828, a convention of so-called 'seceding Masons' was held in Genesee County. They denounced Masonry's pretentions to teach morality, endorsed exposés of Masonic mysteries and aligned themselves with the anti-Masonic movement.

Through 1827 and into 1828, anti-Masonry evolved from a local moral crusade into a political movement that reached into many other states. The movement set up newspapers. It had been an article of faith among anti-Masons that Masonic editors were part of the conspiracy: news of the full scale of the Morgan scandal was being suppressed. The solution was an 'impartial' and 'independent' anti-Masonic press. By the end of 1827, there were twenty-two such papers in New York State; many more would follow thereafter.

The Morgan affair gave rise to numerous popular prints, newspapers and almanacs. The illustration purports to show the moment when Morgan was kidnapped.

Spurred on by their press, the anti-Masons made a bid for power. In the autumn of 1827 nominating conventions were held to select anti-Masonic candidates for the New York State Legislature. The centrepiece of the programme was the abolition of the Craft by means of a ban on all non-judicial oaths. In August 1828, anti-Masons put forward a candidate for governor. The first national anti-Masonic convention was held in Philadelphia in 1830, on the fourth anniversary of Morgan's abduction. In 1832, William Wirt, a former Freemason, stood for President on an anti-Masonic ticket. The following year, former President John Quincy Adams was the anti-Masonic candidate for governor of Massachusetts. Three states – Vermont, Massachusetts and Rhode Island – passed laws banning extra-judicial oaths.

Intimidation and violence from both sides stoked the political tensions. In Rhode Island in 1831, an armed crowd of Masons chased an anti-Masonic campaigner out of Providence and hounded him all the way to Massachusetts. In Boston the following year, an anti-Masonic rabble vandalised a new temple, and tried to set it on fire.

The anti-Masonic party had genuine political leverage at a time when national party organisations were in flux, and when state-based political factions often did not overlap neatly with the national battle lines. Their appeal was accentuated by the fact that the dominant statesman of the era, President Andrew Jackson, was a former Grand Master of the Grand Lodge of Tennessee. The man who stood against him for the presidency in 1832, Henry Clay, was the former Grand Master of Kentucky.

All told, however, anti-Masonry's political impact was short-lived. Its weakness was made apparent by William Wirt's abject presidential campaign in 1832: he tried to back out of the nomination after accepting it, and blamed the electorate for his lack of appeal. As Jackson romped home, Wirt finished a distant third, and only managed to carry the anti-Masonic stronghold of Vermont. Anti-Masonry was hobbled by its own contradictions, split between single-issue idealists who were convinced that the entire system was riddled with Freemasonry, and political realists who wanted to strike bargains to get anti-Masons into office. In the end, even in those states where extra-judicial oaths were banned, the laws were never enforced. The fundamental problem was that anti-Masonry came to seem superfluous: its great enemy was fading away of its own accord.

Freemasonry collapsed first in New York State: Brothers resigned in droves. The triumphal capstone ceremony at Lockport in 1825 now seemed to belong in a different age. At that time, there were 480 Lodges in New York with some 20,000 members. By 1832, there were only eighty-two Lodges left, and barely three thousand members. In Lockport, the one remaining Lodge was forced to assemble its handful of die-hard Brothers in secret, in an attic.

Between the late 1820s and the mid-1830s, there was an estimated two-thirds drop in Lodge membership across the nation. In Philadelphia, where Benjamin Franklin had given such an impulse to early Freemasonry, the Pennsylvania Grand Lodge was forced to sell its headquarters. As one observer commented in 1832, 'as well might they think of establishing Mahometanism in this enlightened land, as to cherish the idea of re-establishing Freemasonry'. The cornerstone ceremonies ceased.

The Morgan case divides opinion to this day. Professional historians with no loyalties to the Craft tend to draw on accounts by the most sober observers of the time: whatever the excesses of the anti-Masonic mania, they conclude, there was undoubtedly something rotten in Freemasonry in the westernmost counties of New York. Masonic historians of today tend to echo what their New York Brethren said in the aftermath of the abduction: they regard the whole affair as a classic instance of anti-Masonic intolerance, and prefer to believe that Morgan arranged his own disappearance as a publicity stunt. The strongest argument the Masons have in their favour takes us back to the fundamental issue of Masonic secrecy. The supposedly momentous secrets at the centre of

Masonic ritual are, in reality, a theatrical conceit. As such, they are hardly worth killing for.

The answer to the mystery of William Morgan's disappearance lies in the Royal Arch Chapters of western New York State, like the one in Lockport to which both Hiram B. Hopkins and Sheriff Eli Bruce belonged. All but two of the men convicted or indicted for involvement in the conspiracy were Royal Arch Masons.

The Royal Arch Degree ritual has its own graphic threats of retribution for those who betray its secrets: any traitor will have his 'skull smote off' and his 'brains exposed to the scorching rays of the sun'. But what most disturbed public opinion at the time of the Morgan affair were the promises that newly initiated Royal Arch Masons had to make – at least according to the versions of the ceremony that were published by recanting Brothers. The most alarming obligation was as follows:

> I do promise and swear . . . that I will promote a companion R[oyal] A[rch] Mason's political preferment in preference to another of equal qualifications. Furthermore, do I promise and swear, that a companion R. A. Mason's secrets, given me in charge as such, and I knowing them to be such, shall remain as secure and inviolable in my breast as in his own, *murder and treason not excepted.*

If these words mean what they seem to mean, Royal Arch Masons were bound together in a gang whose interests trumped any duty to obey the law. In many eyes, the Royal Arch Degree supplied the script for the Morgan murder.

Of course, it is perfectly possible that the seceding Masons were simply making up this version of the Royal Arch obligations to pander to the anti-Masonic phobia. There is certainly no evidence that any such rules were contained in the most widely followed Royal Arch ritual templates. Yet it is equally possible, in *some* Royal Arch Chapters, and in the often factional and self-serving political culture of early nineteenth-century America, that cynical politicians were trying to use the Royal Arch to impose discipline on their local allies. Individual Royal Arch Chapters certainly had the room to tweak rituals as they saw fit. Freemasonry in the United States had lots of local variety. Supervisory bodies like the Grand Royal Arch Chapter of New York had enormous trouble compelling the Brethren to work the authorised rituals.

Something else may have created a climate where a circle of Royal Arch Masons could conceive of abducting and murdering William Morgan: an evangelical revival known as the Second Great Awakening. The western counties of New York were known for the zeal of the Christian sects that thrived there, some of them claiming to restore ancient truths. In the 'Burned-over District', as it would become known, the evangelical fire was so fierce that almost nobody was left untouched. Prophets, preachers, faith-healers and speakers-in-tongues proliferated. That is why there were so many anti-Masons who viewed the Masonic oaths as heretical: because they took them literally, rather than as a part of a vivid parable. Amid such fervour, the Royal Arch's biblical narrative may have been taken literally by some Masons too. Could Morgan's kidnappers have taken their deadly vows in pious earnest when it came to dealing with Morgan's treachery?

Whether the men who abducted Morgan were motivated by political clannishness or religious ardour, or by some poisonous blend of both, will never be known. We are in the realm of speculation – the only realm in which a solution is to be found to the Morgan mystery.

Masons and Mormons

Revivalist Christianity was not the only expression of spiritual fervour in the Burned-over District. Folk magic was widespread too. Hard-pressed farmers clung to amulets and talismanic stones; they believed in warlocks and soothsayers; they used divining rods to find lost possessions, and incantatory rituals to cure one another of disease. The very hills they ploughed held tantalising mysteries. Long abandoned Native-American forts and hundreds of burial mounds were scattered across the landscape. Often a turn of the ploughshare would unearth human bones, or pot shards, or some other artefact made from copper, stone or even silver. The indigenous people were not capable of such sophistication – or so the white settlers assumed – so the land must once have been inhabited by a nobler and more ancient race who fought titanic battles and interred their fallen in vast heaps. The chances were that they had interred gold and silver too. The hunt for buried treasure was an obsession in the western counties of New York. Farmers could hire one of many spiritually gifted treasure-diggers to locate riches that would liberate them from a life of toil.

In March 1830, Joseph Smith Jr, a twenty-four-year-old farmer and treasure-digger from Palmyra, published one of the most influential American books of the century. Palmyra was just nine miles from Canandaigua, where William Morgan had spent a night in jail before disappearing for ever. Smith's book, which was composed as the Morgan affair raged in the towns and villages all around, was the thousand-year history of an ancient American civilisation. Its founding fathers, the family of Lehi, were Israelites who fled the Holy Land and came to America after the destruction of Solomon's Temple in the sixth century before Christ. Their collective epic is a tale of believers and apostates, of prophets and angels, of pillars of fire and divine scourges. Two factions emerge to fight a war for supremacy: on the one hand, the righteous, temple-building Nephites; and on the other, the Lamanites, ferocious unbelievers whom God curses by turning their skin black. After his resurrection, Christ makes a long-prophesied journey to America to preach his gospel and herald an era of peace and prosperity. When two happy centuries have passed, bloody divisions between the Nephites and the Lamanites arise once more. Having forsaken their righteousness, the Nephites succumb and are slaughtered in great heaps. But before the end, the last prophet Moroni buries some gold plates on which the history of his people has been inscribed – mostly by the great Nephite leader Mormon.

Joseph Smith Jr was insistent that his volume, which he called *The Book of Mormon*, was no mere historical fantasy. He could be sure, because fourteen hundred years after the twilight of the Nephites, the prophet Moroni, who was now an angel, had appeared to tell him that the gold plates could be found buried in a stone chest on a small hill a couple of miles from his home. Buried with the plates were the Urim and Thummim: these were crystals bound together to form magic spectacles that enabled the wearer to understand the ancient language in which *The Book of Mormon* was written. Smith's momentous task, explained to him over several visitations by the angel Moroni, was to translate the plates into English, and then to found a new religion. Joseph Smith Jr was a prophet in the mould of the great seers of the vanished Nephite people – a new Moses or even a new Christ – and his book was a new Bible.

The Mormon Church that Joseph Smith founded, officially known as the Church of Jesus Christ of Latter-day Saints, today claims to have sixteen million members. For them, *The Book of Mormon* is holy scripture. For everyone else, it reads uncannily like the kind of story a poor young farmer with a hyperactive imagination might have made up, drawing on the folk culture of the western counties of New York State in the late 1820s, while straining to parrot the high-flown English of the King James Bible. The prose is so turgid that Mark Twain famously called it 'chloroform in print'. The phrase 'and it came to pass' appears more than two thousand times.

The anti-Masonry of the Morgan affair left a deep mark on Joseph Smith's work. His story of the buried gold plates owes something to the Royal Arch ceremony – at least in the form the ceremony was presented in the anti-Masonic almanacs of the period. Like most Masonic Degrees, the Royal Arch acts out a narrative. The story in this case is set after the breaking down

The angel Moroni shows Joseph Smith (1805–1844)
the location of the golden tablets inscribed
with the Book of Mormon. A fanciful
representation from the 1880s.

of the walls of Jerusalem and the destruction of King Solomon's Temple. Three master masons take up work amid the rubble, and discover an underground vault containing a gold box that turns out to be the Ark of the Covenant. Inside it there is the Pentateuch – the first five books of the Old Testament, which had hitherto been lost.

There are other traces of anti-Masonry in *The Book of Mormon*: the 'Gadianton robbers' are an ancient secret society who are just as responsible as the dark-skinned Lamanites for the destruction of the Nephites. It hardly needs exceptional scholarly acumen to work out where the idea came from:

And it came to pass that [the Gadianton robbers] did have their signs, yea, their secret signs, and their secret words; and this that they might distinguish a brother who had entered into the covenant, that whatsoever wickedness his brother should do he should not be injured by his brother, nor by those who did belong to his band, who had taken this covenant.

The Gadianton robbers 'fill the judgment-seats – having usurped the power and authority of the land'. They also have 'a lamb-skin about their loins' – an obvious echo of the white lambskin aprons worn by Masons. Among many other connections between Joseph Smith and anti-Masonry, Martin Harris, a prosperous farmer who financed publication of Smith's work, was on an anti-Masonic committee in Palmyra.

The *Book of Mormon* concludes with dire lessons from the fate of the Nephites: beware 'secret combinations' and dark oaths, for any civilisation that cedes ground to them will inevitably fall. Which turns out to be ironic given the enormous influence that Freemasonry would have on the subsequent development of Mormonism.

Joseph Smith Jr's new religion had a tumultuous early history. His followers migrated to Ohio, Missouri and then Illinois in search of their New Jerusalem. But at each stop their clannish-ness attracted violent hostility from surrounding communities, forcing them to move on. Along the way, the Prophet married Lucinda, the widow of anti-Masonry's martyr, William Morgan. If indeed she was a widow. As it turned out, it mattered little whether her vanished first husband was dead; nor did it matter that she already had a second husband (a Mason, curiously) when the Prophet Joseph Smith became her third: by the early 1840s Mormonism's leaders were embracing polygamy and she would be the first of Joseph Smith's multiple wives – forty-eight is a conservative estimate. Rumours of Mormon polygamy were among the reasons their presence was so resented.

In 1842, Joseph Smith joined a Masonic Lodge in Illinois. His motives are unclear, but the context is undoubtedly a factor: by this time, the Craft was beginning to revive here and there as the impact of the Morgan affair subsided. What we do know is that the Prophet was impressed by Masonry's rich symbolic and ceremonial language and sought to put it to use within his Church. He re-elaborated Masonic ritual into a Mormon version, known as the temple ceremony – a highly sacred blessing that was soon open to women as well as men. The walls of Latter-day Saint temples would display Masonic symbols, such as the square and compass, and the all-seeing eye. Those undergoing the Mormon temple ceremony were presented with new undergarments with the signs of the square and compass stitched over the left and right breast. The temple ritual contained these and other elements familiar from Masonic Degree rituals: a secret handshake known as a 'grip', which involved pressing the thumb to the space between the knuckles of the index and middle fingers; the donning of aprons; oaths of secrecy reinforced by the threat of bloody punishment, which was illustrated by gestures (e.g. the hand drawn across the throat to mimic slitting). It has been suggested that one reason Smith introduced these oaths was to force Mormons to guard the secret of polygamy, since 'celestial marriage', which was often polygamous, formed part of the temple ceremony too.

Thanks to the Prophet's sponsorship, his devotees flocked to the Craft across Illinois: by 1843 there were more Mormon than non-Mormon Craftsmen in the state. Local Freemasons were worried by this expansion, and offended by Smith's appropriation of their rituals. The list of Smith's enemies was growing longer.

Smith was becoming disillusioned with American democracy, because it had proved incapable of protecting him and the chosen people from what he saw as mob rule. In January 1844, he announced that he was standing for President. Meanwhile, in secret, he gathered a new Council of Fifty Mormon leaders to draft a Constitution for a theocracy in which all earthly authority would be vested in him. The Council unanimously approved the following motion: 'That this honorable assembly receive from this time henceforth and forever, Joseph Smith, as our Prophet, Priest, & King, and uphold him in that capacity in which God has anointed him.' This was nation-building with a vengeance. It was also treason. News of Smith's threat to the democratic order was leaked to the press, and anti-Mormon feeling in Illinois reached crisis point.

In 1844 Smith ordered a Mormon dissenter's printing-press to be smashed. Both he and his brother were thrown in jail. But before they could be tried, a mob invaded the jail and shot them dead. One of Smith's wives later said that, as the mob was closing in on him, he gave out the Masonic cry of distress: 'Is there no help for the widow's son?' After the Prophet's death, the bulk of his followers migrated westward with a new leader, Brigham Young, into what is now Utah.

The temple ceremony is still today very much as Joseph Smith designed it – despite the fact that, in 1990, the terrible Masonic punishments (throat-cutting, and the rest) were quietly dropped. Most orthodox Mormons are as unperturbed as was their Prophet by the similarities between their religion and Freemasonry. Smith presented his temple ceremony as a faithful restoration of the rituals practised by the Israelites, from Solomon all the way back to Adam. By contrast, Masonic Degree ceremonies, he explained, were only a later, degenerate version of those original Israelite rituals. If anything, therefore, it was the Masons who copied the Mormons, and not the other way around.

Charleston: **Africans were the Authors of this Mysterious and Beautiful Order**

No bondmen

The Scottish Rites had sprouted in eighteenth-century France as an 'inextricable mess' of rituals and Masonic orders. Early in the nineteenth century, this anarchic proliferation was transformed into a unified Rite of thirty-three Degrees, each with its own stories and mysteries. That process was international, and was set in motion by the remarkable Masonic ambassadorial work of Count Alexandre François Auguste de Grasse-Tilly.

De Grasse-Tilly forged a globetrotting military career after the 1780s. From France, to the Caribbean and the United States, to Italy, Spain and the Low Countries, he knew glory and conquest, captivity and penniless exile. Wherever he roamed, he helped systematise the variegated and profuse Scottish systems into a single Rite of thirty-three Degrees by establishing regulatory authorities, the Supreme Councils. In Port-au-Prince, in what is now Haiti. In Napoleon's Paris, in Milan, and in Murat's Naples. In Madrid, and then Brussels.

All of these bodies were preceded in both time and Masonic authority by the Supreme Council of the Ancient and Accepted Scottish Rite created in the thriving seaport of Charleston, South Carolina. De Grasse-Tilly had arrived there in 1793. He became a naturalised American citizen and immersed himself in the well-established Masonic life of the city. In 1801, along with ten others, he founded the Supreme Council. It is to de Grasse-Tilly that the Charleston Scottish Rite Supreme Council owes the high-sounding title it now enjoys, as Mother Council of the World.

Although the Supreme Council in Charleston was supremely successful in cloning itself abroad, it struggled to establish control over Scottish Rite affairs across the United States. For example, a dispute with a rival body in New York was only resolved in 1815 when Charleston authorised it as the Supreme Council for the Northern Jurisdiction of the United States, thus dividing Scottish Rite America into the two domains that still characterise it to this day. The anti-Masonic wave that followed the disappearance of William Morgan in New York State in 1826 reduced the Supreme Council to virtual inactivity from 1832 to 1842. When it resumed operations, it was a parochial body, with almost all of its officers coming from Charleston. Many of the famous thirty-three Degrees were still short and rudimentary. But from the 1840s, two legends of the Scottish Rite would together assemble a vast body of Masonic law, history, doctrine, liturgy and symbolism that transformed the Scottish Rite into the richest and most evocative Masonic system in the world. Through their selfless devotion to Craft law and esoterica, Albert Mackey and Albert Pike not only made the Scottish Rite what it is today, they also hurled themselves against the forces that were ripping American society apart, and threatening to do the same to the Craft.

Dr Albert Mackey was initiated in Charleston in 1841, and ascended rapidly through the many Degrees and offices. As Secretary General, he ran the day-to-day affairs of the Supreme Council of the Scottish Rite from 1844 until his death in 1881. 'Tall, erect, of spare but vigorous frame' with collar-length grey hair swept back from 'striking features replete with intelligence', he looked every inch the high-minded scholar. In 1854, at the age of only forty-six, he abandoned a successful medical

Albert Mackey (1807–1881), Masonic scholar,
legal authority, and a leading light of
Scottish Rite Freemasonry.

career to invest boundless energy in Masonic study. The massive
Encyclopedia of Freemasonry (1874) is the best known of his
thirteen books. He became one of the Craft's greatest
lawmakers.

In Charleston, on 20 March 1853, Dr Mackey conferred all
but one of the Scottish Rite Degrees on Albert Pike. Born in
Boston, Pike had sought solace from a broken heart in the west.
His adventures culminated in a death-defying 650-mile journey
on foot across Comanche country to reach the safety of Arkansas,
where he would set about making his fortune as a circuit lawyer
plying the Mississippi and Arkansas steamboat routes. Pike could
not have been more different to his Masonic mentor Mackcy:
jovially charismatic, with long hair, a long beard and a gargan-
tuan appetite for food, drink and work, he composed Romantic

poetry, owned and edited newspapers, and commanded a force of Arkansas volunteers in the Mexican–American war (1846–8).

When Mackey initiated Pike, they zipped through all but the thirty-third Scottish Rite Degree ceremonies in a single evening. Mackey recognised his protégé as a man with the intellectual stamina to accomplish the work the Scottish Rite badly needed: a systematic rewriting of its Degree ceremonies, followed by a profound re-elaboration of the lore that those rituals dramatised. The Scottish Rite was to become nothing less than a summation of the wisdom underlying all human cultures.

With Mackey's backing, in 1859, Pike was elected to the Scottish Rite's top job, as Sovereign Grand Commander of the Supreme Council – a post he would hold until his death thirty-two years later. Because American Freemasonry was organised on a state-by-state basis, Pike was the nearest thing the Craft had to a national authority. After rewriting the Degrees and seeing that they were implemented, he began the vast labour that would turn into his most celebrated work, *Morals and Dogma of the Ancient and Accepted Rite of Scottish Freemasonry*, which would eventually see the light in 1871.

Albert Pike's gifts as a Mason were that he was a voracious reader and an exuberant inventor of rituals. His main flaw was that he was a racist, and his racism profoundly shaped his fraternalism. In 1859, Pike wrote that: 'The negro in his best condition is still in his appetites and instincts a wild beast, ready to relapse into all his original barbarism. His sexual appetite, especially, is only controlled by fear; and even the dread and certainty of the most fearful and awful punishment will not restrain it.' Despite being a Yankee by birth, Pike had absorbed the pro-slavery values of the lowland cotton planters of southern and eastern Arkansas, his adopted home. Enslavers were his clients, his friends and his Brothers; he smoked their cigars, drank their whiskey and sat down to 'festive boards' with them. In his editorials, he made known his resentment at northern interference in the South's affairs, railed against 'abolitionist fanatics' and proclaimed his

Albert Pike (1809–1891), Sovereign Grand Commander
of the Scottish Rite's Southern Jurisdiction from
1859 until his death.

belief that wage labourers in the North were much worse off than the negroes of the South.

Pike's bigotry reached out in other directions too. In the mid-1850s, he enthusiastically joined a short-lived anti-Catholic party usually called the 'Know-Nothings' – because members were sworn to deny they were even aware of the group's existence. The Know-Nothing Party, whose slogan was 'America for the Americans', was formed to oppose immigration from Catholic countries like Ireland. Its propaganda claimed that the Pope was covertly orchestrating an invasion that would enslave Protestant America to the Church of Rome. With its oaths, degrees, grips and passwords, the Know-Nothing Party also bore the clear imprint of the Masonic template.

Perhaps surprisingly, given his attitudes to other races, Pike had a certain empathy with Native Americans. A generation earlier, a number of indigenous peoples had been pushed westwards from the south-eastern United States into 'Indian Territory', which lay beyond the western border of Arkansas in what is now Oklahoma. For most of the 1850s, Pike had used his skills as an advocate and his gusto as a lobbyist to try to win compensation for the Creek and Choctaw Nations.

Pike's Freemasonry was a crucial factor in the rapport he enjoyed with the Indian élite. Native Americans had long been welcome in the Lodges. The Mohawk leader Thayendanegea (aka Joseph Brant, 1743–1807) is thought to have been the first American Indian initiated into the Craft: the British inducted him to help win his support in the American War of Independence. Many such episodes of dialogue and mediation through Freemasonry punctuate the grim and shameful story of how the Native-American peoples were dispossessed. Indeed, the Indian Territory of the 1840s and 1850s saw something of a boom in Masonry among the so-called 'Five Civilized Tribes' (the Cherokee, Chickasaw, Choctaw, Creek and Seminole). The first Lodge there, Cherokee Lodge no. 21, was authorised by the Grand Lodge of Arkansas in 1848. In 1852, Choctaws founded Doaksville Lodge, and three years later came Muscogee Lodge, created by Creek Indians.

The élite of the native peoples of America found in Freemasonry the same things that Freemasons from other parts of the world did: fellowship, status, and the rest. But the Craft also brought them the bonus of hobnobbing with influential white Brothers like Albert Pike.

It was, and still is, often claimed that many Native-American peoples had cultural common ground with Masonry: a reverence for numbers and geographical orientation, for example; sun symbolism; secret magic words; sacred regalia. There may be an element of truth in this: some Native-American Masons certainly recognised such shared themes. But then again, by the early nineteenth century, Freemasonry had absorbed so many different myths and motifs from all over the world that it is hardly surprising if more-or-less coincidental correspondences with Native-American belief systems were to be found.

The myth of the noble savage is a more revealing guide to what Pike and other white Masons thought about their Indian Brethren. American Masonic literature of the nineteenth century was particularly fond of tales that pictured a clichéd scene. A triumphant brave, tomahawk raised for the death blow, stands over a wounded white soldier. Through teeth gritted in agony and desperation, the soldier issues a Masonic distress signal. Miraculously, drawing on something deep in the collective uncon-scious of his people, the brave recognises the signal and, instead of scalping his prisoner, treats him with all the respect due to a Brother. Such fables flattered Freemasons' sense that they were the inheritors of ancient truths, common to all humanity – truths that the most noble of the savages of the Americas could somehow feel in their bones. In other words, there was a profoundly arro-gant assumption at work in the white Masonic mind: the Craft, as the highest expression of human wisdom, came to the Americas in fulfilment of the natives' deepest spiritual inclinations. Masons among the colonisers saw themselves, as the leading historian of American-Indian Freemasonry has elegantly argued, as being 'at the vanguard of a historical movement that was preordained, since their arrival was somehow already known to those they came to dispossess'.

Albert Pike's mentor Dr Albert Mackey was intransigent when he was patrolling the boundary between what was, and what was not, properly Masonic. Even his Brothers remarked: 'he made enemies, as men of strong will and positive convictions will always surely do'; 'he did not forgive, not being of a forgiving race'. That prickly quality was especially wont to come to the fore when Mackey formulated and defended the Craft's approach to slavery.

Mackey's home city of Charleston, capital of the Scottish Rite, was built on a peninsula in the bay formed where three rivers ran into the Atlantic. It was a city of wide streets, elegant mansions and waterside promenades whose every verandah and wrought-iron gate was paid for with the profits of bondage. It was a long-established slave market and the place where, in the summer, South Carolina's slaveholding élite would come to escape the swampy heat of their rice plantations and hold sumptuous balls and garden parties.

Enslaved people are not allowed to become Freemasons. The principle was inherited from the Charges of medieval stone-masons, who regarded serfs or 'bondmen' as legally incapable of adhering to employment contracts. In 1723, at the dawn of modern Masonry, the same Landmark was worked into the *Constitutions*: 'The Persons admitted Members of a Lodge must be good and true Men, *free-born*, and of mature and discreet Age, *no Bondmen*, no Women, no immoral or scandalous Men, but of good Report.' In a place like Charleston in the 1840s and 1850s, where white society increasingly defined itself around the right to own other people, such a rule could never just be a technicality or a quaint hangover from a distant past. Freemasonry was, in its founding values, open to all of male humanity, irre-spective of religious creed, political affiliation or race. In the United States, Masons wrestled with the issue of whether black men, and black slaves in particular, counted as part of that humanity.

Dr Albert Mackey's authoritative verdict on the question was legalistic, yet severe. In *The Principles of Masonic Law*, published in 1856, he stipulated that 'The slave, or even the man born in servitude – though he may, subsequently, have obtained his liberty – is excluded by the ancient regulations from initiation.' The principle was clear: no slave or freed slave could ever be admitted to the Craft. The vast majority of the black population of the United States was thereby debarred. It hardly needs saying that such a ruling suited the worldview of Charleston's enslavers. Mackey's racism may have been less raw than Pike's, but it shaped his Freemasonry all the same.

On 12 April 1861, five years after Mackey published these words, Fort Sumter, a Federal stronghold on an island in Charleston harbour, was bombarded by Confederate shore batteries. After a day and a half, the fort's commander, a Freemason by the name of Major Robert Anderson, surrendered to his opponent, General Pierre G. T. Beauregard, also a Freemason. The bombardment marked the beginning of a Civil War that would cost more lives than all of America's other wars put together. It began as a struggle to settle the Republic's aboriginal tension, between the autonomy of the individual states, and the authority of the Federal government – a tension rendered explosive by the question of slavery. But the Civil War also brought to a head a division between the white Freemasonry of Mackey and Pike, and a uniquely American tradition of black Freemasonry whose origins we can trace back to the very beginnings of the United States.

They are ashamed of being on equality

The founding father of African-American Freemasonry was a freedman from Boston, a leather worker, caterer and peddler called Prince Hall; Prince Hall Freemasonry, as this tradition of the Craft is known, takes its name from him.

On 6 March 1775, in Boston, just weeks before the opening skirmishes of the American War of Independence, Prince Hall and fourteen other freedmen became America's first black Freemasons when they were initiated in Boston as members of a British army military Lodge. Some time later, Hall and his Brethren were granted a qualified permit to meet as a Lodge in their own right: thus was born African Lodge no. 1.

Quite why Hall and his Brethren chose to go to the British to begin their Masonic journey is not clear. Boston was a city under occupation, with its 17,000 inhabitants supporting the burden of 3,500 British troops. The suspicion is that the British were making overtures to the black population with a view to enlisting their support in the coming struggle for control of the American colonies. Be that as it may, Hall almost certainly fought on the American side in the war.

For the rest of Hall's life, he was heavily involved in the struggle against the injustices inflicted on African Americans. He and his fellow black Masons petitioned the Massachusetts assembly in January 1787 to demand the end of slavery 'in the Bowels of a free & Christian country'. Their wishes were fulfilled at the end of the Revolutionary War when slavery was abolished in Massachusetts. In 1788, three Boston freedmen were kidnapped and taken away on a slave ship to be sold in the West Indies. Indignant about their plight, Prince Hall petitioned successfully to prevent slave traders operating out of the harbour. The story of the kidnapped freedmen would have a happy ending too, because one of them happened to be a Freemason from Prince Hall's Lodge. When he was offered in sale to a slave merchant who was also a Mason, he made his affiliation known, and the merchant ensured that the three captives were returned to Boston. A great public celebration led by Prince Hall and his Brothers greeted them on their return.

If some of Prince Hall's campaigns ended in triumph, the same cannot be said of his struggle for recognition within the Craft. White Freemasons refused to authorise African Americans either to become members of existing Lodges, or to form separate Lodges of their own. Ironically, Prince Hall had to resort to writing to the old colonial power in the hope of achieving full Masonic legitimacy. In 1787, the Grand Lodge in London granted

African Lodge no. 1 its charter, and renamed it African Lodge no. 459 as a sign that it enjoyed parity with all of the other 458 under London's jurisdiction.

To the end of his life, Prince Hall would strive in vain for reconciliation with white Freemasonry in the United States. As one white clergyman observed in 1795 after he had tried and failed to use his good offices to persuade white Freemasons to give in: 'the truth is, they are *ashamed* of being on *equality* with blacks'. Prince Hall was recognised as black Boston's leading

Prince Hall (c.1735–1807), founder of the African-American Masonic trad-ition. There is no likeness of him from his lifetime. Conventional representa-tions such as this one are displayed in Prince Hall Lodges across the USA.

citizen, a figure of integrity and authority who had also helped establish Lodges in other cities. But by the time he died in 1807, an enduring racial cleavage at the heart of American Freemasonry had been set in place.

Freemasons have always been exhorted to stay away from politics. As Prince Hall himself put it, Masonry 'enjoins upon us to be peaceable subjects to the civil powers where we reside'. Yet by striving to better themselves as men, Prince Hall and the many black Freemasons who have followed in his footsteps cannot help but run up against the discrimination deeply engrained in those 'civil powers'. So Prince Hall Freemasonry was political from the outset. When the Civil War came, ninety years after the foundation of Prince Hall Masonry, we should not be surprised to find a strong Masonic presence among black abolitionists. One of them was perhaps the greatest African-American Mason of the nineteenth century, a Brother who explored the political potential of the Craft more profoundly than any other man: Martin Robison Delany.

Moses

Born a freedman in Virginia, and largely self-taught, Martin Delany developed as an anti-slavery agitator and journalist amid the soot and smoke of Pittsburgh. In 1839–40, at considerable personal risk, he went on a solo journey of discovery across the South, where he explored the range of black experience and culture, from brutalised plantation slaves to the *gens de couleur libres* of New Orleans.

Back in Pittsburgh, Delany trained as a surgeon (a 'cupper, leecher, and bleeder'). He also married and started a family that would eventually number seven children. Toussaint L'Ouverture, his first son, was born in 1846: the boy owed his name to the great leader of the Haitian slave revolution of 1791. Delany's other children would also carry the names of eminent men of colour: like Alexandre Dumas, the author of *The Three Musketeers* and the grandson of a Haitian slave; or St Cyprian, the third-century Christian martyr from North Africa.

Delany founded a black anti-slavery newspaper, the *Mystery*, and went on lecture tours to spread his message; his travelling and lecturing would not cease until old age finally slowed him. In 1847, Delany met Fredrick Douglass, who had escaped enslavement and written a bestselling autobiography that turned him into the international figurehead of the movement for abolition. The two founded a more ambitious newspaper, the *North Star*.

After two years of ceaseless work on this project, Delany returned to his medical books and instruments in Pittsburgh. In 1850, he was one of the first three black students ever admitted to Harvard to study medicine, but he was ejected a few months later following protests by his white peers. He went on to lecture on comparative anatomy, and still found time to invent a component for locomotive engines to help them climb steep inclines; racism ensured that his application for a patent was rejected.

Delany had been a passionate Prince Hall Freemason for a number of years by this time. In November 1846 he was a founder member of the St Cyprian Lodge no. 13 in Pittsburgh. His first newspaper owes its title to Masonic terminology: *Mystery*, like 'Craft', is a synonym for Freemasonry. Delany was also instrumental in spreading Freemasonry to Cincinnati in 1847, and in the same year, according to Masonic historians, the National Grand Lodge of Prince Hall Freemasonry appointed him as its District Deputy of the Western District (covering all territory west of Pennsylvania).

Throughout his life Delany, as the *Mystery*'s founding manifesto stated, aimed at 'the Moral Elevation of the Africo-American and African race, civilly, politically, religiously'. *Elevation* was to remain his lodestar, centring his view of the world on three powerful messages: take pride in being black, work hard, and assert your rights. In Prince Hall Freemasonry, Delany found a way to bring together a black élite who would pioneer elevation and act as role models. It also magnified what has been called his 'near-mystical sense of his potential as a black leader'.

The 1850s, an acutely bleak decade for African Americans, began with the Fugitive Slave Act, which undermined the rights of African Americans nationwide. Delany, like many other Prince Hall Brothers, was active in the Underground Railroad that sheltered escaped slaves and spirited them to Canada. In 1852 he published *The Condition, Elevation, Emigration, and Destiny of the Colored People of the United States* – a pioneering work of political analysis. It viewed blacks as a nation within a nation, whose only hope was to leave the United States *en masse*, and set up a new home elsewhere. At the same time, in his conclusion, Delany issued a call to black Americans to improve their lives in the United States by educating themselves and shaking off the habits of subservience.

In 1853, Delany crystallised his political vision of Freemasonry in a lecture. The man who stood before his Brethren of the St Cyprian's Lodge that day had made his very appearance a message. He was compact, bald-headed and indomitably broad-shouldered. Delany always proclaimed his pride in the fact that he was 100 per cent African: the lustrous dark colour of his skin defied the prejudice that, even among some African Americans, gave mixed-race 'mulattos' a higher status. The lecture he delivered, which became the first study of Prince Hall Freemasonry ever printed, was extraordinarily ambitious. By drawing on a mixture of Old Testament lore and recent history, Delany strove to wrest the whole Masonic tradition out of white hands.

Freemasonry began, he told his Brethren, after the Flood, when the sons of Noah spread across the world founding dynasties and cities. One of those sons, Ham, had black skin, and his descendants peopled Africa. Ethiopians and Egyptians developed a religion that was in crucial respects compatible with Christianity: they were the first to discover that man was made in the image of God; and they had a notion of the Trinity. (As Delany's audience

Martin Delany (1812–1885). Prince Hall Freemason,
anti-slavery agitator and father of black nationalism.

knew all too well, Masonic mythology and symbolism is chock-full of trinities, triangles and the number three.) It was to serve the ends of this religion, and make it useful to society, that ancient Ethiopians and Egyptians invented what would later become known as Freemasonry. There was no doubt, therefore, Delany asserted: 'Africans were the authors of this mysterious and beautiful Order'.

Moses was steeped in African Masonic learning too, Delany continued. For does it not say in the Acts of the Apostles 7:22 that 'Moses was learned in all the wisdom of the Egyptians'? Does not *Exodus* 2:15 tell us that Moses fled to Midian, an Ethiopian kingdom, and there married Zipporah, the daughter of an African ruler?

Solomon inherited the mysteries from Moses, and built a great temple in Jerusalem to give them concrete expression: its foundations lay in an unmistakably *African* knowledge. The implication was clear: Lodges like St Cyprian no. 13 were not just a legitimate expression of Masonic values and Landmarks; they were *more* legitimate than white Freemasons.

Reading the speech now, its subsequent influence among Prince Hall Freemasons seems puzzling. Yet in the nineteenth century, in America in general, and in Freemasonry in particular, Bible-based reasoning of this kind was taken in deadly earnest. Delany was using it to express the 'fraternal indignation' of his Brothers, who had endured repeated snubs whenever they had tried to get their Lodges recognised by the white Masonic authorities. The Masonic values of universal brotherhood surely disallowed any such discrimination. As Delany put it, 'All men, of every country, clime, color and condition, (when morally worthy,) are acceptable to the portals of Masonic jurisprudence.' White Masons wrapped their prejudice in the pages of Masonic lawbooks, citing the venerable principle according to which those who were unfree in body and mind were not worthy of becoming members. Delany's analysis of the story of Moses, a Freemason who was born into slavery and who lived as a slave for many years, was meant to crush this interpretation of the rules: 'Will it be denied that the man who appeared before Pharaoh, and was able to perform *mystically* all that the wisest among the wise men of that mysteriously wise nation were capable of doing, was a Mason?'

For a decade after his lecture to the St Cyprian Lodge in Pittsburgh, Delany threw himself into trying to realise his vision of a black exodus – with himself in the role of the black Moses. When hopes of a Central American homeland proved illusory, he explored other options, including Canada, where a thriving new community in Chatham, Ontario, had been created by formerly enslaved men and women. Delany moved there with his family in 1856.

While in Canada, in May 1858, Delany received a history-making visitor: John Brown, the abolitionist guerrilla leader who was in the process of gathering men and funds to mount a slave uprising in the South. Under the cover of a feigned Masonic Lodge meeting, Delany and Brown gathered a Constitutional Convention to approve a founding charter for the revolutionary republic of freed slaves he intended to set up in the mountains of Virginia. In October of the following year, Brown would carry his Provisional Constitution with him when his small band tried to precipitate an uprising by raiding the Federal arsenal at Harpers Ferry. The raid, as is well known, ended in failure – an episode that greatly exacerbated the tensions that would soon explode in the Civil War. John Brown was executed, becoming an abolitionist martyr whose memory was preserved by the famous Union Army marching hymn.

By the time John Brown met his end, Delany was on his travels again, this time seeking out sites for a settlement in what is now Nigeria. He ventured into the interior, exploring the potential for cotton cultivation and making treaties with local rulers. What he envisaged was a great transatlantic convergence of black experience and expertise when the Africans of America returned to their motherland. On his way back from Africa, Delany visited London and delivered a lecture to the Royal Geographical Society, before embarking on a nationwide speaking tour to abolitionist sympathisers. (And also to cotton barons, who were eyeing a new source of raw materials in West Africa.) Once back in America, using Canada as his base, Delany gave more lectures, extolling the virtues of African civilisation and dressing in clothes he had brought back with him from the Niger valley.

Delany's African plan, which had always struggled to win widespread support among black abolitionists, was buried in 1861 when eleven southern states seceded from the Union to form the Confederacy, thus precipitating the Civil War. A new task now faced him: to make sure that the war was fought, not just to reassert the authority of the Federal government, but to end slavery for ever, and realise the dream of equal citizenship for all.

You have not proved yourself soldiers

On or around 15 September 1863, a ragged group of Union infantrymen wandered among the marshes of Morris Island, at the entrance to Charleston harbour. They were carrying planks and tools. Around them, the palm trees had been shattered by explosions. Despite the sea breeze, the stench of rotting flesh still hovered with the flies in the warm air. Across Light-House Creek to the west, two Confederate batteries continued to lob shells. Out at the harbour mouth, Union ironclads methodically, vengefully, pulverised Fort Sumter.

The group of Union soldiers was led by First Sergeant William H.W. Gray, who was still recovering from his wounds. Under Gray's instruction, when they had found the spot of dry land away from prying eyes that they were looking for, the men erected an oblong wooden shelter, carefully orienting it on an east–west axis. From their knapsacks they then produced a Bible and a square and compasses. Sergeant Gray, Worshipful Master Gray, carried with him a Masonic Charter, obtained in Boston: it bestowed the authority to found a new military Lodge. The shelter was to be their temple: a place to hold the first Lodge meeting, initiate new members, remember fallen comrades and share precious moments of reflection upon the horror they had just endured.

There was a rare poignancy to the moment. For the Union soldiers in question were from the fabled 54th Regiment of the Massachusetts Volunteer Infantry. The unit's fame derived, to be sure, from the bravery it had recently demonstrated. But much, much more importantly, as the *New York Tribune* commented at the war's end, the 54th Massachusetts was 'the first colored regiment organized in the North, and was that one on whose good conduct depended for a long time the success of the experiment of arming black citizens in defence of the Republic'.

Only nine months before the foundation of Sergeant Gray's Prince Hall Lodge, on 1 January 1863, Abraham Lincoln had issued his Emancipation Proclamation, declaring 'that all persons held as slaves' within the rebellious states 'are, and henceforward shall be free'. Freedom would advance with every further step of the Union Army into Confederate territory. The Proclamation also stipulated that African Americans, both escaped slaves and freedmen, could be recruited into the Union forces. Since ancient Roman times, service in the army had brought with it an automatic right to citizenship – as every educated American was well aware.

Armed black men were the stuff of the enslavers' nightmares, so the Confederate government responded with fury to Lincoln's incitement to 'servile rebellion'. Captured black soldiers would be executed, Confederate President Jefferson Davis threatened. Even their white officers would suffer the same fate.

Prince Hall Freemasons immediately grasped the urgency of forming black units. In Massachusetts, the recruitment drive for the pioneer volunteer regiment, the 54th, was led by the Grand Master of Prince Hall Freemasonry, the former slave Lewis Hayden, who would later grant Sergeant Gray's military Lodge its charter. Martin Delany, the would-be Moses of abolitionism, enthusiastically embraced the task of recruiting men by acting as agent for the Federal government across several other states. His oldest son Toussaint L'Ouverture, at just seventeen, volunteered for the 54th, as did two of Frederick Douglass's sons.

Within a few short weeks of enlisting, the men of the 54th Massachusetts were singing 'John Brown's Body' as their ship pulled out of Boston. Soon they found themselves besieging one of the most potent symbols of the injustice they were fighting: Charleston – the place where the Civil War had begun. Sergeant Gray and a few of his Brethren would have been aware that Charleston was important for another reason too: it was the capital of Scottish Rite Freemasonry, from which Albert Mackey, Secretary General of the Supreme Council, and Albert Pike, Sovereign Grand Commander of the Supreme Council, sought to exclude men of African origin. For the Union army, the city was a strategic port in a conflict fought almost as much by sea blockade as it was by land campaign. The battery that guarded traffic in and out of Charleston harbour was shielded by Fort Wagner, a vast, stockaded sandcastle stretching across Morris Island. The fort had to be taken, and the men of the 54th Massachusetts were to lead the assault.

It was during the shockingly bloody assault on Fort Wagner, just a stone's throw from where Sergeant Gray would erect his humble Prince Hall temple, that the 54th Massachusetts destroyed the racist myth that negroes were unfit for combat. Only at Fort Wagner did the American Civil War truly become a fight to end slavery.

On 18 July 1863, the action began as the sun sank behind the dunes. In a broad column, with the troops on the right flank splashing through the breakers, the 54th advanced along the shore for three-quarters of a mile. It was only when the beach narrowed into a defile just short of the fort that, as one survivor recounted, 'Fort Wagner became a mound of fire, from which poured a stream of shot and shell . . . A sheet of flame, followed by a running fire like electric sparks, swept along the parapet.'

Despite horrific casualties, the 54th upped its pace, swerving left towards where the defences were lower. Battle was joined with bayonet, rifle butt, sword and hand-spike. Chronophotographic muzzle flashes captured the grimaces on black and white faces. The 54th's commanding officer, Colonel Robert Gould Shaw, was the Harvard-educated son of one of Boston's leading abolitionist families. He was shot through the heart as he urged his men on.

Forced back down the rampart by overwhelming numbers, the 54th then held their ground, despite the grenades and gunfire raining down on them. But their hope of supporting a further wave of attack proved forlorn. Retreat was the only option – a retreat more terrible even than the attack: a blind stumble through withering fire and over the writhing bodies of fallen comrades.

As morning broke, the count began. Over a third of the six

hundred men who charged Fort Wagner had been killed or wounded. Another sixty had fallen into enemy hands. The Confederates refused to include even the wounded black soldiers in a prisoner exchange. The fate of many of them would remain unknown until the war was over. (In the end, threats of retaliation from the Federal government saved the lives of those whom a harsh imprisonment did not kill.)

The suffering did not finish with the failed assault on Fort Wagner. A siege ensued, lasting fifty-eight days. The soldiers of the 54th and the other African-American units present (most of them comprising freed slaves) were considered more suited to heavy manual labour than white troops, so it was they who were picked to dig the gun emplacements that crept closer and closer to Fort Wagner. The heat and hard labour reduced the men to rags and sinew, tormented by sand fleas. Sniper fire and bombardment were a constant threat. To hamper the siege works, the Confederates had laid 'torpedoes' – buried mines. By the time the Union forces got to within 200 yards of the Fort, so many soldiers were dying that, for fear of demoralising the survivors, senior officers forbade the playing of funeral music during burials.

Only in the early hours of 7 September 1863 did the Confederates finally abandon the charnel house that Fort Wagner had become. The siege was over.

It was during the relative lull that followed that Sergeant Grey and the other Prince Hall Masons founded their military Lodge amid the marshes. None of them can have harboured any illusions that the equality they yearned for, both within and beyond Freemasonry, had come very much nearer. As if to reinforce that point, a running dispute about their pay resurfaced a few days later. Already they had been told several times that they would only get monthly pay of $10 rather than the $13 given to white soldiers. Unanimously, the 54th had refused to accept the money. When the offer was made again after Fort Wagner fell, the troops remained obstinate. Then the brigade commander intervened to find a solution. Colonel James Montgomery was an abolitionist who had taken a leading role in the vicious confrontations between pro- and anti-slavery bands in Kansas in the run-up to the Civil War. A tall, stooping man, he addressed the troops in his usual gentle voice:

> You must remember you have not proved yourselves soldiers
> . . . Nor should you expect to be placed on the same footing
> with white men. Anyone listening to your shouting and
> singing can see how grotesquely ignorant you are. I am your
> friend and the friend of the negro. I was the first person in
> the country to employ nigger soldiers in the United States
> Army . . . In refusing to take the pay offered to you, and
> what you are only legally entitled to, you are guilty of
> insubordination and mutiny, and can be tried and shot by
> court-martial.

An eye-witness to the speech commented that 'the colonel seemed to be unaware that his remarks were insulting, and most of the men he addressed born free'. The men of the 54th continued to refuse the money, and would do so for another year until the injustice of discriminatory pay grades was rectified by law.

The 54th's assault on Fort Wagner quickly coalesced from newspaper report into folklore; it has been fixed in the collective consciousness ever since. In 1989, the story of the assault became *Glory*, a workmanlike movie starring Matthew Broderick, Denzel Washington and Morgan Freeman that won several Academy Awards. The legend of the 54th drew on one of the nineteenth century's most emotive patriotic myths: it was the tale of manhood made in war, of blood sacrifice. As the white North narrated it, the story centred on the martyrdom of the regiment's commander, Colonel Robert Gould Shaw. The Confederates had sought to insult the memory of this 'blue-eyed child of fortune' by burying him in a pit with his black soldiers – a gesture of racist contempt that only served to gild his myth with pathos. The rank-and-file of the 54th remained anonymous by comparison, and prey to an insidious assumption. Much of the sentimentality surrounding the assault on Fort Wagner depended on the notion that African Americans had to *earn* their freedom; that they had to prove themselves *worthy* of citizenship by maintaining the impossible standards of selflessness demonstrated by the fallen of the 54th. Only when the war was over would that assumption work its pernicious effects.

Some sixteen months after Fort Wagner fell, on 18 February 1865, Charleston had become shattered houses, shell-craters, empty wharves and streets strewn with the chattels of terrified white families. The last order executed by the retreating Confederate troops had been to torch any significant assets. Now fire was beginning to spread. Almost all the remaining inhabitants were African Americans, who waited away from the danger in confident expectation of a new age.

Fittingly, the first Union soldiers to land in Charleston were a detachment of the 54th Massachusetts. Fittingly too, one of the first people to greet them was Dr Albert Mackey, Secretary General of the Supreme Council of the Ancient and Accepted Scottish Rite for the Southern Jurisdiction of the United States. He pleaded with the Union soldiers to douse the flames. Thus it was that men from the first regiment of black citizens saved for posterity what was left of a city that was a monument to slavery.

Martin Delany would soon make his way to Charleston too. Just days before, he had gone to Washington to meet President Lincoln and pitch the idea of an expedition deep into the heart of southern territory to gather a black guerrilla army. He had already envisaged just such a plan in his 1859 novel *Blake; Or the Huts of America*: in it, a hero not unlike Delany travelled through the South setting up a secret network, not unlike Prince Hall Masonry, that would prepare the ground for a slave insurrection. At the very moment he and Lincoln were talking, news of Charleston's fall arrived. Delany was quickly granted the rank of major – the highest achieved by any African American during the Civil War – and ordered to recruit more black soldiers to finish off the war. The appointment turned him into an icon: the *Anglo-African* newspaper sold reproduction portraits of him in uniform. He travelled south as the bearer of a patriotic halo.

Martin Delany subsequently recalled his first impressions upon reaching Charleston:

> I entered the city, which, from earliest childhood and through life, I had learned to contemplate with feelings of the utmost abhorrence – a place of the most insufferable assumption and cruelty to the blacks; where the sound of the lash at the whipping-post, and the hammer of the auctioneer, were coordinate sounds in thrilling harmony; that place which had ever been closed against liberty by an arrogantly assumptuous despotism [. . .] into which, but a few days before, had proudly entered in triumph the gallant [General] Schimmelfennig, leading with wild shouts the Massachusetts Fifty-fourth Regiment, composed of some of the best blood and finest youths of the colored citizens of the Union. For a moment I paused – then, impelled by the impulse of my mission, I found myself dashing on in unmeasured strides through the city, as if under a forced march to attack the already crushed and fallen enemy.

A season of triumph had begun for Delany. Thousands of newly freed men and women crowded to hear the celebrity Major speak.

By the spring, the troops that Delany had recruited were no longer needed, because the Confederacy had surrendered. He played an important role in establishing calm in the city after President Lincoln's assassination on 14 April. By now, the 54th Massachusetts was stationed in the Citadel, Charleston's gleaming, stuccoed military college where, for only the second time, the troops were paid their $13.

Just across from the Citadel, in a three-storey civilian house, Worshipful Master Sergeant William Gray brought together his Prince Hall military Lodge once more. There were an estimated twenty-five or thirty Prince Hall Freemasons, among whom non-commissioned officers were prominent. These men had been the backbone of the regiment, and their authority among the troops was moral as well as military – they were an emergent black middle class in uniform. We can put a face to one of them: Quartermaster-Sergeant Peter Vogelsang, age forty-nine, who was a community leader from New York, and the oldest man in the 54th. Vogelsang's organisational efficiency had struck his officers from the outset. He was courageous too: he survived being shot through the lungs two days before the assault on Fort Wagner in July 1863. Despite opposition to the promotion of black soldiers within the military hierarchy and from white field officers, Vogelsang would become First Lieutenant and Regimental-Quartermaster.

In Charleston, Martin Delany was reunited with those he knew in the regiment, including his son Toussaint L'Ouverture. Wounded in a skirmish, Toussaint had missed the carnage at Fort Wagner, but was later wounded a second time. Along with a non-commissioned officer from the 54th, he now became his father's aide. In subsequent years, he would suffer from what was probably shell-shock.

Delany also met up with the friend he called 'brave Vogelsang'. Weeks after his promotion to First Lieutenant, his duties fulfilled, Vogelsang returned to civilian life, and to his career as a clerk in the Customs house in lower Manhattan. But his military Lodge, meanwhile, had seeded the future of black Freemasonry in Charleston. Before 1865 was out it had evolved into a permanent Lodge, authorised in Massachusetts. In South Carolina, as across the former Confederacy, Prince Hall Freemasonry made new converts, many of them inspired by the example of black citizens like Vogelsang from the North. The hope was that, just as the old Lodges of the North had helped forge the black élite who had put paid to slavery, so the new Lodges of the South could create a new élite – living models of virtuous black citizenship. Masonry's cosmopolitanism could also help heal the divisions between black and white.

Later that year, Martin Delany joined the Freedmen's Bureau, a Federal agency set up by Abraham Lincoln to help former slaves. His hopes were clear, and they were those of three million newly liberated African Americans: full citizenship rights, including impartial justice, education, economic opportunity, the vote and political power. The omens seemed positive for what was an unprecedented experiment in forging democracy anew. America's rising economic fortunes funded a vast programme of railway construction that was intended, in part, to buy white support for the new regime in the South. The United States army stood ready to back up the claims of freed slaves. Reconstruction, as it was known, was underway. Delany, who set up a medical practice in Charleston to support himself, intended to play his part.

The leprosy of negro association

When the Civil War broke out Albert Pike, the white Scottish Rite's Sovereign Grand Commander in the South, was sent on a diplomatic mission into Indian Territory to secure the support of the Civilized Tribes for the Confederacy. His task was made considerably easier both by the bonds of Freemasonry he shared with many Indian chiefs, and by the fact that most of those chiefs owned black slaves. Pike was then entrusted with recruiting Native-American troops and leading them into battle against the forces of the Union at Pea Ridge, in March 1862. The engagement was a disaster. Not only did it end in defeat for the Confederacy, but it was discovered afterwards that several Union soldiers had been scalped – a practice regarded as barbaric. There followed a furious row between Pike and his superiors, which led eventually to his resignation. He returned to Arkansas to work in an isolated log cabin for the rest of the war on developing the Scottish Rite.

Pike's *Morals and Dogma* is a series of lectures elucidating the thinking behind each Degree ritual. Much of it, by Pike's own admission, is a cut-and-paste from myriad sacred writings and philosophical texts. Through it all runs Pike's buoyant conviction that the substance of all belief systems can be reduced to common principles. Whether it was classical rhetoric or Jewish mysticism, Eastern religions or medieval literature, alchemy or heraldry, it all boiled down to the same home truths. Pike asserted grand equivalences between anything and everything encountered during years of voracious and eclectic study. The result was highly influential for Freemasons, and unreadable for everyone else:

The important manifestations of Occultism coincide with the period of the fall of the Templars; since Jean de Meung or Chopinel, contemporary of the old age of Dante, flourished during the best years of his life at the Court of Philippe le Bel. The *Roman de la Rose* is the Epic of old France. It is a profound book, under the form of levity, a revelation as learned as that of Apuleius, of the Mysteries of Occultism. The Rose of Flamel, that of Jean de Meung, and that of Dante, grew on the same stem. Swedenborg's system was nothing else than the Kabalah, minus the principle of the Hierarchy. It is the Temple, without the keystone and the foundation.

In his log cabin, Pike filled an anaesthetising 861 pages in this way. The only things of any real clarity in his rewriting of the Scottish Rite are the innumerable truisms: 'Whatever is worth doing at all in this world, is worth doing *well*'; 'To be true, just, and upright is the basis of all virtue.'

Pike probably owes his enormous and lasting success to his sense of theatre rather than his ideas. The Thirtieth Degree of the Scottish Rite provides a vivid example. It confers the title of

Knight Kadosh – a word that supposedly comes from the Hebrew for 'holy'.

The Knight Kadosh Degree takes place through a sequence of four chambers or 'apartments', each hung with cloth of a different hue: black, white, light blue and crimson. The climactic crimson apartment also has contrasting white columns and its eastern wall is hung in black velvet embroidered with silver. A massive collection of incongruous props is deployed in these colourful spaces: a tomb, an altar and a mausoleum; wreaths and crowns; a ladder and a staircase; curtains, banners and ribbons; urns, flames and perfume; daggers; various kinds of cross; a shepherd's crook and a Roman cap of liberty; a decanter and a loaf of bread; several skulls. The costumes are no less arresting: two 'heralds-at-arms' wear full medieval armour, 'gauntleted, and with sword, battle-axe, casque and visor', Pike specifies. The initiate also gets to wear a knee-length white tunic with wide sleeves, a black patent-leather belt, a long cape made of scarlet-lined black velvet, a broad-brimmed hat with a red ostrich-feather plume, yellow morocco boots decorated with gold lace and white tassels, and gold spurs. 'No Apron is worn', Pike concludes, disappointingly.

Despite his opposition to admitting slaves and former slaves into Freemasonry, Dr Albert Mackey remained in Charleston for the duration of the conflict as a supporter of the Union: that is why he was there in February 1865 to welcome the detachment of the 54th Massachusetts and beseech them to save the city from burning. He was rewarded for his loyalty with a plum post as Collector of the Port – his national prominence within Freemasonry seems to have helped him get the job. Mackey, a wily politician, took an active role in Reconstruction as a 'scalawag' – the name given to white southern supporters of the anti-slavery Republican Party by their Democrat enemies. In 1868, Dr Mackey was picked

Albert Pike in one of his extravagant
Scottish Rite costumes.

to be president of the South Carolina Constitutional Convention, which was created to radically revise state laws and thereby earn readmittance to the Union. Seventy-three of the Convention's 124 delegates were black. The Democrat press predictably loathed what they dismissed as a 'negro assembly', and called Mackey a money-grubbing fraud.

During Reconstruction, while he was still working on the Scottish Rite, Dr Mackey's Masonic protégé Albert Pike stuck to the beliefs that had led him into the Confederate fold during the Civil War. Now settled in Memphis, Tennessee, following the break-up of his marriage, he resumed his journalism. During the 1868 presidential election, from the pages of the newspaper he owned, he proclaimed, 'We mean that the white race, and that race alone, shall govern this country. It is the only one that is fit to govern, and it is the only one that shall.'

The years following the end of the Civil War in the South saw a crescendo of torture, mutilation, flogging, rape and murder perpetrated by gangs of white marauders against negroes and scalawags. The most notorious of these bands was the Ku Klux Klan, founded by former Confederate soldiers in Pulaski, Tennessee, in late 1865 or 1866. Their carnivalesque costumes and rites, and the bizarre titles adopted by their leaders (Grand Cyclops, Goblin, Grand Wizard, etc.), made it clear that they were a grotesque take on the many quasi-Masonic fraternal associations still spreading across the States. Indeed, they seem originally to have been founded to stage nasty pranks like pretending to be the ghosts of Confederate soldiers so as to terrify black people. As the conflict over Reconstruction became more brutal, so did the KKK. By 1868, it was a loose network of bands prosecuting a campaign of violence and intimidation across many southern states. There was a national scandal.

There is a longstanding rumour that Albert Pike was a commander of the KKK. Although there is no evidence to support this theory, there seems no doubt that he was an ideological fellow-traveller. In April 1868, he wrote a delicately worded editorial on the Klan for his own paper, the *Memphis Daily Appeal*. After lambasting the northern press for hugely exaggerating the Klan problem, he explained that the KKK had been founded originally for 'fun and frolic', and to scare 'superstitious negroes'. It was 'too demonstrative and courted notoriety too much to have been much in earnest'. Thus, 'It is quite certain that it will never come to much on its original plan. It must become quite another thing to be efficient.' The disingenuous thing about this phrase is that, as was well known, the Ku-Kluxes had *already* come a long way from their 'original plan', and that political terror rather than 'fun and frolic' were their aims. So what did Pike mean by evoking the idea of a more 'efficient' version of the KKK?

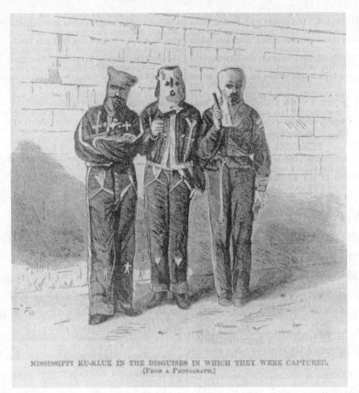

MISSISSIPPI KU-KLUX IN THE DISGUISES IN WHICH THEY WERE CAPTURED.
[FROM A PHOTOGRAPH.]

Pike began his response to the question he had begged by decrying the ever more intolerable 'oppressions' and 'indignities' inflicted on the South by the Freedmen's Bureau and 'negro scoundrels'. 'With negroes for witnesses and jurors, the administration of justice becomes a blasphemous mockery.' For that reason,

> The disenfranchised people of the South, robbed of all the guarantees of the Constitution . . . can find no protection for property, liberty of life, except in secret association. Not in such association to commit follies and outrages; but for mutual, peaceful, lawful self-defence. If it were in our power . . . we would unite every white man in the South, who is opposed to negro suffrage, into one great Order of Southern Brotherhood, with an organization complete, active, vigorous, in which a few should activate the concentrated

will of all, and whose very existence should be concealed from all but its members.

Pike's day-dream was of a secret society that would conduct an élite conspiracy to take the law into its own hands in order to defend white interests and deprive freed slaves of the vote. Perhaps the Ku Klux Klan was not the 'efficient' supremacist brotherhood that Pike envisaged. But the thugs of the Klan could have been forgiven for taking his article as an endorsement.

After the Civil War, Prince Hall Masonry renewed its earnest attempts to gain recognition from the white Masonic establishment. In response, Pike was unbending in his contempt for the very idea that black and white men could join in Masonic fellowship. In September 1875, he wrote to a like-minded Scottish Rite Brother to set out his position. He had no time for any of the legal and historical convolutions invoked by the likes of Dr Albert Mackey in order to justify a refusal to recognise black Freemasonry. Pike believed that a 'Prince Hall Lodge was as regular a Lodge as any created by competent authority, and had a perfect right to establish other Lodges.' Instead, he urged that white Masons act as their prejudices dictated: 'I took my obligations to white men, not to negroes. When I have to accept negroes as *brothers* or leave Masonry, I shall leave it. I am interested to keep the Ancient and Accepted [Scottish] Rite uncontaminated, in *our* country at least, by the leprosy of negro association.'

Meanwhile, Dr Albert Mackey's own racism was also coming to the fore. His job as Collector of the Port gave him, his relatives and his friends a very powerful patronage engine. He proceeded to appoint only white employees, including former Confederate soldiers and others who had refused to take an oath of loyalty to the Republic. He was ousted from the position by an alliance that included black politicians who resented his prejudiced recruitment preferences.

Whenever the issue of black Masonry resurfaced, Mackey stuck doggedly to the letter of Masonic law as he perceived it. Late in 1875, the Grand Lodge of Ohio moved to recognise Prince Hall Masonry. In response, over six months in the pages of *The Voice of Masonry*, Mackey tried to referee a confusing and at times hysterical debate among white Brothers. One contributor complained that admitting negroes to Lodges was tantamount to admitting women. One Brother mentioned that Prince Hall Masons, when rebuffed in the United States, had been awarded recognition by many Grand Lodges in Europe. Mackey eventually lost patience, and wrote an exasperated editorial entitled, 'The Color Question'. He did not have any objection *in principle* to initiating negroes into the Craft. After all, 'Masonry recognizes no distinction of race or color in the qualifications of a candidate'. It was just that Prince Hall Masonry was illegitimate in two ways. First, historically, the original Prince Hall Lodge had not been properly constituted. Second, in terms of Masonic values, the idea of an exclusively negro Masonry ran counter to the Craft's founding, universalist principles. 'Here then, I rest my case, and bid adieu to the subject.'

Mackey's contorted logic was a thin mask for his hatred. In effect, he was saying that Prince Hall Masons could not be proper Craftsmen because, on the one hand, they had always been excluded from American Lodges due to white Brothers' racial intolerance. On the other hand, they could not form their *own* Lodges because that would contravene Masonic rules on racial tolerance. They were damned both ways.

Mackey's erudite references to Masonic legal precedents were not meant to solve the 'Color Question'. Instead, they were meant to save the white Craft, and in particular his beloved Scottish Rite, from destroying itself over race. Mackey must have been aware that Albert Pike's views were shared by very many Masons across the South – and indeed in the rest of the country. Some Grand Lodges maintained an explicit ban on admitting black people. Mackey had identified a way to use Masonic law and tradition to defuse the issue among his white

Brethren, and he was going to stick to it come what may. He, and thousands of less overtly racist white Masons, convinced themselves that, because their fraternity was open in principle to everyone, whatever their race, they could blithely ignore the fact that no sane black man would dare cross the threshold because it was Brothers with views like Albert Pike's who created the climate inside.

Returned with our disapproval

In 1874, Martin Delany made his first bid for elected political office. At the same time, he tried to re-join Prince Hall Freemasonry. Somewhere, he had allowed his membership of St Cyprian's Lodge in Pittsburgh to lapse. Amid his restless travelling and activism, he probably never received the letters reminding him to pay his dues. In any case, Freemasonry for its own sake had never been a mission in life for Delany: his calling was the cause of liberation.

The episode tells us much about the sad end to Delany's career as a political organiser, about the collapse of Reconstruction, and about the more self-serving ends to which the ties of Masonic Brotherhood can be put.

Reconstruction, it turned out, leaned on two props: easy money; and the kind of white, northern anti-slavery sentimentality that had echoed around the Union after the assault on Fort Wagner by the 54th Massachusetts. By the time Delany stood for election, those props had been fatally weakened.

In 1873, the railway boom collapsed into a profound financial and economic crisis that quickly drained Reconstruction of the resources it needed to buy support.

The optimism of 1865 was the hope hallowed by the volunteers of the 54th Massachusetts, and by the sacrifice of nearly two hundred thousand black soldiers during the Civil War. But among white Northerners, the sentimental recollection of the men who had died so nobly at Fort Wagner was never going to survive the moment when the former slaves of the South began to operate within the grimier mechanisms of American democracy: patronage and factionalism; corruption and double-dealing; cheap oratory and squalid compromise. Much of northern public opinion was always doubtful about the wisdom of giving former slaves democratic rights. In the peak years of Reconstruction, Ku Klux Klan raids and other white supremacist outrages had sustained the memories of the war and the willingness of northern public opinion to accept that troops were needed in the South to protect African Americans. But support for army backing for black rights was gradually eroded by a slow feed of propaganda portraying black politicians, officials and voters as ignorant and corrupt. South Carolina, which had the highest percentage of African-American citizens of any state, was held up as a lesson in the futility of entrusting power to 'savages'. One widely read account from 1873 proclaimed South Carolina to be 'a mass of black barbarism . . . the most ignorant democracy that mankind ever saw'.

When Delany, who had always hankered after political office, stood for election as Lieutenant (i.e. deputy) Governor of South Carolina in 1874, he turned a Brother into a political enemy. The incumbent Lieutenant Governor, Richard H. Gleaves, had founded St Cyprian's Lodge no. 13 in Pittsburgh with Delany nearly three decades earlier. He was now Grand Master of the very South Carolina Grand Lodge that had sprouted from the military Lodge of the 54th Massachusetts. Indeed, Gleaves was the most influential Prince Hall Freemason in the country, elected as leader of the National Grand Lodge, a body trying to assert its authority over the black Craft nationwide, at the crucial moment when new Prince Hall Lodges were being set up across the former slave states. Gleaves had travelled widely in the South after the Civil War, inaugurating Lodges as he went. But as it spread among the newly emancipated and enfranchised in this way, the African-American Masonic organisation that had been so crucial to the abolitionist struggle became a tool of political networking and patronage. Gleaves was a divisive figure in Prince Hall Masonry, and the National Grand Lodge collapsed because his leadership was resented for being dictatorial. He was accused of using the Prince Hall movement in the South to create a personal political following – and even of pocketing the subscriptions from the many new Lodges he founded. Gleaves retorted with the accusation that his critics within Prince Hall Masonry were doing the Democrats' job for them, by making out all black Republican politicians to be corrupt. It made for a depressingly unfraternal spectacle.

Delany was desperate to challenge his rival's influence, and wrote to the Prince Hall Grand Lodge of Pennsylvania asking to have his membership renewed. He was met with a blunt refusal: the Grand Lodge 'moved that the appeal of M.R. Delany be returned to him with our disapproval'. Worse still, his former Brothers in Pittsburgh reported that he had borrowed $50 from them and not paid it back. The report was forwarded to Gleaves himself with a request that it be read out in the Grand Lodge of South Carolina.

Delany was rebuffed and humiliated. Whatever remained of his Masonic credibility was obliterated. Richard H. Gleaves, by contrast, had a lot of Masonic friends to call on, and won the election easily. (In July 1877, Gleaves would flee South Carolina shortly before being indicted for a $4,000 expenses fraud; the subsequent trial put an end to his political career.)

Perhaps thwarted ambition clouded Delany's judgement. Or perhaps he sensed that the end of Reconstruction was at hand and believed that some kind of accommodation with entrenched white power was African Americans' only hope. Whatever the reason, Delany was moving away from the Republicans, the party of Lincoln and Reconstruction, and closer and closer to the Democrats, the party of the Confederacy. This last political gamble turned out to be calamitous. In 1876 he publicly supported the notorious Democratic candidate for governor, a Confederate war hero from a slave-owning planter family, Wade Hampton III.

Hampton gave weasel pledges about maintaining black rights if he were elected – pledges that Delany loudly proclaimed he believed. But during the campaign, Hampton was accompanied everywhere by paramilitaries. Across the state, these squadrons of so-called Red Shirts cocked their pistols demonstratively at Republican meetings and sowed terror among black voters in the countryside.

African-American Republicans were understandably infuriated by Delany's betrayal. During one rally, he was shot at. Elsewhere, he was shouted down as a 'damned nigger Democrat'.

Hampton's controversial election victory marked the end of Reconstruction. The Federal government in Washington wanted to move on, and democracy in the former Confederate states was inexorably converted into a white regime based on gerrymandering, ballot-stuffing and the noose.

His dreams shattered, and his political energies exhausted, Delany once more embraced the goal of a return to Africa. But his expedition ended in a commercial and political fiasco. He died in obscurity.

Albert Mackey's arguments against Prince Hall Freemasonry became established policy among white Freemasons, and remained so thereafter. In obeisance to the Masonic belief in the brotherhood of all men, mainstream Freemasonry in the United States would continue to be exclusively white.

Albert Pike spent the rest of his life in quiet but energetic devotion to the Scottish Rite. In 1869, growing impatient with Mackey's administrative inefficiency, he moved the Southern Jurisdiction of the Scottish Rite's headquarters from Charleston to Washington DC. In 1876, having fallen into poverty, he moved into the Supreme Council's building at 602 D Street NW, allowing him to spend every waking hour on Scottish Rite business. But the global currents of Masonic history were not about to leave Pike to enjoy his sunset years in peace. Not long before he died in 1891, back in France where the Scottish Rite began, he would achieve notoriety as Satan's Masonic emissary on earth.

9

Rome–Paris: **The Devil in the Nineteenth Century**

Pandemonium

It was already oppressively humid in the north transept of St Peter's when, on the morning of 18 July 1870, a frail, plump and dignified Pope settled into his throne. Looking back at Pius IX from specially erected tiers of seats were some six hundred senior churchmen; they had been summoned from across the Catholic world to spend months discussing the highest doctrines of the Church. But the business of the day was no longer theological debate, because all misgivings had already been dismissed. Once the tones of the *Veni Creator* had faded, the shrill voice of the Secretary of the Council read out the dogma to be approved. The Holy Father 'is possessed of that infallibility with which the Divine Redeemer willed that his Church should be endowed'. The Pope, when speaking officially on matters of faith and morality, was beyond error and beyond challenge.

One by one, as their names were read out, the cardinals and bishops began to express assent. But before more than a handful had uttered their '*Placet*', the air inside St Peter's went dark and a shattering thunderclap detonated overhead. Soon prolonged flashes of lightning were playing around the cupola as rain descended in Old Testament torrents. Protestant correspondents reporting from Rome could not resist a smirk at the weather's

Pope Pius IX proclaims the doctrine of Papal Infallibility in 1870.
From the *London Illustrated News*.

commentary on the declaration of Papal Infallibility: 'The storm, to many a superstitious mind, might have conveyed the idea that it was the expression of divine wrath.'

The Papacy needed no lessons in the signs of divine wrath. For had not the Lord's displeasure been all too manifest in human affairs ever since the French Revolution of 1789 unleashed a tide of corrosive modern ideas? Were not rationalism, constitutional government, civil liberties, democracy and press freedom themselves signs that humanity deserved punishment? Suffering for their flock, the Popes in person felt the full force of the upheaval. In 1798, the Vatican was trashed by French soldiers, and Pius VI carried off into captivity. Ten years later, Pius VII endured six years of confinement at Napoleon's pleasure. In 1848, two years after his election, Pius IX himself had been forced to flee Rome after revolutionaries cut his Prime Minister's throat in front of the Papal palace. There was no respite even after Pius was restored to his throne in April 1850. In 1859, the newly formed Kingdom of Italy stripped away much of the territory that the Pope-Kings had ruled for a thousand years, leaving only the region around Rome.

The Holy See's response was to brand the Kingdom of Italy a godless state that had 'despoiled' the Church; the faithful were instructed to boycott elections. Pius then turned the calendar back to the Middle Ages. In 1864, the *Syllabus of Errors* listed eighty offences against God's revealed truth: they included religious tolerance, the separation of Church and state and, at number eighty, the scandalous notion that the Pope should 'come to terms with progress, liberalism and modern civilization'.

The Declaration of Infallibility in July 1870 was thus part of an ongoing regressive trend. Yet there was more than a hint of desperation about the act, as if Pius IX were asserting his absolute control of the spiritual sphere just as the world was accelerating far beyond his comprehension. 'Modern civilization' had still more outrages in store.

Three days before the Declaration of Infallibility, France, the foremost Catholic power in continental Europe, had confidently declared war on Prussia. A chain of catastrophes ensued. France was defeated in battle and invaded. The small French garrison in Rome, the only thing preventing what was left of the Pope's lands from being absorbed into the Kingdom of Italy, was summoned home. On 20 September 1870, less than two months after Pius declared himself infallible, Italian troops blasted through the walls of Rome. The Eternal City was now the capital of Italy. Henceforth the Holy Father would have no earthly kingdom but the Vatican.

On the verge of defeat to Prussia, France became a Republic. Paris rose up in revolt against an enfeebled French government. In the spring of 1871, a socialist Commune was declared in the city, and a carnival of sacrilege began. Priests and nuns were harassed and imprisoned. Churches were desecrated, and religious emblems stripped from public buildings. In May, as the Commune neared defeat, the Archbishop of Paris was executed, and Notre-Dame cathedral set ablaze.

There was a remorseless rise in anti-clericalism in Europe in the following twenty years. Governments introduced measures such as secular education, civil marriage, divorce and non-religious funerals. Influenced by Charles Darwin, new trends in science and philosophy sought to cut God out of the physical and social universe. As peasants were sucked into the cities and factories, they lost touch with their immemorial faith. Dangerous new ideologies, like socialism and anarchism, flooded into the spiritual void. A rash of patriotic monuments – statues of national martyrs, imposing ministries, giant secular altars – challenged the Church's traditional dominance of Europe's cityscapes. As the 1880s neared their end, necromancy, spiritualism and black magic became increasingly fashionable in literary circles.

Yet the Papacy was far from defenceless in the face of this onslaught. In France, many believers still thought of their country as 'the eldest daughter of the Church', and saw an alliance of throne and altar as the only secure basis for political authority. Moreover, secularisation generated an opposing religious revival: this was a time of pilgrimages and prophecies, revelations and relics. There was a re-energised cult of the Virgin Mary. In 1858, Bernadette Soubirous, a shepherdess from the French Pyrenees, claimed to see visions of the Virgin. Bernadette's grotto at Lourdes soon became a theatre of miracles. A cult developed around Pius IX too. New media – cheap popular prints, newspapers and books – made him an icon for the faithful.

In this culture war between religion and secularism in Catholic Europe, talk of conspiracies and secret agendas commanded more attention than ever. For the Jesuits, the Freemasons were Catholic enemy number one. In 1850, Pius IX had given the Society of Jesus a vanguard role by putting them in charge of *Civiltà Cattolica* (*Catholic Civilisation*), a new magazine designed to spread the Holy See's message to as big a readership as possible. *Civiltà Cattolica* gave the Craft obsessive coverage over the next four decades, recycling and updating the fears of Masonic conspiracy first expressed by Abbé Augustin de Barruel in 1797.

Civiltà Cattolica launched with a serialised trilogy of anti-Masonic novels by Father Antonio Bresciani: *The Jew of Verona*, *The Roman Republic* and *Lionello* all became bestsellers. They dramatised how Freemasonry and related sects were working in secret to bring about anarchy, Christianity's destruction and Satan's triumph. 'The soul of all the unexpected and rapid changes in European states is the pandemonium of the secret societies.' It was this 'pandemonium' that made the pages of Bresciani's novels turn: a lurid, almost hallucinatory cavalcade of Masonic scheming, moral corruption, sexual deviancy and political turmoil. Despite Freemasonry's notorious sniffiness about women, Bresciani's novels prominently feature malevolent Sisters of the godless sect. None is more malevolent than the cross-dressing communist assassin Babette d'Interlaken, whose many crimes include worshipping Satan and smoking heavily. Divine justice finally catches up with her in a prison hospital run by nuns, whose piety provokes such a fury of self-loathing and demonic possession in Babette that she haemorrhages and drowns in her own blood.

So devilish are the Masons that, according to Bresciani, they have shaped their organisation as an inverted mirror-image of the Church of Christ:

In his perfidious church [i.e. Freemasonry], the devil has created a hierarchy, a priesthood, sacraments, a cult, relics, a calendar, festivals, ferial practices, devotees [. . .], his own temples, his own missionaries, religious vows, unholy orders, congregations, a bible, dogmas, precepts, councils, liturgy, ritual, and liturgical language. Everything; but all of it with a meaning and aims that are diametrically opposed to those of God's Church.

Secularists gave as good as they got when it came to conspiracy theories, often involving the Jesuits. The Church faced a small army of professional anticlerical polemicists. In France the most scurrilous of them was Léo Taxil who, from the late 1870s, churned out a couple of books and half a dozen pamphlets a year, all of them with titles such as *The Bible for Laughs* (1881), *The Secret Loves of Pius IX* (1881) and *A Female Pope* (1882). Taxil was excommunicated by Pius IX's successor Leo XIII in 1879 – quite an achievement for a man who was only twenty-six. But this one-way ticket to hell only encouraged him. He reserved his purest scorn for the Jesuits, such as in the semi-pornographic novels *The Jesuit's Son* (1881) and *The Debauched Confessor* (1883). Taxil was a passionate culture warrior, but he was also unscrupulous and money-grubbing, and had a series of run-ins with the law over plagiarism and slander.

Anti-Catholic polemicist Léo Taxil
(1854–1907), who would undergo
a famous conversion in 1885.

In 1884, Leo XIII issued an encyclical that quickly became the main weapon of the culture war: it was entirely devoted to the evils of Freemasonry. *Humanum genus* was the most extreme of the many condemnations of the Craft that had issued from the Holy See since the first, in 1738. Leo XIII portrays Freemasonry as Satan's instrument against the kingdom of God on earth. The Brotherhood's secrecy shows that none of its public protestations of good faith can be believed: its very essence is deceit. Over the decades, it has grown prodigiously until 'by means of fraud or of audacity [it has gained] such entrance into every rank of the State as to seem to be almost its ruling power'. Through their oaths and rituals, Masons 'bind men like slaves' to an ultimate aim, which is the utter destruction of the Church and the return of paganism. To resist this 'foul plague', the priority for the clergy is to expose its evil secrets, to 'tear away the mask from Freemasonry' so as to expose 'the depravity of their opinions and the wickedness of their acts'.

Humanum genus was a near-delirious overreaction to the fact that, by the 1880s, Freemasonry had indeed acquired far greater influence and visibility. The Craft was now a mass, middle-class movement, integral to the life of increasingly democratic and capitalistic nation-states. In Italy, Masonry had been banned before unification, but it emerged in the 1860s to prosper over the coming decades: there were about a hundred Lodges in the 1870s, and four times that number by 1923. Italian Masonry was politicised, and closely aligned with a state that the Vatican believed had stolen its land. Amid frequent divisions over ideological issues, Italian Masons had common ground: the typical Italian Brother was very patriotic and instinctively in favour of secularist causes like divorce, cremation and non-religious education. Masonic anti-clericalism could be visceral: one Grand Master referred to the Craft's battle against the 'priestly pox'.

Many of the same things applied in France, where Freemasonry openly lobbied for the democratic, secular ideology of the Third Republic formed after defeat to Germany in 1870. In 1877, the

Grand Orient made a radical departure when it voted to lift the obligation for Masons to believe in God. Local Masonic congresses became a forum for political discussion. There was a great deal of overlap between Freemasonry and the country's most influential business and political networks: some 40 per cent of civilian ministers of the Third Republic were on the Square. It was taken for granted within the Craft that the Church was the Republic's enemy. Later, when the threat from political Catholicism grew in the 1890s, the response was the formation of the Radical Party, whose inaugural congress in June 1901 was attended by representatives of 155 Lodges.

Unsurprisingly therefore, Brethren everywhere in the world reacted with a mixture of derision and outrage to the anti-Masonic encyclical *Humanum genus* of 1884. In the United States, former Confederate general and Scottish Rite supremo, Albert Pike, branded it 'a declaration of war against the human race'.

For the Vatican, such reactions only confirmed that the Papacy's message about Freemasonry had hit home. Indeed, before long, *Humanum genus* would bring about the seemingly miraculous conversion of one of Catholicism's most vicious enemies. The celebrity convert would go on to 'tear away the mask from Freemasonry', just as Leo XIII had asked. The Church had never seen his like before.

Léo Taxil's supernatural change of heart

On 14 July 1885, *L'Univers*, the mouthpiece of the most conservative voices in the French Church, published rumours that the notorious atheist militant, Léo Taxil, had converted to the Catholic faith. *L'Univers*, which had often expressed its fury at such works of Taxil's as *Grotesque Cassocks* (1879) and *Mistresses of the Popes* (1884), reserved judgement on his conversion for now: the reports were more appropriately greeted with astonishment than belief, it observed.

Nine days later, a small man with a puffy face, a pince-nez

and unkempt hair pushed back from a balding pate called un-announced at the offices of *L'Univers*. It was none other than Léo Taxil, who was carrying a letter setting forth his thinking: he had indeed repented, and was profoundly ashamed of all he had done during seventeen years as a free-thinker. Nervous but determined, Taxil told the editor that he had placed himself in the hands of the Church.

Taken aback, the editor of *L'Univers* gave a public assurance to Taxil that all good Christians would greet his conversion with compassion and prayer. Many did indeed express their joy at the redemption of this prodigal son. The Paris correspondent of the British *Catholic Times* interviewed Taxil and was moved by his 'supernatural change of heart'. There were doubters, nonetheless. Ever suspicious, some Jesuits warned that the clergy was clasping a viper to its bosom. His former comrades – materialists, atheists, republicans and Freemasons – accused him of converting because his anticlerical books had stopped selling, or because he had been bribed. His distraught wife thought he had had a breakdown.

Taxil was not bothered by the sceptical voices, and at first seemed determined to withdraw from the world and break with his family. He was introduced to Archbishop Camillo Siciliano di Rende, the Papal Nuncio (i.e. ambassador) in Paris, who advised him against such drastic steps, and suggested he begin his spiritual journey with a few days' seclusion. In late August 1885, at a Jesuit retreat outside the city, he spent three agonising days confessing his sins before finally revealing that he had committed a premeditated murder. It went without saying that the Seal of the Confessional prevented the horrified priest from reporting Taxil's crime, but he could at least grant absolution to this tortured soul, and vouch for his sincerity before more senior clergy.

Taxil was determined to atone for his sins, and clear that his atonement could only take literary form. Within days of his conversion he had won the trust of numerous Parisian priests, a job in a Catholic bookshop, a deal with a Catholic publisher, a percentage of the profits from sales of his future books and guaranteed free publicity in the Catholic press. He could now lend his pen to a sacred cause, obeying the exhortation in *Humanum genus* to tear the mask from Freemasonry.

Confessions of a Former Free-Thinker, Taxil's autobiography, came out in 1887. Born Gabriel-Antoine Jogand-Pagès in 1854 near Marseille, he was educated by the Jesuits at the behest of his conservative parents. His journey into the 'inextricable laby-rinth of evil' began at age fourteen when he stumbled upon a Masonic manual; as a result, he quickly became obsessed with the Craft, and lost interest in religious instruction. He took on the name of Léo Taxil at age sixteen when he rebelled against his father and ran away from home, and developed into a polit-ical hot-head who consorted with petty criminals and prostitutes; he was threatened with prison for, among other things, selling phoney aphrodisiac pills. In the end, he was not involved in the Sect for very long because he proved to be too independent minded. Indeed, he left Masonry completely in 1881. But that was long enough to learn the Brotherhood's deepest secrets. Masons were secret devil-worshippers who were prepared to use all other religions as cover for their evil mission. The many patient and wise researchers who had looked into Freemasonry already had left important secrets still shrouded in mystery, notably the Craft's 'grotesque and hateful' rituals. Taxil's future publications were going to fill that gap.

Within two years of his conversion, over many hundreds of pages and four volumes, he set out all thirty-three Degrees of the Scottish Rite, and of various less well-known rites too. He named the officers of all of the Masonic Grand Lodges and Supreme Councils across the world, calculating that there were 1,060,005 Brothers in total. It was clear, Taxil explained, that the 'Great Architect of the Universe' was just a Masonic code-word for the devil, and that the structure and liturgy of the Craft aped the structure and liturgy of the one true Church. The Freemasons had also created an off-shoot, the Charcoal-Burners, in which

Brothers could vent their political ardour. While they were largely dormant at the moment, the Charcoal-Burners stood ready to rise up when the cause of Masonic mischief demanded.

Truth be told, much of what was in Taxil's early works on Masonry had already been published by the Masons themselves. But the sheer quantity of information showed the earnest piety of his purpose. He issued a stern warning to any readers who found Masonic secrets dull or even amusing: 'Do not laugh. Do not believe that Freemasonry is joking. This is a very serious business.' Who could doubt the convert's credibility now?

The most successful of Taxil's first works as a repentant Freemason was *Masonic Sisters* (1886), dealing with the Adoption Lodges, in which both men and women participated. In an opening address to his readers, Taxil declared that, despite his own overwhelming sense of disgust, he would reveal how apparently innocent Adoption Lodges were in reality a ritual device for reducing humanity to bestial forms of carnality and prostitution last seen in ancient Babylon. Given that the moral stakes in Taxil's work were so high, it is not surprising if the last words of his preface were so shrill: 'French mothers! Lock up your daughters! Here come the Freemasons!'

Thankfully, Taxil's sense of decency prevailed over his passion for the truth. Although he did state at the close of each chapter that the next one would expose shocking examples of Masonic sexual turpitude, he wisely withheld any obscenities. Instead, he showed conclusively that the language used in Adoption ceremonies systematically hid immoral intent under a virtuous disguise. When the Masons used a word like 'truth', they meant 'falsehood'; 'good' meant 'evil'; 'friendship' meant 'debauchery'. And so on. Once you understood the code, everything became repugnantly clear. Only in the last few pages of his book did Taxil's exposé become anatomical. He provided a key to Masonic symbolism, which demonstrated that the Craft was in reality a cult of sex, replete with harmless-looking ritual objects that were, in reality, phallic and vulvic symbols. To keep such polluting knowledge out of the hands of innocents, the pages in question were published in Latin.

Thanks in part to his tact, Taxil won the trust and even the admiration of a great many churchmen. Seventeen cardinals, archbishops and bishops sent messages of support. One of Taxil's most ardent backers was the Bishop of Grenoble, who had founded the monthly magazine *Freemasonry Unmasked*. Praise arrived from a great many ordinary clergymen too. A Swiss canon came all the way from Fribourg to meet Taxil, and hailed him as a saint. Shortly after returning home, the canon sent a huge Gruyère cheese with pious mottoes scored into its crust. Taxil reported eating every slice of it with enormous respect.

In June 1887, Taxil made an impromptu trip to the Vatican, in the seemingly naïve hope that he might be able to see the Pope. He was received with joy, and granted an audience with His Holiness for the very next morning. Taxil spent three-quarters of an hour with Leo XIII, and was delighted to hear that the Pope had read all of his anti-Masonic tracts from cover to cover.

Leo XIII's approval, and even affection, won more churchmen over to Taxil. The Jesuit magazine *Civiltà Cattolica* began to cite him as an authority on things Masonic. Translations of his work into several languages made his reputation international.

His next task was to clear up a number of mysterious deaths, which were in reality *Masonic Murders* – as the title of his 1889 book proclaimed. One of the purposes of Freemasonry's ascending scale of Degrees was to slowly induce absolute obedience. Once members achieved the Scottish Rite's Thirtieth Degree of Knight Kadosh, their will was so subservient that they became the Craft's assassins-to-order. The Knights Kadosh had carried out a number of high-profile murders, including those of William Morgan, the American Masonic traitor who disappeared near Niagara Falls in 1826.

Yet none of Taxil's revelations about Freemasonry had the astonishing impact reserved for his next book. Returning to the subject of the Adoption Lodges, *Are There Women in Freemasonry?*

(1891) disclosed horrors unknown even to the highest echelons of the Catholic Church. The most secretive form of mixed-sex Freemasonry was the Palladian Order; and the Palladian Order's most secret obedience, the most hidden of its hidden Lodges, practised sexual debauchery and Satanism in absolutely undiluted forms. Known as the New Reformed Palladian Rite, it no longer disguised its Lucifer-worship behind innocuous code-words: pride of place in its 'Triangles', as the Lodges were termed, went to a statue of Baphomet, the same goat-headed devil venerated by the heretical Templar knights of the Middle Ages. Women who had achieved the highest Palladian Degree of Templar Mistress led its rituals, which involved stabbing the consecrated host and spitting in a communion chalice. The New Reformed Palladian Rite was founded by Albert Pike, whom Taxil described as the anti-Pope of the Masonic 'anti-Church'.

Bravely, Taxil published a profile of one of the leading Templar Mistresses, 'the incarnation of Satanism, as if Lucifer's blood was flowing in her veins'. Sister Sophia-Sapho was an astonishingly precocious devil-worshipper. Before she was out of her teens she had been awarded the five highest Palladian Degrees by Albert Pike himself. She was very pretty, but her siren-like voice acquired an unnerving masculine tone when she was angry. In public, she gave every impression of living an unblemished, spinster's life. Within the Adoption Lodge, she showed she was an 'ardent lesbian' who took part in Masonic orgies coldly, waiting for the moment when she could take a Sister home with her. Sophia-Sapho's real passion, the thing that made her 'cat-like eyes' light up and her voice turn husky, was sacrilege. Not content with spitting on the consecrated host, she would often force a newly initiated Sister to have sex with the sacramental bread stuffed up her vagina.

Taxil clearly had inside sources. Now those sources, heartened by his courage, began to sense that they could talk directly to the public about the hell they were living through. The breakthrough came gradually, beginning in November 1892, with the publication of the serialised exposé, *The Devil in the Nineteenth*

Century. The author, who remained hidden behind the pseudo-nym of 'Dr Bataille' for his own protection, was a ship's doctor who would soon surpass Léo Taxil, so shocking and far-reaching was his discovery of a truly global Satanic conspiracy. (There were some cynics who said that 'Dr Bataille' did not actually exist, and that Taxil was in fact the real author of *The Devil in the Nineteenth Century*. But numerous issues contained categor-ical denials.)

Dr Bataille's story took readers back more than a decade, adding terrifying new details to the picture already painted by Taxil. In 1880, in Ceylon, he had happened across an old Italian friend, Gaetano Corbuccia. Once a well-built man, Corbuccia was now haunted and skeletal. Dr Bataille heard him confess that he had seen the devil manifest himself at a Palladian Triangle in Calcutta.

A man of science and a devout Catholic, Dr Bataille resolved to investigate, posing as a high-ranking Mason and using code-words supplied by Corbuccia. In India, he discovered that such well-known oriental practices as Hinduism, snake charming and monkey marriage were in reality disguised forms of Satanism controlled by British Freemasons belonging to the New Reformed Palladian Rite.

While in Calcutta, Dr Bataille was introduced to a visiting delegate from Charleston, Phileas Wilder, who was one of ten anti-cardinals of the anti-Church, a Lutheran pastor turned Anabaptist turned Mormon turned Satanist. (His daughter Sophia would later be identified by Léo Taxil as Sister Sophia-Sapho, the ardent lesbian Templar Mistress.) Thanks to Phileas Wilder, Dr Bataille began his ascent of the ladder of Palladian Degrees, and embarked on an ever-deeper exploration of the secrets of global Masonic devil-worship.

In Shanghai, for example, Dr Bataille stupefied himself in an opium den so as to gain admission to the demonic rites of the San-ho-hoeï Triad. Its affiliates specialised in assassinating Jesuit missionaries.

On Gibraltar, he was shown the deep caves where, protected by Masons within the British government, the New Reformed Palladian Rite had set up its factories. Dr Bataille himself saw how workers, smoke-blackened and brutishly muscular, crafted all manner of cult objects – swords, magic lamps, pentagrams – in forges powered by the very fires of hell. Gibraltar was also home to laboratories where twenty-one scientists who had been turned towards the cause of evil produced poisons that killed their victims while mimicking the symptoms of heart attacks and cerebral haemorrhages. 'The devil has now turned himself into a bacteriologist', a dismayed Dr Bataille concluded.

But these marvels were as nothing compared to what Dr Bataille discovered when he made it to Charleston, where he met Albert Pike, Albert Mackey and the young Sophia-Sapho. Albert Mackey showed off the Arcula Mystica. Looking like a small drinks cabinet, it opened at the press of a button to reveal a silver toad, a trumpet-like microphone, a bell-shaped ear-piece and seven gold statuettes each representing one of the main centres of the Palladian cult in Charleston, Rome, Berlin, Washington DC, Montevideo, Naples and Calcutta. When Albert Pike wanted to communicate with his emissaries, each of whom had an Arcula Mystica, he just pressed a statuette – at which, on the other side of the world, flames would come out of the mouth of the silver toad to alert the receiver of an incoming message. 'In a word', wrote Dr Bataille in amazement, 'the Arcula Mystica is nothing other than a diabolic telephone.' The worldwide Masonic conspiracy was more tightly coordinated than anyone imagined.

Dr Bataille was shown into the New Reformed Palladian Rite's main temple, the St Peter's of Satanism. Hidden within an unassuming building on the corner of King and Wentworth, it comprised an underground labyrinth at the centre of which was the triangular Sanctum Regnum where Satan was known to materialise once a week, on Fridays.

Perhaps the most dramatic revelation during Dr Bataille's trip to Charleston came when he went for an evening stroll with Sophia-Sapho. She was just talking to him about the demonic legions, when she let slip that she herself was destined to be the great-grandmother of the Antichrist, who would be born on 29 September 1962.

At every stage of his journey, over what would eventually fill nearly two thousand pages, Dr Bataille was at pains to distinguish fact from hearsay. Some things, such as the Arcula Mystica, he had seen with his own eyes. Others he had only been told about: such as the demon dwarf who appeared in a circle of white flame to carry messages for Albert Pike; or the winged, piano-playing crocodile that materialised at a Palladian séance in England. Such things could have been invention: when the devil wants to, he can induce a 'stupefying credulity' in his Palladians, Dr Bataille explained.

Despite this punctiliousness, Dr Bataille would be eclipsed as an authority on Palladism, just as he himself had eclipsed Léo Taxil. The new source came right from the heart of the evil cult

Satanic shenanigans in Masonic Lodges in Paris and Zurich, as reported in Dr Bataille's *The Devil in the Nineteenth Century*.

itself. There was now a palpable sense that the struggle between the Church and Palladism, between good and evil, was moving towards its climax.

In the autumn of 1893, Dr Bataille's memoirs were brought sensationally into the present as news leaked to several Catholic newspapers of a schism at the New Reformed Palladian Rite's secret conference in Rome. The split developed over the election of a successor to Albert Pike, who had died in 1891. One faction was led by a Templar Mistress called Diana Vaughan.

Keen readers of *The Devil in the Nineteenth Century* knew Diana Vaughan's back-story already. Half-French and half-American, she was an anomaly among demonolators. At her initiation to the Degree of Templar Mistress, a ceremony conducted in Paris by Sophia-Sapho, she flew in the face of Palladian orthodoxy by refusing to spit on the consecrated host. Diana believed that Lucifer was in fact a good god, and that Adonai, as the Palladists called the Christian deity, was a force for evil who was incapable of becoming flesh in a communion wafer. Diana's case generated furious debate in the Satanist community. But she was protected from being punished by her personal demon and fiancé, Asmodeus, who had given her a magical lion's tail that flogged anyone who spoke out against her. Diana and Sophia-Sapho became bitter rivals, and Diana went into hiding for her own protection.

In January 1894 came new astonishment. Despite the mystery that normally shrouded Masonic business, Diana agreed with a leading Catholic journalist to give an interview in a secret location in Paris. The Diana who appeared before her interviewer was a tall, attractive woman of twenty-nine, with a serene air and boyish haircut. So open and pure were her features that the interviewer had to remind himself and his readers that, although a virgin, she was a convinced Luciferian who enjoyed uninterrupted hours of infernal ecstasy. In the wake of the interview, published in the Catholic periodical *L'Echo de Rome*, Diana received thousands of letters, many of them urging her to renounce the devil. She typed polite replies to them all, on paper headed with Masonic symbols.

Late in 1894, it emerged that Diana had founded a new Masonic order, The Regenerated and Free Palladium. In March the following year, she took the extraordinary step of going public again, with an attractively priced monthly magazine designed to spread her beliefs.

After only three issues came the news that many prominent Catholics had long been praying for: Diana had embraced the faith. In Rome, *Civiltà Cattolica* spoke for the church hierarchy when it rejoiced at the way divine grace had worked repentance 'in the heart of one of the most implacable enemies of God and his Christ'.

Diana, who was now sheltered in a convent known only to a tiny group, changed the title of her magazine to *Memoirs of an ex-Palladist*. Henceforth she would use it to express her new-found Christianity, confess her past sins and expose the workings of Palladism from the inside. She published a photograph of herself in the male garb of a General Inspector of the Palladium, and gave the intimate story of her relationship with the demon Asmodeus. A series of articles under the heading 'The Great-Grandmother of the Antichrist' contained many revealing anecdotes about Sophia-Sapho, including the time when she had vomited flames after drinking some holy water. It was foretold that Sophia-Sapho would go to Jerusalem where, on 29 September 1896, she would be delivered of a baby girl fated to be the grandmother of the Antichrist. Proof of the prophecy was provided in the form of a letter in Latin from the demon Bitru, the baby's father.

There were signs of divine blessing for what Diana Vaughan was doing: in September 1895 a young woman reported being miraculously cured of a serious affliction after making a pilgrimage to Lourdes in Diana's name. Accordingly, *Memoirs of an ex-Palladist* met with the approval of some of the most authoritative voices in Catholicism, notably *Civiltà Cattolica*, which cited her 'precious' memoirs repeatedly, and said her work

Diana Vaughan, General Inspector
of the Palladium.

was so rigorous that 'it would be a credit to the most erudite historian'.

Freemasons, by predictable contrast, responded to Diana Vaughan either with indignation or forced laughter. One German Brother, the author of a history of the Craft much admired by Masons, denounced her whole story as a Jesuit fabrication aimed at poisoning minds against the Brotherhood.

To the Church, such reactions smelled of panic. The fightback against the sect responsible for all the evils of the modern world was gaining momentum. In the spring of 1896, Diana's journal announced the exciting news that a September date had been fixed for the Church-sponsored International Anti-Masonic Congress. It boded very well that this 'New Crusade' against

Masonry would begin exactly eight hundred years after the First Crusade set out for the Holy Land.

Just at that moment, when Luciferian Freemasonry was on the defensive and the Anti-Masonic Congress was approaching, doubts began to circulate about Diana Vaughan's confessions. Some Catholic newspapers, particularly in Germany, began to make wild insinuations: that she did not exist; or even that the wave of revelations about Freemasonry that followed in the wake of Léo Taxil's conversion was all a gigantic plan to bury the Church under an avalanche of ridicule. Increasingly, the evidence cited in *Memoirs of an ex-Palladist* was challenged: for example, it was pointed out that the letter from the demon Bitru that announced the birth of the Antichrist's grandmother contained lots of grammatical errors. (As if Lucifer's angels would bother to write in flawless Church Latin!)

Many Catholic organs and senior clergy rallied to Miss Vaughan's support. One of the Pope's secretaries sent her a message telling her to carry on her holy work, regardless of her critics. In September 1896, *Civiltà Cattolica* reiterated its belief in her as an instrument of providence.

However, the controversy would not die down. In late September 1896, about a thousand people, among them thirty-six bishops and the representatives of about fifty more, gathered in Trent for the First International Anti-Masonic Congress. The name on everyone's lips was that of Miss Diana Vaughan.

A special session of the Congress was scheduled to discuss the issues arising from her memoirs. Some doubters asked for proof. Who were her confessors? Who were the godparents at her baptism? Léo Taxil, who was one of the few people who had been trusted to know Diana Vaughan's whereabouts, came to the speaker's platform to point out the obvious: publishing such information would endanger Diana Vaughan's life.

Since opinions at the Congress remained divided, a special commission was entrusted with looking further into the issue. But when the commission's report came out some three months later, it said blandly that there was not enough evidence to decide how genuine the *Memoirs of an ex-Palladist* were. There were rumours that the Vatican hierarchy now had serious concerns about Diana, and had put pressure on the commissioners to muffle their conclusions out of fears that exposing her as a fraud would create huge embarrassment.

The controversy only grew louder. The press now alleged that Diana was merely a puppet in the hands of Léo Taxil. More worryingly, 'Dr Bataille' came out from behind his pseudonym – his real name was Dr Charles Hacks – and said that he had been paid to collaborate on *The Devil in the Nineteenth Century*. His paymaster, and the real author, was Léo Taxil. 'I was mocking Catholics', the doctor said. 'Everything I wrote was a fraud.'

Even Diana was feeling the pressure. She only had one option left to prevent the triumph of the Masonic campaign to undermine her: whatever the risk, she owed it to God, the Church and her many loyal supporters to appear in public for the first time.

Early in April 1897 came the announcement that Diana had picked the imminent Easter Monday to hold a press conference. The venue would be the meeting room of the prestigious Geographical Society on the Boulevard Saint-Germain. Léo Taxil would begin proceedings with a lecture entitled 'Twelve years under the banner of the Church'. Diana would then talk on the theme of 'Palladism struck down'. Fifty-five images would be projected by means of the latest oxy-hydric lamp, providing photographic and documentary proof of her claims. This was to be the first event in a tour that would take in many cities in Europe and America. To ensure a good audience, there would be a free raffle: the winner would walk away with a top-of-the-range typewriter generously provided by Miss Diana Vaughan herself.

When the appointed evening came, an invited audience of hundreds packed into the Geographical Society: Freemasons and free-thinkers, clerics and Catholics; most were journalists from both sides in the culture war, and from neither. Many more people crowded the street outside. Projected images of St Catherine and Joan of Arc looked down on the scene from the wall behind the rostrum. The winner of the typewriter was announced: it was Ali Kemal, the young correspondent of the Constantinople daily *Ikdam* (and British Prime Minister Boris Johnson's grandfather). Then, finally, all eyes turned to see Léo Taxil take to the stage. He cleared his throat, and addressed the audience with a broad smile: 'Reverent Fathers, ladies, and gentlemen . . .'

It was, of course, a hoax.

All of it, right from Léo Taxil's conversion, and the murder he had confessed. The New Reformed Palladian Rite did not exist. Satanic Freemasonry was nothing but a fable. Dr Bataille's travels were a fabrication, as were Diana Vaughan's memoirs.

The audience was initially nonplussed as Taxil began to speak. Then, as the truth sank in, a murmuring anger spread through the hall. The claque of friends Taxil had brought with him laughed demonstratively. The first shout to be heard above them was, 'You're just a squalid rascal.' From that point, cries of 'rogue!' and 'scoundrel!' accompanied the speaker's every word, forcing him occasionally to stop until the din subsided. The churchmen present looked at one another, uncertain of what to do. Some wept. Or stared in disbelief. Some began to walk out. Others called them back to continue protesting. When the cry went up, 'Di-a-na!' 'Di-a-na! Where is Diana?', Taxil slapped his chest and replied, 'I am Diana.'

With undisguised relish, he ran through some of the people he had duped, and told the story of his audience with the Pope. He talked about all the times the Vatican had missed the chance to see through his deceit. Such as when the Catholic Bishop of Charleston came all the way to the Vatican to explain that the Freemasons he knew, far from being devil-worshippers, were actually decent folk. Or when a priest from Gibraltar came to explain that the caves described by Dr Bataille, far from containing a diabolical poison factory, did not exist.

Taxil identified his collaborators. 'Dr Bataille' was an old friend from Marseille, a ship's doctor who had been brought in to add some seafaring authenticity to Taxil's ludicrous tales. Diana Vaughan was a secretary in the French office of an American typewriter manufacturer; she had agreed to help by replying to all the letters sent to the famous Templar Mistress. Both were free-thinkers who had gone along with Taxil's scheme to earn some money and have a bit of fun.

There was manifestly something strange about Léo Taxil, as well as merely cynical. He had spent twelve long years cashing in on the Catholic Church's obsession with Freemasonry, and in the process had risked his marriage, and cut ties with many of his friends. Taxil also handled the moment of exposure very badly. The audience were treated to the lengthy spectacle of a man beaming smugly at his own tasteless joke. He considered this 'enjoyable and instructive mystification' to be 'the most fantastic hoax of modern times'. He appealed to the clergymen present not to get angry, but to laugh sunnily along with him.

Nausea, according to one journalist present, was the overwhelming reaction in the hall. When Taxil finished speaking, there was uproar. A good portion of the audience, by no means all of them from the Catholic side, surged towards the speaker. Insults flew, along with gobs of spit. Taxil was only saved from the wrath of the crowd by his friends, and by the policemen who escorted him to a brasserie nearby.

The explosion of Taxil's hoax created news that lasted no more than a couple of days – as if everyone tacitly agreed that the perpetrator did not deserve the notoriety he sought. The Church, for its part, opted for the pretence of dignified silence, wherever it could. *Civiltà Cattolica* had the impressive brass neck to claim that it had never really believed in Léo Taxil and Diana Vaughan. It reassured its readers of the Pope's 'great serenity' when he heard the news, and quoted him as saying that Taxil's fraud was just one more example of how impudent Freemasons could be.

Léo Taxil lived out a comfortable early retirement on the substantial nest-egg that Palladism had earned him. When the opportunity arose, to round out his income, he would republish one or other of the books from his anticlerical days, like *The Secret Loves of Pius IX* (1900) and *The Bible for Laughs* (1901). He died in provincial obscurity in March 1907.

Allahabad: **Mother Lodges of the Empire**

Imperial Brethren

From near to home (Ireland), to the other side of the planet (New Zealand), the British Empire extended over one-quarter of the earth's land surface at its peak, and included more than a fifth of the global population. Its makers were many and diverse: traders and conquerors, freebooters and missionaries, scholars and capitalists, warriors and settlers, bureaucrats and explorers, monarchs and democrats, doctors and drug traffickers. Those who lived under British authority were even more vastly hetero-geneous – albeit within the overarching distinction imposed by the British between white-dominated settler societies on the one hand, and non-white indigenous populations on the other. On the non-white side of the divide, the Empire's subjects ranged from opulent but subordinate partners of the British authorities, like Gulf sheikhs and Indian princes, to hunter-gatherers like the San of southern Africa and the Aboriginal peoples of Australia. British power might bring railways and the rule of law, but it also brought slavery, famine and eradication. The Empire remade the world.

Wherever the Empire went, Freemasonry went too. In February 1728, within five years of the publication of the Craft's *Constitutions*, employees of the East India Company in Fort

William (Calcutta) gathered to petition the Grand Lodge in London to set up the first Lodge in India. The earliest Lodge in the American colonies was founded at the Bunch of Grapes Tavern in Boston, Massachusetts, in the summer of 1733. Five years later came the first Lodge in the Caribbean – Antigua's Parham Lodge. Slowly at first, until the later decades of the eighteenth century, and then with increasing levels of self-confidence and organisation, the Craft reached further and deeper into the Empire's fibres.

There was no grand plan behind the spread of imperial Freemasonry, and still less a conspiracy. There was often rivalry and confusion between the different Grand Lodges of the home nations – English, Irish and Scottish. Yet imperial administrators, soldiers and entrepreneurs found a ready-made support network in the Brotherhood. The Lodge was the local hub of a global welfare system: any Mason who was about to expire in some distant territory had the comfort of knowing that he would get a decent burial, and that his widow and orphans would be helped by his Brethren. The Empire expanded the networking and friend-making opportunities available to Craftsmen to a worldwide scale. Many men joined just before they departed for the colonies, where Lodges had to keep a constant eye out for those with fake Masonic credentials. Freemasonry was a 'passport in all parts of the globe', as the Grand Lodge of Scotland put it in 1896. Providing welcome distraction from the tedium of life in isolated white communities where women were scarce, the Masonic hall often doubled as a bar and theatre. Familiar Masonic rituals conjured up a little piece of home wherever they were performed.

Thus Freemasonry lubricated the machinery of imperial domination. It also turned the Empire into spectacle. Masons did not just build Lodge buildings, each proudly displaying the square and compass over the door; they also funded and/or inaugurated schools, orphanages, bridges, courts . . . To both colonisers and colonised, Masonic parades and monuments could make British rule seem solemn, permanent, mysterious and even scary. 'A common vernacular name for a Masonic hall in India was *jadughar*, or "magic-house". Another common term across North India and in Bombay was *bhutkhana*, or "demon-house".'

Wherever the historian's eye settles, there are vivid and varied cameos of the role Freemasonry played in imperial life.

Masonry was active in late eighteenth-century Barbados, for example. The island was lush, fertile, English in its every pretty house and church, and had grown sumptuously wealthy on the hell-tainted profits of human bondage. Barbadian slave plantations produced the sugar that fuelled the growth of British consumerism. On 10 July 1781, the officers of the Provincial Grand Lodge of Barbados came together under the open Caribbean sky. The Masonic officers were mostly members of the island's planter élite. On 10 October the previous year, the deadliest hurricane ever recorded had killed some 4,500 people – roughly 4 per cent of the population. Every single tree had been uprooted, and most of them even had their bark blasted off. All but a handful of buildings on the island were destroyed, including the Masonic Hall in Bridgetown amid whose ruins the Brethren now stood. There and then they composed a letter to the Grand Lodge of England requesting financial help to rebuild, so that they could once again 'labour in all brotherly love, for the future Welfare and Support of the most ancient and honourable Society'. By February 1783 at the latest, thanks to London's brotherly assistance, a new Freemasons' Hall was in use. The enslavers of Barbados thus restored Freemasonry to its place at the centre of their community life – alongside the racecourse, the bowling green and the literary society.

Just after Christmas 1820, the members of Australian Social Lodge no. 260 celebrated their first St John's Day. In searing heat, they paraded in all their regalia along Sydney's main thoroughfare, George Street, which was then little more than a cart track terminating in the bush. The Lodge, whose warrant had only arrived by ship from Ireland six months previously, was the first permanent Lodge on Australian soil. Remarkably, among the

Brethren in the procession that day was at least one 'Emancipist' – the term used for a transported convict who had either served out his sentence, or whose good behaviour had earned him a pardon. Since the First Fleet of eleven ships, carrying some 700 convicts, had landed in Botany Bay in 1788 to found the colony, the division between Emancipists and those who had arrived as freemen was the engine of Australia's own peculiar form of class conflict. Freemasonry thus demonstrated its broadmindedness for all in Sydney to see. In Australia, as across the Empire, the Craft would continue to soften social divisions, and to help men use the opportunities for bettering their station that life in a new land afforded. As scarcely needs pointing out, Aboriginal peoples were never even considered for Masonic status.

There was nothing Victorian Freemasons liked better than a ball. On Valentine's Day 1854, six hundred fur-clad Brothers and their womenfolk converged on the grand, waterfront Masonic Hall in Halifax, Nova Scotia, for a fancy-dress party that would be a sparkling projection of their civic, imperial and brotherly self-confidence onto the snowy darkness. Inside, gas jets, forming a crown and the letters VR, blazed from one of the walls, their light reflecting on 'a large and handsomely arranged star of bayonets, ramrods, swords, and dirks, the ingenious device of one of the officers of the garrison'. The band of the 72nd Highlanders played a whirling succession of 'quadrilles, polkas, valses, galops, and country dances'. To give the bandsmen of the 72nd an occasional break, their place was taken by the regiment's bagpipers, playing reels. But what stayed longest in the memories of that night were the costumes. The Brothers took the chance to dress up in the splendid aprons, sashes and ornaments of the varied Masonic offices and Degrees, and relished the curiosity their strange garb aroused in the women present. Only when the sun rose at seven o'clock did the revellers make their way out into the biting air. The ball was the summation of a story of personal and collective success. Provincial Grand Master for the past fifteen years was Alexander Keith, just elected as Mayor for the second time. Barely more than a boy when he had arrived from Scotland in 1817 with nothing but a brewing apprenticeship and his Masonic credentials to build on, he was now a beer magnate. Freemasonry had helped turn Halifax from a log-fort garrison, an Atlantic forward base for the Empire, into a proud city running on shipping, timber, cod and Keith's porters and India pale ales.

When the Queen-Empress Victoria celebrated her fiftieth year on the throne in 1887, her Empire was reaching its apogee. The Craft, and the cult of monarchy that it happily endorsed, had grown with Britain's dominions. Victoria's father was an enthusiastic Mason: he had laid the corner stone of the Masonic Hall in Halifax, Nova Scotia, among others. Five of her six uncles were Masons too. She had graciously accepted to become a Patroness of the Masonic Order. Three of her sons were carrying on the Masonic family tradition. Her heir, Prince Edward, had been Grand Master of the United Grand Lodge of England since 1875. In that Golden Jubilee year of 1887, through a Grand Lodge deputation led by Edward, Victoria issued a message to Craftsmen throughout her global realm: 'The Society of Freemasons increases in numbers and prosperity in proportion as the wealth and civilization of my Empire increases.'

English Freemasonry had never enjoyed such prestige. In London, Empire Lodge no. 2108 was founded in 1885 to bolster the ties 'that unite the Dominions with the Mother Country, by bringing the Brethren from Overseas into close relationship with Freemasons in the Metropolis of the Empire'. Several more imperial Lodges embodying the same philosophy were constituted thereafter. The United Grand Lodge in London was approving the foundation of new Lodges at the rate of seventy a year. By 1914 there would be more than 1,700 meeting in England and Wales, and another 1,300 English Constitution Lodges across the imperial territories and in British trading outposts. That figure excludes hundreds more Irish and Scottish Constitution Lodges.

Wherever Craftsmen found themselves, at home or in the

Sir Christopher Wren with St Paul's Cathedral, his greatest creation.
Wren's closest collaborators were members of a secret brotherhood called
the Acception. The completion of St Paul's in 1710, and the accession of
the House of Hanover to the throne in 1714, precipitated the Acception's
transformation into Freemasonry as we know it today.

Scotland's Solomon: King James VI. In 1598, Scottish stonemasons were reorganised and inspired by the Renaissance culture of James's court—a crucial step in the evolution of Freemasonry.

Interior of a typical Lodge. It was under James VI that humble stonemasons' lodges first became memory temples, where rituals are acted out with symbols on a chequered floor. This particular Lodge room in Paris was inaugurated in 1948 and named after Franklin Delano Roosevelt.

Poetry and music have always had a prominent place in Masonic culture.

Freemasons hail Robert Burns as their Poet Laureate in 1787. The scene, set in Edinburgh's Lodge Canongate Kilwinning, the world's oldest purpose-built Masonic temple, is a partly fanciful reconstruction from 1846.

True Concord Lodge, Vienna, 1780s. The Lodge was one of several frequented by Wolfgang Amadeus Mozart. Masons have often claimed that the figure at the bottom right is Mozart himself.

Diplomat, spy, fencing-master and passionate Freemason: the Chevalière d'Éon in a 1792 portrait. Controversy over d'Éon's sex created much embarrassment for English Masons.

Duke Philippe d'Orléans, painted in 1781 as Grand Master of the Grand Orient of France. The Duke, King Louis XVI's cousin, would later embrace the French Revolution and change his name to Philippe Égalité. He was guillotined in 1793.

Masonic charlatan. James Gillray's 1786 caricature of a Lodge meeting featuring Sicilian arch-imposter Count Cagliostro, dressed in red. Cagliostro toured Europe peddling his occult 'Egyptian Freemasonry'.

Initiating a Sister. (Napoleonic Empire, c.1810.) Adoption Lodges, which embraced both Brothers and Sisters, were pioneered in eighteenth-century France.

Napoleon and Josephine as objects of a Masonic cult (mid-19th century). Bonaparte may not have been a Freemason, but as Emperor he used the Craft to reinforce his regime. His wife Josephine de Beauharnais was initiated into an Adoption Lodge in 1792.

Joachim Murat, Napoleon's brother-in-law, in a flamboyant portrait as King of Naples in 1812. Murat was Grand Master of the Grand Orient of Naples. The Charcoal-Burners, a revolutionary secret society closely related to the Masons, developed during his reign.

Two instigators of the Charcoal-Burner revolution of 1820, Michele Morelli and Giuseppe Silvati, are executed in Naples following the revolution's defeat. They would come to be seen as Italian patriotic martyrs, as in this illustration from 1889.

As President, George Washington used Freemasonry as a civic religion.
He would go on to be venerated by generations of American Masons.
The two Brothers featured at the top of this composition from the
1860s are Lafayette and President Andrew Jackson.

The bloody assault on Fort Wagner in 1863 made heroes of the men of the 54th Massachusetts, the first African-American regiment from the North to fight in the Civil War. Freemasons of the Prince Hall tradition led recruitment for the 54th, and many of its NCOs were Masons.

Martin Delany, the abolitionist known as the father of black nationalism, was a prominent Prince Hall Mason.

Léo Taxil caricatured in 1879, when he was excommunicated for his scurrilous anti-Catholic polemics.

After converting to Catholicism in a 'supernatural change of heart' in 1885, Taxil launched exposés of Freemasonry. Masons, he claimed, worshipped the goat-headed devil Baphomet, pictured here.

Prince Edward, Queen Victoria's heir, became Grand Master of the United Grand Lodge of England in 1875. Victoria's reign saw Freemasonry wedded to the twin causes of monarchy and Empire.

In 1872, Prosonno Coomar Dutt, a Bengali produce broker, overcame Freemasonry's prejudice against initiating Hindus.

Masonic processions were a regular feature of British Imperial rule. Here the Grand Master of the United Grand Lodge of England, the Duke of Connaught, leads his Brethren through Bulawayo, Rhodesia, in 1910.

Mocked-up Masonic Lodges were used as propaganda by several Fascist regimes. This one, in Salamanca, can still be visited, and illustrates the enduring anti-Masonic phobia of Spanish dictator Francisco Franco.

ЈЕВРЕЈИН ДРЖИ КОНЦЕ У РУЦИ

ЧИЈЕ И КАКО? — ОДГОВОРИЋЕ ВАМ
АНТИМАСОНСКА ИЗЛОЖБА...

'A Jew is holding strings in his hand. Whose and how? The Anti-Masonic Exhibition will give the answer.' A poster combining anti-Masonic and anti-Semitic themes advertises an exhibition in Nazi-occupied Serbia, 1941.

During Jim Crow and segregation, Prince Hall Freemasonry was an important resource for African-American communities. The photo shows Brothers of the Carthaginian Lodge no. 47, New York, in 1907.

Truman was the most dedicated of the fourteen Masonic Presidents of the USA. This portrait from 1949 shows him in the regalia of Grand Master of the Grand Lodge of Missouri.

Freemasonry has never been as popular as it was in 1950s America—or as open about its rituals. Here Brooklyn Masons re-enact the dedication of Solomon's Temple for *Life* magazine in 1956.

Mississippi, 1963: murdered civil rights campaigner, Medgar Evers, is mourned by Myrlie, his wife, and their children. Evers exemplified the intensely close link between Prince Hall Freemasonry and the struggle for civil rights.

Meanwhile white Freemasons celebrated their contribution to American life in the splendid Masonic Brotherhood Center at the New York World's Fair.

Licio Gelli, the Venerable Master of Italy's notorious P2 Lodge. The terracotta pots in his garden were later found to contain gold bars.

In August 1980 a bomb at Bologna railway station killed 85 people. Venerable Master Gelli was convicted of plotting to cover the culprits' tracks.

Olivia Chaumont, on the throne of a Lodge Master in Paris, 2019. Her struggle to compel the Grand Orient of France to admit women, and give them equal Masonic status, ended in victory in 2010.

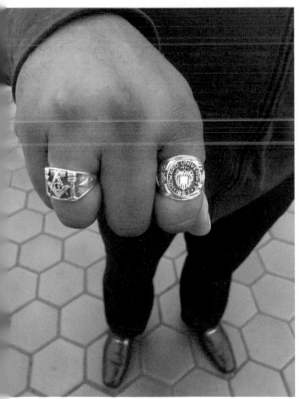

Proud emblems of tradition: Brother James R. Morgan III, Grand Historian of the Prince Hall Grand Lodge of the District of Columbia, displays the rings that proclaim him a Freemason and a Howard University graduate. Washington DC, 2019.

From Rite to Ritual (2009). Leading Australian artist Danie Mellor, a former Freemason, has indigenous heritage. This work explores the common ground between Masonry and indigenous beliefs, as well as the role that the Craft played in destroying Aboriginal cultures.

Empire, songs and poems had a role in their Masonry, both as an aid to memory and as an encapsulation of shared ideals in a rhythmical, almost ceremonial style. The *Constitutions* of 1723 contained long rhymes set to music that encapsulated the Craft's history and values. The high noon of imperial Freemasonry between the 1880s and the First World War produced the poet who was both Freemasonry's greatest literary voice, and 'The Laureate of Empire'. Rudyard Kipling – in his life, work and public image – makes a revealing guide to the theme of Freemasonry and Empire.

Golf in Vermont

Rudyard Kipling passed his first six years of life in India; the first language he spoke was Hindi. The next ten years were spent in southern England, where he acquired an enduring hatred for the damp climate. When he returned to India at age sixteen in 1883 to begin a career as a journalist, he felt he was returning home. He may have left again in 1889 to embrace and augment his literary fame in London, but India had made him, as man and writer.

Kipling's India was always much more vividly imagined than his England. The imperial homeland was less a place than a cause at this stage in his life: 'My affection for England is in large part for the Head Quarters of the Empire and I cannot say that the land itself fills me with comfort or joy.' He plunged himself into literary London but continued to regard it with suspicion, resenting its indifference towards the great project of Empire. He began to conceive a mission: to educate the British about the world, and the sacred duty they had to own large parts of it. 'And what should they know of England who only England know?', he wrote in 'The English Flag' (1891). As he told an admirer, 'Naturally I believe there has been no civilizing experiment in the world's history, at all comparable to British rule in India.'

In 1892, Kipling married an American, Caroline 'Carrie' Starr Balestier. The couple migrated from London to her homeland to start a family, and built themselves a house just outside Brattleboro, in the 'large-boned, mountainous, wooded' Vermont countryside. Here, where the winter snows overtopped the sill of his study window, Kipling's whole sensorium reached out to the India of his mind: to the taste of chillies and mangoes; to the whisper of the breeze in the banana leaves; to the smell of turmeric and cheroots; to the feel of the heat – unending, enfeebling – and of the opium he smoked to counter its effects. *The Jungle Book*, Kipling's timeless collection of children's stories set in India, was written in Vermont.

Freemasonry's most loved poem was also written in Vermont, the fruit of an encounter between Kipling and Arthur Conan Doyle who, like his friend, was a passionate believer in the British Empire. In the autumn of 1894, having recently killed off Sherlock Holmes at the Reichenbach Falls, Conan Doyle took a break from a speaking tour of the United States to spend a couple of days in Vermont teaching Kipling to play golf – despite the lack of a local course.

Conan Doyle and Kipling deepened their friendship as they swished and hacked their way around the open country. The conversation could flow easily between the two writers on a great many topics, including Freemasonry. Conan Doyle had been initiated on 26 January 1887 near his home in Southsea, Hampshire. He resigned in 1889 due to pressure of work and travel, but would later re-join; Masonic motifs crop up in his stories. Kipling was much more captivated by the Craft than Conan Doyle. As one of his biographers has written, he loved the 'soul-cleansing routine' of ritual, and 'to belong to an inner circle, with secret passwords, where he could be safe from the women who fascinated and frightened him, where he could meet odd people who would give him useful copy but not prove a social embarrassment outside the Lodge'.

Kipling repeatedly returned to Masonry in his writing, such

as in the short story 'The Man Who Would Be King' (1888) set in the far-flung frontier of India; it would become a film starring Sean Connery and Michael Caine in 1975. Like so much else, Kipling's Masonry was tied in his mind to the subcontinent: he had been initiated at the Lodge of Hope and Perseverance in Lahore in 1886.

The unique chemistry of those October days with Conan Doyle in Vermont – a combination of friendship, expansive Englishness, memories of India and Freemasonry – charged Kipling with poetic inspiration: he wrote 'The Mother Lodge' in a single sitting. The poem, like a long strand of Kipling's verse, his *Barrack-Room Ballads*, is in the London vernacular voice of an anonymous English foot-soldier who is the salt of the Empire, the epitome of the unsung. He finds himself barred as a trouble-maker from pubs at home, yet in his battered knapsack he carries the light of civilisation to 'the dark places of the earth' (as Kipling called them). The imperial soldier knows the likely reward for his selfless service is to die in a far-off land, either doubled up with dysentery, or writhing on the point of a native spear. Freemasonry is his consolation and his humble philosophy. In 'The Mother Lodge', he wistfully recalls where he was first intro-duced to the mysteries of the Craft, 'out there' in India. The Brethren of his Mother Lodge had no airs: a station-master, a jailer, a shop-keeper and a petty imperial bureaucrat. But what they lacked in resources, they made up for in the diligence of their Craft workings:

> We 'adn't good regalia,
> An' our Lodge was old an' bare,
> But we knew the Ancient Landmarks,
> An' we kep' 'em to a hair . . .

Most importantly of all, in the poem's key stanza and its chorus, the soldier tells us that his Masonic Brothers were men of all colours and creeds:

We'd Bola Nath, Accountant,
An' Saul the Aden Jew,
An' Din Mohammed, draughtsman
Of the Survey Office too;
There was Babu Chuckerbutty,
An' Amir Singh the Sikh,
An' Castro from the fittin'-sheds,
The Roman Catholick!

Outside – 'Sergeant! Sir! Salute! Salaam!'
Inside – 'Brother', an' it doesn't do no 'arm.
We met upon the Level an' we parted on the Square,
An' I was junior Deacon in my Mother-Lodge out there!

The Lodge in the poem seems to embrace every religious and ethnic group in India, as one historian has commented: 'a Parsi, a Moslem draughtsman, a Sikh, an Oriental Jew, a Gangetic Hindu or Rajput, a Catholic Goan, and a Bengali babu'. Within its confines, the command structure of army and empire is temporarily suspended, as these diverse men become Brothers 'upon the Level'.

Masons in Britain and far beyond have read 'The Mother Lodge' as a hymn to global Masonry, to the Craft's ability to embrace men of all cultures, religions and social backgrounds, to accept difference and meld it in fraternal devotion. The author clearly conceived of his verse in that spirit too. The poem replays Kipling's brotherly relationship with the Indians he knew in the late 1880s as a matey dialogue between men of different faiths. In 'The Mother Lodge', even the conventions of British Masonic life are suspended in the interests of inter-community harmony: there could be no banquet or 'Festive Board' because of Hindu and Muslim dietary laws.

An' lookin' on it backwards
It often strikes me thus,
There ain't such things as infidels,
Excep', per'aps, it's us.

For monthly, after Labour,
We'd all sit down and smoke
(We dursn't give no banquets,
Lest a Brother's caste were broke),
An' man on man got talkin'
Religion an' the rest,
An' every man comparin'
Of the God 'e knew the best.

So man on man got talkin',
An' not a Brother stirred
Till mornin' waked the parrots
An' that dam' brain-fever-bird.
We'd say 'twas 'ighly curious,
An' we'd all ride 'ome to bed,
With Mo'ammed, God, an' Shiva
Changin' pickets in our 'ead.

'The Mother Lodge' was not meant to be autobiographical. Yet late in life, by the time he came to look back to when he first joined the Craft in India, Kipling's memory of his earliest Masonic experiences had been colonised by his poetry: 'Here I met Muslims, Hindus, Sikhs, members of the Arya and Brahmo Samaj [Hindu sects], and a Jew tyler, who was priest and butcher to his little community in the city.'

An intolerant world needs all the poems about tolerance it can get. 'The Mother Lodge' is undoubtedly a stirring cameo of the brotherhood of man, one that is deeply flattering to the Craft. But it raises obvious questions about how such a vision could be compatible with the enthusiastic imperialism shown by both

Freemasonry and Kipling. We need to know how 'The Mother Lodge' measures up against the real history of Freemasonry in the Raj in general, and against Kipling's experience in particular.

With Mo'ammed, God, an' Shiva Changin' pickets in our 'ead

'The Mother Lodge' is a memory misty with sentimentality. Yet the records of Freemasonry in Imperial India, and of Kipling's first experiences of the Craft, show that the poem was not divorced from reality. Or at least, not entirely. At times and in places across the Empire, the chessboard floor of the Lodge also became a place where the British met natives on the Square. Nowhere more so than in India – the jewel in the imperial crown and yet never a land of mass white settlement – were those encounters more widespread, more intimate or more dense with political meaning.

Nearly half a century after it arrived in India, the Craft initiated its first Indian Brother in 1775. It is no coincidence that he was a local potentate in southern India and a British ally: Umdat-ul-Umrah Bahadur, the son and heir of the Nawab of Carnatic. Girding a native chief in a Masonic apron could be a good way of knotting an alliance with him against Britain's enemies. The Grand Lodge in London approved of the future Nawab's initiation: it sent him an ornate apron and a finely bound copy of Anderson's *Constitutions*. He responded with a Loyal Address in Persian, with a parallel English translation. The move fitted neatly with East India Company strategy, from the late eighteenth to the early nineteenth centuries, as it progressed from commerce to conquest, ousting rival European and Indian powers, and extending its control far into the interior from its original coastal trading stations at Calcutta, Bombay and Madras.

However, such initiations were extremely rare, and even then did not go unopposed by white Masons on the ground. In Calcutta in 1812, two Brothers refused to be present at the initiation of one Meer Bundeh Ali Khan, despite the fact that his application to join had the backing of a former Governor-General of India. The men protested that 'they were not obligated to be present at the Initiation of a Turk, Jew or infidel'. During the ceremony, two more Masons 'were most unworthily and unmasonically employing themselves in ridiculing the Mahomedan Religion'. The other Masons present, in their embarrassment, and to their credit, gave the new Brother a particularly warm welcome.

Below the level of the indigenous élite, two developments contributed to slowly increasing the number of Indians who gained admittance to Freemasonry. The first was the opening up of niches in the economy for Indian merchants and entrepreneurs. The Parsi community of Bombay were the outstanding beneficiaries here. Originally Zoroastrian refugees from Muslim Persia, since the seventeenth century the Parsis had developed a close relationship with the East India Company, which considered them reliable brokers and suppliers. In due course some Parsi businessmen became bankers and international merchants. From the 1840s, they began to be welcomed into 'Indian Lodges', reserved for them. By the 1860s, they were occupying leadership positions in Bombay Masonry alongside their British Brethren. Parsis were deemed particularly clubbable by the British because they drank alcohol.

The second development was the spread of English education among a tiny but growing stratum of Indians, and the growing number of jobs for educated locals within the imperial state apparatus. Many of the beneficiaries in this case were Bengali Hindus based in the imperial capital, Calcutta. But Hinduism was viewed with suspicion by Freemasons. The overwhelming majority of the Indian initiates before the 1870s were Parsi, Sikh and Muslim. Hindus were different. Indeed, Hinduism was a problem for the whole 'muscular Christian' mind-set of Victorian imperialism. The British, whether Masons or not, clung to offensive stereotypes about India's religious groups. Overwhelmingly, they preferred Muslims (meat-eating, masculine and monotheistic) to Hindus (vegetarian, suspiciously weedy and, well, nobody

was quite sure how many gods or idols the Hindus worshipped).
Freemasonry's *Constitutions* stipulated that polytheism was as
much a Masonic taboo as atheism. It was not clear either what
the Hindu equivalent of the Bible or the Qur'an might be – a
crucial part of the equipment for Craft rituals being a Volume
of Sacred Law from one faith or another. The Hindu caste system
also seemed to many Brothers to be a shocking offence to the
ideal of fraternity. (Some Hindus felt the same way in reverse.)
Thanks in part to such prejudices, no Lodge in Bengal could
initiate an Indian without first seeking approval from the
Provincial Grand Lodge.

All these issues, and the plain old racism blended in with them,
came to a head in 1863 when the indomitable Prosonno Coomar
Dutt, a Bengali produce broker and a Hindu, was proposed for
initiation at a Calcutta Lodge. The Worshipful Master sought
permission from the Provincial Grand Master, which was refused
on the blanket grounds that Hindus were not eligible. However,
Dutt was not a man to be denied: he appealed the decision to
the United Grand Lodge in London, which upheld the great
Masonic principle of tolerance. Hindus were perfectly eligible
for initiation, and no Provincial Grand Lodge veto could change
that fact. There followed nine long years of toing and froing, as
the Provincial Grand Lodge of Bengal vented its bigotry ('our race
differ[s] in every essential point from that of the Asiatic') and tried
to wriggle out of the ruling. Eventually, on 22 August 1872, Brother
Dutt was initiated, thus opening the doors of Lodges across India
to his Hindu co-religionists.

In principle, at least. Nobody should delude themselves that,
after the Dutt affair, Freemasonry became entirely open to
Indians. Individual Lodges still retained the power to admit
whomsoever they liked, and to blackball anyone without giving
a reason. Racial discrimination still had plenty of scope. For all
that, the political climate in India at the time makes the outcome
of the Dutt controversy remarkable. Six years earlier, in May
1857, indigenous soldiers in the Bengal Army had risen up in

rebellion. The imperial authorities lost control of much of northern India, as a whole range of disaffected groups, from princes to peasants, took up arms. It took until late the following year for British forces, amid much indiscriminate savagery, to extinguish the last flames of revolt. In the aftermath, the Crown assumed all the powers that had previously been vested in the East India Company. At the same time, British attitudes lurched. Previous to what they called 'the Indian Mutiny', the British had flattered themselves that they were agents of civilisation, helping their indigenous charges along the path to progress. Now, they preferred to view the Indian population through the intellectually fashionable lens of race. Those old stereotypes about India's different populations acquired a harder edge. Whatever religion they might profess, Indians as a whole were biologically inferior – and therefore fundamentally resistant to improvement. So Freemasonry's open-door policy towards Indians in the aftermath of the Dutt affair ran counter to the dominant ideological trend. Masonic tolerance was not, and has never been, just an empty slogan.

The Craft in India, then, had been on a long, slow journey of adaptation by the time Rudyard Kipling became a Brother. The eighteenth-century tactic of initiating friendly princelings had acquired a new usefulness in the aftermath of the 'Mutiny' of 1857. Kipling's own Mother Lodge, Hope and Perseverance no. 782 in Lahore, was warranted in 1859. Soon afterwards, it initiated the Sikh monarch, Sir Randhir Singh, Maharaja of Kapurthala, who had been zealous in his loyalty to the British during the rebellion. The Maharaja died in 1870, but his younger brother, Sardar Bikrama Singh Bahadur, was still a member when Kipling went through the initiation ceremony, on 5 April 1886. In many parts of the Raj, Indian princes were now proxy rulers or even puppets – deprived of real power, but wealthy and decked in ceremonial trappings intended to give the Raj a traditional Indian façade. Freemasonry was part of the symbolism of this pact with the Crown. By the outbreak of the First World War there were at least ten Brothers in India who put 'Maharaja' in the *Occupation* column of the Lodge register.

Recruitment had broadened greatly since the days when the first indigenous princelings were admitted. Most of the Indians that Kipling exchanged secret grips and passwords with in Lahore were merchants, with the odd doctor or administrator thrown in. They were also ethnically diverse: as well as the Sikh prince mentioned above, the Lodge embraced men such as the Parsi merchant E.C. Jussawalla, the Muslim Assistant Commissioner Mohammed Hayat Khan and the Bengali Hindu lawyer P.C. Chatterjee. But they were still totally outnumbered by white faces: there were *at most* eight Indian Brothers in the Lodge at the time, with one more joining while Kipling was there. So Hope and Perseverance no. 782 was not the celebrated multi-ethnic Mother Lodge of the poem.

In November 1887, Kipling was drawn away from Lahore by a bigger job on a bigger newspaper. His destination, 600 miles to the south-east, was the legal and administrative centre of Allahabad, positioned on a tongue of land where the clear waters of the Jumna flowed into the turbid yellow Ganges. Here, in April 1888, he joined a Lodge that fed his imagination more than Lodge Hope and Perseverance in Lahore had done. Indeed, Kipling's new Lodge, Independence with Philanthropy no. 391, was going through an indigenous recruitment boom. Only one Indian member appeared in the Lodge records before 1883. When Kipling joined five years later, there were at least twenty, with another three joining in the eleven months during which Kipling attended meetings before leaving for England. Of the forty-three men who joined Lodge Independence with Philanthropy in 1887 and 1888, a remarkable eighteen were Indian. Even if the ethnic and religious background of these men was perhaps not as pictur-esquely varied as in the one Kipling would conjure up in poetry six years later in Vermont, they certainly included both Muslims and Hindus.

Some of these new Indian Brothers were merchants; one or

two were doctors or medics of some kind. More were administrators, especially *tahsildars* (local tax collector-cum-magistrates).
But no less than half of the Indian Masons Kipling knew were
barristers or pleaders (a more junior advocate), often referred to
as *vakils*. These were men whose prospects depended on their
contacts and good name among the British legal hierarchy. A
spiritual dialogue among Brethren from different faith communities was not the first item on their list of motives for joining. A
more obvious motive is that among the Brits on the membership
list with them was Sir John Edge. Sir John transferred in from
his London Lodge in December 1886 – just after arriving in
Allahabad to take up his appointment as Chief Justice of the
High Court of India's North-Western Provinces. Whatever their
religion, many Indian *vakils* became Masons for the same reason
that many in Britain did: schmoozing.

However, it would be a mistake to conclude from this mixed
Lodge that all was harmony between the British and the Indian
élite in the city, or even within Freemasonry. For Allahabad was
shaped, and split, by the trauma of rebellion.

After the 'Mutiny' of 1857, in which fifty whites in the city
were massacred, the British felt impelled to live as separately
as possible from the Indian population. Allahabad was turned
into a centre of government and law because it was easily
defensible. No sooner had the violence subsided than a stra-
tegically awkward seventeenth-century mosque was demolished
– without any redress to the Muslim community. This was just
the beginning of what was then British India's most extensive
urban redevelopment. The East India Railway, arriving across
an imposing girder bridge, cut the town in half. To the north
was the 'White Town' or Civil Station, including a new British
quarter baptised Cannington. On the south side lay the old,
Indian city. The contrast between the two areas was glaring.
On one side, inhabited by the 3 per cent of the town's population who were European, there was a grid of wide streets,
expensively maintained, and shaded by teak trees. There were

grand official buildings, hotels, and a hospital and medical school. For the occupants of the stucco-clad bungalows with their ample grounds, the amenities included an Anglican church, a library, a club, a cricket pavilion, a polo field, and of course a 'commodious' Masonic temple, opened in 1875 on Cutcherry Road (where it still stands today). For reassurance, there was also an infantry barracks described as 'palatial' by one British visitor. To the south, there was what the British tended to view as a sump of undifferentiated squalor bisected by a sewer that was 'a noisome ditch, with crawling fetid contents': this was where the Indian population lived, in all their manifold variations of religion, caste and profession. In 1885, shortly before Kipling's arrival in Allahabad, the departing Sanitary Commissioner observed in despair that the prevailing British attitude to the community on the wrong side of the tracks was 'if the natives chose to live amidst such insanitary surroundings, it was their own concern'.

Two small quarters occupied a no-man's land between the Civil Station and the Indian city. The first, by the railway station, was for six or seven hundred mixed-race 'Anglo-Indians'. The second was for educated Bengalis, some of whom occasionally ventured into the Civil Station to attend meetings of Lodge Independence with Philanthropy.

The Masonic Lodge was one of the very few racially integrated institutions in Allahabad. The level of integration in the Lodge was both remarkable, and very circumscribed. In such a segregated city, it would be deluded to think that, when brown-skinned Masons met 'on the Square' with Rudyard Kipling and the other white-skinned Brethren every first and third Tuesday of the month, the encounter bore any resemblance to genuine fellowship. Indeed, in 'The Mother Lodge', Kipling quietly acknowledges that the equality that reigned within the hallowed portals of the Lodge gave way to the normal hierarchies once the meeting was over:

Outside – 'Sergeant! Sir! Salute! Salaam!'
Inside – 'Brother', an' it doesn't do no 'arm.

Brotherhood between whites and natives was *'armless* if, and only if, it remained restricted to the Masonic temple.

The limits of Masonic tolerance in India were a natural fit with Kipling's own contradictory impulses. His writerly empathy was effortless and all-encompassing; he relished tuning into the profusion of India's voices. If he had been a mere bigot, he could not have written *Kim*, his great adventure of Imperial India; it would have been easy for Kipling to avoid joining a mixed Masonic Lodge. But Kipling also hated, in the most un-Masonic way. The list of his hates, which were always trenchantly expressed, grew longer through his life. America: 'barbarism – barbarism plus telephone, electric light, rail and suffrage'. Germans: 'the shameless Hun', 'who at heart follows the dark Gods of the North with the ferocity and darkness of the were-wolf his ancestor'. The Irish: 'the Orientals of the West'. Orientals: see previous quote. One of Kipling's earliest and most long-lasting hatreds, learned in Lahore and particularly in predominantly Hindu Allahabad, was for the *babu*. On British lips, this was a disparaging term aimed at English-educated, Hindu bureaucrats and lawyers who typically came from Bengal. For Kipling, as for many like him, the babus combined 'the obstinacy of men' with the 'unreasoning petulance of small children, always morbidly afraid that someone is laughing at them'. The babu had polish and came dressed in western clothes. But his very *savoir faire* made him untrustworthy – as if he were trying to be more British than the British. 'Babu Chuckerbutty' was one of the Indian character-types embraced by Masonic tolerance in 'The Mother Lodge'. Such tolerance might have been permissible in the Lodge, but it ran out very quickly if the babu in question had any pretensions to political authority.

Kipling gave a caustic portrait of an uppity babu in a tale he began to write in Allahabad, 'The Head of the District'. The story tells of an Indian administrator, the babu in question, who is appointed to govern a frontier province by a well-meaning liberal Viceroy. Bloody chaos ensues. Kipling's story is a parable about the dangers of Indian self-government. India was so vast and heterogeneous a mix of cultures, the argument went, that only the firm hand of a wise *external* ruler could hope to hold the country together.

'The Head of the District' was occasioned by the arrival in Allahabad of 1,248 delegates, 455 of them lawyers, to the fourth Indian National Congress in December 1888. The Congress had been formed in Bombay three years earlier to demand a greater voice in government for the people of the subcontinent. The British authorities in Allahabad took a dim view, and tried to stop the conference. Only when a nawab who owned an empty property with large grounds in the Civil Lines agreed to its being used for the Congress were the delegates able to come and pitch their tents. To Kipling and most of the rest of the white population, it felt like a babu invasion.

Kipling's newspaper, the *Pioneer*, lobbied loudly against the 'seditious' Congress and its 'mischief', and blamed Bengali babu agitators for the trouble. Writing anonymously, Kipling filed a long and contemptuous eye-witness report on the 'specimens from all the Provinces of India' who came as delegates. He noted with distaste that the assembly was 'swamped' by 'vakils': vakils, the Indian lawyers operating at the lower levels of the British imperial system, were a non-Bengali version of the babu, we might say. Kipling's report on the Congress defined the delegates as the 'backwash of the Educational Department'. 'In a language they could not handle [the delegates] wrestled with principles beyond their comprehension.' 'They had come to clamour for equality because their own record betrayed their inferiority.'

The only thing that maintained a semblance of order at the Congress, according to Kipling, was the presence of white and mixed-race delegates. Indeed, he made insistent reference to what he called the 'half-caste persons', the 'second-class Englishmen', the 'whitey-brown men' whom he identified as Congress ring-leaders: '[The Indian delegates] resembled nothing so much as a flock of sheep ready to break away in any direction, but hemmed in and forced to present a close front by half-a-dozen black-and-tan collies.' Understandably upset by the report, one of these 'black-and-tan' Congress delegates, an ex-army officer called Andrew Hearsey, marched straight to the *Pioneer*'s offices, horse-whip in hand, and tried to thrash the editor. He did not discover that it was Kipling who had written the piece.

Another Congress delegate who would have had every right to feel personally offended by the report's language was one of Kipling's own Brothers: a quick-witted and polished young pleader by the name of Motilal Nehru, who had joined Lodge Independence with Philanthropy a year and a half before Kipling. Nehru was a personal friend of Sir John Edge, the Chief Judge of the Allahabad High Court who had drawn so many other Indian advocates to the Craft. If 'The Mother Lodge' was in any way based on Kipling's Allahabad Lodge, then Nehru could easily have been one of the Indian character-types the poem lists. Yet Kipling's article in the *Pioneer* branded him as one of the irresponsible vakils 'swamping' the Congress.

From a high-caste Delhi family that had fallen on hard times after the Mutiny, Nehru had recently been left with sole responsibility for the welfare of his kin following the death of his older brother. He would go on to achieve spectacular success at the bar, and become a leading light in the Indian National Congress, assuming the presidency in 1919 and again in 1928. In 1947, his son Jawaharlal, who was born in Allahabad a few months after Kipling left, became the first Prime Minister of an independent India. His grand-daughter, Indira Gandhi, became India's first woman Prime Minister.

Congress delegates like Motilal Nehru were by no means radicals in the late 1880s. Fealty to the Empire was taken for granted, as it was in the Craft. In the late spring of 1887, Freemasons

Fellow members of Lodge Independence with Philanthropy in Allahabad: Rudyard Kipling (1865–1936) and Motilal Nehru (1861–1931). Sitting at Nehru's feet in this picture from 1894 is his son Jawaharlal, who would become India's first Prime Minister.

from a number of English Constitution Lodges across north-eastern India added their names to a 'Loyal Address' offering the 'warmest and most dutiful felicitations' to Queen Victoria on her Golden Jubilee. The document was typical of the genre: it aligned Freemasonry with the monarchy and the 'Providential' cause of Empire. Among the signatories in Allahabad were most if not all of the Indian Brothers. Motilal Nehru even signed it twice – and this despite the fact that the taxes collected to pay for the Jubilee celebrations were one of the insults to Indian self-esteem that Congress members protested against. Much would have to change in India before Congress would develop from the 'loyal opposition' of the 1880s and 1890s, to the governing party of the 1940s.

Nevertheless, it is a striking coincidence that the arch-imperialist Kipling was a member of the same Masonic Lodge, at the same time, as one of the fathers of Indian nationalism; that the mortal enemy of Indian self-determination sat down in brotherly harmony with the founder of independent India's dominant political dynasty. But there is also more than coincidence at stake. Just as it played a part in the British Empire, Masonry also played a part in the emergence of organised Indian nationalism.

For ambitious, Anglicised Indian intellectuals like Motilal Nehru, the Lodge certainly offered a chance to mix with influential Brits. But more than that, Freemasonry was also a school of political debate and constitutional governance – just as it had been in eighteenth-century Britain and France. The Craft's watchword of brotherly equality might well sound hollow in the mouths of some imperialists, but life in a Lodge could still offer a practical example of parity between educated Indians and their imperial masters. Masonic values also suggested that parity among Indians was possible too. Tolerant without being secular, modern and yet respectful of tradition, Freemasonry offered a way to transcend a major obstacle to the realisation of Indian national interests: the vast cultural differences between its communities, particularly Hindus and Muslims. No wonder Masons were so over-represented among the Indian National Congress's early leaders: between 1885 and 1907, 43 per cent of its presidents were Brothers.

Lodge Rising Star

Freemasons loved 'The Mother Lodge' from the moment it was published in May 1895; in every corner of the dominions, they committed it to memory. As the magazine *Masonic Illustrated* gushed at the time, it 'thrill[s] the heart of every Craftsman' . . . 'Equality, Brotherly Love, the *summum bonum* of Freemasonry, find expression in the refrain'. The power of the poem's sentimentality was that it erased both Kipling's own prejudice, and the harsh limits to Masonic tolerance in India. Instead, it made conquering and ruling the backward regions of the planet seem like a selfless exercise in brotherly generosity and open-mindedness. Again and again in his writing career, Kipling would return to the idea of the Masonic Lodge as a microcosm of the Empire, and a sanctuary where mutual understanding between cultures is sovereign – but only on condition that imperial rule remained unchallenged. The idea caught on in the public mind too, because it captured something about how the British saw themselves and their overseas possessions.

In the 1890s Kipling was rapidly becoming an imperial and Masonic celebrity. His verse, like his public image, was relayed from one end of the empire to the other by the press. In the nineteenth and early twentieth centuries, Masonic magazines were avidly consumed from Dundee to Delhi. They advertised the Craft to non-members, and spread a strong sense of shared news and a shared identity among their readers: Brothers, imperialists, civilisers. Their pages celebrated the great Masonic empire-builders: Richard Wellesley, the Governor-General of India, and his brother Arthur, the Duke of Wellington; Stamford Raffles, the founder of Singapore; Cecil Rhodes, the diamond magnate and 'colossus' of southern Africa; and, of course, Rhodes' close friend, Rudyard Kipling.

Kipling may have learned to be an imperialist in India, but in the years immediately following the publication of 'The Mother Lodge' he came to view South Africa as the Empire's supreme mission. His sense, baldly expressed, was that Britain was running out of territory to conquer, and that its industrial rivals, most notably Germany, were greedy to snaffle what was left. His imperialism was also shot through with the terror that everything Queen Victoria already reigned over could easily be lost. He increasingly adopted an incantatory, Old Testament poetic voice, issuing lofty appeals to patriotic duty in some of his best-known verse. Poems like 'Recessional' (1897) and 'The White Man's Burden' (1899) were published in *The Times* as if they were rhyming editorials. He was hailed the 'Laureate of Empire'.

Freemasons at the time of the Anglo-Boer War (1899–1902)

viewed their Brotherhood through spectacles tinted the same rosy pink as the bits of the Empire in British maps of the world. Like everyone else in Britain, they felt the pull of an unprecedented surge of patriotism fed by a jingoistic press. The downmarket *Daily Mail*, founded only in 1896, reached a million readers by the end of the conflict, making it the bestselling daily in the world. Though far less strident than the *Mail*, Masonic magazines did their bit in the media war, as is clear from their coverage of the two most celebrated Lodge meetings of the day.

Bloemfontein was a town of cheery, tin-roofed bungalows, their flower gardens tended by African servants; it seemed lost in the endless, undulating caramel-brown of the South African veld. Yet it was capital city to the Orange Free State, which, along with its sister Afrikaner Republic the Transvaal, went to war in the autumn of 1899 to remain independent from the British Empire. So it was a momentous day when, on 13 March 1900, a column of thirty-thousand red faced British troops, clad in threadbare khaki and disintegrating boots, marched into the town square. The fall of Bloemfontein looked like the beginning of the end of the war.

Back in London, there were ecstatic celebrations. The members of both Houses of Parliament gathered before Buckingham Palace to serenade the monarch with 'God Save the Queen'. Freemasons were fully entitled to toast this latest triumph of British arms at their banquets: the British commander in South Africa, Lord Roberts, was a Craftsman, and the heroic veteran of campaigns in India, Abyssinia and Afghanistan.

A few weeks later, Lodge Rising Star in Bloemfontein tried to show how brotherly harmony transcended the divisions of the conflict by creating its own version of 'The Mother Lodge'. Twenty-nine members and forty-seven visitors crowded into the town's tiny, dilapidated Masonic temple. Both Afrikaners and Brits were present. Among the visitors were soldiers from all over the Empire. Although Lord Roberts had to send a letter of apology because of illness, other Masonic military luminaries

British troops occupy Bloemfontein in March 1900.
Field Marshal Frederick Roberts (1832–1914), a Freemason,
is shown on a horse in the foreground.

did attend. Among them was Lord Stanley, the Provincial Grand Master of Lancashire, and the army's chief press censor. Most prestigious of all was the severe figure of the Chief of Staff of British forces in South Africa, the District Grand Master of Egypt and Sudan, Lord Kitchener. Kitchener had become a hero eighteen months earlier at the Battle of Omdurman: his army mowed down thirteen thousand dervishes using Maxim guns and new hollow-point bullets manufactured at Dum Dum in India.

The Master of the Lodge, Ivan H. Haarburger, gave an emotional address extolling this 'brilliant manifestation of the raison d'être of Freemasonry' which existed to 'relieve distress all over the great globe' and provide common ground even for those divided by war. Sitting at the Master's right hand, Kitchener moved to the most important business of the meeting, which was to express thanks that Prince Edward, who was both the heir to the throne and Grand Master of the United Grand Lodge of England, had survived an assassination attempt: 'His Royal Highness has done more for Masonry than anybody in the world, and I have no doubt that he heartily joins with us in wishing that peace and harmony should once more reign in South Africa.' The mood of reconciliation glowing from within Lodge Rising Star caught the imagination of the press, both Masonic and mainstream. It flattered the cherished notion that Britain had a gentler imperial manner than other European powers, that it was more inclined to civilise than to oppress and exploit.

The fame of Lodge Rising Star's meeting was also boosted by the fact that the world's two most celebrated writers and spokesmen for imperialism were reported to have been present: Conan Doyle and Kipling. There is some factual basis for the newspaper reports. Conan Doyle volunteered to lend his skills as a doctor to the forces advancing through the Orange Free State. Soon after the capture of Bloemfontein, Kipling responded promptly to a request from Lord Roberts to help edit a newspaper, the *Friend*, aimed at both the forces and the townspeople. After all, how could a Lodge meeting so inspired by the brotherly ideals of harmony between the peoples of the Empire *not* include the famous author of 'The Mother Lodge'?

Lodge Rising Star held an even bigger meeting nine months later, on 31 January 1901: thirty-nine members and sixty-one visitors signed the register. There were no Masonic luminaries this time. The occasion was a sad one: an emergency Lodge of Mourning to express the Craft's sorrow at the passing of Queen Victoria. A Presbyterian minister gave a resonant homily on the Masonic virtues of 'loyalty, reverence and love' that Victoria embodied: 'They are eternal. In our day and generation, [if] we are to practise them, then the Throne shall be kept steady, the Empire made strong, the sovereign helped, and spiritual Masonry enhanced.' Masons in the imperial capital again welled up at the reports from Bloemfontein. As one Masonic magazine reported: 'We are pleased to note that not only were there many Boer

Brothers present, but even several Boer prisoners 'on parole'. It is quite evident that no greater factor in the conciliation of races, which we all hope for, exists in South Africa than Lodge Rising Star.' Yet things in Bloemfontein were not how they seemed, either in the Masonic press, or in the work of Masonic historians who have told the story ever since.

First, it is hardly surprising that both Afrikaners and Brits mixed in fraternal amity in Lodge Rising Star. Bloemfontein's Afrikaner inhabitants were far from unanimously enthusiastic about independence from the Empire because they were heavily linked to the economy of the British-run Cape Colony to the south-west. By the time the British arrived, in any case, those Afrikaners who *were* committed enemies of the Crown had left. Moreover, the British and the Afrikaners had a fundamental shared interest in keeping the non-white population of South Africa subservient – as the peace deal struck at the end of the war would demonstrate. Needless to say, none of the black citizens of Bloemfontein were at either of the celebrated Lodge meetings. 'The conciliation of races' could only go so far.

Second, the story about Kipling's presence at the first Bloemfontein Lodge meeting was fiction. He could not have been there on 23 April 1900, as he had left three weeks earlier, bound for England, where he would set about finishing *Kim*, his tale of a boy brought up in a Masonic orphanage in India.

Conan Doyle was certainly there: he arrived in Bloemfontein just a few hours after Kipling departed, and although he was no longer formally a Mason, his signature can be read on the framed copy of the Lodge's message to the Prince of Wales that hangs on the walls of the Masonic Hall in Bloemfontein to this day. Yet it is striking that Conan Doyle did not mention the famously harmonious Lodge meeting of 23 April in his memoirs. This was probably because he was too desperately busy for it to have made any impression on him. As he later recalled, he was struggling manfully with 'death in its vilest, filthiest form'.

The problem was caused by British commander Brother Lord

Roberts' neglect of logistics and his troops' welfare. He also complacently underestimated the threat of Boer guerrillas, who cut off Bloemfontein's water supply soon after the British arrived. The result was filth, squalor and an epidemic of typhoid that would eventually kill 5,000. The little hospital where Conan Doyle was working, set up in the pavilion of the Bloemfontein Ramblers Cricket Club, was swarming with flies and totally overwhelmed. It was not Masonic harmony that emanated from the town, but the 'sickening smell of the vilest effluvia', as Conan Doyle put it. However, news of the disaster was kept from the public by the army censor, Brother Lord Stanley, the Provincial Grand Master of Lancashire; unlike Kipling, he certainly *was* present at the Lodge meeting of 23 April.

By the time of the second meeting in January 1901, the Lodge of Mourning for Queen Victoria, the British campaign in South Africa had turned into an exasperating struggle against Boer guerrillas, who were creating havoc by blowing up railway lincs and

Wherever Englishmen are to be found in any numbers there will assuredly be a club. The Ramblers' Club at Bloemfontein was a token of the large English element in the town. Before the war the British residents used to gather together in this bungalow. The building is now used by Langman's Hospital for housing the sick and the wounded. Our photograph is by F. J. Mayer

THE RAMBLERS' CLUB, BLOEMFONTEIN, NOW USED AS A HOSPITAL

The hospital where Arthur Conan Doyle (1859–1930) worked in Bloemfontein. From the contemporary British press.

destroying supply depots. Brother Lord Kitchener resorted to tactics of notorious brutality – the 'methods of barbarism', the Liberal opposition leader famously called them. Boer farms were burned. Boer women and children – the families of soldiers and prisoners-of-war, or just the victims of the farm-burnings – were herded into concentration camps, supposedly to make it easier to feed them. An estimated 25,000 inmates, most of them children, would die of hunger and disease in the camps before the war ended.

Bloemfontein had the biggest concentration camp in the Orange Free State. It was visited, at about the same time as the Lodge of Mourning, by the campaigner and feminist Emily Hobhouse. She found ten or twelve people packed into each small tent, no mattresses, no soap, starvation rations, inadequate water supplies and – most worrying of all – foul latrines. The situation was worsening as more women and children arrived. Hobhouse blamed 'crass male ignorance, stupidity, helplessness and muddling'. In such circumstances, the suggestion made by British Masons, then and since – that Lodge Rising Star embraced Boer prisoners-of-war in its solemn commemoration of the life of Queen Victoria and the greatness of her Empire – should be taken for what it is: a grotesque fantasy.

Freemasonry styled a flattering self-image for imperial Britons, a form of manhood that was resolute and self-confident, yet compassionate towards defeated foes and subject peoples. In 'The Mother Lodge', and in stories that grew around episodes like the Lodge meetings in Bloemfontein, Empire was made to seem like the fulfilment of the Masonic ideal of universal brotherhood, a vision of cosmopolitan fellowship. Through the Empire, the Freemasons were extending their moral leadership outwards to embrace a family of peoples from every corner of the world.

Emblems of mortality

After the Anglo-Boer War, Kipling began predicting what he called the 'Great War' against 'the Hun'. He is thought to have turned both of these terms into common parlance. The coming conflict would be a crusade to defend Britain's righteous imperial supremacy against a barbarous challenger. So when the Great War finally came in 1914, Kipling supported it wholeheartedly. He also pulled every string he could to help his son John get the commission he desired, despite the short-sightedness that made the boy unfit. Kipling's old friend Field Marshal Lord Frederick Roberts, the hero of Bloemfontein and a fellow Mason, intervened decisively. In late September 1915, Lieutenant John Kipling of the Irish Guards went into action for the first time amid the slag heaps and chalk pits of Loos. He was a few weeks past his eighteenth birthday, and still three years too young to be admitted to the Craft.

His body was never found in Kipling's lifetime. Only in 2016 did researchers become confident that they had identified his remains.

Kipling set off with his wife Carrie on a desperate, drawn-out quest for news through hospitals, barracks and burial grounds. Conflicting reports about John were all the couple heard. Grief, cruel doubt, and perhaps guilt inflicted immense psychological damage on them. The only consolation came from eye-witness reports that John had fought bravely, and killed Germans. 'It's something to have bred a man', Kipling wrote to a friend.

The poet was ageing, ill and undone. For eight years after his son's disappearance, he wrote almost nothing. But rather than shutting down his creativity, he redirected it, devoting it to a solemn duty that was at once personal, national and imperial: mourning and commemorating the dead of the Great War. Freemasonry would be central to his performance of that duty.

Freemasonry is about death. The noose around the neck, the sword-point at the breast, the skulls, the bones, the tombs, the urns, the coffins . . . A man's journey through Masonic ritual brings him up against endless 'Emblems of Mortality', as the

Brothers call them. Through those emblems, Masons give recognisable shape to a universal mystery. Craft workings use death as an incentive to grow as a moral being; facing up to the fear of death is a sign that one is ready to enter a new life within the Brotherhood.

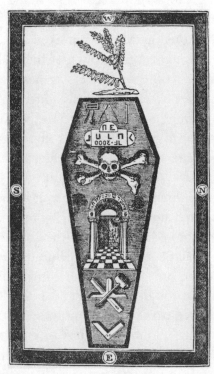

The Tracing Board displayed in Lodges
during the Third Degree (or Master
Mason) ceremony. It acts as a symbolic
aide mémoire and a reminder of mortality.

Death itself is transformed when it is ritualised in these ways. The silent, terrifying prospect of life's vanishing point becomes something that can be contemplated serenely. As philosopher Bertrand Russell once wrote, 'The most refined religions are concerned with the conquest of fear.' Christianity's story of

Christ's death and return to life is a case in point. Indeed, any form of belonging that can give meaning to death is performing essential labour. Nationalism does something very similar through the notion of dying for one's country. Masonic ceremonials sustain the fiction that dying is not a solitary experience, but one that can be faced together, standing shoulder to shoulder with our Brothers. In Masonry, death is a *man* thing.

On 23 September 1919, a Scottish railwayman called Joseph Dickie, lately a Corporal in the Royal Engineers, was initiated into Freemasonry at Lodge St George in Aberdeen. Dickie had been a professional soldier: having enlisted in 1907, he fought all the way through the Great War. After making it home unhurt, he was nearly killed by the 1918 flu pandemic. Family legend has it that he was only revived at the last by a large glass of whisky.

I mention my own grandfather only because he was typical of the many thousands of former soldiers who became Freemasons in the aftermath of the Great War. Men like Joseph Dickie had lived the unimaginable. Before their attack at Vimy Ridge at Easter 1917, some Canadian units insisted on digging their own graves. When the survivors of this industrialised slaughter were demobilised, many of them looked for a surrogate for the comradeship of the trenches, and found it in Freemasonry. The Great War led to an unprecedented spike in Masonic affiliations in many combatant countries. In England and Wales, for example, more than 1,300 new Lodges were established between 1917 and 1929, and membership roughly doubled. The Craft had never been so relevant. Masonic rituals offered a replacement for those routines of military life that make manageable the ever-present fear of death: from shared cigarettes and spit and polish, to hymns, gallows humour and the regimental badge. The Lodge might also provide the contacts needed to get on with a civilian career.

Freemasonry as an institution had long been sympathetic to the soldier's lot, and took its role in the mourning and healing process in solemn earnest. The imposing, sepulchral Freemasons'

Hall that stands today in London's Covent Garden was built as a memorial to the fallen of the Great War. In order to embrace the many mutilated former soldiers, English Freemasonry also issued a clarification to a Landmark that had often been used to exclude the disabled. The eighteenth-century *Constitutions*, echoing their medieval sources, stipulated that no man could be initiated 'unless he be a perfect Youth, having no Maim or Defect in his Body'. The Grand Lodge stated that the rule referred only to brain injuries that rendered a candidate incapable of learning the Royal Art.

Nor was it just former soldiers who found solace in Freemasonry: so too did the bereaved. Among them was Rudyard Kipling.

Since leaving India, he had never been an assiduous Craftsman. His itinerant fame ruled out regular attendance at a Lodge. Nevertheless, Freemasonry had always been an important part of his imaginative tool-bag. He was drawn to the Craft's way of handling lofty moral concerns through humble symbols based on the instruments of the stonemason's trade. Masonry allowed him to hone and texture themes like mourning, manhood and the ideals of Empire. In the poem 'The Widow at Windsor' (1890), Kipling's usual soldier-narrator salutes Queen Victoria (the widow of the title), her Empire, and the troops that made it, by comparing them to a Masonic Lodge:

> Then 'ere's to the Lodge o' the Widow,
> From the Pole to the Tropics it runs . . .

In 'The Palace' (1902), Freemasonry became a way of evoking the importance of tradition and patient labour both to poetry, and to living a good life; Kipling wrote it in the wake of his six-year-old daughter's death from a fever that had nearly killed him too.

One of the few tales that Kipling composed during his long period of mourning for his son John holds the key to understanding why Kipling would henceforth write about Freemasonry more poignantly and more directly than he had ever done. 'In the Interests of the Brethren' was written in September 1917 – exactly two years after John Kipling's death. Set in wartime London, it has little in the way of a narrative. Rather, it is a collective portrait of maimed and traumatised soldiers who find solace, and even fun, by attending a Lodge called Faith and Works. As ever, Kipling excels in his cameos. The Brethren are men of all military ranks and stations in life: they range from a heavily bandaged Scot who had 'only six teeth and half a lower lip to speak to any purpose', to a legless captain in the territorial army who is carried bodily into the organ loft to play Bach. One of the Brethren is a 'shell-shocker' who does nothing but weep; another stumbles in straight off the leave train, his uniform still caked in Flanders mud.

The Lodge of Kipling's story opens, rehearses its ceremonials, and then concludes in a banquet of ham sandwiches. Meanwhile, there is sincerity but little solemnity among the Brethren, who casually discuss what Masonry means to them. One officer in the Engineers, for example, amuses everyone by telling how he and his brothers-in-arms managed to hold a good Lodge meeting in a bombed-out church. They had only two things by way of accoutrements for their rituals. First, rough ashlars. (For Masons, ashlars are symbolic stones, one rough and one cut and smoothed. But in this case the reference is to the ruins of the church.) And second, 'the Emblems of Mortality' – here meaning the bones of dead comrades that lay scattered all around.

'In the Interests of the Brethren' has overlapping messages. Masonry is shown to bring the kind of fellowship that religion brings, but without any theological fuss. For Kipling, Masonry had always been a small *f* kind of faith, a workaday credo for makers and doers rather than thinkers. It offers an accommodating, 'average plan of life' – a cheerful way to negotiate all our trials, big and small. A one-footed corporal in the Royal Army Medical Corps utters a comment close to Kipling's own beliefs: 'I haven't much religion, but all I had I learnt in Lodge.'

The story also imparts a lesson in the healing power of loving, dedicated, painstaking work. The visiting Brethren repay the hospitality they have been offered by sweeping and scrubbing, cleaning and polishing. Years of such generosity have turned the former garage where Lodge Faith and Works holds its meetings into a jewel of Masonic propriety.

Kipling was far too good a writer to make anything he composed merely autobiographical. Nevertheless, one character from 'In the Interests of the Brethren' stands out as a reflection of the author's life. More importantly, the character also reflects what Kipling thought his duty as a writer should now be. Lewis Burges is the Worshipful Master of Lodge Faith and Works. His name is important: for Masons, a 'Lewis' is the son of a Mason. Burges's only son, also called Lewis, has been killed in action in Egypt. Burges is an artisan tobacconist, and a man of delicate hobbies such as fishing and breeding canaries. He knows only too well that he has no heir to inherit his business and his skills. Yet to everything he does, he brings expertise, generosity and good judgement, practising his craft until hard work is grooved into sacrament. 'All Ritual is fortifying,' he says. 'Ritual's a natural necessity for mankind.' This is the ethos that Burges gives to his Lodge. It is also the ethos that Kipling wanted to give to his cultural work during and after the Great War. In the face of personal and collective tragedy, his Masonry and his writing became one.

Freemasonry, as Kipling conceived it, becomes something more than mere consolation in 'In the Interests of the Brethren'. It offers hope that the Great War is not futile carnage, but the path to a more brotherly post-war world. As one character comments, 'And if this war hasn't brought home the Brotherhood of Man to us all, I'm – a Hun!' There are visiting Brothers from Newfoundland, New Zealand, Rhodesia . . . The fictional Lodge Faith and Works is 'as mixed as the Empire itself' – and thus a wartime twin of 'The Mother Lodge'.

Except that the Empire's representatives in Kipling's imaginary

Lodge Faith and Works are all white settlers rather than the religious and ethnic mix he pictured in 'The Mother Lodge' a quarter of a century earlier. During and after the Great War, Kipling embraced a vision of the Empire less as a British imperium and more as a fellowship of white coloniser nations, such as Australia and Canada, which were to enjoy equal status with the homeland. First among the reasons for this change was the contribution in blood and treasure that the dominions made to the war effort. The non-white peoples of the Empire also contributed in huge numbers. For example, among the 90,000 Indian troops who died in the Great War were the more than three thousand who fell alongside Kipling's son John at the Battle of Loos. Yet those non-white troops are invisible to the imagined imperial family of 'In the Interests of the Brethren', as they would be excluded from plans in London to grant greater self-government to some of Britain's possessions.

Within the limits imposed by Kipling's racism, the Masonic values of fellowship and sacramental work pervade everything that he did during his grief-stricken phase: he sought to live by them, and he extolled them in his writing.

'In the Interests of the Brethren' was written just after Kipling agreed to join the Imperial War Graves Commission. The Commission grew from the efforts of a team of Red Cross volunteers led by a teacher, imperial bureaucrat and journalist called Fabian Ware. They began on the Western Front by taking records of the British dead. Their duties expanded to include providing proper inscriptions on the thousands of temporary crosses to be found across the battle lines, then to finding permanent sites for military cemeteries, and finally to liaising with the thousands of relatives of the dead who wanted to come out and visit. By the time the Imperial War Graves Commission acquired its Royal Charter in the spring of 1917, Ware's organisation was active in

Salonika, Gallipoli, Mesopotamia, the Balkans, Egypt and East Africa, as well as France and Belgium. The Charter expressed the imperial philosophy that inspired the Commission's duty towards the dead: 'To keep alive the ideals for the maintenance and defence of which they have laid down their lives, to strengthen the bonds of union between all classes and races in Our Dominions, and to promote a feeling of common citizenship and of loyalty and devotion to Us and to the Empire of which they are subjects.' Reverence for the war dead was meant to set the bonds of Empire in stone.

The Commission's labour required taste and the highest sensitivity; it was immense and detailed. A register of every fallen soldier from across the Empire had to be maintained: there would be over a million of them by the time the war ended. Fragments of evidence about the missing, and about unidentified corpses, had to be compiled and analysed. A design had to be found for a gravestone, and for the layout of each cemetery – a design that would hit the right note with each religion and ethnicity in the Empire that had given its sons to the cause. Even once the cemeteries had been constructed, there was the job of planting and tending them – completing the transformation of bomb-churned battlegrounds into gardens of memory. To guide them through this task, Ware, Kipling and the other members of the Commission had one guiding principle: the fallen were brothers-in-arms. Whatever their station in life, and whatever faith they professed, they were all equal before death. Officers and men, noblemen and nobodies, would have an identical gravestone. Each individual would be distinguished only by his name, rank, age, date of death, a regimental badge and a religious symbol.

Kipling devoted his creative energies to the Commission's work until he died in 1936. He toured the cemeteries of the Western Front as an inspector. He became the Commission's official spokesman, drafted its publications and ghost-wrote commemorative speeches for royalty. Above all, Kipling selected the beautiful, bell-toll inscriptions for the Commission's monuments. He chose the phrase, 'Their name liveth for evermore', which was engraved on the altar-centrepiece of each cemetery. He created, 'A soldier of the Great War / Known unto God', which marked the graves of unidentified soldiers. Kipling's life and work were now dedicated to remembrance more than to writing. So he can be forgiven for picking a writing metaphor to commemorate those among the fallen who, like his son, had no known grave: 'Their glory shall not be blotted out'.

By all reports, Kipling found happiness in his work for the Imperial War Graves Commission. Relishing the teamwork, and confident that he was doing his duty by his country, his dead boy and his author's craft, he could shut out his troubles once the doors to the Commission's meeting rooms were closed.

The work of the Imperial War Graves Commission was unmistakably Masonic. It obeyed an ideal of brotherly equality. It reached out across the Empire. It welcomed men of all faiths, races and walks of life into its posthumous community, its Mother Lodge for the fallen. Each of the Commission's endless, exacting tasks was built on long tradition and directed towards the afterlife in such a way that it had the quality of liturgy. So it is hardly surprising that a Masonic Lodge for the Commissioners and their staff was founded at the Commission's French headquarters, at St Omer, in January 1922. Kipling was one of three Brothers who took the initiative in creating the Lodge. He also came up with its name: Builders of the Silent Cities.

> CITIES and Thrones and Powers
> Stand in Time's eye,
> Almost as long as flowers,
> Which daily die.

Kipling's Masonry, as expressed in the Imperial War Graves Commission, embraced the men of the whole Empire, of whatever colour. Yet, just like the original Mother Lodge of the poem, such broadmindedness had a condition attached: the dead of the

Great War were to seal an immemorial bond of fealty linking the peoples of Empire to their British King-Emperor.

It was not to be. The colonies saw the deal in a different way: they demanded greater independence in return for the service they had offered. Yet, while the white settler societies (Australia, New Zealand, South Africa, Canada) were offered a kind of parity with Britain known as Dominion Status, India was not. Inevitably, the drive for independence gained momentum. Motilal Nehru became more radical during the war, and started a newspaper in Allahabad early in 1919 to express the interests of 'a people ripening into nationhood'. For Nehru, as for so many Indians, a turning-point was the Amritsar massacre of April 1919, when troops were ordered to fire on a peaceful demonstration until their ammunition was exhausted, killing nearly four hundred people. Nehru led the Indian National Congress investigation into the slaughter, a role that propelled him into the front rank of Congress leaders as a proponent of Mahatma Gandhi's civil disobedience campaign. The irony of all of Kipling's Masonic memorial work was that the Empire in whose name he performed it was doomed.

In mainland Europe, meanwhile, Freemasonry was facing its gravest ever threat.

Hamburg: *De Profundis*

In a more sensible world, the Catholic Church would have learned a lesson from the Taxil hoax of the 1890s. Alas, it did not. Several churchmen aired the suspicion that the man who had exposed the hoax in Paris was a Masonic stooge. The real Léo Taxil, and with him the real Diana Vaughan, had been murdered by the Freemasons the previous day. By no means all Catholics were so resolutely gullible. But even among the Church's wiser heads, there was to be no shift in the deep-seated belief that Freemasonry was a byword for heresy, deception and wickedness.

Catholic anti-Masonry encapsulated a fear of the way globalisation, running on steam and electricity, was accelerating to push Christianity's European home from the centre of world affairs. Another reason why anti-Masonry persisted and spread from the late nineteenth century into the twentieth is that it fed the revival of a much older and more poisonous religious hatred. Official Catholicism had despised Freemasonry since the 1730s. It had despised Jews for many centuries longer: they were the killers of Christ.

At the time of the Taxil hoax, the assumption that there was a wicked alliance between Jews and Masons was a routine feature of Catholic invective. Eager as ever to profit from the Church hierarchy's nastiest fantasies, Taxil dedicated a whole chapter of *The Devil in the Nineteenth Century* to Jews in Freemasonry. It claimed that Jewish emancipation was the work of the Freemasons; that the Scottish Rite was founded by Jews; that stamping on a crucifix was part of the ritual for admission into clandestine

Jewish Lodges; and that half a million Jewish Masons were now allied to Luciferian Palladism.

By means such as this, in the late nineteenth century, traditional anti-Semitic themes were re-energised, including the blood libel: the notion that Jews secretly celebrated 'their Easter' with the sacrifice of a Christian child, whose blood was used to make matzos for Passover. Two new themes were also added to the anti-Semitic repertoire. First, the belief that Jews controlled international finance. (The Pope's own financiers, the Rothschilds, figured prominently in this updating of the venerable stereotype of the grasping Jewish money-lender.) Second, the idea that the Jews were a biologically distinct race, an alien and corrupting presence.

There was an obvious temptation for conservative Catholics to merge their anti-Semitism with anti-Masonry. Secrecy. Dark rituals. A lust for world domination. The Freemasons and the Jews seemed to have much in common. Old Testament themes were even prominent in the Craft's vast armoury of symbols: Solomon's Temple and the like. That was evidence enough that the Masons and the Jews were in league. The anti-Masonic conspiracy theory become a model for modern anti-Semitism.

Belief in a Judeo-Masonic conspiracy spread to non-Catholics. In German-speaking countries, for example, it was incorporated into a local variant of extreme nationalism known as the *völkisch* ideology (from *Volk* – people, or soul of the people): it combined anti-Semitism, a hatred of democracy and 'Jewish capitalism', and nostalgia for a fairy-tale Teutonic past. In Vienna, the Judeo-Masonic plot was embraced by Guido von List, a wildly bearded occultist, racial guru and fabricator of folk legends. Von List celebrated a Germanic master race that had originated in the icy north. This 'Aryan' people was locked in a deadly battle for self-preservation against the 'internationals' – meaning Jews, Freemasons, and even the Catholic Church. Von List latched on to the swastika as a symbol of the invincible Aryan saviour, a *Führer*, who was destined to emerge. He also founded a secret society to pursue his mission to 'purify' the master race ready for battle. Ironically, the society was modelled on the Masonic Brotherhood that he so despised. One man in Vienna known to have been a fan of these ideas was an obscure provincial art student who was seen going around for several weeks in 1908 with one of Von List's books tucked under his arm. The student's name was Adolf Hitler.

Twenty-seven years later, in Hamburg, Hitler's hatred achieved its results. Hamburg was the cradle of the Craft in Germany: Lodge Absalom, the first in the country, was founded there by English, Dutch and Swedish merchants in 1737. Under the Nazis, it became German Freemasonry's tomb.

At five minutes to eight on the evening of 30 July 1935, in the neoclassical Grand Lodge on Moorweidenstraße, the last rite began with the lighting of three symbolic candles. Their glow caught the braid on the black uniforms barely visible in the shadowy corners of the temple: the Gestapo had come to make sure the Masons did not try any of their tricks.

The tone for the ceremony was set by a reading from chapter 13 of the First Letter to the Corinthians: 'But now abideth faith, hope, love, these three; and the greatest of these is love.' Grand Master Richard Bröse put forward the motion for immediate dissolution of the Grand Lodge, and ruled out all discussion. After a unanimous vote, the Grand Master was appointed liquidator, with the legal authority to dispose of all Masonic assets. Then three terrible blows from the Grand Master's gavel sealed the passing of the motion. Tears began to flow.

The famous baritone, Brother Robert vom Scheidt, then rose to sing Sarastro's great aria from Brother Wolfgang Mozart's Masonic opera, *The Magic Flute*: 'Within these sacred halls, revenge has no place!' It was a song of forgiveness, from the mouth of the gentle but misunderstood high priest of the temple of Isis and Osiris – which stood for Freemasonry, as everyone knew. On the edge of oblivion, the Brothers were restating their values. Tears turned to sobs.

Grand Master Bröse then gave his farewell address. He recalled that the purpose of Freemasonry was 'to spread love in the name of the Creator and to learn and practise the art of self-knowledge, self-control and self-cultivation'. He cited the national heroes who had taken Masonry's oaths: King Frederick the Great, the first and greatest patron of the Teutonic Craft; Field Marshal Blücher, the vanquisher of Napoleon at Leipzig and Waterloo; titans of German letters like Goethe; and, of course, 'the greatest of all the Masons', Mozart – a genius who was notoriously tolerant in matters of faith and race. The ceremony closed with a prayer: 'A deep and painful grief has now settled on us. Give us the strength to carry it with steadfastness and dignity. In faith, love and hope we conclude our work.' A few days later, the police authorities were able to announce that 'Freemasonry in Germany has been completely smashed'.

Hamburg Grand Lodge was occupied by the Gestapo, who looted its treasures and carried its archives off for investigation. The building was then torn apart by the SS, in a search for hidden evidence that was as maniacal as it was fruitless.

In October 1941, because it was quite close to the cattle station, the former home of Freemasonry in Hamburg was used as an assembly point where the city's Jewish population were held before being deported to the ghetto in Lodz.

Few outside Freemasonry are aware that the Craft endured sometimes brutal oppression at the hands of twentieth-century Europe's dictatorships. The following pages tell the story of that oppression in Mussolini's Italy, Hitler's Germany and Franco's Spain. But these were by no means the only European states to clamp down on the Craft; nor were right-wing authoritarian ideologies the only ones to blame; nor indeed was anti-Semitism always mixed in with anti-Masonry. In Russia, the Soviet regime that came to power in 1917 was ideologically opposed to Freemasonry, but inherited a situation in which the Craft had already been banned by Tsar Alexander I in 1822, leaving very little by way of Masonry for the Bolsheviks to attack. In Hungary, Freemasons were suppressed both by Béla Kun's short-lived Soviet Republic (1919), and by Miklós Horthy's reactionary regency (1920–44). Freemasonry was criminalised by Portuguese dictator António de Oliveira Salazar in 1935. In Vichy France, the Lodges were also raided and ransacked. The list could continue.

However, it is the fate of Freemasonry at the hands of Fascism-Nazism that has since become integral to the Brotherhood's collective memory. Today, when faced with suspicion, as they so often are, Freemasons draw inspiration from the oppressed Brothers of the Fascist generation. For that reason, the closure of Hamburg Grand Lodge in 1935 by the Gestapo occupies a special place in many a Masonic history book. Masons tell the story the way I have just done: as a cameo of the Craft's integrity in the face of the worst adversity; as a demonstration of how Freemasonry and Fascism stand at opposing moral poles. The Masons claim many martyrs to mourn, particularly of Nazism – as many as 200,000, according to some estimates. 'Freemasons were arrested, imprisoned, and exterminated', one recent guide to Masonry states. Assertions like this inevitably evoke images of the Nazi death camps and their skeletal Jewish victims.

So how did it come to this? Just how true are the poignant tales that Masons tell about the suppression of their Brotherhood in the 1920s, 30s and 40s? Does the shutting of the Grand Lodge in Hamburg encapsulate everything we need to know about the way right-wing dictatorships crushed the Craft?

The search for answers begins where Fascism began – in Italy.

Rome: **Roasting the Bedraggled Chicken**

Mussolini and Gramsci

On 27 April 1914, in the Adriatic port city of Ancona, the Italian Socialist Congress debated the proposal that Freemasons should be expelled from the party. The motion's sponsor, and most forceful orator, was a balding, barrel-chested firebrand by the name of Benito Mussolini: 'It may be true that "Masonism" tends towards humanitarianism. But it is time to react against the excessive humanitarianism that has infiltrated the party.'

The leading figure on the party's revolutionary wing, Mussolini spoke with telegraphic gusto. A very physical style was thought to give him a direct connection with the masses. Energetic facial expressions, it was remarked, made him look like a man in the throes of a nightmare. The Ancona speech helped ensure a crushing majority in favour of the ban on Freemasons. Through the party newspaper, *Avanti!*, which he edited, Mussolini rammed home the message: 'the Congress has destroyed the Masonic nests that, in recent years, have been set up in the corners and half-shadows of the Socialist Party'. For Mussolini, breaking demonstratively with Freemasonry meant rejecting all forms of reformist compromise with a corrupt, bourgeois system.

Sixteen months earlier, in Rome, the congress of the extreme right-wing Italian Nationalist Association had passed a motion 'declaring war' on the Craft, which the Nationalists blamed for the small-minded, pacifistic wheeler-dealing of the democracy they sought to overthrow. Anti-Masonry Italian style came in a package with anti-system politics of both Right and Left.

Masonry was indeed part of the Italian system, integral to the country's political life as it had developed over the previous fifty years. There were ten or eleven Masonic Prime Ministers. The leadership of Italian Masonry felt a constant temptation to align the Brotherhood with particular leaders and ideological causes. But because it was rarely obvious what the Craft's high-flown values might actually mean when translated into policy, it repeatedly proved impossible to move the Brotherhood towards one end of the political spectrum without creating dissent among the Brethren at the other. So rather than ideology, what created the impression in the eyes of non-Masons that Craftsmen had undue access to power was that Lodges were often *where* politics was conducted. In the first decades after unification, political parties struggled to take root in the Italian parliament and town councils, so power was brokered between networks of cliques. Like lots of other clubs and associations, Lodges made a good place to do the brokering and networking.

Becoming embroiled in politics also carried reputational risks for the Craft, as became most apparent when wealthy Tuscan businessman Adriano Lemmi was Grand Master (1885–95). Lemmi was a close friend of the dominant political figure of the day, Prime Minister Francesco Crispi, who was also a Brother. Lemmi tried to turn the Grand Orient into a lobby group for Crispi's policies. As a result, he and Masonry also got caught up in two major scandals of the Crispi years. In 1889 it emerged that, thanks to Crispi and the five other Freemasons in the Cabinet, Grand Master Lemmi had helped an American company he represented win the contract to supply the government tobacco monopoly for a year. The company in question then proceeded to hike up the price the government had to pay – and with it Lemmi's huge commission. The rumours from within the Craft were that the money was intended to plug holes in the Grand Orient's finances. Six years later Lemmi was brought down by revelations that he, like other friends and family of Crispi's, had received a loan on extremely relaxed terms from a collapsed bank caught up in a major corruption case. The story helped anti-Masonry break out of the Catholic circles it had previously been confined to, and enter the mainstream. Major newspapers like *La Stampa* would henceforth accuse the Craft of secretive inter-ference in politics.

The cohabitation between Freemasonry and the Italian state entered a crisis in the first years of the twentieth century. The problem was not just that, in 1908, the Grand Orient endured a schism that saw a more right-wing Grand Lodge of Italy split from the democratic Grand Orient of Italy. The country was now changing rapidly. Its northern cities became industrial hubs. Democracy arrived: whereas only 6.9 per cent of the population was entitled to vote in 1900, in 1913 Italy held its first general election in which *all* adult men could have their say. Catholics entered the political arena, and brought their fearful hostility to Freemasonry with them. Political parties grew, and those parties tended to be acutely averse to the established way of doing things: from the Socialist Party, which had a powerful revolutionary wing, to the extreme right-wing Italian Nationalist Association. For these groups, the Craft embodied everything shady and decrepit about the system as it stood.

The Great War pushed Italian politics to the extremes. Benito Mussolini would soon switch from far Left to far Right over the issue of Italy's entry into the war. When peace came, he founded Fascism. Following the Fascist 'March on Rome' in 1922, he became Prime Minister. His underlying views on Freemasonry did not change.

Mussolini's government spent the second half of 1924 in an acute state of crisis created when Fascist henchmen kidnapped and murdered the leader of the Socialist Party. But after the opposition failed to bring the Duce down, he seized the initiative.

On 3 January 1925, he gave a threatening speech to parliament that all but proclaimed his intention to do away with democracy and its freedoms. Just over a week later, on 12 January, he announced the very first step towards that goal: a law to suppress 'secret associations' – meaning the Craft. The bill he presented on 12 January had two provisions: one would stop Masons getting any state job; the other would force secret societies to hand over their membership lists and rulebooks to the authorities if requested – on pain of severe measures. Over the coming ten months, as the bill made its progress into law through the Chamber of Deputies and the Senate, its effects would become more drastic: the utter and violent extinction of Freemasonry in Italy.

Freemasonry was the perfect victim for Benito Mussolini in 1925, for several reasons. The Masons embodied everything that he was intent on sweeping away as he created his dictatorship. Most of the opposition had abandoned parliament in protest the previous summer; in their absence, they were now made to look crooked, pettifogging and sneaky: in a word, *Masonic*. The law would also give the Duce a handy tool to control the many civil servants who were Brothers, thus reducing the state bureaucracy's ability to obstruct him. By contrast, the Church was happy with the policy; the Fascist leader had been making overtures to the Vatican for a while. The various components of the government coalition also approved: right-wing Catholics; and former members of the Italian Nationalist Association, who had made a hobby-horse of their 'war on Masonry'. Hitting the Craft also threw a bone to Fascist 'squads'. These were thuggish, paramilitary gangs who had cudgelled opposition of all kinds in the fields and piazzas. For them, the prospect of ransacking Masonic Lodge buildings and beating up Brethren was lip-smacking.

Indeed, *squadristi* had been ransacking Lodges since the spring of 1923. The violence escalated steadily from January 1924, in incidents dotted up and down the country. From Lucca, in Tuscany, to San Severo, in the southern region of Puglia, where the Masons' archive was stolen before the temple furnishings were heaped onto the chessboard floor and set alight. Soon afterwards, in a coordinated attack, pretty much anything portable was looted from four Lodges in Turin, in the north-west. There was more trouble during the summer of 1924, and it reached a peak in the autumn with devastating attacks on Lodges in eighteen towns and cities, including Milan, Bologna, Venice, Bari and Marsala. Only a cavalry charge prevented a Fascist mob from storming the Roman headquarters of the Grand Orient; a battering ram was used to try to break down the main door, and shots were fired at the building. Early in 1925, another wave of raids on Masons and their buildings up and down the peninsula prepared the ground for Mussolini to launch his anti-Masonic bill. There was no let-up once the parliamentary process began.

The bill was discussed in the Chamber of Deputies in May 1925. The orators took turns to decry Masonry as a 'camorra', a 'parasitic intoxication' of public life. The only group opposed to the legislation was the small number of Communists who, unlike the other opposition parties, doggedly continued to oppose Fascism in parliament. So Communist spokesman Antonio Gramsci made by far the most interesting speech of the debate. The bravest too: many of Gramsci's comrades had been beaten, imprisoned and murdered by Fascists; a Communist Deputy had recently been battered by a Fascist in the parliamentary toilets.

Intellectually and physically, Gramsci was the antithesis of the Fascists' sloganeering machismo. A childhood illness had curved his spine and stunted his growth. One casually nasty newspaper report called him 'a little hunch-back who was all hair and glasses and who, when he stood up, was scarcely as tall as the back-rest of his seat'. He delivered his lengthy and articulate speech in a tiny voice that the parliament could barely hear. So inaudible was Gramsci, in fact, that many Fascists left their seats on the right of the Chamber and crowded the benches round the speaker on the far left. The effect was intimidating, to say the least. But the Fascists' intention was also to listen attentively to what he had to say. For, contrary to what one might expect, the Fascists in the chamber did not ignore Gramsci, or shout him down. Mussolini apparently cupped his ear to catch every word; he also made numerous interjections. It became clear that, while they were sworn political enemies, Mussolini and Gramsci had a fair bit in common when it came to the Masons.

Antonio Gramsci (1891–1937).

Gramsci argued that Freemasonry was 'the only genuine, efficient political party that the bourgeois class has had'. Italy's feeble capitalists, unable to generate the resources to win over large segments of the masses in the open, had to govern from behind closed doors instead, using patronage.

Fascism's intention was not really to crush Masonry, Gramsci went on to say, but to take its place in cornering government jobs and handing them out to its followers. However, the Craft was so integral to the Italian state that, in the end, Fascism would reach a compromise with it, and the two would merge. Gramsci struck a prophetic note: 'Masonry will move *en masse* over to the Fascist Party . . . Freemasonry will become a wing of Fascism.'

For as long as the little Communist leader condemned Masonry as a perverse manifestation of the old order, the Duce could go along with him happily. But Gramsci was now saying Fascism was equivalent to Freemasonry. Mussolini snorted his objection: 'We Fascists burned the Lodges before drawing up the bill!'

Gramsci retorted that *squadrista* violence against Masons was just a phase of the negotiations. He then argued that, because Fascism was destined to fulfil the same role as Masonry, the real target of the bill under discussion was not the Freemasons: it was Communists and the working class.

By this stage, the frail Gramsci was so exhausted that he had to lean on an obliging Fascist to deliver his conclusion. He warned Mussolini and his men that, although they might conquer the state, they could not stop the coming proletarian revolution.

This hollow rallying cry made a fitting end to a dispiriting speech. Gramsci was arguing with the Duce about which of them would inherit the ruins of Italy's democracy, and which was more genuinely anti-Masonic. To really address the issue of Masonry, Gramsci implied, a political movement had to represent the working class, the nemesis of the bourgeoisie and their Masonic 'party'.

Gramsci was right that Fascism's assault on Freemasonry was just the start. He was right, too, in implying that many Fascists were corrupt, and would be further corrupted by greater power. However, his analysis was a wild exaggeration of Masonry's influence over the previous half-century, and its ability to stand up to the Fascist assault.

What neither Gramsci nor Mussolini could see was that Freemasonry was far more than what it looked like from a narrowly political viewpoint such as theirs. No one in the chamber that day could come up with a reason why Freemasonry deserved to survive. Or perceive that the main victim of Fascism's anti-Masonic legislation was to be a part of Italian society that was as weak and flawed as it was precious. Not the working class. Or the bourgeoisie. Not Communists. Or corrupt politicians. But civil society.

Mussolini closed the debate by recalling his long track record of anti-Masonry, dating back to his Socialist days. The Craft was not a mountain that needed to be demolished, as Gramsci had implied, but a mere blister that needed to be popped. This show-piece legislation showed that Fascists were ready to 'do the maximum good to their friends and the maximum harm to their enemies'. Cheering and applause followed.

Then something very odd happened. At eight o'clock in the evening, when the time came to vote on the bill, many members seemed to melt away. Only 206 were left – 30 fewer than were needed for the assembly to be quorate. The vote could not be held. The universal suspicion was that, in a chamber filled almost entirely with Mussolini's allies, the many Masons in parliament had silently asserted their fidelity to the Craft. A couple of days later, after the absent Deputies had been rounded up and encouraged to issue heartfelt apologies, the bill was passed by an overwhelming majority.

What this little gesture of protest demonstrated was that there were plenty of Brothers in Fascist ranks, and that Mussolini's strike against the Craft therefore had the added benefit of imposing discipline on his own party.

In the run-up to the Great War, Italian Masonry's traditional patriotism had morphed into aggressive nationalism in many Lodges. After the war, Masons had moved towards early Fascism for the same reasons that other Italians did: the experience of the trenches, a loathing of Bolshevism and a hankering for 'order'. But in addition to this political drift, there were also specifically Masonic reasons why senior Masons, even those who did not join the Fascist Party, thought that Mussolini might make a useful friend. The two biggest political forces of the immediate post-war years, the Socialists and the Catholic Popular Party, were both openly against Freemasonry. Masons knew that Mussolini was instinctively hostile to them, but he seemed more malleable – and the sheer number of Masons who had been with Mussolini since the foundation of his movement was reassuring in that respect. Perhaps the Brothers could nudge him in the right direction. So we should not be surprised that the Grand Master of the Grand Orient, Domizio Torrigiani, sent Mussolini a congratulatory telegram within days of the March on Rome: he 'ardently and candidly' wished the Fascist leader every success.

The Duce had not entertained the idea of appeasing the Masons for very long. He needed the Catholics more, and soon decided that the Craft made a better enemy than a friend. The Masonic hierarchy had hoped to be able to manipulate Mussolini; in the end, he manipulated them to destruction. The first formal move came in February 1923, when the Grand Council of Fascism, the party's governing body, ruled that being a Mason and being a Fascist were incompatible. There were nineteen men around the table for the vote: twelve were Freemasons, of whom eight voted in favour of the motion, and four abstained. In the entire history of the Grand Council of Fascism, this would be the only decision that was not taken unanimously. Nor was its measure entirely effective. Many Masons remained in the party. Bizarrely, there were even Brothers among some of the Blackshirt raiding parties that smashed up Masonic temples during 1924. In some cases – in Umbria, the Romagna, and perhaps also Tuscany – Masons loyal to one Grand Lodge joined the violence to get one over on their Brothers from a rival branch.

The upshot was that the different strands of Masonry, even those who were not Fascists, were incapable of mounting a concerted opposition to the campaign against them. Should the Craft stress its nationalism and declare its fidelity to Fascism? Or should it oppose Fascism openly and explicitly in the name of its Enlightenment values? Or perhaps negotiating with

Mussolini through personal channels was the answer? All of these options were tried at different times by different Masonic groups before 1925. All failed.

Mussolini's bill was due to be debated in the upper chamber, the Senate, in November 1925. As the moment neared, the campaign against Masonry switched back to the streets.

The demise of Masonry in Fascistopolis

At that time, the second most powerful man in Italy, the General Secretary of the Fascist Party, was the notorious *squadrista* chieftain, Roberto Farinacci. He was also one of Fascism's most outspoken anti-Masons. Starting as a humble railway worker in Cremona, Farinacci rose to prominence through motorised political hooliganism and extortion; he was also a grasping lawyer, who cribbed the thesis submitted to get his law degree. By the autumn of 1925, he had become a man of influence and wealth, a master of graft with close ties to financiers and industrialists. Yet he still exuded violence: he was the very man who had beaten up a Communist parliamentarian in the toilets; he was later to lose an arm while fishing with hand-grenades. With Fascism in government, Farinacci's anti-establishment extremism created problems between Mussolini and Fascism's conservative allies. Then again, it suited Mussolini to pose as the only man capable of keeping the *squadristi* under control. Farinacci joined in the campaign against Freemasonry enthusiastically. In September 1925, his pet newspaper bawled that Masons should be 'shot *en masse* as traitors to the Fatherland'.

Shortly after this article was published, documentation appeared in the press to back up persistent rumours that Farinacci had been a Freemason: he was initiated in 1915, and remained affiliated as late as 1921. In response, Farinacci claimed he had joined the Masons to undermine them from within. This convinced no one. Much more likely, he had become a Brother so as to enter influential business and political circles in his home town of Cremona.

If Farinacci was really hunting for Masons on the make, he needed to look no further than the mirror. It was now even suspected that he was still a Brother, and that he was at the centre of a recent plot among Fascist Masons to replace Mussolini. Quite how true these suspicions were, and how much they were made up by a rival faction within the Fascist Party, is unclear.

Roberto Farinacci (1892–1945), photographed in 1925 (centre of picture).

Squadristi reacted with fury to what they conveniently deemed to be a Masonic provocation aimed at their charismatic boss. Within a week, attacks began on Masons, their temples and their property in many parts of the country. The violence culminated in Florence, which was nicknamed 'Fascistopolis' because it was the main centre of *squadrismo*. On 25 September, an anti-Masonic manhunt began while the police stood by with arms folded – all under the eyes of the city's numerous British and American population. After a brief lull in the beatings, on 3 October, an official Fascist weekly published the following: 'Masonry must be destroyed. This end justifies any means: from the cudgel to the revolver, from smashed glass to purifying fire. The Masons' lives must be made impossible.' Early the same evening, four *squadristi* in search of Lodge membership lists broke into the home of the elderly Venerable Master, beat him and tried to kidnap him. A young neighbour and fellow Mason, Giovanni Becciolini, ran to protect the old man, and succeeded in helping him to escape across the rooftops. However, in the struggle, a revolver went off, killing one of the Fascists. Incandescent with rage, the *squadristi* dragged Becciolini off to their base, where he was pummelled and tortured. They finished him off in public, in front of the central market building, riddling his body with revolver shots. Before the eyes of his widow and young child, his house was trashed.

There then followed an anti-Masonic riot that lasted through the night. *Squadristi* confiscated two taxis and toured the city picking out targets: this was a free-running assault on any potential resistance among the city's middle and upper class. People were also bludgeoned randomly in the street; cafés and theatres were invaded; offices, businesses and private homes were vandalised, pillaged and set alight. Criminals joined in the free-for-all. The next morning, from the hills surrounding the city, smoke could be seen rising above Brunelleschi's cathedral dome. The violence did not stop until later that day. It is thought that eight people were killed.

In dismay at the Florence attacks, Domizio Torrigiani, Grand Master of the Grand Orient, whose country villa 50 kilometres from Florence had been wrecked and burned to the ground, issued an order to close all Lodges in the city. In a measure taken for the Brothers' own safety, he also cancelled their memberships.

At a hastily convened meeting of the Grand Council of Fascism, Mussolini tore a strip off Farinacci for failing to control or condemn this 'grotesque and criminal' violence. It was the beginning of the end of Farinacci's brief period as General Secretary of the Fascist Party. Because Mussolini had increasing control over the police, the extremists needed to be disciplined. Thus the war on Masonry had brought yet another boost to Mussolini's plans to establish a dictatorship, and tighten his control over the Fascist Party in the process.

On 4 November 1925, with the Senate vote on the anti-Masonic bill just days away, Mussolini had a freakish stroke of luck when a Freemason and Socialist politician by the name of Tito Zaniboni tried to assassinate him. Zaniboni's plot was doomed from the outset because he had told a police informer of his plans. But he was allowed to go far enough with it to make for good propaganda. He was eventually arrested lying on his hotel bed, with a sniper rifle ready on its stand by the window. The perfect excuse for a further authoritarian turn had landed in the Duce's lap. The Socialist Party was banned. The 'Fascistisation' of the press accelerated. Masonic Lodges, and other properties belonging to prominent Masons, were occupied by the police. Fascist gangs yet again ransacked Lodges in cities like Brescia, Parma, Mantua, Reggio Emilia, Trieste and Forlì.

When the debate in the Senate finally came a few days later, there were still a few voices prepared to raise doubts. One Senator complained that 'the grandiose and imposing building known as freedom of association has been burned down just to roast the bedraggled chicken that is Freemasonry'. Needless to say, the Senate voted the bill into law by a huge majority. Before the law came into force, the 'bedraggled chicken' had already bowed to the inevitable and begun dissolving itself.

Grand Master Domizio Torrigiani was arrested in the spring of 1927 and sent into internal exile. Blind and gravely ill as a result of his mistreatment, he was released just before he died, in August 1932.

Munich: **The Beer-Hall Strategy**

Protocols and politics

The notion of a Judeo-Masonic conspiracy, for all its apparent virulence in the late nineteenth and early twentieth centuries, could easily have turned out to be a fad – and one marginal to the main currents of secular European ideology at that. Then the Great War and the Russian Revolution pitched much of the continent into turmoil: politics became more uncompromising and violent; nationalism more frenzied in its hatred of internal enemies and scapegoats. When the Great War ended, far-fetched, alarming schemes involving Masons and/or Jews became more compelling than ever – as demonstrated by the most notorious version of the Judeo-Masonic myth, a book that shaped it into a full-blown conspiracy theory. First published in Russia in 1905, *The Protocols of the Elders of Zion* purported to be a speech given at a secret meeting in which Jewish leaders set out their plans to rule the world. In reality, it was as much a fake as Taxil's Palladism, cooked up from a number of French novels in the 1890s. Freemasonry was mentioned at various points in the *Protocols*. Like the press, international finance, socialism, and pretty much everything else, the Craft was portrayed as a tool of the great and despicable Jewish stratagem: 'We shall create and multiply free masonic lodges in all the countries of the world, absorb into them all who may become or who are prominent in public activity, for in these lodges we shall find our principal intelligence office and means of influence.'

The Protocols of the Elders of Zion was ignored outside Russia until translations began to appear in 1920. Thereafter, despite strong evidence that it was a fake, it became a hot topic of discussion internationally. In the United States, automobile tycoon Henry Ford was a passionate advocate, and funded a vast print run – despite the fact that he was a Freemason.

In Germany, the *Protocols* found a ready audience on the nationalist right. The most prominent believer was war hero General Erich Ludendorff. After Germany's defeat, he entered the political arena and spread the 'stab-in-the-back' myth. He believed – as well he might – that defeat was not the fault of German generals. Instead, the blame lay on the home front, where the army had been undermined by a grab-all list of back-stabbers among the civilian population: the Jews were the worst, of course; but there were also politicians and profiteers, strikers and shirkers, Catholics and Communists, Marxists and – last but not least – Masons. Ludendorff had identified a lot of enemies. And all of them were now in charge of the Weimar Republic. Or so he claimed.

Adolf Hitler had been a mere corporal during the war. He greatly admired General Ludendorff, and embraced the stab-in-the-back myth wholeheartedly. There was precious little to separate the two men ideologically: both were exponents of the racist version of nationalism known as the *völkisch* ideology. They met for the first time in Munich in 1922. The following year, Ludendorff, wearing his military uniform and *Pickelhaube* (spiked helmet), took part in a Nazi Party *Putsch* launched from a Munich Beer Hall. It was supposed to trigger a 'March on Berlin' like Mussolini's recent March on Rome. When the coup failed, the former corporal Hitler went to prison. By contrast, the former general Ludendorff was saved from a guilty verdict by his reputation.

Ludendorff, Germany's most prominent peddler of Masonic conspiracy myths, now had the opportunity to assume leadership of the *völkisch* movement, Nazis included. But he fluffed it. He

Adolf Hitler (1889–1945) and, to his right, Erich Ludendorff (1865–1937), posing at the trial that followed the Beer Hall Putsch of 1923.

was falling under the spell of his lover Mathilde von Kemnitz, a nature-worshipping pagan who thought that not only capitalism, Marxism and Freemasonry were tools of the Jew, but even Christianity. This was too much even for most Nazis. It was particularly obtuse of Ludendorff to believe that his message would cut through in Catholic Bavaria when he insisted on including the Jesuits, the Vatican and the church hierarchy in his bulky catalogue of traitors. The Nazi Party fissured among squabbling factions.

Meanwhile, Adolf Hitler's stock began to rise. Despite its failure, the *Putsch*, and especially the rousing speech that he was allowed to give at his trial, increased his prestige. That prestige grew further when he loftily withdrew from politics during his term in the Bavarian prison of Landsberg. He devoted himself instead to drafting *Mein Kampf*, the memoir-manifesto that gave definitive shape to his worldview. The book showed him to be a fervent believer in the idea of a Judeo-Masonic conspiracy. The Jews, Hitler asserted, wanted to 'tear down racial and civil barriers' and so fought for religious tolerance. In Freemasonry they found 'an excellent instrument' for this purpose: 'The governing circles and the higher strata of the political and economic bourgeoisie are brought into [the Jews'] nets by the strings of Freemasonry, and never need to suspect what is happening.' So for Hitler, Masonry was an underhand instrument of the Jew, a means to spread liberalism, pacifism and Jewish material interests.

When Hitler was released in December 1924, he pointedly refused a lift back to Munich in Ludendorff's limousine. A few short weeks later, he re-launched the Nazi Party with a set-piece speech in the Bürgerbräukeller, the very beer hall where he had started his *Putsch* in November 1923. At eight o'clock on the evening of 27 February 1925, a Friday, an audience of 3,000 was crammed under the heavy chandeliers of the Bürgerbräukeller's cavernous grand hall; the balconies, hung with swastika banners, also heaved with supporters; those at the back stood on barrels and chairs to catch a glimpse.

Over the next two hours, Hitler summarised *Mein Kampf*. The German people, he argued, were locked in a life-or-death racial struggle with the evil of Jewry. 'The Jew', who operated both by manipulating international finance and by stirring up Marxism-Bolshevism, was a 'world plague and epidemic', a parasite in the national body, a bacterium to be eliminated. Hitler was the man anointed by destiny to lead his people in a coming racial conflict that could only have one outcome: 'either the enemy walks over our corpse, or we walk over his'.

The self-styled Führer made no mention of the Freemasons. This is curious for several reasons. Mussolini, from whom the Nazis were learning so much, had only just announced his highly successful law against the Craft. As *Mein Kampf* showed, Hitler was a convinced anti-Mason. The notion of a Judeo-Masonic conspiracy was hardly new or unusual in 1925; it was political bread-and-butter for his supporters. So why steer clear of the topic in the Bürgerbräukeller?

Anti-Masonry had proved so addictive a mind-set since the French Revolution partly because it contained ready-made counter-arguments to any objections. Good Masons could be dismissed as dupes, caught up in a façade erected by Grand Masters to hide their sinister plans. The repeated failure to discover nasty secrets in the Lodges did not matter, because the real danger lay in the *hidden* Lodges. Somehow, the true face of this evil never quite came into focus. The Masons seemed all the more cunning and pervasive as a result.

To Hitler, this strength of anti-Masonry was also a weakness: it made the enemy's outlines too fuzzy. He needed to make the phantasmagorical threat to his equally phantasmagorical Aryan race seem real, biological. There could be no excuses, no margin of doubt, no fiddly process of sorting out the innocent from the guilty. He hated Freemasonry, but to let any attack on it clutter the call for a war on Jews would be to rob his ideology of its brutal simplicity. His political instincts trumped his fanaticism, telling him that hatred of Freemasonry was a flexible tool, to be deployed as and when it was useful to spread doubt and confusion. Hitler's anti-Masonry exemplified his ability to combine fanaticism with pragmatism: his overarching, obsessive hatred of 'the Jew' allowed other components of his ideology, notably anti-Communism, to be deployed when they would be most popular and have most impact.

So instead of talking about Freemasonry that evening at the Bürgerbräukeller, Hitler made some trenchant remarks on strategy. It was necessary to simplify things for the masses, 'to choose only one enemy, so that everyone can see that this alone is the culprit'. The single enemy he had in mind was, of course, the Jews, and the 'Jewish Bolshevism' that he saw as their preferred political guise. But as the Nazis in the hall were well aware, the remark about strategy, and the silence on Freemasonry, were a sideswipe at one particular man who was absent that night: Hitler's celebrity rival, General Erich Ludendorff, whose obsession with Freemasonry made him pick on *too many enemies*.

After the Bürgerbräukeller speech, the Nazi leader wasted no time in executing his next move. A few days later he lured General Ludendorff into a trap by flattering him into putting his blathering ideology to the national electorate as the Nazi candidate in the presidential elections. The result was an abrupt humiliation: Ludendorff polled only just over 1 per cent, putting him well on the way to political oblivion.

The following year, Ludendorff married Mathilde von Kemnitz, and the couple dived deep into a bottomless ocean of racial mysticism and conspiratorial delusion. Mathilde would eventually come to believe that the Freemasons, and even those arch-schemers the Jews, were themselves puppets in the hands of the Dalai Lama, who pulled their strings from a laboratory in Tibet. Her husband, the former national hero, became a national embarrassment in the press. In 1927, he published his major work on the Craft, *The Annihilation of Freemasonry through the Revelation of its Secrets*: it claimed that Masonic rituals trained Brothers to be 'artificial Jews', and that the reason they wore aprons was to disguise the fact that they had been circumcised. This was barmy even by the standards of the Masonic exposé genre. But it did not stop it selling in the thousands – about 180,000 by 1940, in fact.

Hitler, who by this time felt able to treat his defeated political rival with contempt, responded to the book by accusing Ludendorff of being a Mason.

Masons and Jews

It should hardly need saying that German Freemasonry could not wield remotely the kind of influence that Ludendorff and Hitler alleged.

In 1925, when Hitler gave his Bürgerbräukeller speech, there were 82,000 Masons in 632 Lodges. Masons in Germany tended to be lawyers, teachers, civil servants, businessmen, Protestant clergy and the like. But they were even more divided than their Italian Brothers: they worked under the authority of no fewer than *nine* different Grand Lodges – including the Hamburg Grand Lodge we visited earlier. These divisions had grown markedly worse amid the polarised politics of the 1920s. The issue of Jewish membership was the main source of the quarrel.

Contrary to what a nostalgic strain of Masonic history-writing would have us believe, most German Masons were not morally opposed to Nazism in the name of tolerance. Indeed, they were increasingly becoming *supporters* of the *völkisch* agenda. Freemasons today might want to believe that their Brotherhood stood by its values in the face of Hitler's terror; the miserable truth of what happened proves them wrong – as the best Masonic historians have now documented with impartial rigour.

The history of the Jews' relationship with Freemasonry really begins in the late eighteenth century, when communities in various European countries made their first moves towards embracing the secular values of the Enlightenment. At the same time, European states began to give Jews more civil rights. The Lodges were a natural halfway house for Jews inclined towards assimilation, because of the tolerant attitude to race and religion expounded by Masonry's British founding fathers. Masonic symbols also felt accessible to Jews: many of them were either non-religious (like the square and compass) or came from the Old Testament (like Solomon's Temple).

During the nineteenth century, the process of integrating Jews into Freemasonry went in fits and starts, in different times and places. When Germany was united in 1871, the Masonic orders from the different pre-unification states, with their distinct approaches to Jewish membership, did not merge; instead, they established an uneasy way of recognising one another and cohabiting under a weak umbrella body. The rise of anti-Semitism and *völkisch* ideas towards the end of the century put that cohabitation under strain.

On one side were six Grand Lodges known as the Humanitarian Grand Lodges. Brothers who recognised the authority of the Humanitarian Grand Lodges tended to be from the centre and centre-Left of the political spectrum, and to be open to accepting Jews. Hamburg Grand Lodge was Humanitarian. However, a large majority of Freemasons – roughly 70 per cent – came under the auspices of three Grand Lodges known collectively as the *Old Prussian* Grand Lodges, which were more historically prestigious. The Old Prussians were also avowedly anti-Semitic, and regarded the Humanitarian Lodges as dangerous centres of 'pacifist and cosmopolitan' thinking. A great many Freemasons in Old Prussian Lodges sympathised with the *völkisch* extreme Right of the political spectrum where the Judeo-Masonic conspiracy myth found its natural home. In May 1923, an Old Prussian Lodge in Munich invited Ludendorff himself to an evening of 'enlightenment' for members of the public. The Lodge's Master was of the opinion that Masonry should have a 'racist base', and wanted therefore to persuade a racist like Ludendorff that the Craft was a friend and not a foe. Ludendorff accepted the invitation, while remaining steadfast in his anti-Masonic delirium.

In 1924, an Old Prussian Lodge in Regensburg adopted the Nazi swastika as its badge. From 1926 – still long before Hitler came to power – two of the three Old Prussian Grand Lodges began to consider reforming their rituals, removing suspiciously Jewish Old Testament references and substituting robustly 'Aryan' symbols sourced from Teutonic folklore. When the Old Prussian Grand Lodges heard accusations that they were a tool of the Jews, they proudly indicated that *they* did not have a single Jewish member – thereby pointing the finger at their Brothers in the more tolerant Humanitarian Lodges.

The Humanitarian Lodges responded lamely that 'only' about one in eight of their members was Jewish. (For what it is worth, this number was about four times larger than the proportion of Jews in the population as a whole – although Jews were more numerous among the upper middle strata of the population from which Lodge members tended to come.) At this time, more and more Humanitarian Lodges were switching their allegiance to the anti-Semitic Old Prussian Grand Lodges. Even in many of the remaining Humanitarian Lodges, the climate became more nationalistic. Jewish Brothers understandably felt exposed; they deserted the Craft in droves in the late 1920s. By 1930 – still three years before Hitler took power – the proportion of Jewish Freemasons in Humanitarian Lodges had fallen from one in eight to one in twenty-five.

The Nazis were now growing in popularity against the background of a calamitous economic downturn precipitated by the Wall Street Crash. While remaining focused on the Jews and their supposed Communist puppets as a national enemy, the Nazis aimed the occasional intimidating noise at the Craft. In the summer of 1931, Hitler urged Nazi Party members to photograph the Freemasons they encountered, and make a record of where they lived.

In response, one Old Prussian Grand Lodge tried to open a personal channel of communication to the Nazi leadership, in the person of Hermann Göring, whose half-brother was a Mason. The aim was once again to try to save the Old Prussian Lodges by branding the Humanitarian Lodges as suspect. The attempt failed, and Göring snubbed the Masons' emissary.

Despite this setback, the Old Prussian Lodges were moving closer and closer to Hitler. In the summer of 1932, one of the Old Prussian Grand Lodges, the Grand National Lodge of Freemasons of Germany, issued a declaration that might just as well have been penned by Hitler's campaign manager, Joseph Goebbels. 'Our German Order is *völkisch*,' it affirmed, before going on to decry the 'slimy, murky waters' of humanitarianism, and the 'mixture and degeneration of all cultures, art forms, races, and peoples'.

We should be clear about what was happening to German Masonry. It was not just a question of Craftsmen reflecting the climate of middle-class opinion in the country at large. In other words, they were not just spooked by Communism and hankering after more order, although that is undoubtedly part of the story. Many of them envisaged a leading role for their Brotherhood in implementing *völkisch* ideas. They wanted to convert Masonry's traditional ethical mission of building better men into a programme to build a purer and more aggressive Aryan race, free of Jews.

Aryanisation

On 27 February 1933, exactly eight years after the Nazi rally in the Bürgerbräukeller, a Dutch bricklayer by the name of Marinus van der Lubbe gave Hitler, newly appointed as Chancellor (Prime Minister), the chance to turn his coalition government into a totalitarian regime. Unemployed and homeless, Van der Lubbe vented his frustrations by burning down the Reichstag. The Nazis dressed the incident up as the beginning of a Communist coup. On this pretext, a decree was passed that drastically curtailed civil liberties. Soon afterwards, an Enabling Act amended the constitution to allow Hitler to introduce any laws he liked, without consulting the Reichstag or the President. The dictatorship had begun.

The first of Nazism's enemies to be targeted were the Communists, who fell victim to a tornado of beating, torture and murder. Then it was the turn of the Social Democrats and trade unions to endure the wrath of Hitler's SA: these brown-shirted 'stormtroopers' were a Nazi army of four hundred thousand. Makeshift penal camps, private Nazi prisons for political detainees, were set up. No law applied here: prisoners could be robbed, raped, sadistically tortured, or shot 'while trying to escape'. The Catholic Centre Party was the last opposition party to be crushed. Then came Hitler's coalition allies, the Nationalists.

As soon as he had incapacitated the Nazis' political rivals, Hitler turned to anyone or anything that threatened to stand in the way of creating a Nazi society. Like clinics or lobby groups that advocated sexual health, contraception or homosexual rights. There was a crackdown on suspected gangsters and vagrants. Local mayors were forcibly deposed; hospitals, law courts and other public institutions invaded. Associations representing the interests of farmers, entrepreneurs, women, teachers, doctors, sportsmen, and even disabled war veterans were taken over and turned into tame emanations of the Nazi Party, with no Jews allowed. Synagogues were raided, pillaged and burned. Jews were attacked in the street. The civil service was 'Aryanised', meaning that Jews lost their jobs. Jewish and politically suspect university professors were sacked. Jews were expelled from orchestras and arts academies, radio stations and cinema production companies. Where the brownshirts led, legislation followed. By the summer of 1933, Germany was a one-party state, and the path to Hitler's racial dystopia had been traced out.

And the Freemasons? They certainly did not suffer the kind of systematic brownshirt assault endured by Hitler's left-wing enemies and the Jewish population. Hitler had his priorities, and they were not the same as Mussolini's had been in 1925, at the equivalent stage in the establishment of the Fascist dictatorship. The Freemasons were a long way from the top of the Nazi list. Even jazz musicians were considered a greater annoyance. Nevertheless, there were sporadic attacks during those first months – albeit nothing like as violent as in Italy. At one Düsseldorf Lodge on 6 March 1933, five uniformed stormtroopers followed by a gang of men in civvies knocked at the door and demanded to see the Lodge's records. When asked to provide some proof of their identity, they replied, 'Loaded pistols are our authority' and forced their way in. They smashed the lock of the cupboard where the records were kept and began loading the papers into a waiting lorry. But they withdrew quietly when they were told that the Lodge was in mourning for a dead Brother. In August, in Landsberg an der Warthe in Prussia, the members of one Lodge were bullied into unanimously voting to hand over all their assets to a local brownshirt unit.

An insidious threat to Freemasonry came from informers – Masons who were happy to betray their fraternal oaths to win favour with the regime. They told the Nazis all kinds of tales about goings on in the Lodges. Whether out of enthusiasm for Nazi ideology, or out of fear, individual Masons began to desert the Brotherhood, and the temples to fall silent. In Hamelin in Lower Saxony, one Lodge Master surprised his Brethren by appearing at a meeting in SS uniform and ordering that the Lodge be disbanded. The Masonic leadership rapidly lost all confidence. As early as the spring of 1933, German Freemasonry was falling apart.

In response to the crisis, all three Old Prussian Lodges united to send a letter to Hitler on 21 March 1933 – the 'Day of Potsdam' when the regime mounted a national celebration to mark its seizure of power. The letter assured that the Lodges would stay true to their 'national and Christian tradition' and be 'unswervingly most loyally obedient to the national government'. The hope was that they would be able to trade political loyalty for some kind of official endorsement. In early April, the Grand Masters finally succeeded in sitting round a table with Herman Göring. Things did not go as they had hoped. Göring banged his fist on the table and roared, 'You damned pigs, I need to throw you and this Jew-band in a pot! . . . There is no room for Freemasonry in the National Socialist State.'

The endgame had begun. Sooner or later, the Nazis would follow the Italian Fascists in banning Freemasonry.

Shortly after the meeting with Göring, one of the three Old Prussian Grand Lodges adopted the swastika as its symbol. Another tried its own ingenious solution to the problem, by ceasing to be Masonic. It abandoned its old name, the 'Grand National Lodge of Freemasons of Germany', and became the 'German Christian Order'; its constitution stipulated that 'only Germans of Aryan descent' could be members. All references to Jewish and Masonic symbolism and vocabulary were cancelled from the statutes. 'We are no longer Freemasons', one circular announced. The other Old Prussian Grand Lodges soon united behind this move.

The Humanitarian Grand Lodges were less coordinated. Three of them, based respectively in Darmstadt, Dresden and Leipzig, followed the Old Prussian Lodges by expelling Jews and ceasing to call themselves Masonic. Another Humanitarian Grand Lodge, the Frankfurt-based Eclectic Union, dissolved itself at around the same time, but then immediately re-formed in an Aryanised version, probably with the intention of saving its real estate from confiscation. The Grand Master of another Grand Lodge, the Bayreuth Grand Lodge of the Sun, announced on 12 April 1933 that the order was Aryanising, and politely asked Jewish Brethren to resign – thanking them in advance for their selfless gesture. Only six days later, the Grand Master decided that this was futile, and opted for the only realistic way to maintain the Masonic dignity of his order in the circumstances: he dissolved the Grand Lodge, asking all the subordinate Lodges to follow suit.

By the autumn of 1933, although it had not been officially banned by the regime, Freemasonry in Germany was a shell. The surviving former Grand Lodges, now Aryanised and reconstituted as German Christian Orders, remained subject to uncoordinated attacks and confiscations. Yet they still hoped that by kowtowing they might earn some form of state recognition. One of the reasons why this hope persisted, and why the Nazis took much longer to stamp out Freemasonry than did the Italian Fascists, was exactly the reason that Hitler had intuited back at the Bürgerbräukeller in 1925 when he chose to focus on a single enemy: deciding just who was and who was not a Freemason was a confusing business.

In the eyes of the Nazis, the creation of the German Christian Orders could just be the Freemasons' latest devious ruse. The issue did not just affect the matter of whether to ban Masonry. What about all the former Freemasons around? Many were also members of organisations that had now been incorporated into the Nazi state. So should they be expelled? Or barred from holding government jobs? Where should the line be drawn? Between the former Old Prussian Lodges and the former Humanitarian Lodges? Or between those who had given up their Masonic ways *before* the Nazi seizure of power, and those who had only conformed afterwards? In some places, the Gestapo suspended anti-Masonic lectures because they thought they were attracting unwanted followers of the aged General Ludendorff. The confusion increased because the SA, the SS, the Gestapo, and other agencies and individuals within the Nazi state jockeyed for control of what was becoming known as the 'Freemasonry Question' – and therefore of the right to plunder the Lodges. For a while, in January 1934, the Führer even suspended measures against Freemasonry to ease the tussling within the Nazi movement. Loyal as ever, the former Old Prussian Grand Lodges chose to interpret this as a hopeful sign. They also saw hope in the fact that a former Freemason by the name of Hjalmar Schacht served in Hitler's government as President of the Central Bank and then Minister of Economics.

In Hitler's mind, political calculation was temporarily outweighing his anti-Masonry, just as it had done in 1925. Some grassroots Masons saw more clearly that the end was nigh. Walter Plessing, like his father and grandfather before him, was a member of an Old Prussian Lodge in Lübeck on the Baltic coast. In September 1933, he resigned in order to join the Nazi Party, and succeeded in becoming a stormtrooper. A few months later, when it was discovered that he had been a Mason, he was forced to leave the party. In March 1934, when he heard that he would be forced out of the SA too, he committed suicide, bequeathing all his money to Hitler. His suicide note protested at being treated as a traitor and a 'third-class German'; neither he nor his former Lodge had any 'connection with Jews or Jewry'.

Nazi Policy on Masons only became unequivocal after July 1934 and the Night of the Long Knives – the savage purge of the SA and other political enemies. Thereafter, the SS assumed control of the Masonic Question. In October 1934, a recent recruit to the SS intelligence agency, Adolf Eichmann, was given a first test of his administrative skills: he was told to compile a central index of Masons. Having convinced his superiors of his talents, he was moved to the SS department responsible for Jews, where he would go on to play a notorious logistical role in implementing Hitler's 'Final Solution' to the 'Jewish Question'.

In the spring of 1935, finally, the former Masonic organisations were told to dissolve themselves completely, or be forced to do so. Either way, their assets would be confiscated. The Grand Masters agreed to this recommendation, on condition that the Craft was publicly absolved of all the accusations of disloyalty that had been made against it. No such absolution was ever granted. The self-dissolutions went ahead anyway during the summer.

All of which brings us back to the mournful scene with which this story began: the final closure of the Grand Lodge in Hamburg, to the sound of weeping Brothers and of Mozart's *The Magic Flute*.

Hamburg, long a centre of a more liberal form of Masonry, was a Humanitarian Grand Lodge – one that admitted Jews, therefore. To his credit, before the Nazis assumed power, Grand Master Richard Bröse did seek to parry Hitler's attacks. He chose transparency as his shield. In August 1931, he wrote a public letter to Hitler offering to grant open access to the Grand Lodge's archives to any investigator mutually agreed between the two of them. Furthermore, he pledged to close the Grand Lodge down if it was found that Masonry had ever done anything against the national interest.

Nazi poster (1935): 'Jews – Freemasonry. Global
politics – World revolution. Freemasonry is an
international organisation in thrall to Jewry.
It has one political goal: through the world
revolution it seeks Jewish rule.'

Bröse's attempt was doomed. No amount of transparency can
reassure a conspiracy theorist. Hitler did not reply. Instead, the
task was taken up by senior Nazi ideologist Alfred Rosenberg,
who dismissed Bröse's offer as a typical Masonic deception; the
Nazis regarded all Masons as traitors, he scoffed.

Once Hitler had taken power, Bröse betrayed his order's
tolerant values as fast as any other Humanitarian Grand Master.
On 12 April 1933, he announced that the Grand Lodge was open
only to 'German men of Aryan descent and Christian religion'.
It was in this Aryanised form that the Hamburg Grand Lodge

shut down, under the eyes of the Gestapo, in the summer of 1935. Clearly, the tale of the closure of the Hamburg Grand Lodge as Masons tend to recount it omits one painful detail: the Craftsmen present in the Hamburg temple that night had already abandoned all trace of Masonic values and embraced Nazi racism in a futile attempt to ensure their survival as a Christian-only fellowship. Mozart would have turned in his grave.

No historian will ever be able to reconstruct the exact mixture of emotions that led Bröse and his Brothers to shed such copious tears on that evening in Hamburg in July 1935. Certainly a sense of loss and injustice. Fear and frustration too, most likely. It may also be that another feeling clouded their eyes as the last rites of their Brotherhood were performed: shame.

The only Masonic group that voiced opposition to Hitler in the name of Masonic values was neither a Humanitarian nor an Old Prussian Lodge. The Symbolic Grand Lodge of Germany was formed in 1930 when some Masons who were determined to stand against the anti-Semitic tide broke off from the Humanitarian Lodges. Virtually alone among German Masonry's leadership, the Grand Master of the Symbolic Grand Lodge, a lawyer called Leopold Müffelmann, resisted courageously, continuing to criticise Nazism even after Hitler took power. Then on 29 March 1933, *in public*, he declared the dissolution of his Grand Lodge, while taking measures to ensure that it could continue to work in secret. However, within a few weeks, Müffelmann had to recognise that the situation was too dangerous. So in June 1933, at a secret meeting in Frankfurt, he and the other leaders of the Symbolic Grand Lodge of Germany decided to transfer their base to Jerusalem, and try to survive in exile.

On 5 September, Müffelmann was betrayed by an informer and arrested in Berlin. He was interrogated by the Gestapo before being sent to the stormtroopers' penal camp at Sonnenburg. There he was beaten and forced to do hard labour, despite having a serious heart condition. He died in August 1934 as a result of his ordeal.

Müffelmann and those who shared his vision of Masonry were, it should be stressed, a tiny minority of fewer than two thousand at the peak. What is more, they were a minority that the institutions of mainstream Freemasonry, both the Old Prussian and the Humanitarian Grand Lodges, categorically refused to recognise as legitimate Masons. So as one historian has pointed out, it is misleading of Freemasons to treat the Symbolic Grand Lodge of Germany as a 'poster child of Masonic victimization and courageous resistance'.

Grand Master Müffelmann was one of the few Masons to be persecuted as a result of his activity within the Craft. Indeed, a vast ambiguity clouds most of the victims of Nazism that Freemasonry claims as its own – whether they are 80,000, or 200,000, or any other number. Take the case of Brother Carl von Ossietzky, who was arrested within hours of the Reichstag fire. Deprived of food, he was forced into hard labour, and beaten and kicked by camp guards who yelled 'Jewish pig' and 'Polish pig' at him. (As it happened, he was neither Jewish nor Polish.) By November 1935, when he was seen by a Red Cross visitor, Ossietzky was 'a trembling, deadly pale something, a creature that appeared to be without feeling, one eye swollen, teeth knocked out, dragging a broken, badly healed leg . . . a human being who had reached the uttermost limits of what could be borne'. It is a testament to his endurance that he only finally succumbed eighteen months later, in May 1938.

Ossietzky was both a Freemason and a victim of Nazism. But he was not victimised *because* he was a Freemason. He was killed because he was a left-wing intellectual, a prominent journalist and critic of Nazism, and a pacifist who had reported Germany's illegal rearmament programme to the international community. He was awarded the Nobel Peace Prize while in a concentration camp in 1936.

How many Freemasons died under the Nazi regime? The research has yet to be done. But it seems very, very unlikely that the total of Masons murdered reached as many as 200,000. That would represent a staggeringly high percentage of the total number of Masons in countries occupied by German forces in the Second World War. What is certain is that the vast majority of those who did die were not killed *because* they were Masons, but above all because they were Jews. Austria, which became part of the Third Reich in the Anschluss of March 1938, is probably typical. When Nazi forces marched in, there were 800 Masons in Austria. The Vienna Grand Lodge was raided and the Grand Master arrested; already ill, he died in custody. The Nazis rapidly proceeded to abolish Freemasonry in Austria as they had done in Germany. It has been calculated that between 101 and 117 Brothers were murdered before 1945. Another 13 committed suicide; 561 went into exile. But these figures only make sense when we realise that most *Catholic* Masons had resigned before the Germans marched in. Hundreds of them had already abandoned the Craft after 1933 because of harassment by the Catholic-Fascistic government that preceded the Nazis. Left behind in the Lodges when the Nazis arrived in 1938 were many Jews – two-thirds of that total of 800.

Although the Nazi state in Germany crushed Freemasonry, it did not persecute individual Freemasons with remotely the same lethal fanaticism as it did other groups. *Mein Kampf*, after all, had given non-Jewish Craftsmen an escape clause. Hitler's memoir had said that ordinary Masons 'never needed to suspect' that the Jews were really in charge behind the scenes. So, in the overwhelming majority of cases, it was enough for a Brother to recant for him to dodge the jackboot and the concentration camp. Even the institutional discrimination against former Masons was lifted, as many Masons with qualifications and skills showed they could be loyal and useful members of Nazi society.

The reasons why Masons have exaggerated what they endured at Hitler's hands are not hard to discern. The Nazis are Hollywood's favourite bad guys. Contrasted against the pitch-black evil that they represent, the Masonic tradition seems to shine more nobly. But Masonry's misleading memories of Nazi repression do a disservice to those who were far more ruthlessly targeted by Nazism: it is as if the Craft were trying to get a foot on the pedestal of history's greatest victims.

Perhaps more tellingly, those Masonic identity narratives draw attention away from a regime that was far more brutal and thorough in its persecution of Freemasonry than were Mussolini's Italy and Hitler's Germany: the Spain of General Francisco Franco.

14
Salamanca: **Hyenas And Concubines**

Long live death!

The mass murder of Freemasons began within days of the start of the Spanish Civil War.

On 17 July 1936, Spanish colonial troops in Morocco revolted against a democratic Republic; the revolt soon spread over the Strait of Gibraltar to barracks on the mainland. The country was cut in two. Where the military uprising failed, including in Madrid and Barcelona, the Republic retained control – albeit in a chaotic state, since no one knew which elements of the army and police would remain loyal, and bands of revolutionary leftists controlled the streets in many places. Where the uprising succeeded, a Nationalist Spain was carved out by martial law. A pocket of Nationalist territory in the south-west quickly expanded as the Army of Africa, a mix of colonial soldiers and Moroccan mercenaries, mounted a bloody advance. In September 1936, the Army of Africa was rewarded for its successes when its commander, General Francisco Franco, assumed supreme military and political leadership of the rebellion. He would soon adopt the title of Caudillo – the Spanish equivalent of Duce or Führer.

In Nationalist Spain, the army and right-wing vigilantes imposed a reign of terror. The intention was loudly proclaimed: to 'cleanse' the Fatherland of its political and cultural 'pollutants'. Anyone associated with the Republic and its institutions, with the political Left, and even with secular modernity, was liable to be arrested, tortured and executed: trade unionists and politicians, workers and peasants, liberals and intellectuals, emancipated women and homosexuals. Tens of thousands died. Among them were many Freemasons.

Most of the Masonic victims were killed in the early months of the Civil War, when the violence was not centrally orchestrated, and left little paperwork behind for historians to work on. The Nationalists would eventually win the Civil War, and thus control the documentary evidence upon which accurate historical reconstruction relies. Today, more than four decades after democracy was restored, the crimes perpetuated against civilians during the Spanish Civil War are still a live and controversial topic of research. The oppression of Freemasons is a neglected aspect. As a consequence, we are nowhere near reaching a calculation of the Masonic body count. The first attempts by historians to reckon the atrocities committed against Freemasons had to wait until after Franco's death in 1975. The earliest picture to be sketched was fragmentary, but shocking. In Zaragoza, thirty Brothers belonging to Lodge Constancia were murdered. In the town of Ceuta on the African coast, Lodge Hijos de La Viuda lost seventeen Brothers. In Algeciras, on the Bay of Gibraltar, twenty-four members of Lodge Trafalgar died. All but a handful of the Brothers in Lodge Vicus in Vigo were killed. In places like Tétouan (Morocco), Las Palmas (Canary Islands), La Coruña, Lugo and Zamora, the Freemasons were exterminated.

The list could continue. But this early panorama of the anti-Masonic atrocities was still fogged by hearsay and Civil War propaganda. Nobody could quite be sure how reliable it was. Yet it established clearly enough that Spanish rightists were uniquely vicious in their campaign against the Craft. The persecution also raises the same awkward question raised by estimates of the number of Masonic victims of Nazism: were these Spanish Brothers all murdered *because* they were Masons? Or were they targeted for other reasons, and just *happened to be* Masons?

Only in a few places have investigations now been carried out to verify the shocking initial sketches. In Granada, for example, we know that 35 per cent of Freemasons died violently. Yet the evidence points to their being executed primarily because they were representatives of democratic parties or the Republican institutions rather than because they were Masons. In early August 1936, when the Nationalist authorities captured membership documents from the city's three Lodges, the ensuing inquiries found that many of the men listed had already been put to death for other reasons. The surviving Brothers were incarcerated.

In Seville, Lodges were raided, and membership lists published in the Catholic and right-wing press: a cue for vigilante violence. Here too, the Masons most likely to be killed were those who occupied prominent positions in the institutions of the Republic. For opponents of the rebellion, being a Mason could be an aggravating factor serious enough to make the difference between being sent to concentration camp and being put before a firing squad. A few, notably the regional Grand Master and his son, were executed for no other reason than that they were prominent in the Brotherhood. By contrast, many Masons scrambled to distance themselves from the Craft and demonstrate their enthusiasm for the rebellion – thereby preserving their freedom and their life. Seville and Granada were both places where the Nationalist violence was particularly intense, yet no Lodge suffered the eradication of all its members.

Clearly, not all the Masons who died were killed because of their Masonry. Yet there was a belief, shared by all the different forces on the Nationalist side, that a conspiratorial Masonic influence permeated the Republic so thoroughly that almost anyone could be an instrument of the Lodges. The brutality was capricious: many were denounced on the basis of false or exaggerated testimonies. Some Nationalist groups, like the Falange (Spain's Fascist movement), compiled their own death lists from any source that came to hand. The inevitable result was that many of the people murdered for being Freemasons had nothing to do with the Craft.

A famous episode from the heart of Nationalist Spain brings this messy tragedy into human focus. In late September 1936, the rebel military élite met in Salamanca to appoint General Francisco Franco as their supreme leader. Salamanca was a good choice to be the Nationalist capital. A place of conservative traditions that enjoyed the prestige of one of the world's oldest universities, it was also close enough to the Portuguese border to give the rebellious generals an escape route if the Civil War went against them. As a sign of the Church's favour, the Bishop of Salamanca offered General Franco his palace as a headquarters. A short time later, and no more than a couple of hundred metres away, a public ceremony was held under the stone arches of Salamanca University's great hall, to honour Columbus's 'discovery' of America and Spain's imperial heritage. The bishop was there, as was Franco's wife. The main speaker was the Caudillo's most savage commander, General José Millán Astray, who had lost an arm and an eye in colonial fighting. Millán Astray's splenetic harangue climaxed with the battle cry of the Spanish Foreign Legion, '¡*Viva la Muerte!*' ('Long live death!').

The slogan shocked and angered the old man who was presiding over the event: Miguel de Unamuno, one of Spain's great writers, and the Rector of the University. Unamuno had initially supported the Republic, but was appalled by the disorder that seemed to reign under it. Then he supported the military rebellion – until he witnessed its unbridled violence. As General Millán Astray spoke, Unamuno reached into his pocket, where he had put a plea for help he had received from the wife of a friend; the friend in question was the city's Protestant pastor and had been arrested for being a Freemason. Unamuno took the letter out and scribbled some notes on the back – the basis for what would become his last speech, and the most memorable of the Civil War.

With breathtaking bravery, Unamuno rose to his feet and called Millán Astray a cripple, who wanted to see Spain crippled. He went on to warn the General that the Nationalists had brute

General Francisco Franco (1892–1975) with his
wife and daughter in Salamanca during the
Spanish Civil War.

force on their side, but not reason or right. 'You will conquer,
but you will never convince.' The slogan would echo through the
long years of Franco's dictatorship.

Unamuno was lucky to get out of the university alive. For his
insolence, he was sacked and placed under house arrest. In
December 1936, he sent an anguished letter to a friend. Here in
Salamanca, he wrote, there had been 'the most bestial persecution and murders with no justification'. What claimed to be a
war on Bolshevism was actually a war on liberalism. Anyone
could be caught up in it: Freemasons, Jews, members of the
League of Human Rights. 'Lately they've killed the Protestant
pastor here, for being a Mason. And for being my friend. Clearly

these dogs – and among them there are some real hyenas – have no idea what the difference is between Freemasonry and anything else.' So the Protestant pastor did not make it. Neither did twenty-nine of his Brothers in Lodge Helmántica, Salamanca.

Miguel de Unamuno, his spirit broken, passed away two and a half weeks after writing the above words. We can only guess at what his feelings would have been had he known that the atrocities of 1936 were only the beginning. Hatred of Freemasonry was set to drag the Caudillo and his followers down a remorseless slide into an obsession unique in the history of the Craft. But before we trace the arc of that descent, we need to take a step back and ask what it was about Spain's right-wingers that made them repress Masonry with more brutality than did their counterparts in either Italy or Germany. The short answer is: the Catholic Church. The forces that fell in behind Spain's military rebellion in the summer and autumn of 1936 inherited the full force of the Spanish Church's legacy of anti-Masonic rage and fear.

A perfectly Masonic political revolution

Freemasonry had had a troubled early history in Spain – the Inquisition saw to that. Only after Napoleon Bonaparte invaded in 1808 were Lodges allowed; but they were banned again following the restoration of the monarchy in 1814.

Thereafter, in Spain as elsewhere in Catholic Europe, the history of Freemasonry was part of a protracted culture war between the Church and the forces of secular liberalism. The Spanish Church was actually pretty successful in defending itself against the threat of secularism. While Freemasonry may have been unbanned in 1868, Catholicism remained the religion of state under the constitutional monarchy (1876–1923): education was Catholic, and public expression of other religions was banned. Despite this comparatively very privileged position, the Church in Spain resented the gains the secularisers had already made – including the legalisation of Freemasonry. Catholics were politically divided by many things, such as the vexed issue of regional autonomy. Yet they were united in their loathing of Freemasons. In the 1880s, Léo Taxil's invented exposés of Satanism in the Lodges was rapidly translated into Spanish. There was a rash of home-grown anti-Masonic publications.

The Church was not entirely wrong to identify Masonry with secularism. In the last quarter of the nineteenth century, Spanish Masonry prospered for the first time – although it remained much smaller and less powerful than in other Catholic countries like France and Italy. Membership increased to over ten thousand; there were eight Masonic newspapers. Freemasons viewed themselves as an enlightened minority, holding out against mass religious fanaticism. They were active in anticlerical newspapers and in running lay schools. However, as elsewhere in Europe, Spanish Freemasons were divided between several competing Grand Lodges, and were thus unable to exercise any influence collectively.

A turning-point came in 1898 with Spain's traumatic military defeat at the hands of the United States, which led to the loss of its last remaining possessions in the Americas. Four centuries of New World empire were at an end. Catholics blamed this national humiliation on the Masons – whether at home, or in Cuba and the Philippines. Police raided the Madrid headquarters of the Grand Orient of Spain and the National Grand Orient, the country's two most important Masonic governing bodies. Masonic membership went into decline. In the wake of 1898, the military developed its own strain of anti-Masonry. Two generations of officers would grow up believing that a fifth column of Masons had caused Spain's defeat, and were actively impeding attempts to carve out new territories in Morocco.

The accelerating social changes of the early twentieth century then hardened opinions on the Church-versus-state issue, as on many others. Although the advance of Masonry had been checked, the Church's fear of the Craft increased regardless. For the more the system was permeated by the Catholic hierarchy's vision of a society based on religion, property, order and family, the less able it was to meet the challenges of modernity, and the more enemies the Church acquired. Liberals mounted a secularising drive and the threat of atheist socialism loomed. There were a number of anticlerical riots. During the upsurge of working-class violence in Barcelona in 1909 known as the 'Tragic Week', radicals, socialists and anarchists beheaded religious statues, desecrated graves and burned churches. Nor would this be the last attack against religious personnel and property. By the end of the Great War, entire sectors of Spanish society hated the Church: notably the urban working class, and the brutalised peasantry of the great estates of the south. Spanish Masonry's destiny was in the balance: it was wedded to the fortunes of liberal ideas – which would increasingly be treated with scorn by both Right and Left.

In 1923, amid strikes, disorder and the international fear of Bolshevik revolution, a military dictatorship under Miguel Primo de Rivera abandoned constitutional government, much to the satisfaction of many in the Church. Masonry was harassed, although not banned. *The Protocols of the Elders of Zion*, with its report of a Judeo-Masonic conspiracy, was first translated into Spanish during the dictatorship. The Jews were henceforth the Masons' regular partners in imagined plotting. But partly because there was only a very tiny and almost invisible Jewish population – they had notoriously been expelled in 1492 – their threat remained an abstract one. The Masons, by contrast, seemed all too real.

Primo de Rivera's dictatorship fell because its attempts at conservative reform only increased the opposition to it, even within the military; as it fell, it also brought down the Church's historical ally, the monarchy. When a democratic Republic was declared in April 1931, the forces of secular modernity finally had the chance to steer Spain into the future, and away from the Church. Many Freemasons, true to their Brotherhood's longstanding constitutional sympathies, took a leading role. Of 468 members of the Constituent Assembly elected in June 1931 with the task of drawing up the Republic's Constitution, 149 are thought to have been Freemasons – just under a third. This prominence was all the more remarkable given that there were only about five thousand Craftsmen in the whole country. Yet they viewed the Republic as their own creation, as an editorial in a magazine for members of the Scottish Rite made clear: 'There has been no more perfectly Masonic political revolution than Spain's. Everything was temperance, justice, order, moderation, humanitarianism, tolerance, and piety.'

To Catholics, even those who supported the Republic, such triumphalism confirmed the worst alarms about a Masonic plot. As did the Republic's Constitution itself. Civil marriage and divorce were introduced, along with freedom of worship. Religious orders of monks, nuns and priests were barred from any role in education. 'Spain has ceased to be Catholic,' as the prominent Republican minister Manuel Azaña crowed in October 1931. To the dismay of Catholics, Azaña would go on to serve as the Republic's Prime Minister and then President. The government issued provocative directives forbidding religious burials and processions.

Such measures only stoked opposition to the Republic. Anti-Masonic hatred became a token of rightist identity that was guaranteed to raise a cheer among supporters of all the different factions among the Republic's enemies. The volume of the propaganda was now turned up several notches. The Catholic newspaper *El Debate* had no doubt that 'the spectre of the Lodges' was operating behind the scenes. A leading figure among the Carlists, a group that wanted to return to an almost theocratic version of the monarchy, told a rally in Palencia, 'We are governed by a small number of Freemasons, and I say that any means are permitted against them if they continue trying to de-Christianize us.' In 1932, a Catholic youth movement launched with a manifesto 'declaring war' on Communism and Masonry. Catholic resistance to the Republic centred on a new party, CEDA (standing for Spanish Confederation of Autonomous Rights), which increasingly imitated the rhetoric and style of Nazism. There was an anti-Masonic drumbeat in CEDA's propaganda: 'The country is writhing in the anguish of a tragic agony, because of crimes and outrages committed by lunatics who are paid for and commanded by the Masonic Lodges and international Judaism. With the cooperation of Marxist sectarianism, they have broken the sacred bonds of Church and state.'

For a while, a right-wing electoral victory in 1933 checked the secularist advance. In October 1934, CEDA's leader became Minister of War and immediately moved to ban Masons in the military: six generals were dismissed. New elections in February 1936 saw anti-Masonry once again become a battle cry for the Right. 'They shall not pass! Marxism shall not pass! Freemasonry shall not pass!'

For all this stridency, the 1936 election result brought the Left to power once more, and with it the forces of anti-clericalism. The polarisation of Spanish society accelerated dramatically. Militias were formed on both sides. There was a rash of tit-for-tat assassinations.

Plans for an army rebellion against the Republic were soon hatched. The man at the centre of those plans, General Emilio Mola, believed that the Republic itself had come about through 'one race's hatred, as transmitted through a skilfully managed organization: I am referring specifically to the Jews and Freemasonry'. On 30 June 1936, Mola issued a long list of instructions to his fellow conspirators in Morocco, where the revolt would begin; they included the following: 'Eliminate leftist elements: communists, anarchists, trade unionists, Freemasons, etc.'

When the fighting started two weeks later, a cruel vengeance was unleashed on both sides. Hatreds sedimented over decades burst to the surface. There was a wave of anticlerical killings in the Republican zone: close to seven thousand clergy died, including thirteen bishops and two hundred and eighty-three nuns. These murders often took a sadistic, symbolic form. In Torrijos, near Toledo, the parish priest was stripped and flogged, and then forced to drink vinegar, wear a crown of thorns and carry a beam on his back. In the end, his tormentors decided to shoot him rather than nail him to a cross. There is little or no evidence that Masons were involved in the many episodes of anticlerical violence that Spain saw before and during the Civil War. But that made little difference.

On the Nationalist side, bishops hailed the right-wing uprising as a 'crusade'. The guns of soldiers and militiamen were blessed as instruments for the defence of Christian civilisation. More than a century of Catholic anti-Masonic venom made the Brothers a target, part of the 'anti-Spain' that had to be crushed. According to one newspaper belonging to the Falange, in September 1936: 'All of Spain is calling for exemplary and rapid punishment for Masons, those cunning and bloodthirsty men.' To make matters worse, by a tragic historical coincidence, the British influence that had radiated up from Gibraltar meant that the Craft was concentrated in the southwestern corner of Spain, around Cádiz, Huelva and Seville – the very area that was most savagely 'purged' in the first months of the war. So it was that decades of religiously infused anti-Masonic rhetoric culminated in the brutal persecution of Masons at the start of the Civil War.

Mussolini had a long track record as an anti-Mason. But his Fascist movement was not a Catholic force and, except when it came to political tactics, religion played no part in his anti-Masonry. Nor did anti-Semitism. Although Hitler was of course an anti-Semite, he was no more religious than was Mussolini in his anti-Masonry. Like the Duce, the Führer was tactically flexible. His animus against Masonry was always subordinated to his strategic goals: winning power; crushing all sources of actual or potential opposition; waging a race war. By contrast, the Spanish style of Fascism, as it took shape under General Franco, was Catholic through-and-through. Anti-Masonry, and the persecution of Freemasons, were essential to Nationalist propaganda and action.

From APIS to DERD to TERMC

As the military acquired stable control in Nationalist territory, Craftsmen were more likely to end up in a prison camp or labour unit than staring down the barrel of a gun. However, brutal treatment continued to be meted out to them here and there throughout the Spanish Civil War: it is reported that in Málaga, in October 1937, eighty prisoners were executed just for being Masons. Such ferocity was remarkable enough. More remarkable still was the repressive drive that began during the war and continued well beyond its end. Neither the Duce nor the Führer, once they had broken the Brotherhood as an organisation, were particularly zealous in persecuting individual former Masons. The Caudillo, by contrast, was remorseless to the point of obsession.

As a Catholic, and a professional soldier who had made his career in the Moroccan campaigns, General Francisco Franco carried a predictable baggage of anti-Masonry. He may also have had a personal rancour against the Craft. Some testimonies suggest that he twice tried and failed to join a Lodge, in 1926 and 1932, in the hope of accelerating his military career. It is claimed that he was blackballed on the second occasion by his brother Ramón, a celebrated aviator with Republican sympathies; the two had a very tense relationship. Be that as it may, Franco certainly blamed Masons in the military for blocking his advancement.

Once the Civil War began, Franco put his anti-Masonry into practice even before he assumed supreme leadership of the Nationalist side. In mid-September 1936, he outlawed the Craft in the territory under his command, and declared that persistent members were guilty of the 'crime of rebellion'. In December

1938, he announced that all Masonic motifs and inscriptions that 'could be judged offensive to the Church' would be destroyed.

As the Francoist forces ground out their victory, which they owed in large part to German and Italian military support, the Caudillo began to take measures to purge all Spain of the Masonic plague. The notorious Law of Political Responsibilities, issued in February 1939, made it a crime to have supported the Republic and decreed that the culprits should have their property confiscated; Masons were included within its provisions. A new school curriculum issued in 1939 included lessons on how, under the Republic, the Judeo-Masonic conspiracy had handed the country over to Communism.

Franco acquired the habit of using the sexually loaded term *el contubernio* to refer to the way Masons plotted with all kinds of subversive elements: it means 'concubinage' – a squalid *mésalliance*, like that of a concubine with her lover. This was the vocabulary of a ravenous phobia. Before long, somebody decided that Franco's phobia needed feeding.

The Civil War ended in April 1939. The Second World War, in which Francoist Spain would remain neutral, began in September. At around this time, a network of informers began to pass high-level information on the international Masonic conspiracy against Spain directly to Franco. The network was highly mysterious: it was referred to as APIS in official communications, but no historian has yet discovered what the letters stood for. What is known is that, over the next quarter of a century, the Caudillo read intelligence briefs of astounding quality. Among the highlights of the APIS papers are letters to or from Roosevelt, Churchill, Montgomery, Eisenhower and the Secretary General of NATO. But more valuable still was the substantial body of revelations about the Freemasons' persistent operations in Spain, and their attempts to infiltrate the Francoist regime.

The main flow of this precious intelligence arrived through three intriguing women. The deep throat was a woman who had access to Masonic strategy at the highest levels. She referred to herself only as A. de S.; her husband, known only as R., was a high-ranking member of the Association Maçonnique Internationale – a federation of Grand Lodges in many different countries. A. de S.'s liaison with the APIS base in Madrid was her children's nanny, known as Elisa. And the woman in Madrid who edited the reports and prepared them for the Caudillo was Marìa Dolores de Naveràn, who led a second life as a professor in a teacher-training college. The Caudillo frequently intimated to his entourage that, thanks to such spies, he had inside knowledge of Masonic schemes.

Evidently, he trusted his sources. This was unfortunate for him because pretty much all the significant information provided by APIS about Masonic conspiracies was fake.

There are a number of clues. The Association Maçonnique Internationale fell apart in 1950, but APIS reports of its mischiefs continued to arrive on the Caudillo's desk until 1965. There were never any original copies of the English-language documents that APIS agents had supposedly stolen, only Spanish translations. When those translations quoted the original for effect, the quotes often contained howlers in English spelling and grammar. The deep throat A. de S. may well have been completely fictional.

APIS was the espionage equivalent of the great Taxil hoax of the late nineteenth century. Franco fell for it utterly. Researchers currently working on the documents do not know who was behind it. The most that can be said is that Marìa Dolores de Naveràn, who edited the reports, may have been involved. The most likely scenario is that somebody, probably somebody deep in the dicta-torship, was hoodwinking the Caudillo to manipulate his anti-Masonic mania against political rivals. Whatever the origins of the APIS deception, Freemasons, or those suspected of being Freemasons, would pay the price.

Salamanca today is a beautiful backwater: a medieval city carved ornately from soft Villamayor stone that glows like butter in the early morning sunshine, to the delight of selfie-snapping sightseers and foreign students on Erasmus scholarships. Some of the more thorough visitors find their way to a museum that lies down a small street behind the cathedral, on the opposite side to the university where Miguel de Unamuno gave his final speech. The little museum's centrepiece is a windowless Masonic Lodge room. Or at least it purports to be a Lodge room. Accessed through heavy double doors, and arranged around a chessboard floor, it is a lamp-lit box crammed with Masonic stuff: squares and compasses, stone blocks, columns, and an altar emblazoned with the double-headed eagle of the Scottish Rite. The blood-red walls carry pictures of decapitated heads, zodiac signs, Hebrew inscriptions and black gravestones: 'Here lies Jubelo: ambition made him the murderer of Hiram Abiff'. From the far wall, three seated dummies in black robes stare back at you with goggly eyes painted onto their hoods. The dummy in the centre has a skull-and-crossbones on his chest, and a miniature skull with luminous eyes on the desk in front of him. It is all meant to be spine-tingling. Most tourists are just baffled or amused.

The Salamanca Lodge is the last surviving example of its kind in Europe. It was built as propaganda by the Francoist authorities in the 1940s. Everything in it is a genuine artefact confiscated during police raids on Lodges. Franco's men took bits and pieces from their hoard to create the spookiest ensemble they could. It is not very hard to make Freemasonry seem weird.

The Nazis mounted similar shows in Germany and countries they occupied. Having closed the Lodges, the SS put skeletons in some, and invited the public in to take a look. Across Fascist Europe, the message was that the nation's saviours had finally vanquished the Masonic menace, exposing the Craft's secrets for all to ogle.

The Salamanca Lodge exhibit is housed on the ground floor of the General Archive of the Spanish Civil War. Only scholars ever make it to the archive itself, located on the first floor. Here, among many tons of the regime's papers on Franco's enemies, can be found much grimmer evidence of the Caudillo's Masonic fixation. Lining the walls of one room are a number of card-index cabinets in dark wood, their drawers worn by decades of bureaucratic labour. The letters T. E. R. M. C. are printed across the top of each cabinet: *Tribunal Especial para la Represión de la Masonería y el Comunismo* – Special Tribunal for the Repression of Freemasonry and Communism. The card-index system is the cranking handle of a lumbering machine of bureaucratic subjugation.

The original nucleus of the collection in Salamanca was the private archive of the most rabid of the many anti-Masonic polemicists of the early 1930s, the Catalan theologian Father Juan Tusquets Terrats. Lanky, blond and hyperactive, Tusquets developed his own network of spies to sniff out the Lodges' secrets and amass documentation; on one occasion he even stole paperwork from a Barcelona Lodge after starting a fire to cause a distraction. In 1932, Tusquets wrote a bestselling account that blamed Jews and Freemasons for setting up the Republic. General Franco was an avid reader.

Once Franco was installed in Salamanca, he made Tusquets his daughter's tutor, and put him in charge of the Judeo-Masonic Section of the rebellion's intelligence service with a mission to gather information on Freemasons from all possible sources.

For Tusquets, this was a licence to indulge an all-consuming mania. He became convinced that he could spot the symptoms of Masonic affiliation in the way a handkerchief was folded into a breast pocket. Such was his zeal that he did not only investigate the Republican side. As one nervous Falangist noted, 'Tusquets saw Freemasons everywhere.' Late in 1936, with Franco's help, Tusquets set up a publishing house, Anti-Sect Editions, that served as an outlet for his findings. Many of the titles sold in huge numbers. He toured Nationalist Spain to promote his ideas, alleging that nudists, vegetarians and speakers of Esperanto were all in on the Masonic plot. The lectures ended with a call for Masons to be exterminated.

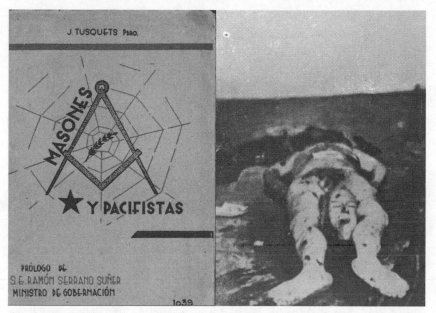

The cover of *Masons and Pacifists* (1939), a work typical of the output of Father Juan Tusquets Terrats (1901–1998). This grisly image from the book shows the corpse of General Eduardo López Ochoa, who was lynched by a left-wing mob in 1936. Tusquets claimed his death was an act of ritual Masonic vengeance.

In June 1937, investigations into Freemasonry were geared up when one of Franco's friends was put in charge of a militarised research unit that became known as the State Delegation for Document Recuperation (DERD, in the Spanish acronym). Tusquets was bitter about being marginalised in this way, but eventually agreed to hand over his archive. By the end of 1938, DERD reported that it had collected five million documents in what was once a seventeenth-century orphanage – the building in Salamanca that still houses the collection today. This growing mountain of paper was put to practical use. The Francoist authorities purged the civil service of 'anti-Spanish' elements – including Masons. Even loyal Nationalists lost their jobs. Republican prisoners found to have taken part in the 'red rebellion' could be singled out for execution if they were suspected of being in the Craft.

In March 1940, at around the time the APIS network started to supply the Caudillo with intelligence, he set up a Special Tribunal for the Repression of Freemasonry and Communism. Only a tiny minority of the cases heard before the Tribunal would involve those labelled Communists: as everyone acknowledged, Freemasons were the real target. The archive in Salamanca, which continued to grow, would henceforth be used to bring all members of the Craft before a dedicated court in Madrid. Over twenty-six thousand verdicts would be issued against Freemasons over the next dozen years.

The judges who sat in the Special Tribunal for the Repression of Freemasonry were nominated by the regime. They assumed that pretty much everyone brought before them was guilty: acquittals were a great rarity. The maximum sentence available was thirty years in prison, and the minimum a very harsh twelve years and a day. For a Mason to get his sentence cut, he would have to fully renounce the Sect, ideally before a bishop. But it was extremely hard to prove that any recantation was genuine. After all, Craft rituals made dissemblers and liars of all the men who underwent them – or so the judges assumed, imbibing the lesson of all anti-Masonic propagandists since the Abbé Barruel. One way for a suspect to add credence to his confession was to implicate other Freemasons. The lucky few who spilled the most damning accusations could even escape prison this way, and merely be sacked from their public sector jobs. Unsurprisingly, therefore, most defendants confessed, thus feeding more evidence into the paper machine in Salamanca.

Most of the Masons arraigned before the Special Tribunal were entirely harmless middle-class men. Not a few were supporters of the Nationalist cause. Some were just members of the Rotary Club or the League for the Rights of Man, which counted as Masonic front organisations for the purposes of the law. Many of the accused had only had the briefest of encounters with the Craft, and had quickly dropped out because they were too busy, too bored, or too cash-strapped to pay their dues.

This has always and everywhere been the case: only a small minority of those who are put through the first rituals stay on to become committed Craftsmen. Winston Churchill, often held up by Freemasons as one of their own, was one such drop-out. But these mundane facts did not shake the Special Tribunal's founding conviction that Spain was the target of a disciplined international conspiracy. All they proved was that only the small fry had been caught. So sentencing was not savage – at least within the severe limits set out by the law. One estimate is that 76 per cent of the accused received the shortest stretch. The longer tariffs were applied exclusively *in absentia*, to the senior Freemasons who had fled into exile – presumably taking the Craft's most dastardly secrets with them, and joining forces with the global conspiratorial leadership to manipulate the western democracies against Spain.

One case from among the thousands must serve to highlight the cruel absurdity of the whole process. Atilano Coco Martín was the Protestant pastor and friend of Miguel de Unamuno who was murdered for being a Freemason while in detention in Salamanca in the autumn of 1936. In the anti-Masonic archives in Salamanca, however, it was falsely stated that he had gone on the run after being released, and so paperwork about him continued to accumulate. In March 1940, two Masons denounced him as a Brother in their confessions. The police in both Madrid and Salamanca dutifully reported to the Special Tribunal that their efforts to track down the pastor had proved fruitless: whereabouts unknown. The dead man was put on trial *in absentia* before the Special Tribunal in 1942, and sentenced to sixteen years.

Masonry was a slippery beast. The men around Franco seem to have viewed their struggle to pin it down as a heroic labour – much trickier than the Nazi war against Jews. Mauricio Carlavilla, a specialist anti-Masonic investigator, remarked in 1945: 'Lucky Hitler! When it comes to granting or denying anyone nationality, he can be guided by the sign of a hooked nose or a

Talmudic rite. Poor us! To deny anyone nationality we have to rely on less pronounced indicators: a Masonic confession, which is never really confessed.'

The more meticulous was the Special Tribunal's work of repression, the more terrifying the spectre of Masonic conspiracy grew. When Harry S. Truman, a well-known Freemason, became President of the United States in 1945, the Caudillo interpreted this development as a significant advance towards Freemasonry's goal of 'fusion within the Presidency of the United States of supreme executive power and the supreme Masonic powers'. Writing under a pseudonym in 1951, Franco implied that there could be no victory over Freemasonry this side of the Day of Judgement: 'Daughter of evil, its demonic spirit survives the defeat and comes to life in new beings.'

There were roughly five thousand Brothers in Spain at the start of the Civil War. Before it ended, many of those Craftsmen who had not been killed or captured fled abroad. Nobody knows how many were left when the Nationalist victory came. A thousand, at the very most? The Craft as an organisation had certainly been destroyed on Spanish soil. The Masonic threat was an illusion. Yet the card-index system in Salamanca would eventually contain the profiles of 80,000 suspected Brothers.

The Special Tribunal only ceased to operate in 1964, but the Salamanca archive was still consulted when it came to deciding which political prisoners to release, and which exiles to allow home. Franco demanded eternal vigilance against his imaginary foe.

In 1975, Spain was a very different society to the one torn apart by Civil War in the late 1930s. One sign of change was the invasion of northern European tourists that filled the beaches every summer. Another was TV, which was now Spaniards' favourite pastime. On 1 October 1975, millions tuned in to see a muzzy transmission of a speech given from the balcony of the Royal Palace in Madrid by the man who had been Head of State for thirty-nine years. General Franco, who was suffering from Parkinson's disease, was manifestly frail. His wizened face was hidden behind an outsized pair of Ray Bans. His right hand wobbled feebly by way of a wave. His voice, amplified to the masses in the Plaza de Oriente below him, was reedy and tremulous. Yet the message he issued could not have been more steadfast. He warned the nation against 'a leftist-Masonic conspiracy amid the political class, in concubinage with socialist-terrorist subversion in society'.

Anti-Masonry was embedded in the Caudillo's being, and he built it into the very structure of his dictatorship. While giving the speech, he caught a chill that provoked a collapse in his health. He would never appear in public again. Only the superhuman efforts of his doctors kept him alive until 20 November.

Freemasonry remained a crime in Spain until democracy returned. Only after 2007, with the promulgation of a Law on Historical Memory, was the Masonic Lodge exhibit in Salamanca accompanied by a video to explain that it was Francoist propaganda.

15

New York: **A Golden American Century Closes**

NOVUS ORDO SECLORUM

In the United States, after the Civil War of the 1860s, there began a golden age of fraternalism that would last until the end of the nineteenth century. Apart from a brusque and temporary dimming in the 1930s, its glow would last until the 1960s.

An astonishing 235 brotherhoods were founded in the United States between 1865 and 1900, with as many as six million members – the vast majority of them men. By one estimate, that amounted to 40 per cent of the male population aged over twenty-one. The Improved Order of Red Men, the Knights of Pythias, the National Grange of the Order of Patrons of Husbandry, the Benevolent and Protective Order of Elks, the Loyal Order of Moose, the Woodmen of the World. The Tribe of Ben-Hur was founded in Indiana in 1894 with rituals styled on Lew Wallace's 1880 novel of early Christianity. These and dozens of other bodies were not Masonic, but they had clearly learned a lot from the Craft. In 1899, *The Cyclopaedia of Fraternities* produced a genealogical tree of all America's many fraternities, with Freemasonry, the 'mother fraternity', at its root: 'Few who are well informed on the subject will deny that the Masonic fraternity is directly or indirectly the parent organization of all modern secret societies, good, bad or indifferent.'

344

The fraternal urge reached down towards the lower end of the social scale. The Independent Order of Odd Fellows, the so-called 'poor-man's Masonry', had more members than the Freemasons by the mid-1890s. Catholics joined in: the Knights of Columbus was founded in Connecticut in 1882 as a Catholic alternative to the Craft; within 25 years it had nearly 230,000 members. But Freemasonry, growing rapidly, retained its place at the centre of the fraternal world. The Masonic parades and cornerstone-laying ceremonies of the early Republic resumed. On 5 August 1884, the Grand Master of the State of New York performed one such ceremony on Bedloe's Island in Upper New York Bay – the chosen site for the Statue of Liberty. Cathedral-sized Grand Lodge head-quarters were built in prime urban spots, such as the Philadelphia Masonic Temple, completed in 1873, right across the road from City Hall. Such buildings typically contained meeting rooms, offices, banqueting halls, libraries, smoking rooms and ladies' lounges. Those ladies' husbands had become the world's proudest joiners of fraternal organisations, takers of fraternal oaths, wearers of outlandish fraternal costumes, and – not coinciden-tally – givers to charitable causes.

Philanthropy, or at least mutual assistance, provides much of the explanation for America's unstoppable upsurge in brotherly love. The middle classes had more disposable income than ever before, but they had no safety net. The Freemasons and other fraternities offered a sense of stability and a kind of welfare system at a time of accelerating change: orphanages, retirement homes, life insurance, health insurance, burial insurance. Masonry also offered a nationwide network of friendship for a population that was highly geographically mobile: Lodges had germinated along the railroads as they rolled out into the west. Each wave of inward migration to the United States saw the creation of mutual benefit societies and brotherhoods for Swedes, Jews, Poles, Hungarians, Slovaks, Hispanics, and so on.

Masonry was fun too. In New York, a special second-floor table at Manhattan's Knickerbocker Cottage on 6th Avenue became a regular venue for beery Masonic revelries. Here, over lunch in 1870, thirteen Craftsmen dreamed up the Ancient Arabic Order Nobles of the Mystic Shrine. The Shriners, for short, were 'the playground for Masons'. Their rituals, hammed up for laughs, were based on an Arabian Nights pastiche of Middle-Eastern culture, including mock punishments supposedly derived from the Muslim criminal code. The red fez was the order's ceremonial headgear, and its leader carried the title of Imperial Potentate. The Shriners are still today the most visible of the many branches of Masonry, with their trademark miniature cars joining in parades of all kinds. Their humour is not to everyone's taste, but the Shriners do donate vast amounts to their network of children's hospitals; the first one was built in Louisiana in 1922. The Shriner emblem – an assemblage of oriental motifs including a scimitar, a crescent, a sphinx's head and a star – became one of the most recognisable badges of fraternal affiliation in America.

Growth in the Masons and other brotherhoods continued in the early twentieth century. The Scottish Rite, re-invented by the Confederate General Albert Pike, enjoyed a huge expansion in the years after his death in 1891. Pike had imagined the Scottish Rite as a moral academy for a Masonic élite. But its prestige inevitably attracted wannabes, and the leadership soon gave in to the pressure. The ethical lessons of Pike's thirty-three elaborate and grandiose Degrees, right up to the famous Thirty-third, were originally absorbed by each individual Brother as he underwent a ritual in a temple. Now those same rituals were performed as a spectacle before crowds of initiates in an auditorium. Membership consequently skyrocketed.

Other brotherhoods found ways to meet the needs of a new audience too. The Rotary Club, founded in 1905, stripped the Masonic idea of its ceremonies, regalia and titles; its exclusively professional membership just wore business suits, and concentrated on meeting up and working for the community. In 1915, D.W. Griffith's movie *The Birth of a Nation* sparked the re-emergence of the most notorious of American fraternities, the Ku Klux Klan. However, despite these innovations, the rate at which new brotherhoods were generated tailed off. The growth curve of Masonic membership became less hurtling too. Much of the reason was simply the cycle of generations: to some younger men, a grey-haired leadership made the air in the Lodges seem a little staid.

As in Europe, the aftermath of the Great War saw Craft membership swell once more: the number of Masons passed three million in 1924. Being a Mason became a calling card of credibility and fair-dealing for America's burgeoning legions of businessmen. The local Lodge, and the wider Masonic network, also offered a way of spreading one's reputation that could be useful when it came to standing for election to a low-level judicial or administrative post – the bottom rung of the political ladder. Such was the case with Harry S. Truman, the struggling businessman son of a struggling Missouri farmer who would in time become a President of the United States – a classic instance of the common-man President. Initiated at age twenty-five, in 1909, Truman was later recalled as a 'very good Lodge man', who had a lifelong love of Masonry's fellowship, ritual, spiritual teachings and tradition. His Masonic and early political careers progressed in tandem: in 1922 he became eastern judge of Jackson County and the following year he was elected Deputy Grand Master of the 59th Masonic District, Jackson County. Truman, like many men of his ilk, was an eager joiner of clubs: in addition to the Masons, by the early 1930s he belonged to the American Legion, the Veterans of Foreign Wars, the Elks, the Eagles and the International Acquaintance League. The Harry Trumans of America were behind a renewed wave of temple building, with imposing edifices inaugurated across the States. In 1926, in St Louis, Missouri, 50,000 people attended the inauguration of a twelve-storey temple, with a 3,000-seat banqueting hall, its exterior adorned with huge colonnaded porticoes at both its base and summit. St Louis Masons were outdone by their

Brethren in Detroit, however: later the same year, 60,000 were there to witness the dedication of the largest Masonic building in the world; its 1,030 rooms extended over half a block, and its kitchens could serve 5,000.

A young Harry S. Truman (1884–1972),
future President of the United States,
proudly wears a Masonic lapel pin.
Photo taken soon after his initiation.

Soon afterwards, however, the Great Depression put the growth of Masonry temporarily into reverse: struggling to pay their dues, over six hundred thousand Brothers left between 1930 and 1935. Other brotherhoods fared even worse, and went into terminal decline.

It was at this low point that the United States acquired its best-known Masonic symbol: the all-seeing eye, set inside a triangle, sitting atop a pyramid, which is printed on the back of the dollar bill. There are two accounts of how it ended up in such a prominent place. The first suggests that the Illuminati put it there because they founded the United States, and secretly control it to this day. The Latin motto set below the pyramid, NOVUS ORDO SECLORUM, proclaims the Illuminati plan to establish a 'new order of the ages' or 'New World Order'. There is a potentially significant weakness in this theory: it is hard to understand what an occult power like the Illuminati would have to gain by advertising its intentions so openly. To be fair to the theory's proponents, however, we can safely assume that anything is possible when you can exercise mind control through triangles.

The second account of the symbol's origins has more evidence to support it. The all-seeing eye is a way of representing an omniscient god that has been common to many cultures for a very, very long time. That was what the Founding Fathers of the United States meant when they incorporated the Eye of Providence (as it was then termed) into the design of the Great Seal in 1782. The idea was to show God watching over the new republic, which was represented by the pyramid (meaning it was built to last) with its thirteen levels (representing the thirteen original states). At this point in history, none of the very many genres of Masonic symbolism had yet given the all-seeing eye a specific meaning for Freemasons. As far as we know, given the patchy historical records, none of the men who designed the definitive version of the Great Seal was a Mason. The design on the reverse was not used for any official purposes thereafter, and was widely ignored.

The Great Seal, both front and back, was only put on the dollar bill during a redesign in 1935, under the Presidency of Franklin Delano Roosevelt. The idea seems to have come from the then Secretary of Agriculture, Henry A. Wallace. He mentioned it to Roosevelt, who proposed the dollar redesign. Both men were 32nd Degree Freemasons, and both knew that the all-seeing eye had become established as a Masonic symbol for the Almighty. However, it was *not* the Masonic meanings of the motif that most attracted them, but rather the motto, NOVUS ORDO SECLORUM. For the Founding Fathers back in 1782, these words alluded to the new American age inaugurated by the Declaration of Independence. Wallace and Roosevelt thought it could be loosely translated as New Deal – which, of course, was the slogan FDR had invented for his policy of state intervention in the economy. Far from wanting to stamp a Craft logo on the national currency at all costs, Roosevelt was actually rather concerned that using the Masonic all-seeing eye would offend Catholic voters. He gave the design the go-ahead only after his Catholic Postmaster General reassured him that no offence would be taken.

When the Second World War ended, soldiers, sailors and airmen returning from the European and Pacific theatres re-ignited the national passion for Masonic fellowship. In the fifteen years after 1945, membership of the Freemasons increased by a million, reaching a total of over four million. At the dawn of the 1960s, one in twelve adult males was a Brother. There were nearly twice as many Freemasons in the United States as there were in the whole of the rest of the world combined. The figure is certainly extraordinary. But it becomes positively eye-popping when we remember that it *excludes* the other American fraternal organisations that had taken the Craft as their template. Moreover, many Americans still lived below the income threshold at which the costs of Masonic membership became affordable. Of a United States population of 139.9 million in 1945, many also had origins in European Catholic countries where there was a deep tradition of hostility to the Craft, such as 2.3 million Irish, 2.9 million Poles and 4.5 million Italians. In short, in middle-class, male, Protestant America, aprons and strange handshakes were the norm.

America in the 1950s and early 1960s was afraid of many things, like reds under the bed, Russian atomic bombs, Martians and teenagers. But in the States, unlike most of the rest of the world, Freemasonry aroused no suspicions. Indeed, it felt like a guarantor of freedom. Its core values reassured Americans about the essential goodness of their society and the universality of its aspirations. Roosevelt, Truman, Johnson: people grew used to having a Freemason as President.

The Craft placed itself at the heart of a nation that had never been so bullish about its future. IBM announced the dawn of the computer era. With Project Mercury, its manned space-flight programme, the USA embarked on what *Life* magazine called 'man's greatest adventure'. Everyday marvels filled spanking new suburban homes: air-conditioning and freezers, ballpoint pens and tape recorders. Middle-class America became a land of automatic transmission and four-lane highways. This was the Googie nation fondly caricatured in the cartoon series *The Flintstones*, which set a suburban family in a stone-age world filled with gleefully anachronistic tech. Needless to say, Fred Flintstone and his friend Barney Rubble regularly got away from their stay-at-home, shopping-dependent wives at the local Lodge of the Loyal Order of Water Buffaloes – a nod to the American man's mania for Masonry.

Freemasonry's astounding popularity bred self-assurance and openness. *Empire State Mason*, the New York Fraternity's magazine, advertised status symbols that were also proud displays of affiliation: Masonic cruises, and gold watches with Craft symbols on the face. Freemasonry began to present itself more openly to the profane world than it had ever done. One New York Lodge sponsored a kids' baseball team that played with 'MASONS' proudly printed across their chests. In 1957 *Life* magazine published a celebratory collective portrait of Freemasons that included unprecedented photographs of initiation rituals. The Masons did not even seem to object when the magazine nonchalantly affirmed that becoming a Mason was a smart career move: 'Masons enjoy each other's company, sometimes find it useful in business, almost indispensable in social life.' There seemed to be famous Masons everywhere: men like Gene Autry, Audie Murphy, Douglas MacArthur, J. Edgar Hoover, Roy Rogers and Arnold Palmer. Norman Peale, author of the multi-million-selling 1952 self-help guide *The Power of Positive Thinking*, was a Thirty-third Degree Scottish Rite Mason. Positive thinking was at the centre of Peale's Masonry, as he explained to his Brethren in a lecture given as part of a 'Masonic Showcase' in Ohio. The Craft 'teaches that problems are for the creation of great human beings': 'Any man who is afflicted with a sense of defeat in the problems of life [will] find within the confines of Masonry that faith, character and ruggedness of spirit which [will] help him to act like a man and be strong. That's what Masonry means to me.'

The last, flamboyant celebration of mid-century American

optimism and Masonic self-confidence came at the New York World's Fair. With its theme of 'Peace Through Understanding', the World's Fair was a colossal showcase of American leadership in technology and lifestyle. Held in Flushing Meadows Corona Park in Queens over two April-to-October seasons in 1964 and 1965, it attracted 51.6 million people – equivalent to more than a quarter of the American population. Visitors could watch the first colour TV at the RCA Pavilion. Or ride a gleaming new model called the Mustang at the Ford pavilion. Bell Telephones brought their 'Picturephone'. Formica built a World's Fair House on the site: this seven-room home made every conceivable use of plastic, including wipe-clean walls inside and out. Sweets were factory-made before spectators' eyes in the Chunky Candy Corporation Pavilion. Walt Disney's 'Audio-Animatronics' – talking robots – amazed all comers when they were deployed in several pavilions. General Motors epitomised the spirit of the event with the vast and highly popular 'Futurama' attraction, a cavalcade of awe-inspiring technologies that lay just over the horizon, including lunar crawlers, commuter suburbs in space, underwater motels and laser tree cutters to slice down the world's forests with ease. The Hall of Magic, sponsored by General Cigar, expressed 'the magic of the future' with a machine that blew twenty-foot smoke rings high in the air.

Dozens of countries across the world grasped the chance to show off their wares in the homeland of modernity: Japan offered its miniaturised electronics, and from the Swiss pavilion you could take trips over the fair on cutting-edge 'Sky Ride' cable cars.

Art and heritage were well represented too. South Africa offered exciting Zulu dancers, and Thailand a Buddhist temple. Spain's pavilion combined flamenco dancers, paintings by the likes of Velázquez and Picasso and a full-scale replica of the ship that carried Christopher Columbus from Spain to the New World. The pavilion was so successful that the World's Fair's president even flew to Europe to present Generalissimo Francisco Franco with a congratulatory gold medal. But even the Spaniards were outdone by the Vatican, which shipped Michelangelo's *Pietà* over from St Peter's basilica. The UK's lazy effort was a 'British Lion Pub'. The Soviet Union refused to come.

The World's Fair had an undeniable magic, and would live long in popular memory. At its heart stood the Unisphere – a 140-foot-high steel model of Planet Earth that became an instant icon. Great loops of metal circling it suggested the flight paths of orbiting rockets. Just a short walk from the Unisphere, across from the Swiss Sky Ride, and next to the British Lion Pub, there was a luminously white, curved building set in a landscaped garden: the Masonic Brotherhood Center, the work of the Grand Lodge of New York State.

To approach it, one went through a fibreglass arch, five storeys tall, in the form of a giant square and compass, with a golden G suspended below it. (G, of course, stood for Geometry and Great Architect of the Universe.) Visitors then crossed an arched bridge over an oval reflection pond, where pumps sprayed curves of water into the air. They entered the Center by a tall glass gate under gilded grill-work. The interior, all walnut panels, air-conditioning and deep carpets, was dominated by an eleven-foot marble statue of George Washington in his fraternal regalia – the 'master builder of our country'. At the great man's feet, Briliantined Brothers wearing sky-blue armbands were ready to show their guests around the display cases.

The story told in the Masonic Brotherhood Center was of a fraternity that was more than six hundred years old – 'with roots in even remoter centuries'. To prove it, there were medieval manuscripts about stoneworkers and pictures of Gothic cathedrals. There was even a model of what Solomon's Temple looked like. Possibly. A first edition of the *Constitutions* was on display, alongside Benjamin Franklin's 1734 reprinting.

Very many of the cherished artefacts in the Brotherhood Center attested to Freemasonry's role in the birth and growth of the nation. There was George Washington's apron, a lock of his hair and the Masonic Bible on which he swore his oath of office. The ceremonial tools the first President used to lay the cornerstone of the Capitol building in 1793 were set below a poster proclaiming that 'Masons are Champions of Liberty. For this reason, no tyrant or dictator will tolerate Masonry in his country.' Portraits of fourteen Brother Presidents of the United States were displayed.

The Center had its slogan spelled out in large, gold letters at both ends of the building: 'BROTHERHOOD: THE FOUNDATION OF WORLD PEACE'. Quite how Masonry's closed form of brotherhood could practically achieve peace in the world at large was unclear. Yet we cannot deny that such a message was in tune with some of America's deepest hopes and fears. Its author was Grand Master Harry Ostrov, an eminent lawyer and the first Jew to rise to the summit of Masonry in the Empire State. He came up with the plan for a Masonic Brotherhood Center shortly after the Cuban missile crisis had taken the West to the very brink of nuclear war in October 1962. As he explained to his Brethren at the time, 'Unless the world accepts this challenge, and embraces brotherhood as part of its living, civilization as we know it will not survive.'

The Center brochure gave a Cold War edge to the Masonic love of liberty: 'Our Grand Lodges and Lodges are found all over the world outside the iron and bamboo curtains.' This claim was substantially correct – as a short historical detour from the Masonic Brotherhood Center shows.

The light of Masonry had indeed been extinguished everywhere within the Soviet Empire. In many places, such as East Germany, Czechoslovakia and Romania, the Craft had only just revived after the Nazi repression when the orders came from Moscow to close it down again. Tragically, when Freemasonry was banned in Hungary in 1950, the Grand Senior Warden of the newly reconstituted Grand Lodge committed suicide rather than fall into the hands of the secret police. It is reported that he and his twin brother, who was the Worshipful Master of a Lodge, clasped hands and jumped from a window when the dreaded knock at the door came. For the authorities in Hungary, the Lodges were 'meeting places of the enemies of the people's Communist republic, of capitalist elements, and of the adherents of Western imperialism'. The same was true across the Eastern bloc.

There was no Freemasonry in mainland China either. Before the Communist takeover in 1949, the Craft there had been almost entirely restricted to the British colonial population. In 1950, Masonic Lodges were required to register with the authorities and go through the troublesome business of translating their rulebooks and minutes into Chinese. But rather than actively crushing the Craft, Chairman Mao seems to have largely ignored it and allowed it to wither.

Curiously, the only Communist one-party state that did not ban Freemasonry was Cuba, where Fidel Castro closely monitored the Lodges, but allowed them to continue working. He recognised that Freemasonry was important to the culture and historical memory of the Cuban Left. Masonic Lodges had been incubators of the movement for Cuban independence from Spain at the end of the nineteenth century, and many Masons played a leading role in the struggle. José Martí, the 'Apostle' of Cuban independence, who became a national martyr when he died fighting the Spanish in 1895, was a passionate Mason. Castro's regime venerated Martí as a herald of its own ideology.

At the time of the Masonic Brotherhood Center, Freemasonry was repressed in much of the Muslim world too, as it had been for long periods during the old Ottoman Empire. Anti-Masonry was a much more successful import from the West than was Masonry itself, which had mostly remained limited to colonial enclaves. France was the dominant power in much of the Middle

East, and French Masons there tended to be more reluctant to fraternise with locals within the Lodges than were the British in India: their fear was that the Arabs might end up taking all the talk of brotherhood and equality rather too literally. Only in a few places did westernising intellectuals and elements of the indigenous élite embrace Masonry. Such was the case, for example, with many members of the Young Ottomans in Istanbul in the 1860s and 1870s, and with their successors the Young Turks in the early twentieth century.

Masonic traditions in most of the Muslim world disappeared when many former colonies achieved statehood. President Sukarno, the leader of Indonesia's struggle for independence from Holland, banned Freemasonry in 1961. President Gamal Abdel Nasser of Egypt did the same in 1964. Nationalists saw Masons as agents of western imperialism and capitalism. Monarchs saw them as agents of Marxism. The deprived saw them as agents of the wealthy. Islamic clerics saw them as agents of Satan. And, after the foundation of the state of Israel in 1948, pretty much everyone who had any kind of inkling about who the Freemasons might be saw them as agents of Zionism and/or the international Jewish conspiracy.

So through the Masonic Brotherhood Center, Freemasonry put forward a strong claim to being an emblem of freedom and democracy. Alongside a picture of the Capitol building, visitors could view an impressive cohort of Craftsmen who occupied leading positions in American politics at the time: 42 per cent of Congressmen, and more than half of all Senators and State Governors.

Inevitably, the Center also contained long honour rolls of distinguished Brothers of past and present: from Paul Revere and the Marquis de Lafayette, to Buffalo Bill, Ty Cobb and Irving Berlin. The very many eminent Masons of the world were name-checked:

Robert Burns, José de San Martín, Franz Joseph Haydn, Edward VII . . . Some were honoured with busts (Sir Walter Scott, Voltaire . . .), and some with paraphernalia (Simón Bolívar's apron, Garibaldi's will, a gavel Rudyard Kipling had sent to his Mother Lodge and musical scores handwritten by Wolfgang Amadeus Mozart and Jean Sibelius). Lest anyone suspect that the Freemasons were locked in the past, other items on display showed their ancient values to be an asset in shaping the kind of man needed for the space race: one of the most popular was the Masonic flag that accompanied Brother Gordon 'Gordo' Cooper when he orbited the earth twenty-two times in May 1963 – Project Mercury's boldest mission.

Mississippi Goddam

The Center's mission was to set Freemasonry at the heart of the American way of life, of what it meant to be an American man. Yet at the same time, it gave a garish demonstration of how that way of life excluded some 10.6 per cent of the population. For the faces on the walls in the Masonic Brotherhood Center were all as startlingly white as the building's exterior. There were plenty of notable black Freemasons who could have been celebrated: Booker T. Washington, Nat King Cole and Sugar Ray Robinson, to name but a few. The problem was, of course, that all of these greats were *Prince Hall* Masons – members of the African-American tradition shunned by the white Craft establishment everywhere in the United States.

Through the long golden age of fraternalism, African Americans had shown themselves to be joiners just as enthusiastic as their WASP compatriots. Indeed, given the discrimination and insecurity they experienced in their everyday lives, they had a particularly strong impulse to find support networks and mutual aid. As African-American social settlement activist Fannie Barrier Williams wrote in 1905:

Next to the Negro church in importance, as affecting the social life of the people, are the secret orders. These affect every phase of their social life and represent the best achievements of the race in the matter of organization . . . In no form of organization do the terms of brotherhood and mutual obligations mean so much.

Because white insurance companies often refused to sell policies to blacks, fraternal associations became a crucial source of financial security. Because blacks were often barred from white cemeteries, the need to band together to buy a burial ground was often the prompt for the creation of a mutual benefit society, church or fraternity.

There were some uniquely African-American fraternities, such as the Knights of Tabor, founded in 1872. But many mirrored the equivalent organisations created exclusively for whites: hence there were black Odd Fellows, Knights of Pythias, Woodmen, Elks and Moose. Prince Hall Freemasons developed their own Scottish Rite and Shriners, and their own Order of the Eastern Star – a male-designed auxiliary to Freemasonry for female relatives of Brothers. Founded in 1874, the Sisters of the Prince Hall Eastern Star built much closer and more egalitarian ties to their Brothers than was the case in the mainstream Craft.

Being a Mason was as much a marker of bourgeois identity for African Americans as it was for their white fellow citizens. Aspiring Prince Hall Brothers were carefully vetted to ensure that they were sufficiently respectable. Interviewers were given model questions to ask the candidates: 'Is he a clean, right-living man, sober and industrious? Has he any habits which tend to degrade his morals? Does he live with and support his family as a husband should?' About one-third of the men included in the 1950 edition of *Who's Who in Colored America* were Prince Hall Brothers.

Nowhere more than the black United States was political

struggle a natural facet of brotherly belonging. Not only did African Americans face discrimination, segregation and disenfranchisement in society at large, but white Masonry's exclusionary membership practices were a painful affront to the Craft's most sacred principles. Following the example of their abolitionist founder, Prince Hall Masons had always been involved in the struggle for black rights. It is no coincidence that a Prince Hall Mason, W.E.B. Dubois, was one of three creators of what would become the most effective agency for pursuing civil rights through the courts, the National Association for the Advancement of Colored People (NAACP, 1909). The NAACP was where African-American Freemasons' training in leadership and their carefully cultivated respectability could be leveraged most effectively.

By the 1960s, the struggle for civil rights had become the pivotal political issue of the day. In the deep South, both black and white Masonic traditions made their position abundantly clear.

Take Alabama, for example. The state's white Masons held their 1967 Annual Communication (a kind of AGM) in Montgomery in a hotel named after Jefferson Davis, the President of the Civil War Confederacy. The Grand Orator delivered a pyretic address that portrayed 'racial integrity' as an American heritage that was now under threat. Invoking the need for racial pride on all sides, he claimed that the scriptures did not advocate racial 'mongrelization', and exhorted parents to teach racial integrity to their children. It is hard to imagine anything less Masonic than such a speech. It was a disingenuous manifesto for segregation which, while supposedly involving 'separate but equal' status for black and white, was actually the grimly familiar cover story for bigotry enforced by violence. The assembled white Brothers of Alabama gave the Grand Orator a sustained standing ovation.

The same year, at the Prince Hall Grand Lodge of Alabama's Annual Communication in Mobile, the Grand Master declared as follows:

Let me impress upon you my brothers, that the Negro must become an integral part of the American Body Politic. That somehow, he must regain his right of a free, effective and untrammeled use of the ballot in Mississippi, as well as in Massachusetts; in Alabama as well as in Arizona; in South Carolina as well as in New York . . . In this day and time with the government (which is Politics) more and more concerning itself with the economic set-up of the country, the Negro without a ballot will soon be without a worthwhile job, a mere ward of the social set-up depending for a livelihood upon the crumbs which fall from the well-laden tables of the more politically-minded groups.

The latest generation of Prince Hall Masons were as good as these words. In 1951, black Grand Masters had united to create the Prince Hall Masons Legal Research Fund under the control of the NAACP. The NAACP's history-making legal victory over 'separate but equal' segregation in public schools, Brown vs Board of Education (1954), was partly funded by Prince Hall donations, and was argued before the Supreme Court by one of the great men of Prince Hall Masonry, Thurgood Marshall. In 1958 Marshall, who had been heavily involved in the foundation of the Prince Hall Masons Legal Research Fund, publicly thanked his Masonic Brothers, and said that without their help, many of the civil rights cases disputed before the Supreme Court would not have been won. In 1965, during the New York World's Fair, Marshall was appointed Solicitor General of the United States – the first African American to hold the position. In 1966, he spoke before a gathering of Prince Hall Grand Masters from across the nation at a 'Testimonial Dinner' in Washington DC to mark his being appointed a Thirty-third Degree Prince Hall Freemason. The theme of the evening was 'Thurgood Marshall: Symbol of Change'.

Thurgood Marshall (1908–1993):
Prince Hall Freemason and champion
of civil rights. (The Prince Hall Brother
in the hat is unidentified.)

Down in Alabama, the secretary of the NAACP chapter in Montgomery was also a member of a Masonic organisation. Rosa Parks is now hailed as the mother of the civil rights movement, and held up as a role model to children far beyond the United States. In December 1955, the prim, bespectacled Parks famously triggered the Montgomery bus boycott by being arrested for refusing to give up her seat to a white passenger. She was the daughter and grand-daughter of Prince Hall Masons, and an active member of the Order of the Eastern Star – the female adjunct to Freemasonry. The Eastern Star had a proud history of preparing black women for leadership roles in racial uplift endeavours.

At the time when the Masonic Brotherhood Center was conceived, Medgar Evers was the NAACP Field Secretary in Mississippi, where 95 per cent of African Americans were denied the vote by means both crooked and violent, and where black people were more likely to be beaten up, clubbed by the police, lynched or made to disappear than in any other state. Since 1954, Evers had toured Mississippi investigating racially moti-vated murders and building the collective will to resist. He clocked up thousands of miles in his V-8 Oldsmobile – a car chosen because it was big enough to sleep in where all the motels were whites-only, heavy enough to resist being run off the road and fast enough to make a quick getaway. He knew he was a target.

Evers had a background typical of many Prince Hall Masons: he was a veteran of the Normandy campaign in the Second World War, and had a career as an insurance salesman. His case also illustrates just how closely the black Craft was woven into the fabric of the civil rights movement. His NAACP office was housed in the local Prince Hall temple at 1072 Lynch Street, Jackson. Dedicated by none other than Thurgood Marshall in 1955, it was built to answer the need for a relatively safe place where blacks could work politically. Much the same was true of other Lodge buildings in other southern states. The Mississippi NAACP organised events at the Lynch Street Masonic Temple, such as the Lena Horne benefit concert where Evers gave his last speech: 'Freedom has never been free. I love my children and I love my wife with all my heart, and I would die, die gladly, if that would make a better life for them.'

Evers was shot dead in front of his family five days later. The assassin, Byron De La Beckwith Jr, was a white supremacist, Klansman – and Freemason. Indeed, several witnesses at the scene identified De La Beckwith's car by the distinctive Shriner emblem – scimitar, crescent, sphinx's head and star – in the window. Twice acquitted by all-white juries in the 1960s, he would even-tually be convicted in 1994.

After Evers' body had lain in state at the Masonic Temple for three days, five thousand people braved police dogs and 39-degree heat to set off for the two-mile march to the funeral home. The ceremony received nationwide newspaper coverage. Nina Simone's 'Mississippi Goddam' was inspired by Evers; her performance of it at Carnegie Hall a month before the World's Fair was released as a single and quickly became a civil rights anthem. Bob Dylan's 'Only a Pawn in Their Game' was also about Evers, and was also released in 1964.

Evers was murdered nine months before the World's Fair opened in New York. His contribution to civil rights and Prince Hall Masonry may have escaped the attention of the white Brothers planning the Masonic Brotherhood Center, but the same was not true of Prince Hall Masons in New York. In 1963, under the title 'Martyr to Freedom', Evers' picture adorned the front page of the *Prince Hall Sentinel*, the Prince Hall Grand Lodge of New York's magazine. New York Prince Hall Brothers sent $500 to Evers' widow, and its condolences to the Prince Hall Grand Lodge of Mississippi; it then set up a Freedom Now Fund to support the struggle. In 1964, a Freedom Now Fund Rally in Harlem, attended by Martin Luther King, raised $10,000 to be distributed among civil rights organisations including the NAACP. The rally also saw the awarding, for the first time, of a Medgar Evers Memorial Award to honour Brothers who had distinguished themselves in the fight for rights.

The *Prince Hall Sentinel*, which gave constant coverage to the civil rights struggle and to Prince Hall Masonry's place in it, did not once mention the white Craft's Masonic Brotherhood Center during its two-year run.

The final gasp of American innocence

The New York World's Fair has been called 'the final gasp of American innocence'. The civil rights movement was only one sign during the World's Fair that the innocence it embodied was coming to an end. In August 1964, the Gulf of Tonkin incident marked the beginning of much more direct American involvement in the Vietnam war. In 1964, 42 per cent of Americans smoked – the statistical maximum. But in January of that year the Surgeon General's report on the dangers of cigarettes proved to be a watershed in public attitudes. Tobacco was not the 'magic of the future' after all. In August 1965, six days of rioting in Watts, Los Angeles, exposed the ghettoisation resulting from racism in housing. Across America, laying down roads to reach all those fine new ranch homes in the suburbs had spurred white flight, leading to 'chocolate cities and vanilla suburbs' – as funk musician George Clinton would later call them.

Try as it might, the New York World's Fair could not keep the tumult at bay. Protestors opposed discriminatory hiring practices by picketing the United Nations building with placards saying 'End Apartheid at the Fair' and 'African Pavilions Built with Lily White Labor'. President Johnson's speech on the opening day was interrupted by hecklers shouting 'Jim Crow Must Go!' A howlingly inappropriate minstrel show at the Louisiana Pavilion shut down after two days. Twelve of the Zulu dancers at the South Africa Pavilion claimed asylum from apartheid, and their cause was taken up by the likes of Harry Belafonte and Martin Luther King. Refugees from Franco's Spain mounted a protest outside their country's pavilion under the slogan 'Amnesty for All Political Prisoners'.

The corporate dominance of the fair also attracted criticism. Art critic Robert Hughes angrily dismissed it as 'a promotional orgy for American business . . . From the moment you enter Flushing Meadow[s], you become a fetus in the bulging womb of commerce, suspended in an amniotic fluid of ballyhoo and gimmickry.' Many more commentators just felt that the fair was out of date. The feeling was crystallised by the musical entertainment on offer: the Beatles were there only as bad waxworks; the real thing was shunned in favour of Guy Lombardo and his Royal Canadians, who had been playing the same 'sweetest music this side of Heaven' since 1924.

The Masonic Brotherhood Center's worthy exhibits could not compete with what *Time* magazine called the 'whoosh and voom' of the World's Fair, its 'gimcrack sorcery'. The Masons did not get near the visitor numbers of the biggest attractions: General Motors' massive investment in 'Futurama' paid off with 29 million visitors, and 27 million rode the conveyor belt past Michelangelo's *Pietà*. But a tally for the Masons of 1.25 million was highly respectable. The Grand Lodge of New York was rightly proud of the show it had put on, and of the $52,875.32 made for charity in the first season alone; the beneficiaries would be the children in an upstate Masonic care home. Indeed, when much of the fair had 'a tacky, plastic, here-today-blown-tomorrow look, as if it were a city made of credit cards', the Masonic Brotherhood Center radiated contemplative permanence. To visit it was to feel that the august patriotism and sense of tradition that had sustained the Craft through its hundred-year golden age was set to take it to ever-greater heights.

Yet the changes that arrived in the 1960s were to have effects as profound for Freemasonry as they did for America at large. The Masonic Brotherhood Center stood at a peak from which Freemasonry's membership and influence would face an inexorable decline. Gerald Ford, the last Masonic President to date, took office in 1974: by that time there were 3.5 million Masons – down from a 1959 high of 4.1 million. The fall was steady but relentless. By 1984, membership was below three million. In 1998, it fell to under two million. In 2017, the last year for which figures are available, the number of Brothers totalled only just over one million – a quarter of the figure half a century earlier. The Craft began to look more and more superannuated. Prince Hall Masons have faced a comparable decline, although precise numbers are not easy to come by. The same trend can be identified in many countries. One attempt to dig deeper into the data across the Anglosphere suggests that the Craft's most serious weakness was that Masons remained Masons for an ever-shorter period. Masonry has increasingly become a phase that men go through rather than a long-term commitment. Lifelong Freemasons are greying, and dying, and not being replaced.

The problems causing the decline are many and deep-seated – part of trends that are visible in other parts of society.

The gleaming image of the American lifestyle that the New York World's Fair projected onto the future was a fake. Propping up that image, just as it propped up Freemasonry, was a silent assumption. One of the most talked-about books of the day called it the Feminine Mystique. Betty Friedan's feminist classic of that name, published in 1963, was an eloquent and documented demolition of the notion that the best that life could offer was being a suburban housewife surrounded by consumer gewgaws. And a husband who was a respected member of the local Lodge, we might add.

The Masonic Brotherhood Center did its bit to propagate the feminine mystique by holding up a man in a silver spacesuit as its paragon of contemporary American manhood. Gordon 'Gordo' Cooper, like all the other astronauts, was supposed to be clean-cut, dependably macho and devotedly married. His Freemasonry dovetailed nicely with the image NASA wanted. The reality was very different. Because of his infidelity, he and his wife Trudy were well on the way to divorce when his chance to take part in Project Mercury came along. The couple decided to put on a façade of marital bliss so that they could together reap the rewards that came with space stardom. Like the other astronaut wives, Trudy, who was a trained pilot, smiled at the cameras, radiated vapid glamour and dutifully proclaimed her pride in her man. Meanwhile, Gordo had a number of dalliances with 'astro-groupies' – or 'Cape Cookies', as the heroes of the space race called their many female admirers.

Far beyond Cape Canaveral, the weekend and evening hours that men spent building a better self with their Brethren – memorising and performing rituals and absorbing their ethical lessons, discussing which charities to support, eating, drinking and back-slapping – were all paid for by more time in the kitchen for their wives. It could not last. Over the coming decades, the feminine mystique mouldered. Women went back into education and the workforce. They got married later. They had fewer children. They got divorced. Tellingly, in the early 1970s, there was a rash of marital break-ups among NASA astronauts. Men changed too. Bringing up a family became more of a two-carer enterprise. And the nine-to-five, college-to-the-retirement-carriage-clock pattern of white-collar work became increasingly rare, eating further into the free time available for fraternalism. The Lodge room also had to compete for men's time with a growing leisure industry that offered more fun in return for less cost, rigmarole and gender exclusivity: TV, restaurants, gyms and sports clubs, concerts, car trips, and so on.

Another change that was beginning to bed down in the early 1960s was the growth of a generational divide. Teenagers and twenty-somethings were acquiring an identity of their own, defined as distinct from and even opposed to the mind-set of older folk. They listened to different music, wore different clothes, watched different movies, expressed different values. It all served to reduce the appeal of an ideal life-narrative cherished by Freemasonry: the young man, following his father into the Craft, and beginning a journey towards maturity and wisdom under the benevolent eye of older Brethren.

There were very practical reasons for Freemasonry's decline too. The welfare safety net that was one of the main attractions of membership became superfluous when the benefits were increasingly provided by the state and/or employers. Medicare, to cite just one example, was introduced by President Johnson during the second season of the New York World's Fair. In the private sector, financial security became one of the biggest growth industries of our era. The finance industry has often directly supplanted fraternalism. Several of the fraternal societies founded in the late nineteenth century have now morphed into financial services organisations: examples include the Woodmen of the World (aka WoodmenLife), the Lutheran Brotherhood (aka

Thrivent Insurance) and the Tribe of Ben-Hur (aka Ben-Hur Life Association).

For all these reasons, the story of Freemasonry in America became one of managed decline.

Arezzo: **The Man Who Would Be Puppet-Master**

A list of friends

Licio Gelli seemed born to pass unobserved: on the small side of medium stature, respectably bespectacled, with tidy grey hair tidily side-parted, he managed a clothing factory in small-town Tuscany. Yet in the late 1970s, this colourless man had a hypnotic hold over the Italian press. 'In the gallery of unreachable personalities, he is among the most unreachable.'

Gelli lived in a secluded villa that was not far from his factory, just outside Arezzo. Powerful friends came to stroll in the gardens with him. He often stayed in a suite in the five-star Hotel Excelsior on the grand, curving slope of Rome's via Veneto. There he received the VIPs who came for an intimate chat.

His power was as obvious as it was obscure. He was known to be poorly educated, and to have been a passionate Fascist when young: at seventeen, he volunteered to go and fight on Franco's side in the Spanish Civil War. Much of the rest was rumour. He was reputed to be personal friends with both US President Jimmy Carter and Argentinian dictator Juan Perón. Yet investigative journalists suspected aloud that Gelli was mixed up in everything from bank fraud and kidnapping to political graft and neo-Fascist terrorism. All that anyone knew for certain was that his influence derived in some way from the Masonic

Lodge known as Propaganda 2, or P2, of which he was the Venerable Master. P2 was both notorious and unknown – a new variant of Masonic secrecy.

Licio Gelli (1919–2015),
Venerable Master of the
Lodge Propaganda 2, or P2.

On 5 October 1980, *Corriere della Sera*, Italy's most prestigious daily, pulled off a scoop by publishing an in-depth interview with Gelli. 'What is P2?', he was asked. 'A centre that welcomes and unites only people endowed with intelligence, a high level of education, wisdom and, above all, generosity.' With evident satisfaction, Gelli told the *Corriere* that the negative publicity surrounding him and his Lodge had only served to draw in more applications to join. But he would not reveal anything about his Brothers in P2, or how he communicated with them: 'A classy lover never reveals his methods for meeting his woman.' Did he have an 'occult power'? He had never thought of himself that way, but he couldn't stop other people imagining that he did. 'I can count a great many friends both in Italy and abroad. But having friends is one thing, and having power is quite another.' Any insight into the man and his mysteries was shrouded in Masonic waffle, name-dropping and hints. Only the interview's final exchange gave a glimpse of the truth:

'As a child, when they asked you what you wanted to be when you grew up, what did you answer?'

'A puppet-master.'

Italy is prominent in the pages of this book because nowhere have more different strands of the Masonic story converged. As the home of the Papacy, Italy has a tradition of anti-Masonic phobia that remains unbroken since the first time Freemasons were excommunicated in 1738. In the early nineteenth century, under its Napoleonic regimes, Italy saw Freemasonry used as a tool of authoritarian government. Yet, in the Charcoal-Burners, Masonic-style brotherhood became a vehicle of revolutionary plotting. Later, quasi-Masonic fraternities degenerated into the mafia. Early in Italy's history as a unified country, its Lodges also developed into the antechamber of power. The birthplace of Fascism, Italy was also the first country where Freemasonry was crushed by a totalitarian regime.

The innovations did not stop when Fascism fell. In the 1970s, one Brother spun a web of influence so pervasive that it was deemed to pose a mortal threat to Italian democracy. Here, it seemed, was everything the most alarmist conspiracy theorists had ever warned about. The Brother's name was Licio Gelli, and his Lodge was P2.

In 1945, Italian Freemasonry re-emerged from under the Fascist ban to find that the new Italy was almost as uncomfortable as the old one. The Italian Craft had always gained much of its prestige from a close relationship to politics. But the post-war political stage was dominated by two opposing giants who together closed off Freemasonry's access: the *Democrazia Cristiana* (the DC, or Christian Democrats), which was aligned with the Vatican and the western, capitalist bloc; and the *Partito Comunista Italiano*, or PCI, which was Western Europe's largest Communist Party and was initially aligned with the Soviet Union. The Christian Democrats would be the central component of Italy's governing coalitions until the end of the Cold War. Meanwhile, the PCI loomed in perpetual opposition. For two generations Italian politics was dominated, and paralysed, by the overriding need to keep the Communists out of power.

Few things united Italy's Christian Democrats and Communists across the Cold War chasm, but one of them was a suspicion of Freemasonry. The DC inherited the Church's historic anti-Masonry. For the PCI, the Craft had always been a bourgeois cabal. Neither party would allow Masons in its ranks. These sentiments found expression in Italy's Constitution, which both Christian Democrats and Communists helped to design. When it came into force on 1 January 1948, its Eighteenth Article banned secret societies. Neither the DC nor the PCI could quite bring itself to include Freemasonry in the ban – to do so would have had uncomfortable echoes of Fascism. But they also rejected proposals to exempt it. Without a law to clarify exactly what counted as a secret society, the Brotherhood was left in a constitutional no-man's land.

Post-war Italian Freemasonry also had to contend with a host of internal problems. Because it looked out of step with the times, it struggled to recruit. Worse still, precisely because it had been victimised by Fascism, it now attracted cynical former Fascists eager to cover up their past. Masonry was also divided. The older and bigger of the two main lineages – the one that would be caught up in the P2 storm – was the Grand Orient of Italy. The other was the Grand Lodge of Italy. The doctrinal issues that separated the two versions of Freemasonry need not detain us. Suffice it to say that both suffered schisms, and the differences between them took new forms – notably in 1956 when the Grand Lodge of Italy created a women's Lodge. Both branches of the Masonic hierarchy still hankered after the kind of prominence that Italian Craft had enjoyed in the late nineteenth century. Some leaders pinned their hopes on just restating the old opposition to Catholicism. Others sought friendship and favour from Britain and the USA by posing as a bulwark against the Communist menace. No clear strategy emerged from the confusion.

Only in the early 1960s did Freemasonry begin to grow in numbers and reach. The Christian Democrats, who were permanently in government but permanently unstable, tentatively opened to coalitions with the parties of centre and centre-Left within which Masons were more welcome. Under Pope John XXIII, the Vatican took a more liberal turn, and a cagey dialogue be--tween some intellectuals from both Freemasonry and the Church began.

Just as in other countries where the Craft was much stronger, Italian Masonry also had to contend with momentous social transformations in the 1960s and 1970s. Italy was now an industrial power, its cities swelling with immigrants from the countryside, its homes filling with consumer goods, its workers hungry for their share of the country's increased wealth, its women restive for rights, its young people experimenting with new lifestyles and political identities. The Italian situation had its peculiarities too. The state badly needed reform, but the Christian Democrats and their coalition partners seemed too mired in convoluted bargaining and in handing out state jobs to their friends to implement change. Inefficiency, patronage, corruption and mafia influence seeped further into the institutions. Scandals broke out repeatedly. Partly as a result of such cases, the PCI gradually accumulated electoral support by building a reputation for honesty. In the 1963 general election, it

attracted a quarter of the votes cast. In 1976, against the background of an economic crisis, it reached its maximum of more
than a third of the votes. In Italy's proportional system, that was
easily enough to stake a claim to power.

Meanwhile, outside of parliament, politics had become far
more volatile. At the end of the 1960s, social stresses erupted
into student revolt and strikes. Then, in December 1969, Italian
political life entered a fearful and violent new era when a bomb
exploded in a bank in Piazza Fontana, a square around the corner
from Milan cathedral; there were sixteen fatalities. Police attempts
to blame anarchists unravelled over the coming weeks and months
– but not before one anarchist suspect had fallen to his death
from the fourth floor of police headquarters in circumstances
that looked deeply suspicious. Investigative journalists soon
produced a more plausible explanation: the police had deliberately ignored evidence that the real culprits were not anarchists,
but right-wing terrorists with close contacts to the secret service.
This looked for all the world like the Strategy of Tension, which
was a secret plan to use terror to create the climate for a decisive
turn to the Right, or even for a right-wing *Putsch*. Further atrocities followed.

The decade after the Piazza Fontana bomb also saw street
fighting involving militants of the Left and Right and, particularly
from 1976, assassinations. In March 1978, the country came to
a standstill when a terrorist group called the Red Brigades
kidnapped Aldo Moro, a former Christian Democrat Prime
Minister. After fifty-five days during which Moro underwent a
kangaroo trial, and politicians argued about what to do, the Red
Brigades murdered their captive.

On 2 August 1980, just when the Communist vote had begun
to decline and the Strategy of Tension seemed to have been
dropped, eighty-five people died when a massive bomb devastated
the railway station in the Communist-run city of Bologna.

So Licio Gelli's interview with the *Corriere della Sera*, published
two months after the Bologna station explosion, came at a grim

and acutely twitchy moment. His sibylline pronouncements showed that he was only too happy to augment the unease. He made no secret of the fact that he was a man of the Right, but he dodged a question about his suspected links to the secret services, and hid his precise views behind an unnerving anecdote. Asked what he thought of democracy, he recalled a conversation with Aldo Moro, the former Prime Minister killed by the Red Brigades two years previously. Moro, who was known for the extreme caution of his approach to reform, apparently told Gelli that democracy was like beans in a pot: to be done properly, they had to cook very, very, very slowly. Gelli interrupted Moro to tell him: 'Watch out that the beans don't run out of water, because you'll run the risk of burning them.'

Just when Italy's democratic institutions were in grave peril, and trust in those institutions had plummeted, Gelli chose to ignore Masonry's time-hallowed aversion to 'politicks', its loyalty to the governing institutions, and to make murky allusions to burning democracy. The Brotherhood had rarely appeared more sinister.

Within months of Gelli's notorious *Corriere della Sera* interview, the true face of P2 began to emerge during the investigation into Michele Sindona, a Sicilian tax lawyer who owned a complex web of banks and offshore finance companies. When the fortunes of his empire became precarious, Sindona took more risks in currency speculation and upped his ambitions. In 1972, despite rumours that he had links to the mafia, he acquired a controlling share of the Franklin National Bank, then the twentieth biggest bank in the United States. Two years later, when the Franklin National Bank hit the rocks, Sindona came under investigation in the USA for fraud. The Bank of Italy ordered his Italian banks to be wound up, and a request was issued to extradite him.

Sindona became increasingly desperate to save his empire, and began paying large sums to the ruling Christian Democrat Party in the hope that it could engineer a salvage plan. He also laundered and invested vast amounts of mafia narco-dollars. In July 1979, the liquidator appointed by the Bank of Italy to look into Sindona's affairs, having resisted various attempts at bribery and corruption, was murdered by a professional hitman.

Soon afterwards, Sindona vanished from New York and reappeared in Sicily, posing as the victim of a kidnapping by a non-existent 'Subversive Proletarian Committee for a Better Justice'. In reality, a mafia network heavily involved in the transatlantic heroin trade had orchestrated everything. To add colour to the far-fetched charade, Sindona even had himself anaesthetised and shot in the leg by a compliant doctor. The point was to issue sensitive information from 'captivity' as a way of blackmailing politicians into saving him, his banks and the mafia's money. It didn't work. Still maintaining the kidnapping fiction, Sindona then had himself found, suitably wounded and dishevelled, in a Manhattan phone booth. In 1980, he was sentenced to twenty-five years for financial crimes by an American court.

Back in Italy, in Milan, investigations into Sindona continued. A number of clues pointed in the direction of Licio Gelli and P2. Gelli's private contact details were in Sindona's diary. His loyalty to Sindona cropped up in the *Corriere della Sera* interview. The Venerable Master also wrote an affidavit for the disgraced banker in the hope of blocking extradition from the United States: he claimed that a fair trial was impossible in Italy because the judiciary had been infiltrated by Communists. The doctor who anaesthetised Sindona and shot him in the leg – a man who described himself as 'a sentimental international Freemason' – had travelled to and fro between Sicily and Gelli's home during the kidnapping farce. Evidently the Venerable Master had invested a great deal of his mysterious cachet in trying to save Sindona.

So it was that, in March 1981, amid hermetic confidentiality, a small team from the *Guardia di Finanza* (Finance Police) travelled down from Milan to raid Gelli's properties in Arezzo. They found what they were looking for – much more than they were looking for – in the offices of his clothing factory. Next to the desk was a suitcase containing thirty-three envelopes full of documents; each envelope was signed across the seal by Gelli, and labelled with names associated with some of the major business and political scandals of recent years. In the safe – once the key had been confiscated from Gelli's secretary, who had tried to run off with it – there was a roster of P2 members. Understandably, a folder labelled 'FINANCE POLICE' caught the attention of the finance policemen carrying out the search. Its contents showed that five of their most senior commanders were members of P2. Indeed, while the search was still underway, the officer in charge received an urgent message to contact his General Commander, the top man in the whole *Guardia di Finanza*, who told him: 'I know you are there and that you've found some lists. You should know that my name is on them. Tread carefully, because the top echelons [of the state] are there too. Watch out, because the whole force will be brought down.' The men who searched Gelli's office had arrived in a humble FIAT Ritmo. Arrangements were quickly made for them and their explosive cargo of documents to be escorted back to Milan by two Alfa Romeos filled with heavily armed police.

The two investigating magistrates in charge of the case were so worried by what they read that they took time to number every page, and run off copies to place in different secure locations. Then they made an appointment to see the Prime Minister. When the time came, they were shown into the antechamber of his office by his private secretary, who was a model of smiling courtesy – despite the fact that he was one of the 962 men on the P2 membership list, and already knew the highly confidential news that the magistrates had come to divulge. They found the Prime Minister, Arnaldo Forlani, blinking behind the boxy frames of his glasses, ready to make a show of being unruffled. He did not make a very good job of it, according to one of the magistrates: 'He tried to say something to us, but for a good couple of minutes he couldn't articulate a single word. Guttural sounds came out of his mouth, leaving us with the unconfirmed impression that he was trying to pooh-pooh the subject, without succeeding in mastering his words.' After this strange encounter, Prime Minister Forlani decided to buy time, and left it to a committee of three wise men to decide if P2 counted as a secret society under the Italian Constitution. Meanwhile, news and rumours began to leak out.

Only on 22 May 1981, more than two months after the search of Gelli's factory in Tuscany, did newspaper readers get to see the jaw-slackening roll-call of P2 members.

There were three currently serving government ministers, as well as forty-odd Members of Parliament, several of whom had held office.

Far more disturbing than the number of P2 politicians was the Lodge's reach into the state apparatus. The *piduisti* ('P2-ists') – as Italians quickly learned to call them – included the heads of *all* branches of the civilian and military secret services, in addition to the Chief of the Defence Staff, and no less than 195 officers from the army, navy and air force – of whom 92 were generals or colonels. Three of the P2 generals had been implicated in an abortive military *coup d'état* in 1970.

The top strata of Italy's various law-enforcement agencies were well represented: as well as the five men from the *Guardia di Finanza*, there were nine generals from the *Carabinieri*, and two from the State Police. It was profoundly disquieting that, during the fifty-five days that Prime Minister Aldo Moro had been held captive by the Red Brigades, ministers were advised by a coordinating committee of high-ranking law-enforcement officers that included six P2-ists – a majority. Could their presence explain the tragic outcome of the kidnap?

Over sixty high-ranking civil servants and nine senior diplomats were named. In the Treasury Ministry, including the nationalised banks it controlled, there were sixty-seven P2-ists.

As well as within the state, Gelli also had lots of 'friends' in society and the economy. The entrepreneurs included a member of the Agnesi pasta dynasty and, with membership number 1816, a forty-five-year-old Milanese construction and TV businessman called Silvio Berlusconi. There were also bankers from the private sector, such as the fake kidnap victim Michele Sindona, member no. 501. Sindona's pupil and rival, Roberto Calvi, was also in P2 (and also laundered money for the mafia through his Banco Ambrosiano, as would later be revealed).

Gelli had menacing international connections, like the man who had been, until 1979, the chief of the Shah of Iran's secret police. Over forty affiliates were from, or based in, South American countries. The strong Argentinian contingent included Admiral Emilio Eduardo Massera, a leading figure in the military coup of 1976: he was currently engaged in masterminding the *junta*'s Dirty War against political opponents in which some 30,000 people are thought to have been murdered.

Among the many prominent figures in the media that had joined P2, the stand-out names were the proprietor and the managing director of the company that owned the *Corriere della Sera*, as well as the paper's editor, and the journalist who had conducted the 'puppet-master' interview.

Shock and outrage followed the publication of the P2 list. Events moved fast, and had long-lasting repercussions. The government fell, brought down by Forlani's dithering. A Parliamentary Commission of Inquiry into the P2 Masonic Lodge was set up under the remarkable Christian Democrat Tina Anselmi – a hero of the Resistance against the Nazis and the first woman in Italy to become a government minister. P2 was soon banned under the so-called 'Anselmi Law', based on Article 18 of the Constitution.

The Venerable Master bolted to Switzerland, where he was later arrested; in August 1983 he escaped from a Geneva prison and made his way to South America on an Argentinian diplomatic passport. Only in 1988 would he return to Italy to face justice. Further investigations were already underway across a whole host of cases of corruption and right-wing subversion in which P2 involvement was suspected; legal proceedings and public controversies would last for many years.

A nervous Roman establishment made its counter-moves early – or so those on the Left alleged. In September 1981, the prosecutors in Milan who had conducted the search of Gelli's factory were ordered to surrender their documents to magistrates in Rome, where the prosecutors' office had a reputation for slowing

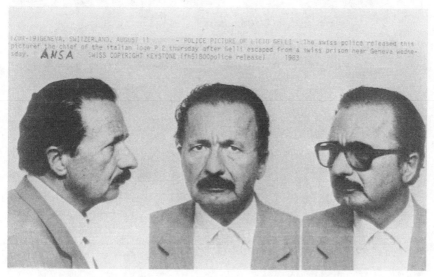

Licio Gelli, in a picture distributed by police
soon after his escape from a Swiss prison in 1983.

down and defusing politically sensitive cases.

The exposure of P2 removed the protection previously enjoyed by P2-ist Roberto Calvi. His Banco Ambrosiano collapsed the following year, and in June 1982 Calvi was found hanging by his neck under London's Blackfriars Bridge. To this day, no one is sure whether he was murdered or committed suicide. In 1984, the fake kidnap victim Michele Sindona was finally extradited to Italy to be tried and jailed for financial crimes. In March 1986, he was also found guilty of commissioning the murder of his

381

bank's liquidator. Sindona died in prison two days later after drinking an *espresso* laced with cyanide. Although he probably killed himself, speculation was rife that he had been silenced.

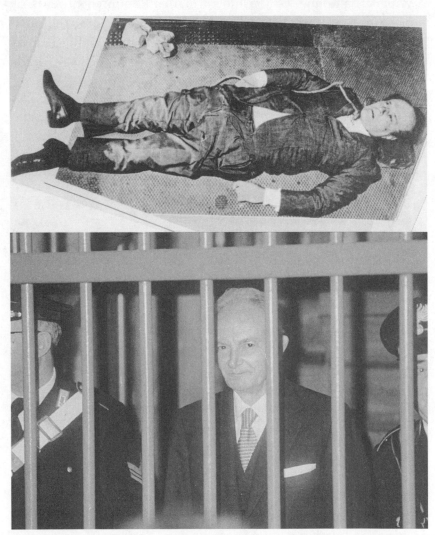

Roberto Calvi (1920–1982), whose body was found hanging under Blackfriars Bridge, London, and Michele Sindona (1920–1986), who drank a coffee laced with cyanide after being sentenced to life for murder. Both bankers were members of the P2 Masonic Lodge.

Gelli's offices in the Uruguayan capital Montevideo were searched, revealing, among other things, highly confidential papers belonging to the Italian secret services. Only a small part of this Uruguayan trove would ever make it into the hands of the authorities back in the peninsula. The suspicion remained – and remains to this day – that the list of P2 members found in Gelli's factory in Arezzo was incomplete, and that hundreds more VIPs were also affiliated.

The P2 affair, which has never really come to an end, is plagued with such uncertainties. As Tina Anselmi, the President of the Parliamentary Commission of Inquiry, put it: '[The P2 story] is uniquely rich in ambivalence and in facts with a double meaning. Together with evidence that supports one theory, [. . .] circumstances almost always emerge to justify the opposite theory.' As if to demonstrate her point, the members of the Inquiry could not agree: when they produced their findings in 1984, they issued a majority report and no fewer than five dissenting minority reports.

Years later, participants in the drama and historians both still take wildly varying lines on Gelli's Lodge. For some, it was a subversive Fascist conspiracy. For others, far from being subversive, the P2 Lodge was a way of propping up the system from within. Many perceive the shadow of the CIA somewhere in the background of either scenario. Tina Anselmi famously described P2 as part of a 'double pyramid'. The lower pyramid was P2, with Licio Gelli at its apex. But Gelli was also placed at the point of an inverted pyramid, most of which was safely hidden within the state. The real culprits in the whole story, Anselmi was implying, were shrouded figures in the inverted pyramid. Many think of P2 as the true face of power, and of the P2 scandal as the only time in Italian history when citizens caught a glimpse of where the real decisions are made. By way of contrast, one eminent historian of Freemasonry has recently argued that there was no P2 conspiracy at all: the whole affair was cynically cooked up by the Left. There is no consensus on whether Licio Gelli was a puppeteer, or a puppet in the hands of more powerful men; a crime-boss, or a blagger

Tina Anselmi (1927–2016),
who presided over the Parliamentary
Commission of Inquiry into P2.

whose power was no more real than the Wizard of Oz's; an illicit
lobbyist, or the latest in a long line of misunderstood Masons.

Over more than three decades, Gelli was investigated and/or
put on trial for a long list of crimes: involvement in a subversive
organisation; funding terrorist attacks; financial misdemeanours;
political corruption; slander; perverting the course of justice;
complicity in murder (for having Roberto Calvi hanged under
Blackfriars Bridge); working with both the Sicilian mafia and the
Neapolitan camorra; arms and currency trafficking; tax avoid-
ance. Given the vast legal arsenal unleashed against him, and
given the initial expectations that P2 was the key to all the era's
mysteries, the final total of guilty verdicts against his name was
underwhelming:

- In 1994, Gelli was given a ten-year sentence for 'aggravated slander with a terrorist aim' in relation to the Bologna station bomb of 1980. The courts found that Gelli had conspired with four secret agents to throw investigations into the massacre off-track. The plan involved planting a suitcase containing the same explosive as that recently used in the Bologna station massacre, with a view to implicating foreign terrorists rather than the Italian neo-Fascists who were actually responsible.

- In 1998, Gelli went on the run just after the Supreme Court confirmed a twelve-year sentence for his role in the collapse of the Banco Ambrosiano – the bank run by Roberto Calvi, of Blackfriars Bridge notoriety. The Venerable Master was recaptured four months later in the South of France; he had a beard and was wearing a beret.

- Gelli was also convicted of slandering the magistrates investigating his case. But the conviction was cancelled under the statute of limitations. He was ordered to pay legal costs.

- The Venerable Master was successfully sued for defamation by a journalist, and had a minor conviction for offending the honour of the Italian President.

Taken together, these verdicts do not unambiguously support any of the various interpretations of P2. Neither does the fact that, in 1996, the Supreme Court acquitted Gelli and the P2-ists of conspiring against the Constitution and the state institutions. Many saw this verdict as the end-result of an establishment cover-up; others objected that conspiring against the state was only the most far-fetched theory about what P2 was up to.

We shall never know the full truth. What follows, presented with all due caution, is my attempt to go back over the years before the raid on Gelli's factory near Arezzo, and tell the P2 story.

The covert Lodge

P2 was not Licio Gelli's creation. It was originally set up nearly a century earlier within the Grand Orient of Italy under the name of Lodge Masonic Propaganda. Its first affiliates were leading figures of the 1880s, including two Prime Ministers and the un-official poet laureate, Giosuè Carducci. Lodge Masonic Propaganda had a special status: based in Rome, it exempted its famous, busy, much-travelled members from the duties imposed by their territorially based Lodges. Propaganda affiliates were also afforded much more privacy, since they could be admitted to Masonry directly by the Grand Master; the procedure was known as 'initiation on the sword-blade'. The Grand Master also kept their identity to himself, or 'in his ear', in Grand Orient jargon. Propaganda was thus a 'covered Lodge' (Masonic jargon again).

All this showed just how keen Italian Masonry was to accom-modate powerful friends. Part of the reason for the privacy granted to its members was so that they could guard their repu-tations. No chancer in an ordinary Lodge would be able to vaunt his intimacy with the great and the good of the Grand Orient.

However, there were also aspects of Lodge Propaganda's history that foreshadowed later troubles. The Lodge was most closely associated with Grand Master Adriano Lemmi, recruited into the Lodge in 1877, and his close friend Prime Minister Francesco Crispi, who was also a member. As mentioned briefly in an earlier chapter, their political alliance damaged the Craft's reputation when they were caught up in scandals relating to the government tobacco monopoly and a failed bank.

When Italian Freemasonry resurfaced after the Second World War, Lodge Propaganda was given the number two, as a mark of its importance. (Lodge no. 1 was the oldest in the country.) In the course of time, the Lodge would become known simply as Propaganda 2 or P2.

Licio Gelli was first initiated into Masonry in 1965. Two years later he transferred to P2. By the late 1960s, he was already a close collaborator of the Grand Master. Gelli had charm and even charisma, according to those who knew him; and he brought with him a range of real and/or boasted contacts with a number of good candidates for Masonic initiation.

In 1970, Gelli was put in charge of P2, and vested with the authority to initiate new members 'on the sword-blade' – hitherto the exclusive privilege of the Grand Master. In 1971, his role was formalised when he was given the unprecedented role of Organisational Secretary of P2. A Management Council created to work with him remained powerless. P2 was well on the way to becoming Gelli's personal domain.

Any Freemasons in Britain or America who are reading this will have already felt their eyebrows reach their hairline on hearing about the original, nineteenth-century Lodge Propaganda. Nothing like a covered Lodge has ever existed in Britain or America, and it was clearly a structure ripe for abuse. Under Licio Gelli, the abuse happened. Before Gelli, P2 was little more than a select list of distinguished Brothers. Under him, it became a parasitical body within Freemasonry that was entirely under his control. The *covered* Lodge Propaganda was turned into the *covert* Lodge P2. For those who hold Masonic values dear, the truly shocking thing about this system was that Gelli laid its foundations with the collaboration of the Grand Orient Leadership, and the complicity of many senior Freemasons.

The fascinating central figure here is Giordano Gamberini, the Grand Master of the Grand Orient for most of the 1960s, and a power behind the throne of the Grand Orient under his two successors. Gamberini was the man who took Gelli under his wing, gave him responsibility for revitalising P2, and then sponsored and protected him. Yet Gamberini was anything but stupid or corrupt. He was a refined Protestant scholar with a goatee beard and an aristocratic bearing that he owed to his noble family from Ravenna. He was also searingly honest about Italian Masonry's weaknesses. His writings analysed the way in which

387

Italian history, unlike the history of England or the United States, had prevented Masons from creating a great tradition rooted just in the Craft's ability to build better men. He made it plain that he regretted, but could ignore, how political Italian Masonry had always been – right since Murat and the Charcoal-Burners. Gamberini passionately believed that the Craft should resist becoming 'a political force, a power-centre, an ideological school'. It also needed to grow out of its bad old habits of secrecy and its 'inclination towards favouritism between Brothers'.

Grand Master Giordano Gamberini
(1915–2003).

Evidently Gamberini thought of Masonry in terms diametrically opposed to what P2 became. Which makes it all the stranger that this honest man entrusted such power to a devious character like Gelli. The explanation lies in other weaknesses of Freemasonry that Gamberini was incapable of recognising. Like many Italian

Masons, he was a passionate anti-Communist. He welcomed an open battle with Communist intolerance, since it would help free the Craft of 'false Brothers' who deluded themselves that they could remain neutral. In Gamberini's mind, anti-Communism was a Masonic test of manhood.

Masons everywhere have always had a tendency to think of themselves as the ethical *crème de la crème*. Gamberini displayed that tendency in abundance: put bluntly, he was a snob. There was a certain high-minded machismo to his conception of Masonry too. The Craft's way of perfecting character was not suitable for women, he believed, because they were 'different' and had a 'different road to travel'. He was coy about precisely how women were different, although there is a clue in his contempt for feminism. For Gamberini, the ideal Craftsman was a morally superior being, prepared to stand fast against the brute cravings of the mob: 'Masonic teaching exclusively addresses the individual, and aims to help that individual to become a "person" in the full sense of the word. When the time comes that every individual is truly a person, the crowd – with its stupidity, its cruelty, its monkey-like incoherence – will no longer exist.' Gamberini also disliked the profane press, which did nothing but spread harmful misconceptions about the Craft.

Grand Master Gamberini's hauteur was flattered by Licio Gelli's ability to insinuate himself into exalted company. For their very different reasons, they both wanted to attract the same men: not politicians, who were too caught up in the factional game, but top-level servants of the state. In Gamberini's eyes, these were real men, endowed with a sense of duty and order, and not susceptible to the whims of the masses. That degree of shared ground between Gamberini and Gelli was the basis of the initial trust between them. Then, as the Italian political climate became more strained from 1969, Gamberini grew to appreciate Gelli's fervent anti-Communism. In Gamberini's mind, a re-energised P2 could make brotherly values into a moral stiffener for the conduct of public business in a society menaced by corruption and the Left. *Politics* weakened Masonry, he thought. But the *state* badly needed what Masonry had to offer. In that sense, the Italian Craft could still consider itself as being above and outside the political struggle, as the Landmarks had always required.

So it was that Grand Master Gamberini gave his blessing to Licio Gelli's control over P2. Gelli then quickly moved the Lodge towards much greater secrecy and a right-wing orientation. He gave members code names, and the Lodge was referred to by an innocuous cover designation in Gelli's letters: 'the Centre for Contemporary Historical Studies'. He arranged special meetings of P2 members who had senior positions in the same branch of the state to discuss the political situation.

According to Gelli, the danger was that Catholics and Communists, Masonry's old adversaries, had formed an unholy 'clerico-Communist' entente. He bullet-pointed the political agenda as follows: 'The threat of the Communist Party, in agreement with clericalism, which is close to conquering power. The powerlessness of the police. The uncontrolled spread of immorality . . . Our position in the event that the clerico-Communists came to power. Relationship with the Italian state.' In a circular to P2 members about these discussions, Gelli talked darkly of 'emergency plans' that might be needed if the 'clerico-Communists' gained the upper hand.

At around the same time as these meetings, on 29 December 1972, the top officers of P2, including Gamberini's successor as Grand Master, met in the four-star Hotel Baglioni in Florence. Gelli put forward a plan to manage information within the Lodge: news would be funnelled up from Brothers, evaluated by a committee of P2 experts, and then passed on to a friendly press agency. There was no mystery about what the purpose would be: blackmail.

Democrats and traditionalist Masons within P2 grew increasingly alarmed. Gelli had been heard to boast that he possessed information that could ruin the Grand Master. At that very time, the Strategy of Tension was pushing Italy into a moment of supreme danger. In May 1974, in Brescia's Piazza della Loggia, a bomb killed eight people and mutilated dozens more during a demonstration against right-wing terrorism. In August of the same year, twelve more were killed when a bomb exploded on a train passing through a tunnel under the Apennines. Yet despite this climate, and the distinct whiff of skulduggery that emanated from P2, almost all P2 members and senior Grand Orient Craftsmen decided not to go to the authorities. The P2 affair was to be kept private – a matter for Masons alone.

In December 1974, a Grand Orient Assembly took on board the democrats' concerns, and voted to convert P2 into an ordinary, regular Lodge: there would be no more cloak-and-dagger Masonry. But the following spring, when the decision was supposed to be ratified, it was reviewed after off-stage manoeuvres. Gelli is thought to have circulated documents implicating the Grand Master in financial malpractice. Soon afterwards, he was anointed as Venerable Master of the regular Lodge P2, which had no more than a handful of members, while behind the scenes he continued to run his private version of P2, with hundreds of other covert members 'in his ear'. He would even be given packs of blank membership cards to fill in as he saw fit. The cuckoo had command of the nest.

The Grand Orient leadership clearly thought that their constitutional manoeuvres had provided a cover story to insulate any risk that Gelli's P2 might pose to Masonry as a whole. Interviewed amid growing press concern in 1977, former Grand Master Giordano Gamberini disingenuously claimed that P2 was now just a normal Masonic Lodge, no more secret than any other.

Meanwhile, Gelli was investing a huge amount of time in face-to-face meetings either at his Rome hotel suite, where he had three telephones installed, or in the Bar Doney next door. He initiated so many members 'on the sword-blade' that the Lodge had to be restructured. Until this point, he had relied on a few close collaborators, who were among the earliest recruits. From 1979, while the most powerful Brothers remained directly tied to Gelli and to him only, he distributed the rest of the P2 membership, about half of it, into local groups whose leaders would pass requests upwards.

These cells formalised the miniature networks that were one of the secrets of P2's success throughout. The Venerable Master would recruit an individual who was eager to use P2 connections to gain an unfair advantage in his career, or the like. That recruit would then recommend to Gelli one or two others they knew who had a similar outlook. In this way, lots of clusters of men were built into the P2 system. Groups of perhaps three or four gained access to a much wider world of contacts. In return, Gelli found ever larger numbers of people who, unlike most Masons, had important favours to trade, and could be relied upon not to raise any quibbles if he asked them to perform a service for a P2 member they did not know. The Venerable Master was turning himself into a human switchboard of favours.

When the *Guardia di Finanza* raided Gelli's factory they found 200 letters in the P2 archive, two-thirds of which were requests for Masonic solidarity. In most cases the solidarity took the form of what Italians call a *raccomandazione*: a personal letter to an employer recommending someone else for a job. A *raccomandazione* is something distinct from a job reference. Typically wrapped in friendly and polite language, the *raccomandazione* is an implicit request to bend the rules for the person being recommended. It involves one powerful figure asking another powerful figure for a favour in return for other favours. Such letters were the Venerable Master's day-to-day business.

Gelli was also able to keep the Grand Orient leadership on side by diverting some of P2's abundant supply of Masonic solidarity and *raccomandazioni*. In the spring of 1980, at a meeting of the Grand Orient, the Grand Master (the third during Gelli's reign) fielded yet more expressions of concern about P2 by explaining that 'only by turning to P2, that is to Mr Gelli, could he satisfy the numerous requests for solidarity that came his way from various Brothers'.

Where possible, Gelli reinforced his system with coercion. He built up a vast private archive on actual or potential members of P2. Information was a tribute that Gelli demanded of his men: the more compromising the material, the more valuable it was. Some members later reported that Gelli browbeat them into joining the Lodge by threatening to expose their secrets. As one high-ranking civil servant would testify, '[Gelli] made me realize that he was able to acquire knowledge of anything that I had done that was against the rules, and that only he would be able to protect me properly.'

P2 gave Gelli all kinds of options for tactical meddling. Sometimes all he needed to do was to put P2-ists in touch with one another. In the late 1970s there was a scandal involving a tax-dodging oil importation scheme worth hundreds of billions of lire. The northern Italian companies engaged in the scheme found protection from the law in a network of senior finance policemen in P2, who in turn laundered their profits with the help of bankers in P2, and protected *themselves* from investigation with the help of secret agents who were in P2. Thanks to the P2 network, a criminal initiative became a system.

Through his men at the top of the Finance Police, Gelli could offer protection to anyone who might be apprehensive about having their financial affairs scrutinised. This seems to have been the case when he intervened to help resolve a dispute over a $5 million business debt incurred by construction tycoon Anna Bonomi from P2 member Roberto Calvi's notorious Banco Ambrosiano. Gelli's mediation was a quicker, cheaper, safer option than resorting to the courts, where greater transparency would be required.

Gelli had the power to turn commercial financial deals into exchanges of favours between 'friends'. The Rizzoli Group bought the *Corriere della Sera* in 1974. In doing so, it racked up oversized debts and was unable to obtain more credit to implement its restructuring plans through conventional channels. That is when Gelli appeared on the scene. Rizzoli's owners and top managers joined P2, and the Venerable Master procured the capital they needed from a small cluster of banks, all of which were headed by other P2 affiliates: three of them were state-controlled, and the other was once again Banco Ambrosiano under Roberto Calvi. By the Rizzoli general manager's own admission, the group paid Gelli a commission of 6 or 7 billion lire between 1975 and 1980 (very roughly, €25 million today). Through the Banco Ambrosiano, which was itself running into serious financial and legal trouble, P2 would gradually take control of Rizzoli behind the scenes: Gelli's financial right arm, Umberto Ortolani, was put on the board, and Gelli himself became the company's South American representative.

All of which brings us to the enigma of P2's politics. Contrary to what one might expect, Gelli's influence over the *Corriere della Sera* did not lead to a glaring change in editorial line. Even the Gelli interview, burned beans and all, did not seem out of place when it was published in October 1980, because it was part of a series on the hidden sources of power in Italy. Many expressed concern about what Gelli said, but nobody at the time blamed the *Corriere* for giving him a platform. Whatever else it might have been, Italy's biggest daily was not a P2 megaphone between 1975 and 1981. To understand Gelli's subtle political game, we need to look elsewhere.

Democratic rebirth

In the summer of 1981, soon after the P2 list was discovered in Tuscany, Licio Gelli's daughter landed at Rome on a flight from Brazil. She was carrying a suitcase whose seams had been opened and crudely stitched shut again. Inside, under a rudimentary false bottom, customs officers discovered two sets of documents: the raw material of fake allegations involving Swiss bank accounts that were concocted to discredit the investigating magistrates working on the P2 case; and the *Plan for Democratic Rebirth* – the P2 programme for an authoritarian turn in Italian politics.

The question of P2's politics remains the most controversial and enigmatic aspect of the whole affair. A delve into the *Plan for Democratic Rebirth* is the best way to tease out the political aims to which Gelli turned his Lodge. The Plan was not, it should be said from the start, a scheme to destroy democracy entirely. If it were boiled down into a formula, it might be defined as authoritarian conservative rather than Fascist. It sets out policies whose masthead values are family, nation and economic freedom. There would be a brisk round-up of 'ordinary and pseudo-political thugs'; the police would use less fussy interrogation methods than those currently allowed. The judiciary would be brought under greater government control. The news media would be managed through a state press agency. And so on.

The most eye-catching bits of the *Plan* do not relate to policy. Instead, they come in Gelli's diagnosis of Italy's political failings. His picture of his enemies is *conspiratorial*. It is a truism that all conspirators are also conspiracy theorists.

The Italian Communist Party was P2's supreme enemy. Gelli portrays the PCI as cynically pretending to be a respectable, democratic, enlightened party, acceptable to the middle classes: its 'true face', by contrast, was brutally 'Hungarian or Czechoslovakian'. (The reference here is to the repression of an uprising against the Soviet-backed Communist Party in Hungary in 1956, and to the crushing of the 'Prague Spring' by a Soviet-led invasion in 1968.) According to Gelli, small militant Leftist groups engaged in a public critique of the Italian Communist Party for not being left-wing enough were secretly operating a coordinated strategy with it. Worse still, the hand of the Soviet secret police, the KGB, was at work in arranging 'savage massacres' on Italian soil with a view to bringing the PCI to power. The Strategy of Tension, in other words, was a scheme of the mainstream Left and not the far Right.

Stopping the PCI was therefore the *Plan*'s overriding aim. The Christian Democrats were not up to the job: they were too tied to the Vatican, too factional, too corrupt, and too impervious to the real needs of business to be of much use.

Following this logic, because there was a left-wing conspiracy already underway, P2 was perfectly entitled to weave a right-wing counter-conspiracy. Gelli's first step towards a solution would be to set up a club – styled on the Rotarians, and with strong links to 'international Masonry'. Its members would be a group of thirty to forty, selected from the top levels of business, finance, the professions, the law and the civil service. Only a very few, carefully vetted, politicians would be part of the team. Gelli tells us his chosen men should be 'homogeneous in their discernment, impartiality, honesty and moral rigour'. This 'Rotarian Club' – as we could term it – was an élite group *within* P2, a committee of 'guarantors' who would watch over the politicians tasked with implementing the *Plan for Democratic Rebirth*.

The next stage would be to infiltrate the governing Christian Democrat Party so as to 'rejuvenate' it, ousting at least 80 per cent of its leaders. A legion of young public servants and professionals would be trained in local DC clubs or institutes supervised by the Rotarian Club. They would be installed within the institutions, which they would guide in the right direction. Thus, Gelli claims, Italy could reach a situation where 'an honest political power imposes clear directives', which are then carried out by state functionaries out of patriotic duty and 'a spirit of Rotarian purity'.

Gelli's *Plan* is as bizarre as it is sinister. His view that the Rotary Club is a good model for the heroes of a stealthy right-wing takeover is distinctly odd. As are the unimpeachable ethical standards required of his fellow conspirators, to whom he planned to give a huge budget for buying influence. Presumably only men of marble morals can bribe their way to power with a clean conscience.

In short, passages of the *Plan for Democratic Rebirth* are a child-like 'puppet-master' fantasy, of the kind that the Venerable Master alluded to in his infamous *Corriere della Sera* interview.

The *Plan for Democratic Rebirth* also has a distinct Masonic flavour – or at least the kind of Masonic flavour that would appeal to someone like former Grand Master Gamberini. The

Plan's Rotarians look a lot like Gamberini's vision of what true Freemasons should be. Gelli is concerned to keep the Grand Orient leadership on board, and attract men within the institutions who are intrigued by Gamberini's ideas about what P2 could help Masonry achieve. It would also win over some sincere anti-Communists and those who might sympathise with Grand Master Gamberini's vision of using Masonry to inject a new ethical energy into the state.

But that was not the core of P2's mission. Indeed, the *Plan*'s real intentions were not made explicit. It is important to keep in mind that the *Plan* was not particularly secret: it was not some coded instruction booklet sent out by an evil mastermind to his slavish co-conspirators. It is likely that Gelli *wanted* the contents of the suitcase his daughter was carrying to be found, although possibly not all at once. Moreover Gelli had aired the ideas in the *Plan* before; and in 1975 he had shown an early version of them, known as 'Schema R', to the President of the Italian Republic. The *Plan* did not need to be highly confidential, because there were plenty of people not just within P2, but also within the Italian institutions, who might be sympathetic. As we shall see, the *Plan* was sending carefully pitched signals to Gelli's actual and potential friends.

In making sense of the *Plan* and the P2 affair, much depends on how genuine we take the 'red menace' to be. Many people in 1970s Italy sincerely feared and loathed anything to do with Communism. However, the Italian Communist Party had proved its democratic credentials again and again: not least by helping to design the Italian Constitution. By the 1970s, the PCI was decidedly *not* a 'Hungarian' or 'Czechoslovak' threat to liberal values or to Italy's place in the western alliance against the Soviet Empire.

Nonetheless, in the post-war Italian system, a large section of the electorate was frozen out of the national power-game by voting Communist. A smaller but still substantial section was frozen out by voting for the MSI, the neo-Fascist party – which was just as unelectable as the PCI. Therefore, an amorphous centre, dominated by the Christian Democrats, was left to occupy power by default. The Communist menace, exaggerated as and when necessary, suited the purposes of many politicians and their business friends who operated within that amorphous centre. As one historian of the P2 affair has put it: 'for fifty years, in the shelter furnished by the struggle against Communism, people built dazzling political and economic careers'. A big threat posed by the Communists was that they might insist on reform and a corruption clean-up if they got access to power.

Another key issue in the context of the P2 affair was the Strategy of Tension. There was, without doubt, an element within Italy's secret services in the 1970s who sought to use the threat of violent subversion to scare voters back towards the amorphous centre and give that centre a rightward shove. Several senior secret servicemen have been convicted for what Italians call *depistaggio* – deliberately creating false trails for investigators so as to protect right-wing terrorists.

A good many of the secret servicemen involved in the Strategy of Tension were P2-ists. But the exact nature of Gelli's relationship with them is one of the foggiest aspects of the whole P2 affair. Tina Anselmi's Parliamentary Commission of Inquiry detected signs that Gelli had a very strained relationship with the intelligence services, who had extensive files on his past. It emerged during the Parliamentary Commission of Inquiry that, in the Second World War, Gelli had acted as a liaison officer between Italian Fascist forces and the SS, and took an active part in round-ups of anti-Nazi activists who were later executed. But he had also passed information to the Communist Resistance, and subsequently worked for Allied intelligence too, giving him a foot in every camp: he was hedging his bets. In 1950, a report claimed that Gelli had been an agent of Eastern European

Communist intelligence since 1947. Strangely, this lead was not followed up. Even more strangely, the secret services sat on Gelli's file and did not pass it on to the investigators who first began sniffing around P2 in the mid-1970s. Were secret agents using Gelli's history to control him? Were they protecting their man by failing to pass on what they knew?

The plot thickened in 1979, when Gelli's file was given to a journalist he had previously used to publish compromising information on people. The journalist, Mino Pecorelli, began to drip-feed bits of what the secret services knew about the Venerable Master into the public domain. The full dossier could have ruined Gelli's credibility as an anti-Communist, but Pecorelli was murdered before he could publish it. Had the secret services grown tired of the Venerable Master and decided to bring him down by passing documents to Pecorelli? Why was Pecorelli murdered? (Gelli, it should be stressed, was far from the only person to have plausible reason to want him out of the way.) Tina Anselmi could only shrug her shoulders: 'we can formulate all kinds of abstract hypotheses, and no conclusion is obviously absurd'.

The most likely conclusion goes something like this. Licio Gelli clearly had no scruples about the Strategy of Tension, as his conviction in relation to the Bologna station bomb shows. Through the *Plan*, as through his hints about burning pots of beans, Gelli let it be known that he had no qualms about the dirty work involved in the anti-Communist crusade. But the Strategy of Tension was not a P2 conspiracy. Or Gelli's ultimate aim. Whether they were P2-ists or not, the secret servicemen who enacted these despicable perversions of justice were doing what they would have done anyway: as they saw it, it was their job to stop Communism. Gelli helped them, but he was not their mastermind.

Instead, Gelli's objective was to appeal to powerful men within the amorphous centre. To do that, he had to be anti-Communist enough to be credible, and cynical enough to be useful. The *Plan for Democratic Rebirth* was designed for that purpose: it was a calling card to win friends who had 'built dazzling political and economic careers' in the amorphous centre. Such men did not care about the impractical aspects of the *Plan* – the Rotarian Club and all that. What counted for them was that they could trust Gelli's services as a fixer.

So the Venerable Master put subversive scheming at the service of networking. The aim was to win enough credibility to accumulate money and power by orchestrating the exchange of favours – most lucratively, favours between politicians and shady bankers like Michele Sindona and Roberto Calvi, or between bankers and struggling companies like the Rizzoli Group.

Terracotta pots

P2 was created by meticulously dismantling all of the inbuilt anti-corruption safeguards that make Freemasonry harder to use for dishonest ends than we might assume; such safeguards are by no means foolproof, but they are nonetheless significant. New members have to swear that they are *not* joining for selfish purposes, for example, and that they will not break the law. In themselves, such oaths might not deter the most determinedly dishonest. But they do create an expectation of straight dealing within Freemasonry that makes it difficult for a crooked Mason to know whether any of his Brethren are as crooked as him, or whether they are prepared, at least, to be discreet.

Freemasonry has other anti-corruption antibodies. Because Masonic meetings take place behind the closed doors of a Lodge room, many people guess that this opens the door to surreptitious wrongdoing. It is certainly true that, because the members of any given Lodge can blackball aspiring members they don't like, a Lodge can create its own style. In theory, that style could be corrupt. But Lodges *are* open and transparent in one important sense: they must be available to be visited by Brothers from other Lodges in the same branch of the Craft. The people who do the most visiting are senior Masons whose job it is to ensure good practice and sound financial management. It would also be hard to maintain a corrupt culture within a Lodge because, following the principle of equality between Brethren, the leadership positions change regularly. Officers are appointed only for one year, and before taking a turn in the big chair as Worshipful Master, a Brother has to have done five or six other jobs.

The last, but not the least, of the ways in which the Craft wards off anyone with iffy intentions is the sheer amount of time spent on ritual, Masonic jurisprudence, raising money for charity, and simply talking. Most Lodge business is an extravagant waste of effort if you are only interested in lining your own pockets.

Gelli stripped P2 of all the Craft's ritual, moral and esoteric accoutrements. Once the initiation ritual was out of the way, there were no P2 ceremonials. Masonry's long tradition of internal democracy was also excised: P2 had no elections or constitution. There were no membership records: only Gelli knew who all the members were. Furthermore, there were no Lodge meetings at all after about 1974, thus ensuring that individual members could only get to know other P2 Brethren through the Venerable Master. He transformed the centreless mesh of fraternal contacts within the conventional Craft into a highly centralised information brokerage.

The ideal P2 recruit was a man whose ambitions trumped his principles, who wanted to get ahead and get back at his enemies. Applicants were given a form that asked for information on 'injustices (if any) suffered during your career' . . . 'the resulting harm' and 'the people, institutions or environments that you believe that harm can be attributed to'. Gelli sent new affiliates a 'Summary of Rules', which had only a light dusting of Masonic pieties about 'trying to improve the whole of humanity'. The rest blended exhortations to strict confidentiality with a blunt statement of P2's aims: 'to work to help friends acquire an ever-greater degree of authority and influence, because the stronger each one of them becomes, the more power will accrue to the organization as a whole'. Power reinforced by secrecy: that was P2's mission. Gelli's methods turned the vague and subtle Masonic principle of secrecy into something akin to the mafia code of *omertà*.

Through all these means, the Venerable Master reversed the ethical polarity of the trust among Freemasons. Building a career in the Craft is supposed to be about building a good reputation by selflessly devoting time and effort to the life of the Lodge; it is about learning from men you respect, and becoming respected by younger Masons in your turn. A career in P2, by contrast, was about building a reputation as a trustworthy provider of favours and sensitive information.

When Gelli turned P2 into the creature of his designs, he did so by preying on precisely the historic weaknesses of Italian Masonry that Grand Master Gamberini pinpointed: its incurable meddling in politics and love of powerful friends; its fear of repression and its insecure status under the Italian Constitution; and a 'jobs-for-the-boys' mentality that had become much worse in Italy's increasingly tainted political culture.

In sum, Gelli was not a Bond villain. Like all fixers, the Venerable Master had every interest in exaggerating his connections and influence, as he did when he styled himself as a puppet-master in the *Corriere della Sera*. He made countless other boasts in private to his P2-ists. Italian Freemasonry's reputation as a club for wheeler-dealers only gave him more publicity along the same lines. Indeed, when it came down to it, that is what Gelli was: a wheeler-dealer with a devilish insight into how he could re-engineer Lodge Propaganda to serve his purposes.

In response to the P2 crisis, the Grand Orient tried to cauterise the wound to its reputation by expelling Gelli. In due course, they would also expel former Grand Master Giordano Gamberini. To no avail. Most Italians were utterly indifferent to the nuances of the Venerable Master's relationship with mainstream Freemasonry, and had already decided what they thought long before the many trials against Gelli reached their final verdict.

An equation that was as rigid as it was simplistic took hold of the public mind: P2 = conspiracy = Freemasonry. The damage to the Craft in the peninsula will probably never be repaired.

Licio Gelli expired in his Tuscan villa in December 2015, aged ninety-six, having spent the previous fourteen years under house arrest: legal technicalities and his advanced age ensured that he had never spent more than a few days in an Italian jail. His most eloquent epitaph is perhaps the list of his assets compiled in 1990 for one of his many trials. In addition to his various properties in Italy and France, worth €5.5 million in 2019, he had deposits in various Swiss banks including 250 kg of gold ingots (€3.5 million), $8.5 million US (€15 million) and a mammoth 117 million Swiss francs (€125 million). We can add to the inventory the 165 kg of gold bars (€2.3 million) found hidden in six terracotta flowerpots on the terrace of his Arezzo villa eight years later. Not the kind of money you make managing a medium-sized clothes factory.

17

Legacies

What is the state of Freemasonry today? It should be obvious by now that nobody can answer that question comprehensively. The Masonic idea manifests itself in so many different ways across the globe, and even self-identified Freemasons obey so many conflicting codes and governing bodies, that a constantly updated encyclopaedia running into dozens of volumes would be required as a starting point.

Nevertheless, in a heroic attempt to reach an answer, Belgian documentary-maker Tristan Bourlard recently spent two years touring the world. The result was a portrait of the 'Masonic Earth' in a stirring 2017 film *Terra Masonica: Around the World in Eighty Lodges*.

I have said very little about Masonry in South America, whereas Bourlard toured Brazil and Argentina, and even visited Lodge Fin del Mundo, founded in a former prison in Ushuaia on Tierra del Fuego – only 1,238 kilometres north of the Antarctic peninsula. For reasons of space, I have had to pass over Scandinavia's strong Christian-only Masonic tradition in silence. The dauntless Bourlard took his camera to the world's northernmost Lodge in Hammerfest, Norway, deep in the Arctic circle. Most of Africa has been off my map of the Craft's history, but not of Bourlard's. Just south of the Sahara, in the Republic of Mali, he found a tiny Masonic enclave where members of the Muslim majority share brotherly relations with Protestants, Catholics and Jews.

Bourlard is honest enough to own up to his disappointing failure to visit the most remote Masonic Lodge of them all, which is based 384,400 kilometres from earth. Tranquility Lodge no. 2000 was established when Brother Buzz Aldrin landed on the moon in July 1969 carrying a Special Deputation from the Grand Lodge of Texas.

Bourlard is a Freemason, and he has his biases. Nevertheless, his globetrotting more than earns him the right to make a senti-mental film. As a historian, I have aims in this final chapter, as throughout this book, that are less celebratory. I seek to measure Freemasonry in different parts of the world against its founding Enlightenment values. In so doing, I challenge some of the misconceptions that 'Cowans' (non-Masons) have about Freemasonry, and also challenge the way Craftsmen have tended to narrate their collective past. To that end, bringing some of the stories told in previous chapters up to date, I briefly revisit the countries that have made Masonic history most forcefully over the past three hundred years: Britain and its former Empire, France, the United States and Italy.

'The mafia of the mediocre'

This book began with a story from 1743 about Masonic secrecy, and the Inquisition's deep suspicion of it. Today, while the Catholic Church may have abandoned the rack and the *strappado* as means of theological persuasion, the same old dogma on Freemasonry is still officially operative. In 1983, Cardinal Ratzinger (the future Benedict XVI) issued the following statement in his capacity as head of the Congregation for the Doctrine of the Faith (as the Inquisition is now known): 'The Church's negative judgment in regard to Masonic associations remains unchanged . . . member-ship in them remains forbidden. The faithful who enrol in Masonic associations are in a state of grave sin and may not receive Holy Communion.' The excommunication stands. In 2013, Pope Francis, the most liberal Pope in decades, muttered darkly in an interview about a mysterious 'Masonic lobby' conspiring against the Church. There is even the odd clerical voice still denouncing Satanism and sexual perversion concealed within the Lodges. To many people it will seem that, in matters of 'sexual perversion', the Church does not have a solid pulpit to preach from.

Catholicism is not the only home for religious anti-Masonry. In the early 1990s, some evangelical Protestant groups in the United States expressed an anti-Masonic phobia not seen since the Taxil hoax of the 1890s. Their propaganda alleged that Masons in the highest Degrees all worshipped Baphomet, the goat-headed avatar of the devil supposedly revered by the Templars in the fourteenth century, as by Taxil's fictional Palladian rite in the nineteenth. Albert Pike, Confederate general and guru of the Scottish Rite in the Civil War era, was portrayed as the anti-Pope of the Masonic anti-Church.

Although the Southern Baptist Convention ruled in 1993 that Masonic membership was a question for each individual Christian's own conscience, the spread of the Internet in subsequent years ensured that there would always be a home for such ravings. For example, Albert Pike's strange afterlife as the star of conspiracy theories looks set to continue. Pike hit the news recently, because in 1871 he supposedly made a prophecy about a Third World War between the Christian West and Islam. British tabloid newspapers the *Sun* and the *Star* first reported the story in 2016. In their wake, a long list of websites now tells us that the secret goal of the Illuminati is to make Pike's prophecy come true. Which is indeed 'chilling', as the *Sun* called it. As long as you are extremely naïve and entirely without historical memory.

There are many parts of the world where anti-Masonry is a much darker force. Since the 1960s, Freemasonry has disappeared from almost all of the Muslim world. When the Raj ended in 1947, the Craft survived the partition of India. However, in Pakistan, the number of members and Lodges fell dramatically with the migration of most of the white British population. There were about one thousand Freemasons left, many of them Muslims, when an ominous series of press attacks began in 1968: the Craft was accused of being a Zionist front group financed by the CIA. It was outlawed by President Zulfikar Ali Bhutto in 1972. The Masonic Temple in Lahore, where Rudyard Kipling was initiated, is now a general-purpose government building.

In Iran, to cite just one more example, Freemasonry reappeared as an aristocratic club in 1951 under the new Shah, Mohammad Reza Pahlavi, who used it to build loyalty to his regime among the elites and middle classes. The Islamic Revolution of 1979 swept the Lodges away, and many Brothers, particularly those close to the deposed Shah, were executed.

As of 2019, Freemasonry is banned everywhere in the Muslim world except Lebanon and Morocco. The Charter of the Palestinian Islamic Resistance Movement, better known as Hamas, describes Freemasonry, the Lions and the Rotary Club as 'networks of spies' created by the Jews to 'destroy societies and promote the Zionist cause'.

In western democracies, Freemasonry's reputation for secrecy continues to provide an awkward test for tolerance. Masons have some justification in regarding themselves as the pit canaries of freedom of association and the rule of law. Even Britain, the very cradle of the Craft, provides a demonstration.

In 1976, a young provincial journalist called Stephen Knight claimed that a Masonic conspiracy was responsible for Jack the Ripper's series of unsolved murders in 1888. Knight's book, *Jack the Ripper: The Final Solution*, was dismissed as laughable. Nonetheless, it captured the imagination enough to go through twenty editions. Its echoes endured: the gloriously spooky graphic novel *From Hell* (1989), and a slasher movie of the same title starring Johnny Depp (2001), were both inspired by Knight.

At the time of *Jack the Ripper: The Final Solution*, the United

Grand Lodge of England had a longstanding policy of maintaining a dignified silence in the face of conspiracist accusations. Stephen Knight's subsequent book, *The Brotherhood* (1983), would expose the limits of that policy.

The Brotherhood was an odd mixture. There were painstaking and tedious protestations of good faith ('we should not judge Freemasonry by the actions of a few individuals'), together with ambiguous evidence of workaday misdeeds by Masons within the police force. But there were also absolutely false claims that Knight had unmasked upper tiers of Masonry so secretive that even the vast majority of Brethren had no idea they existed. Based on an error-strewn summary of the P2 story, Knight went on to propose that Soviet intelligence had masterminded Gelli's plot so as to discredit an enemy government. He concluded that, in the UK, the 'KGB's use of Freemasonry for placing operatives in positions of authority' was 'almost certain'.

Knight became a follower of the Indian cult leader Bhagwan Shree Rajneesh in the year *The Brotherhood* came out. He died two years later after refusing conventional medical treatment for a tumour. Despite his lack of authority, and his book's glaring shortcomings, *The Brotherhood* had a huge impact. As conspiracy theories began to circulate about Knight's death, another journalist took up his work on Masonic scheming within the police. The same old refrain began: if the Freemasons are as innocent as they say, why all the secrecy? In June 1988, Jeremy Corbyn, Labour Party leader between 2015 and 2020 but then a back-bench MP, declared in parliament:

> Many of us are gravely suspicious about the influence of Freemasonry. I am utterly opposed to it and to the influence of other secret organisations because I believe them to be a deeply corrupting influence on society . . . Masonic influence is serious . . . Freemasonry is incompatible with being a police officer . . . I am suggesting that the power of a Masonic Lodge on any organisation is sinister and insidious.

The British public was ready to stretch its credulity a long way when it came to a police force that had a shabby reputation, especially for framing Irish people for IRA bomb attacks. These were the years of the notorious Guildford Four, Maguire Seven and Birmingham Six cases, as well as of Operation Countryman (an investigation into collusion between the City of London Police and professional criminals). This distrust of the police made a potent cocktail when combined with the centuries of suspicion surrounding Masonic secrecy. Henceforth, newspaper editors were all on the lookout for a Masonic angle to stories of wrong-doing.

The strongest evidence of Masonic foul play that Knight had to offer was the United Grand Lodge's refusal to dignify his allegations with a reply. So in response, the English Masonic leadership looked hard at its own culture of secrecy. It turned out that even rank-and-file Masons thought that they were supposed to keep silent about their membership, despite there being no such rule in place; some had not even told their families. Henceforth, they were encouraged to speak openly. A post of Director of Communications was created. Freemasons Hall in Covent Garden opened its doors to visitors for the first time in 1985. English Freemasonry's lax disciplinary procedures were also tightened, and the number of expulsions rocketed from 12, between 1934 and 1986, to 277, between 1987 and 1996. In the early 1990s, non Mason historians would begin to delve into the archives of the Grand Lodge.

However, this Masonic *glasnost* failed to stop the suspicion, which took parliamentary form in 1992 with an all-party Home Affairs Select Committee set up to investigate any influence the Craft might have within the criminal justice system. Every imaginable insinuation against Masons and Masonry was aired – with anticlimactic results set out in the Select Committee's report. Yes, individual Freemasons had committed crimes, and some of those Freemasons were policemen. But no, these indi-viduals were not representative of Masonry as such, nor was

Masonry a factor in what they had done. The overwhelming majority of witnesses who alleged that there was illicit networking by Masons had no proof. The number of Brothers in the police and judiciary was far smaller than suspected, and was falling. A certain kind of secrecy was part of Freemasons' rituals, but the organisation itself was no more secret than a sports club or professional body.

In the end, everything boiled down to an image problem. Widespread mistrust of British Freemasonry, groundless as it was, nevertheless damaged public confidence in the institutions. So the solution was for all Masons in the judiciary to make a declaration of interest, the Select Committee advised in 1997.

This final recommendation sounded sensible enough, and the Labour Party, which came to power in 1997, set about trying to implement it. Wielding the sword of transparency against a stuffy institution like the Craft would help justify the 'new' in New Labour, as leader Tony Blair had rebranded the party. From 1998, judicial appointees were obliged to declare if they were Freemasons.

However, the policy never escaped a tangle of practical issues and legal objections. If there was no evidence that the Craft was a source of trouble, why target it? Would the declaration-of-interest policy not lead to prejudice against Masons, a presumption of guilt? If it applied to Masons, what reason could there be for not applying it to other forms of belonging that might conceivably lead to bias, like religions, or Oxford colleges? In the early 2000s, the European Court of Human Rights ruled on two cases in Italy where local government had tried to apply a similar policy to Freemasons: the Court decided that the measure was discriminatory and contrary to the right of free association. In 2009, on the verge of losing power, the Labour government very quietly gave up on the scheme, acknowledging that it had achieved nothing.

Meanwhile, an assumption had long since bedded down in the public mind: Freemasonry was 'the mafia of the mediocre', a coterie of paunchy men pursuing preferment in their careers and protection from scrutiny. We Brits are still saps for urban legends of Masonic skulduggery. Recent headlines in the press have alleged that Freemasons were responsible for a whitewash at the inquiry into the sinking of the *Titanic* in 1912, and for concealing the dreadful police misconduct at the Hillsborough stadium disaster, which led to the death of ninety-six Liverpool football fans in 1989. Such 'revelations' typically cite little or no supporting evidence, and die with the first headline. In both of these cases, the conspiracy interpretation looks feeble on even a cursory second glance. The British marine establishment of 1912, and the South Yorkshire police of 1989, both had compelling motives for covering up their own mess and scapegoating – respectively – the captain of the *Titanic* and a mass of innocent soccer fans. There are no loose ends for the Masonic conspiracy theory to explain. Yet such stories regularly make it past the bullshit detectors of reputable newspapers.

Gotha

Nowhere, among the western democracies, is hostility to Freemasonry more widespread than in Italy. Nowhere more than in Italy has Freemasonry been tainted with corruption. Now the conviction has taken root in Italy's poorest region that the Freemasons are in league with the mafia, that bastard branch of the fraternalist tradition.

Calabria, the region in the 'toe' of the Italian 'boot', is home to the 'ndrangheta. Of all the world's gangster fraternities, the 'ndrangheta has the best claim to being global: it has colonies in northern Italy, northern Europe, North America and Australia. Regional and local government has been beset for decades by organised criminal influence, and the dilapidated rural communities of Calabria are home to some of Europe's biggest drug traffickers. The 'ndrangheta is no mediocre mafia.

In October 2011, in a farm building in one of those rural communities, police listening devices recorded the local 'ndrangheta boss, Pantaleone 'Uncle Luni' Mancuso: 'The 'ndrangheta doesn't exist any more!. . . The 'ndrangheta is part of Freemasonry . . . let's say, it's under Freemasonry. But they've got the same rules and stuff . . . Once upon a time the 'ndrangheta belonged to the rich folk! After, they left it to the poor sods, the clodhoppers, and they created Freemasonry instead!' If nothing else, Uncle Luni's words testify to the fact that the history of the Masonic idea is still being made in Calabria. Limbadi, where the recording was made, lies about 25 kilometres as the crow flies from Pizzo, where Joachim Murat uttered his famous final words: 'Aim at the heart. Spare my face.'

There has been a great deal of talk in Calabria recently about links between Freemasonry and the 'ndrangheta. Not all of it is easy to interpret, but all of it is very worrying. Take the testimony of Giuliano Di Bernardo, the university professor who, between 1990 and 1993, was the Grand Master of Italy's biggest and most prestigious Masonic order, the Grand Orient. In June 2019, speaking through the beard that makes him resemble an Armani-suited Karl Marx, Di Bernardo testified before a Calabrian court. He recalled his shock when, as Grand Master, he looked into the state of Masonry in Calabria: 'I discovered that twenty-eight of thirty-two Lodges were governed by the 'ndrangheta. So at that moment, I decided to leave the Grand Orient.'

Calabria has provided plenty of fuel for conspiracist newspaper headlines that are as confusing as they are inflammatory – along the following lines: 'Mafia boss says, "Freemasons run the 'ndrangheta!"' 'Former Grand Master confesses, "The 'ndrangheta runs the Freemasons!"'

On 1 March 2017, on the orders of the permanent Parliamentary Commission of Inquiry into the Mafia, police mounted dawn raids on the offices of the four biggest Masonic orders, and confiscated membership lists. Their search concentrated on Freemasonry in Calabria and Sicily, Italy's most notorious mafia hotbeds. The raids by the Parliamentary Commission of Inquiry brought back Masons' memories of similar raids twenty-five years earlier. At that time, a sprawling criminal investigation had sought to map hundreds of criminal and wheeler-dealer networks over the impossible tangle of different Masonic orders, Lodges and rites – both regular and irregular, open and covert. In 1993, the confiscated membership lists were leaked, and Italy's Freemasons were named in many newspapers. Some Brothers reported receiving anonymous threats in the aftermath; others said they were cold-shouldered by friends. (Strangely, the lists in the press excluded all but a tiny number of the women Masons from mixed orders.) Eventually, in 2000, a court in Rome halted the investigation, declaring that it owed more to the 'collective imaginary' about Freemasonry than it did to any evidence that Freemasons were infiltrating the public institutions for illicit ends. Many dismissed this ruling as a cover-up. Masons were left bitter.

Given this history, in 2017 there was a complete breakdown in trust between the members of the Parliamentary Commission of Inquiry and the Masonic leadership. The Commission's report accused the chief Masons of being in denial about mafia infiltration, and of being 'far from transparent and cooperative': all four Grand Masters had refused to hand over their membership lists. Soon afterwards, the Grand Master of the Grand Orient published a pamphlet that compared the Parliamentary Commission to the Inquisition. (As coincidence would have it, the Commission's hearings are held in the same Roman palazzo where Galileo was forced to recant his scientific findings.)

Because I have spent more than five years researching the history of Freemasonry, and even longer researching the history of the 'ndrangheta, I may stand half a chance of seeing some meaningful shapes through the mists of this polemic. So in the summer of 2018, I accepted an invitation to speak at a gathering of Freemasons 800 metres up in the Calabrian mountains. The venue was a cavernous one-storey hotel in the woods, its walls painted in a nauseating combination of tangerine, terracotta and fresh pork. But the welcome, as I have invariably found in the company of Freemasons around the world, was open and warm.

To anyone whose automatic reaction to the Brotherhood is a smirk or a sneer, I recommend sitting down with a Mason and simply asking what it is all about. All the many times I have now done just this, I have never encountered any reticence. Moreover, as often as not, a Brother doesn't get very far into his explanation before his eyes moisten and his lower lip begins to tremble.

Over a buffet, one nervous man in his twenties spoke to me with a flaming sincerity in his eyes. Several years earlier he had very nearly succumbed to Hodgkin lymphoma – a blood cancer that also undermined his sense of what he wanted out of life. When the threat to his health passed, he began a search for existential answers that only reached its conclusion when he became a Mason. In the Craft, he found the fellowship of older, wiser men, and a unique environment where they could listen to his story and share their experiences of life. Together with them, he could begin to direct his energies out towards the wider world.

Masonry's mixture of ritual, moral instruction and male bonding can still impart dignity, and a plan for self-improvement that is about more than ego. Only the laziest of cynics would scoff away Masonry's claim to 'make good men better' – even in Calabria, a region that desperately needs civil society organisations like the Freemasons.

Aside from the décor of the hotel, and the warmness of the welcome, I was struck by the collective anger – at least among the most vocal Brothers there. One accused the Parliamentary Commission of wasting public money in a drive to destroy Freemasonry. The episode set off 'an alarm bell for freedom and democracy'.

My trip to Calabria gave me a strong sense that the Craft's dispute with the Commission of Inquiry was fuelled by political grandstanding from both sides. It is worth remembering that the most senior Masons are elected: they are the Prime Ministers and Presidents of their little democracies. Denouncing anti-Masonic prejudice and evoking the memory of Masonic martyrs have always been rallying cries among the Brethren, and thus a useful electoral gambit. On the other side, it would have taken a strong-willed parliamentarian on the Commission of Inquiry to face up to the public animosity towards the Craft. In February 2017, for example, Italy's leading current affairs magazine carried the front-page headline, 'Let's abolish Freemasonry'. The populist Five-Star Movement, which came to power in June 2018, has a policy of expelling Freemasons from its ranks, and Masons are often listed among its 'establishment' enemies.

Amid the misunderstanding and grandstanding, our best hope of reaching the truth lies with the judges presiding over a huge case, known as the 'Gotha Trial', which is now running through the Calabrian courts. It has already consumed thousands and thousands of pages of evidence and legal argument in an effort to dispel the confusion.

A tough reading task awaited me when I got back from Calabria: the 2,500-page ruling issued by judges to explain their verdict on a small but significant part of the Gotha Trial. The verdict is being appealed, so we are still quite some distance from a definitive legal truth. Nevertheless, leaving aside the guilt or innocence of the individuals involved (I will not even name them here), the ruling offers a plausible account of what has really been going on. As we will see, it has uncanny echoes from the history of Freemasonry.

The 'ndrangheta is a curious organisation, having more than twice as many members as Sicily's Cosa Nostra, and a much more complicated structure: for example, each stage in the career ladder of an *'ndranghetista* is marked by a new rank with its own elaborate initiation ritual. The Calabria mafia is an underworld mirror of the Craft, which blends local autonomy for the Lodges with national and international 'brand' control. What we could call the 'ndrangheta brand or franchise – meaning its rules, ranks and rituals – are all centrally controlled by a body called *il Crimine* ('the Crime'). Even when they are based outside Calabria, *'ndranghetisti* seek authorisation from the Crime to set up new cells. But the 'ndrangheta is also decentralised, in that its individual clans and cells pursue all kinds of criminal activities at their own initiative. Nobody is answerable to the Crime when they smuggle in a shipment of drugs, for example.

Things began to shift in the 1970s, when the 'ndrangheta grew vastly richer on the profits of kidnapping, narcotics and infiltrating public works contracts. As the money flowed in, the criminal brotherhood's structure evolved: unbeknownst to the mass of the membership, ever more upper ranks were invented. By creating them, the most senior bosses were trying to monopolise access to the money derived from infiltrating public works, and keep the peace among themselves while they did so. But they could never settle on a definitive formula, just as at various times in the history of Freemasonry, there was runaway inflation in the number of Degrees and rituals, and a fight over who got to authorise them. Such internal wrangles were one of the reasons behind savage 'ndrangheta civil wars in the 1970s and 1980s.

In the end, around 2001, an alliance of the most powerful bosses founded an entirely separate and highly secretive group within the 'ndrangheta – so investigators believe. The group's members include men with the kind of white-collar, political skills needed to get on with brokering corrupt deals with business and the state, while the crime bosses were left free to use their own less specialised skills to best effect. A few bosses who knew about this group have been bugged using various names to describe it: 'the invisible ones', for example. And because, like everyone else, Calabrian gangsters love to think of the Freemasons as the last word in occult power, they also refer to the new group, according to one supergrass, as 'something analogous to Freemasonry'.

That is what the 'ndrangheta boss Pantaleone 'Uncle Luni' Mancuso was doing when he was recorded in 2011 saying that the Freemasons had taken over the 'ndrangheta. He was using a *metaphor* – as almost no one pointed out when Uncle Luni's words were splashed over the newspapers.

But now is not the time for the Freemasons of Italy to shout their outrage at the way their reputation has been attacked because of a mere metaphor. The Gotha Trial may yet hold damning surprises in store. It is also crucial to understand that when *'ndranghetisti* refer to Freemasonry they are not *just* speaking in metaphor. Masonic Lodges – real Masonic Lodges – are part of the Calabrian mafia's pervasive networking system.

Here is how the judges think it all works. The 'ndrangheta loves to get its hands on state contracts for collecting and disposing of rubbish, building and maintaining roads and hospitals, and so on. *'Ndranghetisti* use mediators to wheedle their way into winning these contracts: politicians, administrators, entrepreneurs and lawyers. Indeed, mafia organisations are only as strong as the mediators they can call on; they have a constant hunger to co-opt new ones, and will use any mix of bribery, blackmail and intimidation to do so. This is where Masonic Lodges fit in.

Especially since the P2 scandal, Freemasonry has attracted unscrupulous men from the same kind of professional background as the honest Masons I met in Calabria, most of whom were doctors and lawyers. Many of the unscrupulous new arrivals get bored and go elsewhere when they realise what honest Masons actually do. But within the confused world of Calabrian Freemasonry, there are plenty of niches where clusters of them can find a base. Most of the Lodges cited in the judges' ruling in the Gotha Trial are the kind of 'covert' or 'irregular' Lodges not authorised by the main national orders. They act like dating agencies, matching *'ndranghetisti* to mediators from among the professional classes, and can offer a route to the very top of the grey zone where the criminal underworld meets the upperworld of politics and business. But regular Lodges are at risk too: by accepting a banal favour from a Brother secretly in league with the 'ndrangheta, even an honest Mason can be drawn into a web of blackmail.

If the first Gotha Trial ruling is right, then there is an obvious way that the interests of Freemasonry could be harmonised with the fight against the mafia. The main Masonic orders could seek the help of the law in policing the boundary between regular and irregular forms of Masonry. Alas, no such approach will be adopted any time soon. There are too few people on either side who have an interest in collaboration. Masonry and anti-Masonry seem doomed to carry on their centuries-old slanging match.

A Sister with fifty thousand Brothers

Women's experience of Freemasonry is rich, and speaks powerfully of the forms of self-realisation they have been able to achieve within the formidable constraints of their time and place – as I tried to show through my treatment of the Adoption Lodges of eighteenth-century France. Since the end of the Second World War, inspired in part by the example of the Adoption Lodges, more mixed and women-only strains of Freemasonry have appeared.

Yet if this book has not followed the history of female Freemasonry since the eighteenth century in more depth, it is because women in the Craft have always been the exception that proves the historical rule: you have to be a man to be a Mason. Whether it be in Adoption Lodges, or in the various female-centred bodies such as the Order of the Eastern Star in the United States (for which women qualify only by being relatives of Masons), women have almost always been allowed only into subordinate branches with a circumscribed role in Masonic life. The Lodges that *have* given women full Masonic status at various points in history belong to minority branches not recognised by the major institutions of Freemasonry.

Moreover, the roles that most forms of Freemasonry set aside for women are stereotypically sexist. Dutiful wives. Totems of male respectability. Angels of compassion. Widows worthy of charity. Spectators of costumed male performance. Men continue to monopolise power within Freemasonry as an institution. Inasmuch as Freemasonry has influence in society, men monopolise that too.

418

Because, overwhelmingly, Freemasonry has been and remains an exclusively male society, its history tells us important and sometimes unflattering things about male identity. It seems highly improbable that a genuinely mixed form of Freemasonry could have produced the smugness of the British imperial Craft, or the ugly perversion of Masonic ideals that was P2. It is also worth pondering on the fact that it is almost always men who indulge in paranoid fantasies about Masonic plots. As one recent study speculates, 'conspiracy theories may be hysterias for men'. My history of Freemasonry perhaps deserves the provocative subtitle, 'Four centuries of male eccentricity'.

So it was an extraordinary moment when, in 2010, for the first time in two and a half centuries, the Grand Orient of France finally welcomed women as Sisters with equal Masonic status to their Brothers. In the little world of Freemasonry, this was a revolution – and a revolution embodied in one woman. In September 2019, I travelled to Grand Orient headquarters to meet her.

The restaurant on the seventh floor of the Grand Orient enjoys a glorious view across Paris, and offers a menu of French classics: I ate a pleasing andouillette with sauté potatoes. There are no such concessions to the appetites of the flesh in the lugubrious Freemasons' Hall in London. Enjoying a long and chatty lunch with me was Olivia Chaumont, an architect in her late sixties who is youthful, happy in her skin and enthusiastic about her Masonry. Hers is a progressive, lay vision of the Craft, one only catered for by the French Grand Orient's republican values, and its freedom from religious dogma. (It famously abolished the duty for Masons to believe in a Grand Architect of the Universe in 1877.) 'I'm pretty libertarian, in my way of looking at the world,' she says; she has also been an LGBT rights activist for years. The Lodges, for Olivia, give members the space to live out the universal values of *Liberté*, *Egalité* and *Fraternité* among themselves, and then go out to act as a spur to the rest of society.

So for Olivia, the moment when the Grand Orient made her its first Sister with full Masonic status in February 2010 was the moment it began living up to its principles at last. Just a few months later, in September 2010, her Brothers in Lodge L'Université Maçonnique elected her the first woman ever to sit on the throne of a Lodge Master. Many more women have followed the trail she has blazed. 'There are now fifty-four thousand members, and two thousand, perhaps two and a half thousand, women – I don't know exactly. It's not a lot, but it's not bad.' Some of these new Sisters made a point of thanking Olivia. 'There were women who dreamed of joining Masonry, but didn't do it because they only wanted to join the Grand Orient. I received very warm, touching messages from Sisters who said I had changed their lives.' Partly because of this change, Olivia tells me, French Grand Orient Masonry has none of the problems attracting younger recruits that face the Craft in Britain and the United States. Among the candidates for initiation whose photos I saw displayed in the lobby where I met Olivia, perhaps 20 per cent were women. She tells me that the problems of Masonry in the anglophone world are only destined to get worse:

> The more society has egalitarian relations between men and women, the more there will be clubs that will close themselves into masculine practices, entrenching themselves behind walls that allow their members to safeguard the privilege of being among men alone. That's the case with English Freemasonry . . . They don't want to let Eve into their paradise.

Some of my own encounters support Olivia's pessimism. One senior Mason in the United States explained his belief that Freemasonry is a defence against the 'feminisation of the culture', and the 'grossly feminine' over-protectiveness of contemporary mores. There is a risk that, the longer Freemasonry excludes women, the longer its decline in some countries will continue, and the more concentrated will its sexism become. After being a club for men for most of its history, a Freemasonry in decline could become a club for misogynists.

Olivia is a feminist, and believes masculine gender identity has often been constructed in a harmful way that condemns women and homosexuals to an inferior place in society. Mixed Masonry can help here, Olivia argues, by bringing other 'canons of behaviour' into the controlled space of the Lodge, thus helping male Masons 'emancipate themselves from the myth of the virile hero'. This is Freemasonry's original mission of building better men, updated in the cause of sexual equality.

Olivia knows a thing or two about constructing masculine identities, because she spent the best part of fifty years constructing an artificial one for herself. When she was first initiated into Freemasonry in 1992, she was biologically male. And she felt constrained to remain so by a society in which trans women could only be themselves at the price of becoming either cabaret entertainers or prostitutes. So she kept her real identity hidden until she felt ready to transition in 2002, at the age of fifty-one. The process was completed with an operation in Thailand in 2007, and with the court case that changed her civil status from male to female in 2009. I asked her why, as a trans woman, she was drawn to a male-only fraternity in the first place. She explained that, before she transitioned, she was just like other women attracted by the ethos of Grand Orient Masonry while it was still exclusively male – with the difference that she was biologically qualified to join: 'for once, having a man's body was useful to me'. Not surprisingly, when I mention the Chevalière d'Éon, the cross-dressing eighteenth-century spy, Olivia smiles: she is proud that 'one of the first documented trans women in history' was on the Square.

The most moving moment in Olivia's autobiography, *From*

One Body to the Other, describes when she came out to the Brothers of her own Lodge in 2007. Following a stunned silence, there was nothing but warm support – even though many of those present barely knew what a transsexual was. 'They had accepted me as a Brother, they would continue to accept me as a Sister. And it mattered little to them that, by becoming mixed, the Lodge became illegal [under Grand Orient law].' To a man, the members of Olivia's Lodge even vowed to back her up in the dispute that would inevitably follow when the news reached the Council of the Grand Orient. Over the next three years, Olivia and the Grand Orient negotiated their way through a maze of issues. The Masonic hierarchy tried to persuade her to switch to a different fraternal order that admitted women: she refused. Although they were legally obliged to recognise her new civil status as a woman alongside her status as a Mason, they hoped that they could treat her case as an exception, justifying themselves with the argument that, because she had been initiated as a man and was still genetically male, no change to Masonic law was required to accommodate her. The climax of the battle came in 2010 when Olivia's Lodge elected her as their representative at the Grand Orient's annual Convention in Vichy. Although anger and even a physical confrontation had been feared, when she spoke before the other 1,200 delegates she was well received. Shortly afterwards, the Convention finally voted to allow any Lodge that wished to do so to initiate women.

Olivia is far from triumphant about what she has achieved. There is still resistance in many provincial Lodges to admitting women, and a desire to keep women confined to Lodge level and away from the senior positions in the Grand Orient: 'the glass ceiling is worse than in profane society'.

The splendid Museum of Freemasonry on the ground floor of the Grand Orient building betrays a collective embarrassment about what Olivia has done. A great deal of space is given over to the Adoption Lodges of the eighteenth century. There is a beautiful female apron, for example, with the Tree of Knowledge and the snake printed onto its flimsy, faded silk. There is also a whole display case recounting the decision in 1877 to admit atheists. Yet the even bigger decision in 2010 to admit women is described in two sentences, which are bald, unillustrated and unexplained: only the most thorough visitors to the museum will notice them. There is no mention of Olivia, let alone a photograph of her. Even when Freemasonry changes, it would seem, it is reluctant to change its story.

Monuments

In 2009, Grand Lodges across the United States were in a state of fibrillation. Six years earlier, Dan Brown's *The Da Vinci Code*, a cloak-and-dagger thriller about earth-shattering truths supposedly concealed by the Catholic Church, had sold in Harry Potter quantities and been adapted into a hit movie. Now Brown's sequel, *The Lost Symbol*, was imminent: set in Washington DC, its theme would be the secrets of Freemasonry, and the initial print run a record-breaking 6.5 million copies. The fear was that, just as the Vatican had been besieged by cranks in the wake of *The Da Vinci Code*, so the Masonic establishment would be made answerable for whatever portentous baloney Dan Brown had made up this time around. Even before *The Lost Symbol*, the Scottish Rite headquarters in Washington DC regularly had to report threatening letters to the police. (Meanwhile, Freemasons' Hall in London diverted its stream of post from oddballs into a file called 'Nutters'.)

The Lost Symbol sold a million copies on its first day alone. But it proved to be a false alarm. Within a few short weeks, the tide of interest in Freemasonry had subsided to normal levels. Part of the explanation for the anticlimax lies within the novel itself. Whatever its flaws, which were gleefully nailed by reviewers at the time, *The Lost Symbol* has a clever way of feeding our enduring obsession with Masonic secrecy, without making too many concessions to the silliest myths. In the end, it is only the novel's deluded, psychopathic villain who believes that the Masons are guarding momentous mysteries. By contrast, the hero, 'symbologist' Professor Robert Langdon, gives the Brothers a glowing press: 'For the record, ma'am, the entire Masonic philosophy is built on honesty and integrity. Masons are among the most trustworthy men you could ever hope to meet.' The real star of *The Lost Symbol* is Washington DC, which is reimagined as a Masonic maze of unknown tunnels, high-security laboratories, underground sanctuaries and coded inscriptions.

In the real world, Masonic Washington certainly has plenty of history. However, far from being hidden, it could scarcely be less ostentatious. Most of it consists of huge monuments from the golden age when Masonry was central to male life across the nation. More than any other Freemasons across the western world, Craftsmen in the United States have a huge architectural patrimony to administer.

The most magnificent Masonic edifice in the capital is the House of the Temple (1915), the headquarters of the Scottish Rite (Southern Jurisdiction). With a Mesopotamian ziggurat roof, and a columned façade guarded by sphinxes, it is modelled on the Mausoleum at Halicarnassus – one of the seven wonders of the ancient world – which was intended to bestow god-like status on a Persian imperial satrap. The man immortalised in the House of the Temple is Confederate general Albert Pike: his ashes are walled in next to a shrine dedicated to big donors. The heart of the building is the Temple Chamber, the holy of holies of Scottish Rite Masonry: a lavish square hall of black marble, purple velvet, Russian walnut and bronze – all dramatically lit by high windows and a skylight. It is open to visitors.

Atop a hill across the Potomac, a Metro ride away in Alexandria, Virginia, stands the George Washington Masonic National Memorial (1932), which rises where the great man was a member of the local Lodge. It too is a copy of one of the seven wonders of the ancient world: the Lighthouse of Alexandria in Egypt. In its atrium stands a titanic 5.2-metre bronze statue of the first President, Brother George Washington, in his apron; it was unveiled in 1950 by the thirty-third President, Brother Harry S. Truman.

Freemasons today have a less heroic outlook than the monuments bequeathed to them by earlier generations. With the Craft in decline, they now seem almost embarrassed by the grandeur that surrounds them. The House of the Temple is a massive financial burden for the Scottish Rite: $45 million has been raised in a decade to fund a renovation, but much more is needed to endow ongoing repairs. The George Washington Masonic National Memorial is forlorn, struggling for a purpose. While it holds one or two genuine artefacts from the life of the great man, most of the rest is the detritus of Washington's posthumous Masonic personality cult. The Director told me when I visited that '90 per cent of the stuff that is on display in this building is contrived, it's fake'.

Ironically, cinema is important to the survival of these buildings: they make atmospheric sets for movies and adverts, and the resulting income helps cover maintenance bills. Although filming of a movie based on *The Lost Symbol* has been put on ice, it seems hard to imagine that it could be made anywhere else but the House of the Temple: the book's climactic scene – a typically Brownian blur of cyphers, smashing glass and helicopter blades – is set in the Temple Chamber itself.

The Masonic monument that I was most looking forward to seeing when I went to Washington recently was much less magniloquent than either the House of the Temple or the George Washington Masonic Memorial. Nobody would think of setting an advert in the Prince Hall Grand Lodge of the District of Columbia (1929): it is a five-storey grey box with a row of Masonic symbols engraved around the top; a pharmacy occupies much of the ground floor. As their architecture shows, African-American Freemasons have never been able to call on the same resources as their white Brethren.

The Prince Hall Grand Lodge tells us about a very distinctive conception of what Freemasonry is about. It stands at the centre of U Street, and was at the heart of the black community with which U Street was synonymous. Beginning life as an encampment of freed slaves after the Civil War, the U-Street area was a town-within-a-town in the era of segregation. At a time when white capital was denied to African-American businesses, they were funded by the Industrial Bank: created in 1934 by Most Worshipful Past Grand Master Jessie H. Mitchell, it was and is located just across from the Grand Lodge. U Street was once known as the 'Black Broadway', where the likes of Brother Cab Calloway came to play. Brother Duke Ellington was at home here: he was a member of Social Lodge no. 1, which met (and still meets) in the Grand Lodge building. A few blocks away, Howard University trained a black intellectual élite: Brother Thurgood Marshall graduated from the Law School in 1933. Indeed, civil rights was built into the very fabric of the U-Street Grand Lodge. The plan for the building was suggested by Brother Booker T. Washington when he came to speak in 1912. The lower floors were to contain a big dining hall and shop spaces that could be rented out to provide sustainable funding for the Masonic activities on the upper floors: hence the pharmacy. Still today, at the end of a corridor within the Grand Lodge building you can find a door guarded by fluted columns and encased in mirrored plastic: it is marked 'Washington DC Branch NAACP'.

Yet U Street is no longer the force it once was. The heart was ripped out of the community in 1968 by the desperate revolt following the assassination of Martin Luther King. Much has changed in the lives of African Americans. U Street has made a slow recovery, which has been driven by yuppification in recent years; the place now lives on its heritage. The Prince Hall Craft has seen better days too: in United States Masonry, white and black are as one in having a greying membership.

I came to Washington primarily to find out about the ongoing racial division within American Freemasonry. Brother Alton G. Roundtree, the elderly former Grand Historian and Archivist of the Prince Hall Grand Lodge of DC, has done as much as anyone to chart its history. He is a Howard graduate and, like so many Masons I met in the USA, a former military man. His ringtone, which occasionally interrupts our conversation amid the dusty files of the Grand Lodge's archive, is the theme from the movie *Shaft*.

Alton explains to me that a merger between white and black Masonry is 'not on the agenda': the dream that one day they might form a single multi-racial Brotherhood, as Masonic values prescribe, has died. The two branches simply have too long a history of independence to think of uniting. There are too many vested interests on both sides, and Prince Hall Masons, who are fewer in number, have no desire to be submerged in a majority white fraternity. Rather than unification, the issue at hand is *recognition* – acknowledging one another as legitimate Freemasons, in other words. Recognition may also go as far as 'intervisitation': so that Brothers from one order can sit in on meetings held under the auspices of the other. This kind of relationship is the stuff of Masonic diplomacy the world over. Only in the United States is it shaped by the deeply rooted and subtle dynamics of race relations and the long shadow of slavery. Some American churches, notably the Methodists, have a very similar history of racial division.

Both Prince Hall and mainstream (i.e. predominantly white) Masonry are organised on a state level, so any moves towards recognition are necessarily made state by state, by individual Grand Lodges. Only in 1989, more than two hundred years after the original schism, did the first mutual recognition come, in Connecticut. Progress was slow thereafter. By 2006, there were still eleven states in which white Masonry had failed to recognise its black equivalent. Not coincidentally, they were the same eleven states in the South that formed the Confederacy during the Civil War. As of 2019, seven white Grand Lodges were still holding out. Alton strikes a resigned note in conclusion:

The situation is shameful. The former slave states are late in recognizing Prince Hall Freemasonry. Having grown up in the midst of segregation, and even worse my family were sharecroppers, I don't expect much. Change has only come as some of the older white Masons from the former slave states have passed on. The white Brothers who grew up after the integration law passed [1965] tend to have a different view towards recognizing Prince Hall Freemasonry. Still, they are fighting an uphill battle.

The mainstream Masonic leaders I visited in both Washington DC and Charleston, South Carolina (a state where there is still no mutual recognition), shared similar feelings. They acknowledge that the 'technical' reasons that Albert Mackey devised to avoid recognising Prince Hall Masonry were just a pretext for racism. But they view persuading the old men who are the grass roots of Freemasonry in the former slave states as a lost cause. One senior white Mason, who would gladly see mutual recognition become universal, quipped to me that, 'We just need a few more Masonic funerals.'

There are also optimistic signs. When I met Worshipful Grand Master Quincy G. Gant in the U-Street Grand Lodge, he had just been a guest of honour at a concert of Mozart's Masonic music organised by mainstream Masons. The two Grand Lodges, white and black, had recently formed a partnership to sponsor the DC special Olympics. 'We're in a good place in DC,' he told me.

While in Washington I also shared a Thai meal with Oscar Alleyne, an epidemiologist working on public health programmes, a Masonic historian, a charismatic lecturer, and the first man of colour to be elected to a leadership role within the mainstream Grand Lodge of New York since its foundation in 1782: he is currently Junior Grand Warden. With any luck, the very Grand Lodge that organised the glaringly white Masonic Brotherhood Center at the New York World's Fair of 1964–5 could soon have a man of colour as Grand Master. Oscar described the joyful scenes when he was overwhelmingly voted into office as 'pande-monium . . . There were tears. The feeling in the hall was simply "it's time".'

Chequered

No force more than the British Empire was responsible for creating the 'Masonic Earth' celebrated in Bourlard's documentary. So perhaps the most appropriate theme to finish with is the legacy of the Empire in Masonry.

In the autumn of 2019, over lunch near Freemasons' Hall in London, I discussed the present state of the Craft in India by catching up with a visiting senior Brother. Bharat V. Epur radiates an inner calm appropriate in a man who has held a number of exalted offices within the Grand Lodge of India, including that of Regional Grand Master for Eastern India. Hailing from Chennai (Madras in imperial times), and initiated into the Craft in 1998, Bharat sold his insurance company a few years ago and now travels the world on Masonic business. He also found time to write the *Penguin India Quiz Book*. He sees Masonry as the 'distilled wisdom of all ages presented in a multi-layered form'. Its rituals, which he dismisses as 'amateur theatrics', derive from western experience, but its profoundest truths are Indian in origin.

Bharat is high-minded in his Masonry, but gives a down-to-earth assessment of the state of the Craft in his homeland: 'we're muddling along'. Compared to the early days of the Grand Lodge of India, the Lodges no longer attract the 'very highest echelons' of society. Partly as a result, money is a problem too. Indian Lodge buildings often betray their origins in the infrastructure of the Empire: they are on land leased long term from the railways or the military. Many such plots have rocketed in value as India has prospered. With the leases coming up for renewal, the Brothers face a tough challenge to stay in their collective homes.

There are also looming recruitment problems. Many educated

young men simply do not have time for Lodge business: those employed in the burgeoning IT industry work extremely long hours, often on American or European time, in facilities situated far from the historical city centres where the Temples are.

One thing that is decidedly not a problem for Indian Freemasonry is intolerance. The very first Grand Master elected at the foundation of the Grand Lodge of India in 1961 was a Muslim; recent Grand Masters have included a Sikh and a Parsi; and the current head of the Southern Region is a Syrian Christian. Indian Lodges all recognise no fewer than five different Volumes of Sacred Law: the Bhagavad Gita, the Qur'an, the Bible, Guru Granth Sahib (for Sikhs) and the Zend-Avesta (for Zoroastrians). Bharat even has words of understanding for Rudyard Kipling, author of 'The Mother Lodge', whose racism he says was no more than 'a reflection of the time'. Indeed, Kipling's portrait adorns the home page of the Grand Lodge of India website, side by side with that of his Brother from Allahabad days, Motilal Nehru.

Thus, in India at least, the legacy of Freemasonry's role in the British Empire is largely a positive one. Elsewhere, Freemasons have a tougher task coming to terms with the shadows in their past. Australia is a case in point. One of the many troubling aspects of the inhuman treatment of Aboriginal peoples over the centuries since the first whites arrived in 1788 is the abuse of indigenous burial sites, which all Aboriginal nations regard as essential to their bond with the landscape. Identifying and re-interring ancestral remains is a cause pursued with passion by Aboriginal groups. In 2002, following an amnesty, Freemasons handed over to the Melbourne Museum a large but uncatalogued collection of indigenous remains, 'usually crania and arm or leg bones'. For many years, the Lodges of the state of Victoria had been using Emblems of Mortality stolen from Aboriginal graves. A member of the Museum's Indigenous Advisory Committee was appalled:

This material has turned up without information on the source of these remains or why they were collected. It's scandalous that so many of our ancestors were held by the Freemasons, but it's made worse by the fact that the Freemasons cannot tell us where they come from. How are we to rebury our ancestors when we don't know where they came from?

No wonder that the Craft was recently called to account for its role in colonisation by one of Australia's leading artists, in a prize-winning work that now hangs in the National Gallery of Australia. Danie Mellor's *From Rite to Ritual* depicts a Masonic Lodge and its associated symbols: columns, chessboard floor, coffin and the skull-and-crossbones. The scene is painted in the same blue as the Willow pattern crockery decorated with kitsch Chinese scenes that was first produced in Britain in the late eighteenth century – a typical consumer commodity of the imperial economy at the time when the Craft was being transplanted across the globe. Standing out incongruously against this background are colour cameos of Australian animals, such as koalas, kangaroos and red-winged parrots. At the centre of the temple floor are ghostly Aboriginal men enacting a ceremonial dance. The picture reminds us of how the Craft provided a solemn and harmonious cover story for the lethal and greedy business of carving out colonies.

Yet Danie Mellor is aware of the Craft's insistent contradictions: not only is he a former Freemason, he is also of mixed indigenous and European heritage. As he told me: 'it's correct there is inclusivity in Masonry, and my feeling while I was part of the organisation was that a core of tolerance and recognition of us belonging to a "human family" was real'. *From Rite to Ritual* also dwells on the fragile common ground between western Freemasonry and indigenous Australian cultures, notably the way knowledge is embedded in ceremonies, and death is seen as central to the experience of being human.

Australian Freemasons point to some Aboriginal community leaders who have been on the Square, such as Sir Douglas Nicholls, the élite Aussie rules footballer, campaigner and Governor of South Australia in the mid-1970s. A glance at the indigenous press suggests that Nicholls is not an entirely isolated case. Historically, Freemasons may have poached symbols from other cultures around the world for use in their ceremonies, but the Lodges have proven again and again that they are also cradles of cultural dialogue.

A sense of history has always been crucial to Freemasonry. But all too often, as I have tried to highlight, the Masons have squeezed their history into rosy identity narratives. Like Danie Mellor, I believe they would be truer to their values if they explored ways to write their story that have a bit less Masonic harmony and a bit more social tension. Freemasonry's past is as chequered as a Lodge floor.

Even those of us who would never dream of being initiated can find lessons to learn by viewing history through a Masonic lens. Globalisation and the Internet are forcing us to rethink and reinvent a fundamental human need: community. At such a moment, our pursuit of wellbeing may be well served by contemplating the tragi-comic tale of how a form of community born in an earlier global age tried to live out some of our most precious ideals.

ACKNOWLEDGEMENTS

One of my great hopes for *The Craft* is that its readers will be able to share some of the pleasures I derived from researching it. In the front rank of those pleasures was the chance to follow the Freemasons into times and places that were unfamiliar for me as a historian and writer. Letting curiosity lead the way is both thrilling and risky. *The Craft*, I am sure, will betray the signs of those risks in its flaws, for which I alone am responsible. I can only ask my readers to keep in mind the risks I took when they point out the mistakes I have made. However, many people have helped me identify so many opportunities and avoid so many pitfalls along the way that the book simply would not have been possible without their generosity. To the following Freemasons, academic colleagues, and friends old and new I owe a much bigger debt than can be repaid by the only gesture of gratitude that space permits me here: mentioning their names. But I feel I do have to single out the two people who have done more than anyone to enable my research: Martin Cherry and Susan Snell at the Museum of Freemasonry in London are the kind of librarian / archivists that scholars dream of encountering. Their colleagues at the Museum of Freemasonry, and the staff of the British Library and the other libraries and archives where I worked, also deserve special praise.

Oscar Alleyne	Stephen Bennetts	Thomas K. Byrd
Gioia Avvantaggiato	Michael Berkowitz	Roger H Bullard
Franco Benigno	Stefano Bisi	Alessia Candito

Jim Carroll

Olivia Chaumont

Lloyd 'Curly' Christopher

Catherine Clarke

Ken Collins

Claudio Cordova

Nicholas Cronk

Enrico Dal Lago

Simon Deschamps

Bharat V. Epur

Tehuti Evans

Adrian Fleming

John Foot

Vahid Fozdar

Quincy G. Gant

Emilio Gin

Christian Goeschel

Andrew Hadfield

Rick Halpern

Jessica L. Harland-Jacobs

Peter Hinks

Stephen Hiott

Stephen Katrowitz

Deirdre Leask

George Lucas

José Luis Hernández Luis

Bob James

Prue James

Andy Jameson

Dilwyn Knox

Rupert Lancaster

Carl Levy

Giuseppe Lombardo

Olivia Loperfido

George Lucas

Giuseppe Lumia

Mario Maritan

Giuseppe Maviglia

Danie Mellor

Peter Mellor

Thomas R. Metcalf

Radojka Miljevic

Guillermo Mira

Lucio Mollica

James R. Morgan III

Brent Morris

Stefano Musolino

Florian Mussgnug

Kerry Nicholls

Gaetano Paci

Salvo Palazzolo

Giovanni Pandolfo

Ghanshyam M. Patel

Sarah Penny

Thad Peterson

Clive Priddle

Jackie Ranston

Alton G. Roundtree

Francesco Ruis

Julius Ruiz

Ivan Scott

Gajendra Singh

Simon Southerton

David Stevenson

Mark Tabbert

Doug Taylor

Benedetta Tobagi

Fabio Truzzolillo

James Van Zyl

Fabio Venzi

Gareth Wood

BIBLIOGRAPHY WITH BRIEF NOTES AND CITATIONS

In an effort to make *The Craft* as accessible as possible, I have not used footnotes or endnotes. Those of us who are university professors and therefore lucky enough to read for a living all too easily forget the huge efforts that many people have to make to find the time to read – and to read non-fiction in particular. Perhaps the least we can do to meet such readers halfway is to produce a narrative unencumbered by references, nods to obscure academic debates, and the name-checking of academic allies and opponents.

That said, footnotes fulfil many duties and afford many pleasures. The following pages can be but a poor substitute for them. My hope is that they will at least serve as a stimulus to further reading, a recognition of my many intellectual debts, an indication of what sources I have used to formulate and substantiate my arguments, and a clue to interesting issues that I did not have time to explore or treat fully. Any scholar curious to know more about my sources is welcome to contact me by email.

All translations are my own unless stated.

I have used the following abbreviation: *AQC* = Ars Quatuor Coronatorum.

Chapter 1: Lisbon: John Coustos's Secrets

R. Beachy, 'Club Culture and Social Authority: Freemasonry in Leipzig, 1741–1830', in F. Trentmann (ed.), *Paradoxes of Civil Society: New Perspectives on Modern German and British History*, 2nd edn, New York, 2003.

F. Braggion, 'Managers and (Secret) Social Networks: The Influence of the Freemasonry', *Journal of the European Economic Association*, 9 (6), 2011.

R. Burt, 'Freemasonry and Business Networking during the Victorian Period', *The Economic History Review*, 56 (4), 2003.

G.M. Cazzaniga, 'Il complotto: metamorfosi di un mito', in Cazzaniga (ed.), *Storia d'Italia. Annali, 21. La Massoneria*, Turin, 2006.

J. Coustos, *The Sufferings of John Coustos, for Free-Masonry, and for His Refusing to turn Roman Catholic, in the Inquisition at Lisbon*, London, 1746. 'That he has infring'd the Pope's Orders', p. 52. (The original quote varies between the first and third person. I have made it uniform throughout for ease of reading.) 'As Secrecy naturally excited Curiosity', p. 33. 'Not a little honoured in belonging to a Society', p. 27. 'Charity and Brotherly Love', pp. 25–31. 'If this Society of Free-Masons was so virtuous', p. 33.

J.A. Ferrer Benimeli, *Masoneria, Iglesia e Ilustracio. Un conflicto ideologico-politico-religioso*, Madrid, 1976, vol. 2. For inquisition trials in Lisbon, pp. 133–94, esp. pp. 183–91 for Coustos.

J.A. Ferrer Benimeli, 'Origini, motivazioni ed effetti della condanna vaticana', in G.M. Cazzaniga (ed.), *Storia d'Italia. Annali, 21. La Massoneria*, Turin, 2006.

J.-C. Flachat, *Observations sur le commerce et sur les arts d'une partie de l'Europe, de l'Asie, de l'Afrique, et même des Indes Orientale*, vol. 1, Lyon, 1766, p. 420; on hatred of Masons in the Ottoman Empire.

W. McLeod, 'John Coustos: His Lodges and His Book', AQC, 92, 1979.

G. Simmel, 'The Sociology of Secrecy and of Secret Societies', *American Journal of Sociology*, 11 (4), 1906.

G. Tarantino, 'The mysteries of popery unveiled: Affective language in John Coustos's and Anthony Gavin's accounts of the Inquisition', in S. Broomhall (ed.), *Spaces for Feeling: Emotions and Sociabilities in Britain 1650–1850*, London, 2015.

S. Vatcher, 'John Coustos and the Portuguese Inquisition', AQC, 81, 1968. Contains a translation of Coustos's interrogation and other papers. 'In [our] Fraternity, it is not permitted to speak of religious matters', p. 56.

Chapter 2: Nowhere: The Strange Death of Hiram Abiff

Anon., *The Scottish Ritual of Craft Freemasonry: With Tracing Boards*, Edinburgh (no date). I consulted the rituals followed by my grandfather in 1919 in my outline of the Craft ceremonies.

L. Corsi, *Tommaso Crudeli, Il calamaio del Padre Inquisitore*, Udine-Florence, 2003. Masturbation ritual, p. 121.

M.C. Duncan, *Duncan's Masonic Ritual and Monitor*, New York, 1966. The source of all the images in this chapter.

S. Vatcher, 'John Coustos and the Portuguese Inquisition', AQC, 81, 1968: 'As the

Sun gives light to the day', p. 71. 'To be recognised in any part of the World', p. 48. 'Placing his thumb on the first knuckle-joint', p. 62. '[Coustos] said: that the only purpose they have', p. 54. 'Abbreviated, evasive and deceitful', p. 73.

M. Vigilante, 'Crudeli, Tommaso', *Dizionario Biografico degli Italiani*, 31, Rome, 1985.

Chapter 3: Edinburgh: The Art of Memorie

D. Allan, 'Moray, Sir Robert (1608/9?–1673)', *Oxford Dictionary of National Biography*, Oxford University Press, 2004, online edn, October 2007 [http://www.oxforddnb.com/view/article/19645, accessed 23 February 2017].

P. Beal, 'Dicsone [Dickson], Alexander (bap. 1558, d. 1603/4), philosophical writer and political agent', *Oxford Dictionary of National Biography*, consulted online 21 February 2017.

I. Campbell and A. MacKechnie, 'The "Great Temple of Solomon" at Stirling', *Architectural History*, 54, 2011. Earliest Renaissance building of its kind in Britain, p. 91.

H. Carr and J.R. Dashwood, *The Minutes of the Lodge of Edinburgh, Mary's Chapel, no. 1, 1598–1738*, Masonic Reprints, vol. XIII, London, 1962. Initiation of Civil War officers in Edinburgh, pp. 118–19.

I.B. Cowan and D. Shaw (eds), *The Renaissance and Reformation in Scotland*, Edinburgh, 1983.

P. Croft, *King James*, Basingstoke, 2003.

T. De Moor, 'The Silent Revolution: A New Perspective on the Emergence of Commons, Guilds, and Other Forms of Corporate Collective Action in Western Europe', *International Review of Social History*, 53(S16), 2008.

S. Epstein, 'Guilds and Metiers', in J.R. Strayer (ed.), *Dictionary of the Middle Ages*, New York, vol. 6, 1985.

W. Fraser, *Memorials of the Montgomeries, Earls of Eglinton*, vol. 2, Edinburgh, 1859, pp. 239–44. Contains the text of the Schaw statutes. 'Tryall of the art of memorie', p. 243.

D. Harrison, *The Genesis of Freemasonry*, Addlestone, 2014.

M. Hunter, 'Ashmole, Elias (1617–1692)', *Oxford Dictionary of National Biography*, Oxford University Press, 2004, online edn, May 2006 [http://www.oxforddnb.com/view/article/764, accessed 23 February 2017].

G.P. Jones, 'Building in stone in medieval Western Europe', in M.M. Postan and E. Miller (eds), *The Cambridge Economic History of Europe*, vol. II: *Trade and Industry in the Middle Ages*, 2nd edn, Cambridge, 1987.

C.H. Josten, 'Elias Ashmole, FRS (1617–1692)', *Notes and Records of the Royal Society of London*, vol. 15, July 1960.

C.H. Josten (ed.), *Elias Ashmole (1617–1692): His Autobiographical and Historical Notes, his Correspondence, and Other Contemporary Sources Relating to his Life and Work* Oxford: Clarendon Press, vol. IV, 1966. 'I was the Senior Fellow among them', p. 1701.

A.L. Julhala, 'The Household and Court of King James VI of Scotland', PhD Thesis, University of Edinburgh, 2000.

D. Knoop and G.P. Jones, *The Genesis of Freemasonry*, Manchester, 1947.

D. Knoop and G.P. Jones, *The Mediaeval Mason: An Economic History of English Stone Building in the Later Middle Ages and Early Modern Times*, Manchester, 1967.

D. Knoop and G.P. Jones (eds), *The Early Masonic Catechisms*, Manchester, 1963. 'Secrets which must never be written', quoted p. 5. 'Being buried within the floodmark, where no man shall know', quoted p. 36. The 'Sisterhood of Free Sempstresses', reproduced pp. 226–8.

M. Lynche (ed.), *Oxford Companion to Scottish History*, Oxford, 2001. See the entry on the Royal court.

D. MacCulloch, *Reformation: Europe's House Divided, 1490–1700*, London, 2003. For a summary of the Scottish Reformation, see pp. 291–5 and *passim*. 'The great temple of Solomon', quoted p. 110.

E. Miller and J. Hatcher, *Medieval England: Towns, Commerce and Crafts 1086–1348*, London, 1995.

R. Plot, *Natural History of Stafford-shire*, Oxford, 1686, The account of the Acception quoted here, pp. 316–18.

L.F. Salzman, *Building in England Down to 1540: A Documentary History*, Oxford, 1967.

M.D.J. Scanlan, 'Freemasonry and the mystery of the Acception, 1630 to 1723 – a fatal flaw', in R.W. Weisberger et al. (eds), *Freemasonry on Both Sides of the Atlantic*, New York, 2002. This important study also contains the best explanation of the meanings of the term freemason.

M.D.J. Scanlan, 'The origins of Freemasonry: England', in H. Bogdan and J. Snoek (eds), *Handbook of Freemasonry*, Leiden, 2014.

M.K. Schuchard, *Restoring the Temple of Vision: Cabalistic Freemasonry and Stuart Culture*, Leiden, 2002. On Hermeticism and the Scottish court, pp. 200–206.

D. Stevenson, *The Origins of Freemasonry: Scotland's Century, 1590–1710*, Cambridge, 1988. I have drawn heavily on this classic study throughout this chapter. For the figure of 80 per cent of Schaw Lodges still being around today, see p. 216. For that of there being thirty Schaw Lodges across Scotland by 1730, see p. 213. 'Som secret signe delivered from hand to hand', quoted p. 143.

D. Stevenson, 'Schaw, William (1549/50–1602)', *Oxford Dictionary of National Biography*, Oxford University Press, 2004 http://www.oxforddnb.com/view/article/24799, consulted 21 February 2017.

D. Stevenson, 'Four Hundred Years of Freemasonry in Scotland', *The Scottish Historical Review*, XC (2), 2011, p. 230.

H. Swanson, *Medieval Artisans: An Urban Class in Late Medieval England*, Oxford, 1989.

S.L. Thrupp, 'The gilds', in M.M. Postan, E.E. Rich and E. Miller (eds), *The Cambridge Economic History of Europe*, vol. III. *Economic Organization and Policies in the Middle Ages*, Cambridge, 1963.

E.M. Veale, 'Craftsmen and the economy of London in the 14th century', in R. Holt and G. Rosser (eds), *The Medieval Town, 1200–1540*, London, 1990.

F.A. Yates, *The Art of Memory*, London, 1966. The classic study of the art of memory and its Renaissance adaptations.

The text and translation of the Regius Poem are available at http://www.freemasons-freemasonry.com/regius.html, consulted 3 April 2017.

Chapter 4: London: At the Sign of the Goose and Gridiron

J. Anderson, *The constitutions of the Freemasons: Containing the history, charges, regulations, etc. of that ... fraternity*, London, 1723.

J. Anderson, *The New Book of Constitutions of the ... Fraternity of Free and Accepted Masons ... collected and digested, by order of the Grand Lodge, from their old records ... and lodge-books*, London, 1738.

Anon, 'Cunningham, James, fourteenth Earl of Glencairn (1749–91)', *The Burns Encyclopedia*, consulted online, http://www.robertburns.org/encyclopedia/CunninghamJamesfourteenthEarlofGlencairn174915191.255.shtml, on 14 April 2017. 'My first, my dearest Patron'.

R. Beachy, 'Masonic apologetic writings', in M. Fedelma Cross (ed.), *Gender and Fraternal Orders in Europe, 1300–2000*, Basingstoke, 2010.

F. Benigno, 'Assolutezza del potere e nascita della sfera pubblica: critica di un modello', in M. Rospocher (ed.), *Oltre la sfera pubblica: Lo spazio della politica nell'Europa moderna*, Bologna, 2013.

R.A. Berman, 'The Architects of Eighteenth-Century English Freemasonry, 1720–1740', University of Exeter PhD Thesis, 2010. Especially on Desaguliers and Whig networks. 'Many London Freemasons represented precisely the type of men the Whig government would have favoured', p. 155.

R.A. Berman, *The Foundations of Modern Freemasonry: The Grand Architects, Political Change and the Scientific Enlightenment, 1714–1740*, Brighton, 2012.

J. Black, *Eighteenth-Century Britain, 1688–1783*, 2nd edn, Basingstoke, 2008.

M. Blackett-Ord, *Hell-Fire Duke: The Life of the Duke of Wharton*, Shooter's Lodge, 1982.

'Boniface Oinophilus' (pseud. of A.-H. de Sallengre), *Ebreitatis Encomium, or The Praise of Drunkenness*, London, 1812. 'When the King Enjoys his Own Again', p. 90. "'Tis wine, ye Masons, makes you Free', p. 83.

A.T. Carpenter, *John Theophilus Desaguliers: A Natural Philosopher, Engineer and Freemason in Newtonian England*, London, 2011. Walpole as Mason, p. 104.

W.J. Chetwode Crawley, 'Notes on Irish Freemasonry, no. VI, The Wesleys and Irish Freemasonry', *AQC*, 15, 1902.

J.C.D. Clark, *English Society 1660–1832*, Cambridge, 2000.

P. Clark, *British Clubs and Societies 1580–1800*, Oxford, 2000. The authority on the area, upon which I have drawn heavily. On Burns's networking, pp. 230–1. Two thousand coffee houses, p. 163.

R. Clutterbuck, *The History and Antiquities of the County of Hertford; compiled from the best printed authorities and original records preserved in public repositories and private collections: Embellished with views of the most curious monuments of antiquity, and illustrated with a map of the County*, vol. 1, London, 1815. On the Strongs, pp. 166–70.

H.T. Dickinson, 'Whiggism in the eighteenth century', in J. Cannon (ed.), *The Whig Ascendancy: Colloquies on Hanoverian England*, London, 1981.

K. Downes, *Christopher Wren*, London, 1971. For a death notice mentioning Freemasonry, p. 182.

P. Elliott and S. Daniels, 'The "school of true, useful and universal science"? Freemasonry, Natural Philosophy and Scientific Culture in Eighteenth-Century England', *The British Journal for the History of Science*, 39 (2), 2006.

A. Everitt, 'The English Urban Inn, 1560–1760', in A. Everitt (ed.), *Perspectives in English Urban History*, London, 1973.

M. Goldie, 'The English system of liberty', in M. Goldie and R. Wokler (eds), *The Cambridge History of Eighteenth-Century Political Thought*, Cambridge, 2006.

J. Habermas, *The Structural Transformation of the Public Sphere: An Inquiry into a Category of Bourgeois Society*, Cambridge, MA, 1989.

D.G. Hackett, *That Religion in Which All Men Agree: Freemasonry and American Culture*, Berkeley, CA, 2014. Another fundamental study. Accounts of Masonic procession in Charleston, quoted p. 19. The book also has a fine chapter on Native-American Masonry.

E. Hatton, *New View of London: or an Ample account of that City*, London, 1708. A 'fraternity of ... many of the Nobility and Gentry', p. 611.

J. Herron Lepper, 'The Earl of Middlesex and the English Lodge in Florence', *AQC*, 58, 1945.

C. Hobson, 'Valentine Strong – Cotswold Stonemason', *Fairford History Society Occasional Paper*, 3, 2006.

M.C. Jacob, *Living the Enlightenment: Freemasonry and Politics in Eighteenth-Century Europe*, Oxford, 1991. A ground-breaking study I have drawn on across the London and Paris chapters. On Masonry as a 'phantom' of Liberty, see p. 203.

M.C. Jacob, *The Origins of Freemasonry: Facts & Fictions*, Philadelphia, PA, 2006.

L. Jardine, *On a Grander Scale: The Outstanding Career of Sir Christopher Wren*, London, 2002.

D. Knoop and G.P. Jones, *The London Mason in the Seventeenth Century*, Manchester, 1935.

B. Krysmanski, 'Lust in Hogarth's *Sleeping Congregation* – Or, How to Waste Time in Post-Puritan England', *Art History*, 21, 3 September 1998; on a cartoon of Desaguliers giving a boring sermon.

J.M. Landau, 'Muslim Opposition to Freemasonry', *Die Welt des Islams*, 36 (2), 1996.

J. Lane, *Masonic Records 1717–1894* (2nd edn), London, 1895.

J. Lang, *Rebuilding St Paul's after the Great Fire of London*, Oxford, 1956.

N. Leask, 'Robert Burns', in G. Carruthers and L. McIlvanney (eds), *The Cambridge Companion to Scottish Literature*, Cambridge, 2012.

J. Macky, *A Journey Through England in Familiar Letters from a Gentleman Here, to his Friend Abroad*, 2nd edn, London, 1722, i. 'An infinity of CLUBS, or SOCIETIES', p. 287.

R.K. Marshall, 'Davison [Davidson], Jeremiah (c. 1695–1745)' *Oxford Dictionary of National Biography*, Oxford, 2008. Online version consulted 23 April 2017.

H. Morrison, '"Making Degenerates into Men" by Doing Shots, Breaking Plates, and Embracing Brothers in Eighteenth-Century Freemasonry', *Journal of Social History*, 46 (1), 2012. Covers Mozart and Haydn's revels in their Lodge.

M. Mulvey Roberts, *British Poets and Secret Societies*, London, 1986; on Burns.

A. Newman, 'Politics and Freemasonry in the Eighteenth Century', *AQC*, 104, 1991.

R. Péter, 'The "Fair Sex" in a "Male Sect": Gendering the Role of Women in Eighteenth-Century English Freemasonry', in M. Fedelma Cross (ed.), *Gender and Fraternal Orders in Europe, 1300–2000*, Basingstoke, 2010.

A. Pink, 'Robin Hood and Her Merry Women: Modern Masons in an Early Eighteenth-Century London Pleasure Garden', *Journal for Research into Freemasonry and Fraternalism*, 4 (1–2; single issue), 2013.

M.G.H. Pittock, *Inventing and Resisting Britain: Cultural Identities in Britain and Ireland, 1685–1789*, Basingstoke, 1997.

W. Read, 'Let a man's religion … be what it may', *AQC*, 98, 1985. Cites the case of English Freemasonry's first Catholic Grand Master.

C. Révauger, 'Les femmes et la franc-maçonnerie, des origines à nos jours', *REHMLAC: Revista de Estudios Históricos de la Masonería Latinoamericana y Caribeña*, 4 (2), December 2012 to April 2013. On some exceptional early cases of female Masons.

M.D.J. Scanlan, 'Freemasonry and the mystery of the Acception, 1630 to 1723 – a fatal flaw', in R.W. Weisberger et al. (eds), *Freemasonry on Both Sides of the Atlantic*, New York, 2002, 'A Great Convention at St Paul's of the Fraternity of Accepted Masons', quoted p. 171.

S. Schaffer, 'The Show That Never Ends: Perpetual Motion in the Early Eighteenth Century', *The British Journal for the History of Science*, 28 (2), 1995. Very useful on Desaguliers.

J.M. Shaftesley and M. Rosenbaum, 'Jews in English Regular Freemasonry, 1717–1860', *Transactions & Miscellanies (Jewish Historical Society of England)*, 25, 1973–5.

J.M. Shaftesley, 'Jews in English Freemasonry in the 18th and 19th Centuries', *AQC*, 92, 1979.

D.S. Shields, 'Franklin and the republic of letters', in C. Mulford (ed.), *The Cambridge Companion to Benjamin Franklin*, Cambridge, 2008.

Ev. Ph. Shirley, 'Remarkable Clubs and Societies, 1748', *Notes and Queries*, 27 July 1878. For names of strange clubs, p. 65.

L.B. Smith, 'Wharton, Philip James, duke of Wharton and Jacobite duke of Northumberland (1698–1731)', *Oxford Dictionary of National Biography*, Oxford, 2008. Online version consulted 3 May 2017.

W. Speck, 'Whigs and Tories dim their glories: English political parties under the first two Georges', in J. Cannon (ed.), *The Whig Ascendancy: Colloquies on Hanoverian England*, London, 1981.

D. Stevenson, *The Origins of Freemasonry: Scotland's Century, 1590–1710*, Cambridge, 1988. 'An exclusive cell within the London Company', p. 281. '1000 ridiculous postures and grimmaces', quoted p. 137.

D. Stevenson, 'James Anderson, Man and Mason', *Heredom: Transactions of the Scottish Rite Research Society*, 10, 2002.

P. Sugden, 'Veil, Sir Thomas de (1684–1746)', *Oxford Dictionary of National Biography*, Oxford, 2004. Online version consulted 1 May 2017.

A. Tinniswood, *His Invention So Fertile: A Life of Christopher Wren*, London, 2001.

A. Vickery, *The Gentleman's Daughter: Women's Lives in Georgian England*, New Haven, CT, 1998.

E. Ward, *A Compleat and Humorous Account of All the Remarkable Clubs and Societies in the Cities of London and Westminster*, London, 1756. 'Crepitations', p. 31.

S. Wren (ed.), *Parentalia Or Memoirs of the Family of the Wrens Viz. of Mathew Bishop of Ely, Christopher Dean of Windsor ... But Chiefly of --- Surveyor-general of the Royal Buildings ... Now Published by Stephen Wren*, London, 1750. For the account of the topping-out ceremony, p. 293.

J. Wright, *Phoenix Paolina: A Poem on the New Fabrick of St Paul's Cathedral*, London, 1709.

Chapter 5: Paris: War on Christ and His Cult; War on Kings and All Their Thrones

L. Aimable, *Une Loge Maçonnique d'avant 1789: les Neuf Soeurs*, Paris, 1897.

Anon., *L'adoption ou La maçonnerie des femmes*, Paris(?), 1775. The opening quotation, from pp. 10f., has been reorganised to be clearer in this context.

P. Barbier and F. Vernillat, *Histoire de France par les Chansons*, vol. 4, *La Révolution*, Paris, 1957. 'We Masons have a zealous Brother', pp. 20–1.

A. Barruel, *Mémoires pour servir à l'histoire du jacobinisme*, 5 vols, Hamburg, 1798–9. 'Everything in the French Revolution, everything right down', vol. 1, p. viii. 'If Jacobinism triumphs', vol. 1, p. 3. 'War on Christ and his cult', vol. 2, p. 280. Final stages of the conspiracy convergence in vol. 4, ch. XI. On losing incriminating letters, vol. 2, p. 465. 'Exterminating Angel', vol. 2, p. 468.

P.-Y. Beaurepaire, *L'autre et le frère: L'étranger et la Franc-Maçonnerie en France au XVIII siècle*, Paris, 1998; 'all those profanes [i.e. non-Masons] who have the misfortune to be Jews', quoted p. 566.

R. Berman, *The Foundations of Modern Freemasonry: The Grand Architects, Political Change and the Scientific Enlightenment, 1714–1740*, Brighton, 2012.

J.H. Bloch, 'Women and the reform of the Nation', in E. Jacobs et al. (eds), *Woman and Society in Eighteenth-Century France*, London, 1979.

C. Brinton, 'Revolutionary Symbolism in the Jacobin Clubs', *The American Historical Review*, 32 (4), 1927.

J.M. Burke, 'Through Friendship to Feminism: The Growth in Self-Awareness Among Eighteenth-Century Women Freemasons', *Proceedings of the Annual Meeting of the Western Society for French History*, 14, 1987.

J.M. Burke, 'Freemasonry, Friendship and Noblewomen: The Role of the Secret Society in Bringing Enlightenment Thought to Pre-revolutionary Women Elites', *History of European Ideas*, 10 (3), 1989. 'She was imprisoned and summarily executed', p. 289.

J.M. Burke, 'Leaving the Enlightenment: Women Freemasons after the Revolution', *Eighteenth-Century Studies*, 33 (2), *Colonial Encounters* (Winter, 2000). 'There is no question that an incipient type of feminism', p. 256.

J.M. Burke and M.C. Jacob, 'French Freemasonry, Women, and Feminist Scholarship', *The Journal of Modern History*, 68 (3), 1996.

S. Burrows, J. Conlin, R. Goulbourne, V. Mainz (eds), *The Chevalier D'Eon and his*

Worlds: Gender, Espionage and Politics in the Eighteenth Century, London, 2010.

J. Casanova de Seingalt, *Histoire de ma vie. Suivie de textes inédits*, Paris, 1993. 'In this day and age, any young man', tome I, vol. 3, ch. VII p. 553. 'Fine suppers in the company of pretty girls', tome III, vol. 12, ch. VI, p. 957.

R. Chartier, *The Cultural Origins of the French Revolution*, London, 1991. On Masonry and secularization, pp. 92–110.

E. Chaussin, 'D'Éon and Tonnerre', in S. Burrows, J. Conlin, R. Goulbourne and V. Mainz, 2010, *op cit*. 'Despite her transformation', p. 78.

W.J. Chetwode Crawley, 'The Chevalier d'Éon', *AQC*, 16, 1903. 'If we are permitted to conjecture', p. 251.

P. Chevallier, *Les Ducs sous l'Acacia. Les premiers pas de la Franc-Maçonnerie française, 1725–1743*, Paris, 1964.

P. Chevallier, *Histoire de la Franc-Maçonnerie Française. Tome I. La Maçonnerie: École de l'Égalité, 1725–1799*, Paris, 1974. 'Inextricable Scottish mess', Gaston Martin, quoted p. 185.

L.F. Cody, 'Sex, Civility, and the Self: Du Coudray, D'Eon, and Eighteenth-Century Conceptions of Gendered, National, and Psychological Identity', *French Historical Studies*, 24 (3), 2001.

R. Darnton, *Mesmerism and the End of the Enlightenment in France*, London, 1968.

R. Darnton, 'Cherchez la Femme', *New York Review of Books*, 10 August 1995. Review of *Monsieur d'Eon is a Woman: A Tale of Political Intrigue and Sexual Masquerade* by G. Kates.

S. Desan, 'What's After Political Culture? Recent French Revolutionary Historiography', *French Historical Studies*, 23 (1), 2000.

C. Francovich, 'Balsamo, Giuseppe', *Dizionario biografico degli Italiani*, vol. 5, Rome, 1963.

P. Friedland, *Seeing Justice Done: The Age of Spectacular Capital Punishment in France*, Oxford, 2012.

G. Giarrizzo, *Massoneria e illuminismo*, Venice, 1994.

D. Goodman, *The Republic of Letters: A Cultural History of the French Enlightenment*, Ithaca, NY, 1994. On Guillotin's Masonry, *passim*.

R.F. Gould, *The Concise History of Freemasonry*, revised by F.J.W. Crowe, New York, 2007 (1920).

R. Halévi, 'Les origins intellectuelles de la Révolution française: de la Maçonnerie au Jacobinisme', in É. François (ed.), *Sociabilité et société bourgeoise en France, en Allemagne et en Suisse, 1750–1850*, Paris, 1986.

G. Hivert-Messeca and Y. Hivert-Messeca, *Comment la Franc-Maçonnerie vint aux femmes: Deux siècles de Franc-Maçonnerie d'adoption féminine et mixte en France, 1740–1940*, Paris, 1997. Eighty-two per cent of Adoption Lodge women were aristocrats, pp. 115–21.

R. Hofstadter, 'The Paranoid Style in American Politics', *Harper's Magazine*, November 1964.

O. Homberg and F. Jousselin, *Un aventurier au XVIIIe siècle. Le Chevalier d'Éon (1728–1810)*, Paris, 1904. 'I enclose an invitation to this ceremony', from d'Éon's unpublished papers cited p. 279. 'His – or her – chin is adorned', quoted p. 206.

S.J. Horowitz, 'What's Behind Hip Hop's Illuminati Music Obsession?', http://www. complex.com/music/hip-hop-illuminati-obsession; consulted 2 March 2017.

J.I. Israel, *Democratic Enlightenment: Philosophy, Revolution, and Human Rights 1750–1790*, Oxford, 2011. 'Traitorous and hostile to religion', quoted p. 842.

A. Joly, *Un mystique Lyonnais et les secrets de la Franc-Maçonnerie, 1730–1824*, Macon, 1938. On Willermoz.

C. Jones, *The Great Nation: France from Louis XV to Napoleon, 1715–99*, London, 2002.

F. Jupeau Réquillard, *L'initiation des femmes, ou, Le souci permanent des francs-maçons français*, Monaco, 2000. 'Oh my Sisters! How sweet it is', quoted p. 300.

G. Kates, 'The Transgendered World of the Chevalier/Chevalière d'Eon', *The Journal of Modern History*, 67 (3), 1995.

M.L. Kennedy, *The Jacobin Clubs in the French Revolution: The First Years*, Princeton, NJ, 1982.

R. Le Forestier, *Les Illuminés de Bavière et la Franc-Maçonnerie Allemande*, Paris, 1914.

R. Le Forestier, *La Franc-Maçonnerie templière et occultiste aux XVIIIe et XIXe siècles*, Paris, 1970.

E. Lever, *Philippe Égalité*, Paris, 1996.

D. Ligou (ed.), *Chansons Maçonniques 18e et 19e siècles*, Paris, 1972.

D. Ligou, *Dictionnaire universel de la Franc-Maçonnerie*, Paris, tome 2, 1974. Among my sources for the strange varieties of rites and Degrees, pp. 1105–31.

D. Ligou (ed.), *Dictionnaire de la Franc-maçonnerie*, Paris, 1987. On Chaillon de Jonville, pp. 209–10. On Orléans/Égalité, pp. 874–5. On Condorcet, p. 289. On Guillotin, p. 550. On Égalité's wife and sister, p. 154.

D. Ligou (et al.), *Histoire des francs-maçons en France 1725–1815*, Toulouse, 2000.

K. Loiselle, *Brotherly Love: Freemasonry and Male Friendship in Enlightenment France*, Ithaca, 2014. On the prominence of suspicions of sodomy surrounding French Freemasonry, pp. 94–5. On the use of Masonic terms in gay subculture, pp. 94–8; 1777, Adoption procedures used as a pretext to invite prostitutes into Lodges, p. 99.

S. Mandelbrote, 'Ramsay, Andrew Michael [Jacobite Sir Andrew Ramsay, baronet] (1686–1743)', *Oxford Dictionary of National Biography*, Oxford, 2004, online edn, consulted 21 July 2017.

D.M. McMahon, *Enemies of the Enlightenment: The French Counter-Enlightenment and the Making of Modernity*, Oxford, 2001. 'The whole of the wonderful narrative', quoted p. 113.

P. McPhee, *The French Revolution, 1789–1799*, Oxford, 2002.

D. Menozzi, 'Cattolicesimo e massoneria nell'età della Rivoluzione francese', in Cazzaniga (ed.), *Storia d'Italia. Annali, 21. La Massoneria*, Turin, 2006.

P. Négrier (ed.), *Textes fondateurs de la tradition maçonnique 1390–1760: Introduction à la pensée de la franc-maçonnerie primitive*, Paris, 1995. Ramsay discourse reproduced pp. 303–35.

C. Porset, 'Cagliostro e la massoneria', in Cazzaniga (ed.), *Storia d'Italia. Annali, 21. La Massoneria*, Turin, 2006.

J. Quéniart, *Culture et Société Urbaines dans la France de l'Ouest au XVIIIe siècle*, Paris, 1978. On priests and curates as Masons in Angers and Mans, p. 450.

M. Rapport, 'The international repercussions of the French Revolution', in P. McPhee (ed.), *A Companion to the French Revolution*, Oxford, 2013.

M. Riquet, *Augustin De Barruel: Un jésuite face aux Jacobins francs-maçons, 1741–1820*, Paris, 1989.

H.G. Riqueti, comte de Mirabeau, *De la monarchie Prussienne sous Frederic le Grand*, tome 5, London, 1788. 'Oddities, contradictions and mysteries', and other quotes on German Masonry, pp. 64–9.

J.M. Roberts, *The Mythology of the Secret Societies*, London, 1972. The classic history, which I have drawn on repeatedly in the eighteenth- and early nineteenth-century chapters of this book. On Shelley and Barruel, pp. 211–13.

J. Robison, *Proofs of a Conspiracy against all the Religions and Governments of Europe, carried on in the secret meetings of Freemasons, Illuminati and Reading Societies*, New York, 1798 (1797).

D. Roche, 'Sociabilitiés et politique de l'Ancien Régime à la Révolution', *French Politics and Society*, 7 (3), 'Commemorating the French Revolution' (Summer 1989).

J.M.J. Rogister, 'D'Éon de Beaumont, Charles Geneviève Louis Auguste André Timothée, Chevalier D'Éon in the French nobility (1728–1810)', *Oxford Dictionary of National Biography*. Online version dated 4 October 2012, consulted 4 August 2017.

J. Smith Allen, 'Sisters of Another Sort: Freemason Women in Modern France, 1725–1940', *The Journal of Modern History*, 75 (4), December 2003. On the difficulties of calculating the number of female Masons, p. 803.

J. Snoek, *Initiating Women in Freemasonry: The Adoption Rite*, Leiden, 2012.

J. Snoek, 'The Adoption Rite, its Origins, Opening up for Women, and its "Craft" Rituals', *REHMLAC: Revista de Estudios Históricos de la Masonería Latinoamericana y Caribeña*, 4 (2), December 2012 to April 2013.

W.R.H. Trowbridge, *The Splendour and Misery of a Master of Magic*, London, 1910. On Cagliostro's initiation, pp. 111ff.

R. Van Dülmen, *The Society of the Enlightenment: The Rise of the Middle Class and Enlightenment Culture in Germany*, Cambridge, 1992. Sixty-four of the 454 members clergymen or theologians, p. 109. 'Princes and nations shall disappear', quoted p. 113.

J. Van Horn Melton, *The Rise of the Public in Enlightenment Europe*, Cambridge, 2001.

R.W. Weisberger, *Speculative Freemasonry and the Enlightenment: A study of the Craft in London, Paris, Prague, and Vienna*, New York, 1993.

R.A. Wells, *The Rise and Development of Organised Freemasonry*, London, 1986.

W.D. Wilson, 'Weimar Politics in the Age of the French Revolution: Goethe and the Spectre of Illuminati Conspiracy', *Goethe Yearbook*, 5, 1990.

G.S. Wood, 'Conspiracy and the Paranoid Style: Causality and Deceit in the Eighteenth Century', *The William and Mary Quarterly*, 39 (3), 1982.

https://vigilantcitizen.com/ 'Symbols Rule the World', consulted 4 August 2019.

Chapter 6: Naples: A Raving Sickness

J.-C. Bésuchet de Saunois, *Précis historique de l'ordre de la franc-maçonnerie: depuis son introduction en France jusqu'en 1829*, Paris, 1829, vol. 2. 'Perhaps never was an Adoption Lodge', p. 153.

J.H. Billington, *Fire in the Minds of Men: Origins of the Revolutionary Faith*, London, 1980. 'The modern revolutionary tradition', p. 87.

D. Bocchini, 'Breve storia filosoficha delle sette del Regno di Napoli', in Archivio di Stato di Napoli, Archivio Tommasi, busta XI. Now reproduced in Gin, *L'aquila, il giglio e il compasso*. Twenty-three thousand Trinitarians, p. 204.

M.A. Caffio, *Il gioco delle appartenenze. Strategie associative e pratiche del potere in Terra d'Otranto (1760–1821)*, Bari, 2007.

A. Capece Minutolo (Duke of Canosa), *Abbozzo riservato di un piano politico-morale onde neutralizzare il Sistema massonico, paralizzarne i progressi e farlo divenire utile ai sovrani, alla religione cattolica ed ai stati*, in Carte Canosa, Archivio di Stato di Napoli, Archivio Borbone, vol. 729, 'Memorie ed opuscoli antirivoluzionari ed anti liberali (1797–1832)'.

'Career', entry in *The New Shorter Oxford English Dictionary*, Oxford, 1993.

C. Cassani, 'De Attellis, Orazio', in *Dizionario Biografico degli Italiani*, vol. 33, 1987.

N. Castagna, *La sollevazione d'Abruzzo nell'anno 1814*, Rome, 1884.

G.M. Cazzaniga, 'Origini ed evoluzioni dei rituali carbonari italiani', in Cazzaniga (ed.), *Storia d'Italia. Annali, 21. La Massoneria*, Turin, 2006.

E.M. Church, *Chapters in an Adventurous Life: Sir Richard Church in Italy and Greece*, London, 1895.

Z. Ciuffoletti, 'La Massoneria napoleonica in Italia', in Z. Ciuffoletti and S. Moravia, *La Massoneria. La storia, gli uomini, le idee*, 2nd edn, Milan, 2016.

F. Collaveri, *La franc-maçonnerie des Bonaparte*, Paris, 1982.

P. Colletta, *Storia del Reame di Napoli dal 1734 al 1823*, tomo III, Capolago, 1834. Murat's entry into Naples 1808, p. 93. 'Aim at the heart. Spare my face', p. 53. 'If the accused are Charcoal-Burners', pp. 63–4.

F. Conti, 'La Massoneria e la costruzione della nazione italiana dal Risorgimento al fascismo', in Z. Ciuffoletti and S. Moravia, *La Massoneria. La storia, gli uomini, le idee*, 2nd edn, Milan, 2016.

N. Cortese, 'Le prima condanne murattiane della Carboneria', *Archivio Storico per le Province Napoletane*, 34, 1955. 'Cultivating democratic principles', quoted p. 234. 'These clandestine unions use brotherly love', quoted p. 306.

N. Cortese, 'Il Murat e la Carboneria napoletana nella prima metà del 1814', *Studi Storici in onore di Gioacchino Volpe*, vol. 1, Florence, 1958.

J.A. Davis, *Naples and Napoleon: Southern Italy and the European Revolutions (1780–1860)*, Oxford, 2006.

M. Dayet, 'Pierre-Joseph Briot. Lucien Bonaparte et les Carbonari', *Annales Historiques de la Révolution Française*, 1, 1953.

A. De Francesco, *Vincenzo Cuoco. Una vita politica*, Rome/Bari, 1997. Caroline Bonaparte believed Maghella was behind the creation of the *Carbonari*, p. 115.

A. De Francesco, 'La Carboneria in Sicilia: notabilato politico o politica notabilare', in G. Berti and F. Della Peruta (eds), *La Carboneria. Intrecci veneti, nazionali e internazionali*, Rovigo, 2004.

C. De Nicola, *Diario napoletano dal 1799 al 1825*, Archivio Storico per le Province Napoletane, 1903.

J. Dickie, *Cosa Nostra: A History of the Sicilian Mafia*, London, 2003. 'An intangible sect whose organization', quoted p. 69.

O. Dito, *Massoneria, Carboneria e altre società segrete nella storia del Risorgimento italiano*, Turin/Rome, 1905.

J.-P. Garnier, *Murat. Roi de Naples*, Paris, 1959.

F. Giampietri, 'Rapporti Giampietri al Re', Archivio di Stato di Napoli, Ministero di Grazia e Giustizia, busta 2083. 'Rapporti su carbonari fra popolani e carcerati, e massoni', ibid., busta 2080. 'Men hardened by the path of crime', Giampietri to King, 8 June 1818 in busta 2083.

J.-C. Gillet, *Murat 1767–1815*, Paris, 2008.

E. Gin, *Sanfedisti, Carbonari, Magistrati del Re. Il Regno delle Due Sicilie tra Restaurazione e Rivoluzione*, Naples, 2003. 'Ready to plunge itself into anarchic horrors', quoted p. 53.

E. Gin, *L'aquila, il giglio e il compasso. Profili di lotta politica ed associazionismo settario nelle Due Sicilie (1806–1821)*, Salerno, 2007. 'I tell you again, Sire', quoted p. 67. Murat contemplated simply killing the leadership, p. 75.

V. Haegele, *Murat. La solitude du cavalier*, Paris, 2015.

Y. Hivert-Messeca, *L'Europe sous l'Acacia. Histoire des franc-maçonneries européennes du XVIIIe siècle à nos* jours, 2 *Le XIXe* siècle, Paris, 2014.

R. Lansdown, 'Byron and the Carbonari', *History Today*, vol. 41, 1991. 'The C[arbonari] seem to have no plan', quoted p. 24.

D. Laven and R. Riall (eds), *Napoleon's Legacy: Problems of Government in Restoration Europe*, Oxford, 2000.

F.M. Lo Faro, 'Maghella, Antonio', *Dizionario biografico degli Italiani*, vol. 67, Rome, 2006. For descriptions of Maghella as 'shadowy' and 'enigmatic' see *passim*.

A. Lucarelli, *Il brigantaggio politico del Mezzogiorno d'Italia*, Bari, 1942. 'A raving sickness', quoted p. 153. Descriptions of Ciro Annicchiarico, quoted p. 107. Six thousand Cauldron-Beaters in 1815, p. 24.

B. Marcolongo, 'Le origini della Carboneria e le Società segrete nell'Italia Meridionale dal 1810 al 1820', *Studi Storici*, Pavia, vol. XX, nuova serie vol. II, Pavia, 1911–12.

G. Masi, 'Federici, Vincenzo, detto Capobianco', in *Dizionario biografico degli Italiani*, vol. 45, Rome, 1995.

F. Mastroberti, *Pierre Joseph Briot. Un giacobino tra amministrazione e politica (1771–1827)*, Naples, 1998.

W. Maturi, *Il principe di Canosa*, Florence, 1944. 'By the different sects and by perverse philosophy', quoted p. 3.

C. Porset and C. Révauger (eds), *Le Monde maçonnique des Lumières*, vol. 1, Paris, 2013. On Josephine and Masonry, pp. 289–93.

A. Postigliola, 'Capece Minutolo, Antonio, principe di Canosa', *Dizionario Biografico degli Italiani*, vol. 18, Rome, 1975.

A.M. Rao, 'La massoneria nel Regno di Napoli', in Cazzaniga (ed.), *Storia d'Italia. Annali, 21. La Massoneria*, Turin, 2006.

R.J. Rath, 'The Carbonari: Their Origins, Initiation Rites, and Aims', *The American Historical Review*, 69 (2), 1964; for estimate of numbers of Carbonari at the peak.

G. Rota, 'Società politica e rivoluzione nel Mezzogiorno: la Carboneria palermitana, 1820–22', *Rivista Italiana di Studi Napoleonici*, 1991.

A. Scirocco, *L'Italia del Risorgimento*, Bologna, 1990.

J. Smyth, 'Freemasonry and the United Irishmen', in *The United Irishmen: Republicanism, Radicalism and Rebellion*, D. Dickson et al. (eds), Dublin, 1993.

R. Sòriga, 'Gli inizi della Carboneria in Italia secondo un rapporto segreto del Generale Giuseppe Rossetti', in *Le società segrete, l'emigrazione politica e i primi moti per l'indipendenza*, Modena, 1942.

R. Sòriga, 'Le società segrete e i moti del 1820 a Napoli', in *Le società segrete, l'emigrazione politica e i primi moti per l'indipendenza*, Modena, 1942.

J. Tulard, *Murat. Ou l'éveil des nations*, Paris, 1983.

A. Valente, *Gioacchino Murat e l'Italia meridionale*, Turin, 1965.

A. Zazo, 'Il principe Canosa e le sette nel Regno di Napoli (1815–1818)', *Samnium*, VIII, 3–4, 1935.

Chapter 7: Washington: A Lodge for the Virtues

C.L. Albanese, *Sons of the Fathers: The Civil Religion of the American Revolution*, Philadelphia, PA, 1976.

A. Allyn, *Ritual of Freemasonry*, Philadelphia, PA, 1831. Version of Royal Arch ceremony, pp. 127–8.

Anon., *An account of the reception of General Lafayette in Savannah*, Savannah, GA, 1825.

G.J. Baldasty, 'The New York State Political Press and Antimasonry', *New York History*, 64 (3), 1983. By the end of 1827, there were twenty-two anti-Masonic papers in New York State; p. 266.

D. Bernard, *Light on Masonry*, Utica, NY, 1829. Version of Royal Arch ceremony, p. 130. 'I do promise and swear ... that I will promote a companion R[oyal] A[rch] Mason's political preferment', ibid.

Book of Mormon, https://www.churchofjesuschrist.org/study/scriptures/bofm/, consulted 15 November 2017. 'And it came to pass that [the Gadianton robbers] did have their signs', The Book of Helaman, ch. 6, verses 22 and 24. 'Fill the judgment-seats–having usurped the power and authority of the land', The Book of Helaman, ch. 7, verse 4. 'A lamb-skin about their loins', 3 Nephi, ch. 4, verse 7.

K.R. Bowling, *The Creation of Washington, DC: The Idea and Location of the American Capital*, Fairfax, VA, 1991.

F.M. Brodie, *No Man Knows My History: The Life of Joseph Smith*, 2nd edn, New York, 1995. Two thousand repetitions of 'it came to pass', p. 63. Number of Smith's wives, pp. 334–47. 'Is there no help for the widow's son?', reported pp. 393–4.

J.L. Brooke, *The Refiner's Fire: The Making of Mormon Cosmology, 1644–1844*, Cambridge, 1996. On the Smith family's Masonic connections, and other links to his early followers, see pp. 140–4 and pp. 157–9. On Masonic and other influences on the portrayal of Gadianton bands, pp. 149–83.

H. Brown, *A Narrative of the anti-Masonick Excitement*, Batavia, NY, 1829. 'The masons arrayed in robes of royalty', quoted p. 151.

S.M. Brown, *In Heaven as it is on Earth: Joseph Smith and the Early Mormon Conquest of Death*, Oxford, 2012. On Smith's marriage to Morgan's widow, p. 11.

D.J. Buerger, 'The Development of the Mormon Temple Endowment Ceremony', *Dialogue: A Journal of Mormon Thought*, 20 (4), 1987. On Masonic ceremonies as a copy of those of the Mormons', p. 92.

S.C. Bullock, *Revolutionary Brotherhood: Freemasonry and the Transformation of the American Social Order, 1730–1840*, Chapel Hill, NC, 1996. A fundamental study I have drawn on heavily in this chapter. 'The first temple dedicated to the sovereignty', quoted pp. 137–8. There were more Lodges in America than there had been in the whole of the rest of the world, p. 138. Figures on the expansion of Masonry in New York State before 1825, pp. 187–8.

R.L. Bushman, *Joseph Smith: Rough Stone Rolling*, New York, 2006.

E. Bussiere, 'Trial by Jury as "Mockery of Justice": Party Contention, Courtroom Corruption, and the Ironic Judicial Legacy of Antimasonry', *Law and History Review*, 34 (1), 2016.

J.A. Carroll and M.W. Ashworth, *George Washington*, vol. VII, *First in Peace*, London, 1957. GW's funeral, pp. 627–31.

J.J. Ellis, *His Excellency George Washington*, New York, 2004. For GW's religious beliefs, p. 45.

R.P. Formisano and K. Smith Kutolowski, 'Antimasonry and Masonry: The Genesis of Protest, 1826–1827', *American Quarterly*, 29 (2), 1977.

K.W. Godfrey, 'Joseph Smith and the Masons', *Journal of the Illinois State Historical Society*, 64 (1), 1971. By 1843 more Mormon than non-Mormon Masons, p. 89.

P. Goodman, *Towards a Christian Republic: Antimasonry and the Great Transition in New England, 1826–1836*, Oxford, 1988. On the religious roots of anti-Masonry, pp. 54–79. On the evolution of anti-Masonic politics, pp. 105–19.

D.G. Hackett, *That Religion in which All Men Agree: Freemasonry in American Culture*, Berkeley, CA, 2014. A key study I have drawn on repeatedly here. Forty-two per cent of GW's generals, p. 287. In the first quarter of the nineteenth century, membership more than tripled, p. 72.

C.M. Harris, 'Washington's Gamble, L'Enfant's Dream: Politics, Design, and the Founding of the National Capital', *The William and Mary Quarterly*, 56 (3), 1999.

S. Hayden, *Washington and His Masonic Compeers*, New York, 1869. 'See WASHINGTON, he leads the train', quoted p. 51. 'With unspeakable pleasure we gratulate you', quoted p. 132. 'The fabric of our freedom is placed', p. 135. 'A sanctuary for brothers, and a lodge for the virtues', quoted p. 165. GW's funeral, pp. 197–208.

M.W. Homer, *Joseph's Temples: The Dynamic Relationship between Freemasonry and Mormonism*, Salt Lake City, UT, 2014.

H.B. Hopkins, *Renunciation of Freemasonry*, Boston, MA, 1830. 'Supported by all the wisest and best of men in every age', and on Hopkins' Royal Arch exaltation, pp. 5–8.

G.E. Kahler, *The Long Farewell: Americans Mourn the Death of George Washington*, Charlottesville, VA, 2008. 'Genius of Masonry', pp. 86–104.

O. Lohrenz, 'Thomas Davis, Jr.: Officiating Clergyman at the Funeral and Burial of President George Washington', *Anglican and Episcopal History*, 73 (2), 2004.

P.K. Longmore, 'The Enigma of George Washington: How Did the Man Become the Myth?', *Reviews in American History*, June 1985.

P.K. Longmore, *The Invention of George Washington*, Berkeley, CA, 1988.

W.D. Moore and J.D. Hamilton, 'Washington as the Master of his Lodge: History and Symbolism of a Masonic Icon', in B.J. Mitnick (ed.), *George Washington: American Symbol*, New York, 1999.

S.P. Newman, *Parades and the Politics of the Street: Festive Culture in the Early American Republic*, Philadelphia, PA, 1997.

B.E. Park, 'Joseph Smith's Kingdom of God: The Council of Fifty and the Mormon Challenge to American Democratic Politics', *Church History*, 87 (4), 2018. 'That this honorable assembly receive from this time henceforth', quoted p. 1048.

D. Persuitte, *Joseph Smith and the Origins of the Book of Mormon*, Jefferson, NC, 2000. For borrowings from the Morgan affair, pp. 192–8.

J.H. Pratt, *An authentic account of all the proceedings on the fourth of July, 1815, with regard to laying the corner stone of Washington monument*, Baltimore, MD, 1815. 'Honourable sir, on behalf of the free and accepted masons', p. 15.

S. Pruitt, 'Contents of Boston Time Capsule Buried by Samuel Adams and Paul Revere Unveiled', 7 January 2015, http://www.history.com/news/contents-of-boston-time-capsule-buried-by-samuel-adams-and-paul-revere-unveiled, consulted 7 August 2017.

S.J. Purcell, *Sealed with Blood: War, Sacrifice, and Memory in Revolutionary America*, Philadelphia, PA, 2002. On Lafayette's tour, pp. 171–209.

E.L. Queen II, et al. (eds), *The Encyclopedia of American Religious History*, Boston, 2009. Entry on Church of LDS, pp. 127–8, includes figure of 16 million members.

D.M. Quinn, *Early Mormonism and the Magic World View*, Salt Lake City, UT, 1998.

C. Raible, '"The threat of being Morganized will not deter us": William Lyon MacKenzie, Freemasonry, and the Morgan Affair', *Ontario History*, Spring 2008. 'To be executed with savage cruelty', quoted p. 18.

K.L. Riley, *Lockport: Historic Jewel of the Erie Canal*, Charleston, SC, 2005. On the ceremony at the locks, p. 46.

K. Smith Kutolowski, 'Freemasonry and Community in the Early Republic: The Case for Antimasonic Anxieties', *American Quarterly*, 34 (5), 1982.

K. Smith Kutolowski, 'Antimasonry Reexamined: Social Bases of the Grass-Roots Party', *The Journal of American History*, 71 (2), 1984.

K. Smith Kutolowski, 'Freemasonry revisited: Another look at the grassroots bases of antimasonic anxieties', in R.W. Weisberger et al. (eds), *Freemasonry on Both Sides of the Atlantic*, New York, 2002. On the social and religious profile of Masons in Genesee County, pp. 589–92.

F. Somkin, *Unquiet Eagle: Memory and Desire in the Idea of American Freedom, 1815–1860*, Ithaca, NY, 1967. On Lafayette's tour, pp. 131–74.

H.G. Spafford, *A Gazetteer of the State of New York*, Albany, NY, 1824. 'American Mediterranea', p. 102.

W.L. Stone, *Letters on Masonry and Anti-Masonry*, New York, 1832. The most important contemporary account. 'Morgan is considered a swindler', quoted p. 133. 'Two swivels, fifteen or twenty guns, and several pistols', p. 153. Judge Enos T. Throop's remarks, p. 201. 'Mountebank Anti-masonic professors of Masonry', p. 294. 'As well might they think of establishing Mahometanism', p. 563. All but two convicted were Royal Arch Masons, p. 414.

L. Travers, '"In the greatest solemn dignity": the Capitol cornerstone and ceremony in the early Republic', in D.R. Kennon (ed.), *A Republic for the Ages: The United States Capitol and the Political Culture of the Early Republic*, Charlottesville, VA, 1999. The best account of the ceremony.

M. Twain, *Roughing It*, Hartford, CT, 1873. His account of Mormonism, pp. 127–35. 'Chloroform in print', p. 127.

W.P. Vaughn, *The Antimasonic Party in the United States, 1826–1843*, Lexington, KY, 1983. 'There is blood upon the order of Masonry', and for religious anti-Masonry, pp. 14–24. On collapse in Masonic membership, p. 52 and *passim*.

D. Vogel, 'Mormonism's "Anti-Masonick Bible"', *The John Whitmer Historical Association Journal*, vol. 9, 1989.

Watch Tower, Cooperstown, NY. For anti-Masonic newspaper coverage of the Morgan affair. 'A profanation and a mockery of sacred and holy ordinances', article on Anti-Masonic convention held in Cooperstown in county of Otsego, 14 July 1828. 'The hand of an overruling Providence', 29 October 1927.

T.S. Webb, *The Freemason's Monitor; or, Illustrations of Masonry*, Salem, MA, 1818. 'Indescribably more august, sublime, and important', p. 127.

G.S. Wood, *The Creation of the American Republic, 1776–1787*, New York, 1993 (1969).

G.S. Wood, *Empire of Liberty: A History of the Early Republic, 1789–1815*, Oxford, 2009.

See http://www.mormonthink.com/temple.htm#didthemasons, consulted 16 November 2017, for a detailed table of parallels between Mormonism and Masonry, and changes made in 1990 to the Temple ceremony.

Chapter 8: Charleston: Africans were the Authors of this Mysterious and Beautiful Order

T. Adeleke, 'Martin R. Delany's Philosophy of Education: A Neglected Aspect of African American Liberation Thought', *The Journal of Negro Education*, 63 (2), 1994.

T. Adeleke, 'Race and Ethnicity in Martin R. Delany's Struggle', *Journal of Thought*, 29 (1), 1994.

T. Adeleke, '"Much learning makes men mad": Classical Education and Black Empowerment in Martin R. Delany's Philosophy of Education', *Journal of Thought*, 49 (1–2), 2015.

K. Allerfeldt, 'Murderous Mumbo-Jumbo: The Significance of Fraternity to Three Criminal Organizations in Late Nineteenth-Century America', *Journal of American Studies*, 50 (4), 2016.

T. Anbinder, *Nativism and Slavery: The Northern Know Nothings and the Politics of the 1850's*, New York, 1992.

N.L. Bailey, et al. (eds), *Biographical Directory of the South Carolina Senate, 1776–1985*, Columbia, SC, 1986, vol. I. Entry on Gleaves.

R. Blackett, 'In Search of International Support for African Colonization: Martin R. Delany's Visit to England, 1860', *Canadian Journal of History/Annales Canadiennes d'Histoire*, 10 (3), 1975.

W.L. Brown, *A Life of Albert Pike*, Fayetteville, AR, 1997.

The Builder, December 1922, reproduced at http://www.masonicdictionary.com/mackey.html, consulted 29 April 2018. On Mackey: 'he made enemies', 'he did not forgive'.

M.C. Carnes, *Secret Ritual and Manhood in Victorian America*, New Haven, CT, 1989.

G.M. Cazzaniga, 'Nascita del Grande Oriente d'Italia', in G.M. Cazzaniga (ed.), *Storia d'Italia. Annali, 21. La Massoneria*, Turin, 2006.

M.R. Delany, *The Condition, Elevation, Emigration, and Destiny of the Colored People of the United States* (1852), New York, 1968.

M.R. Delany, *The Origin and Objects of Ancient Freemasonry: Its Introduction into the United States, and Legitimacy among Colored Men: A Treatise Delivered Before St. Cyprian Lodge No. 13 June 24th AD 1853–AL 5853*, in R.S. Levine, *Martin R. Delany: A Documentary Reader*, Chapel Hill, NC, 2003. 'Africans were the authors of this mysterious', p. 55. 'Learned in all the wisdom of the Egyptians', p. 53. 'All men, of every country, clime, color and condition', p. 57. 'Will it be denied that the man who appeared before Pharaoh', p. 64.

M.R. Delany, *Blake; or, The Huts of America* (ed. J. McGann), Cambridge, MA, 2017 (1861–2).

P.L. Dunbar, 'Hidden in Plain Sight: African American Secret Societies and Black Freemasonry', *Journal of African American Studies*, 16 (4), 2012.

R.L. Duncan, *Reluctant General: The Life and Times of Albert Pike*, New York, 1961.

L.F. Emilio, *A Brave Black Regiment: The History of the 54th Massachusetts, 1863–1865*, Boston, MA, 1894. For an account of the Lodge meeting after the attack on Fort Wagner, pp. 129, 313. 'The first colored regiment organized in the North', quoted p. xi. 'Fort Wagner became a mound of fire', p. 80. 'You must remember you have not proved yourselves soldiers', quoted p. 130. Description of Montgomery, p. 40.

M.W. Fitzgerald, *Splendid Failure: Postwar Reconstruction in the American South*, Chicago, 2007.

E. Foner, *Reconstruction: America's Unfinished Revolution, 1863–1877*, New York, 1988. 'A mass of black barbarism', from J.S. Pike, *The Prostrate State*, quoted p. 525.

E. Foner, 'South Carolina's black elected officials during Reconstruction', in J.L. Underwood and W.L. Burke Jr (eds), *At Freedom's Door: African American Founding Fathers and Lawyers in Reconstruction South Carolina*, Columbia, SC, 2000.

W.L. Fox, *Lodge of the Double-Headed Eagle: Two Centuries of Scottish Rite Freemasonry in America's Southern Jurisdiction*, Fayetteville, AR, 1997. On Northern and Southern Jurisdictions of the Scottish Rite, pp. 30–1. On the Masonic affiliation of officers at Fort Sumter, p. 70. 'We mean that the white race, and that race alone, shall govern', quoted p. 439. On Pike and KKK, pp. 81–3. Pike's move to Washington DC, pp. 99–103.

R. Freke Gould, *A Concise History of Freemasonry*, London, 1904. For Port-au-Prince, p. 507, and for the spread of the Scottish Rite around the world, *passim*.

P. Gilroy, *The Black Atlantic: Modernity and Double Consciousness*, Cambridge, MA, 1993.

C.E. Griffith, *The African Dream: Martin R. Delany and the Emergence of Pan-African Thought*, University Park, PA, 1975.

R.B. Harris, *Eleven Gentlemen of Charleston: Founders of the Supreme Council,*

Mother Council of the World, Ancient and Accepted Scottish Rite Freemasonry, Washington DC, 1959.

W.C. Hine, 'Black Politicians in Reconstruction Charleston, South Carolina: A Collective Study', *Journal of Southern History*, 49 (4), 1983.

T. Holt, *Black over White: Negro Political Leadership in South Carolina during Reconstruction*, Urbana, IL, 1977. On Mackey's job as Collector of the Port, pp. 117–18.

W.L. Jenkins, *Seizing the New Day: African Americans in Post-Civil War Charleston*, Bloomington, IN, 1998. On Delany's role in establishing calm after Lincoln's assassination, p. 40.

R.M. Kahn, 'The Political Ideology of Martin Delany', *Journal of Black Studies*, 14 (4), 1984.

S. Kantrowitz, '"Intended for the better government of man": The Political History of African American Freemasonry in the Era of Emancipation', *The Journal of American History*, 96 (4), 2010.

S. Kantrowitz, *More than Freedom: Fighting for Black Citizenship in a White Republic, 1829–1889*, New York, 2012. On Gleaves and the National Grand Lodge, pp. 376–82.

S. Kantrowitz, 'Brotherhood denied: black freemasonry and the limits of reconstruction', in P. Hinks and S. Kantrowitz (eds), *All Men Free and Brethren: Essays on the History of Africa American Freemasonry*, Ithaca, NY, 2013. On accusations against Gleaves, pp. 1019–20.

S. Kaplan and E. Nogrady Kaplan, *The Black Presence in the Era of the American Revolution*, revised edn, Amherst, MA, 1989. For a biography of Prince Hall, pp. 202–14. 'In the Bowels of a free & Christian country', quoted p. 202. 'They are *ashamed* of being on *equality* with blacks', quoted p. 212. 'Enjoins upon us to be peaceable subjects', quoted p. 205.

A.M. Kass, 'Dr Thomas Hodgkin, Dr Martin Delany, and the "return to Africa"', *Medical History*, 27, 1983.

E.J. Kytle, 'African dreams, American realities: Martin Robison Delany and the emigration question', in *Romantic Reformers and the Antislavery Struggle in the Civil War Era*, New York, 2014.

P.D. Lack, 'An Urban Slave Community: Little Rock, 1831–1862', *The Arkansas Historical Quarterly*, 41 (3), 1982.

R.S. Levine, *Martin Delany, Frederick Douglass, and the Politics of Representative Identity*, Chapel Hill, NC, 1997.

R.S. Levine, *Martin R. Delany: A Documentary Reader*, Chapel Hill, NC, 2003. 'Near-mystical sense of his potential as a black leader', p. 9.

D. Ligou, *Histoire des francs-maçons en France*, vol. 1, 1725–1815, Toulouse, 2000. On de Grasse-Tilly, pp. 230–2.

A. Mackey, *The Principles of Masonic Law: A Treatise on the Constitutional Laws, Usages and Landmarks of Freemasonry*, New York, 1856. 'The slave, or even the man born in servitude', ch. I: 'Of the Qualifications of Candidates'.

A. Mackey, *The Voice of Masonry*, Debate on 'The Color Question', moderated by Mackey, January–June 1876. 'Masonry recognizes no distinction', 'Here then, I rest my case, and bid adieu', June 1876, pp. 424–5.

A. Mackey, An *Encyclopedia of Freemasonry and Its Kindred Sciences: Comprising* the Whole Range of Arts, Sciences and Literature as Connected with the Institution, new and revised edn, Philadelphia, PA, 1884.

The News and Herald, Winnsboro, SC, 'In the toils', 11 June 1877. Among many newspapers that cover the Gleaves trial.

[A. Pike], *Thoughts on Certain Political Questions by A Looker On*, Washington, DC, 1859. 'The negro in his best condition', pp. 31–2.

A. Pike, 'The Ku-Klux Klan', *Memphis Daily Appeal*, 16 April 1868.

A. Pike, *Morals and dogma of the Ancient and accepted Scottish rite of freemasonry: Prepared for the Supreme council of the thirty-third degree, for the Southern jurisdiction of the United States, and published by its authority*, Charleston, SC, 1871. 'The important manifestations of Occultism coincide', p. 823.

[A. Pike], *Liturgy of the Ancient and Accepted Scottish Rite of Freemasonry for the Southern Jurisdiction of the United States*, part IV, Charleston, SC, 1878. 'Whatever is worth doing at all in this world, is worth doing *well*', p. 247. 'To be true, just, and upright is the basis of all virtue', p. 243. Knight Kadosh Degree ending in 'No Apron is worn', p. 231.

A. Pike, *Foulhouzeism and Cerneauism scourged: dissection of a manifesto*, New York, 1884.

A. Pike, *Indo-Aryan Deities and Worship as Contained in the Rig Veda* (1872), Washington DC, 1930.

J. Porter, *Native American Freemasonry: Associationalism and Performance in America*, Lincoln, NE, 2011. On similarities between Masonry and Native-American belief systems, pp. 140–52. 'At the vanguard of a historical movement that was preordained', p. 179.

B.E. Powers Jr, *Black Charlestonians: A Social History, 1822–1885*, Fayetteville, AR, 1994. Fifty-fourth Regiment paid in the Citadel and establishing school, p. 139. Delany's medical practice, p. 171.

L. Reece, 'Righteous lives: a comparative study of the South Carolina scalawag leadership during Reconstruction', in M.B. Bonner and F. Hamer (eds), *Southern Carolina in the Civil War and Reconstruction Eras*, Columbia, SC, 2016.

F.A. Rollin, *The Life and Public Services of Martin R. Delany*, Boston, 1883. 'I entered the city, which, from earliest childhood', quoted pp. 197–8.

A.G. Roundtree and P.M. Bessel, *Out of the Shadows: The Emergence of Prince Hall Freemasonry in America – Over 225 Years of Endurance*, Camp Springs, MD, 2006.

A.G. Roundtree, 'Richard Howell Gleaves', *The Phylaxis*, XLV (1), 2018.

H. Rubin III, *South Carolina Scalawags*, Columbia, SC, 2006. On 'negro assembly' and Mackey as a money-grubbing, drunken fraud, pp. 26–30.

T. Shelby, 'Two Conceptions of Black Nationalism: Martin Delany on the Meaning of Black Political Solidarity', *Political Theory*, 31 (5), 2003.

T.D. Smith, 'Indian territory and Oklahoma', in F.E. Hoxie (ed.), *The Oxford Handbook of American Indian History*, Oxford, 2016.

D. Sterling, *The Making of an Afro-American: Martin Robison Delany – African Explorer, Civil War Major, & Father of Black Nationalism*, New York, 1971. 'The Moral Elevation of the Africo-American', p. 81. 'Damned nigger Democrat', quoted p. 312.

W.H. Upton, *Negro Masonry: Being a Critical Examination of Objections to the*

Legitimacy of the Masonry Existing Among the Negroes of America, Cambridge, MA, 1902. Pike's views on 'negro Masonry' from 1875 quoted, pp. 214–15.

W.C. Wade, *The Fiery Cross: The Ku Klux Klan in America*, New York, 1987. On Pike as nominally KKK commander in Arkansas, p. 58.

C.D.B. Walker, *A Noble Fight: African American Freemasonry and the Struggle for Democracy in America*, Chicago, IL, 2008. For *Blake* and the influence of the Masonic model on it, pp. 107–15.

J.A. Walkes Jr, *Black Square and Compass: 200 Years of Prince Hall Freemasonry*, privately published, 1979. For Vogelsang biography, pp. 46–9.

M.O. Wallace, '"Are we men?": Prince Hall, Martin Delany, and the black masculine ideal in black Freemasonry, 1775–1865', in *Constructing the Black Masculine: Identity and Ideality in African American Men's Literature and Culture, 1775–1995*, Durham, NC, 2002.

C.H. Wesley, *The History of the Prince Hall Grand Lodge of the State of Ohio 1849 to 1971*, Columbus, OH, 1972.

Chapter 9: Rome–Paris: The Devil in the Nineteenth Century

J. Bernauer and R.A. Maryks (eds), *'The Tragic Couple': Encounters Between Jews and Jesuits*, Leiden/Boston, 2014.

M. Borutta, 'Anti-Catholicism and the culture war in Risorgimento Italy', in S. Patriarca and L. Riall (eds), *The Risorgimento Revisited: Nationalism and Culture in Nineteenth-Century Italy*, Basingstoke/New York, 2012.

A. Bresciani, *Della Repubblica Romana. Appendice a L'Ebreo di Verona*, 2 vols, Milan, 1855.

A. Bresciani, *L'Ebreo di Verona*, 2 vols, Naples, 1861. 'The pandemonium of the secret societies', vol. 1, p. 74. Death of Babette d'Interlaken, vol. 2, p. 52. 'In his perfidious church', vol. 1, p. 84.

A. Bresciani, *Lionello*, 3 vols, Milan, 1877.

The Catholic Times and Catholic Opinion, 'Leo Taxil interviewed', 31 July 1885. 'Supernatural change of heart', p. 5.

La Civiltà Cattolica, Rome. 'Le logge israelitiche segrete pienamente illustrate', 1896: 'It would be a credit to the most erudite historian', p. 160. 'Le mopse. Origini, riti, gradi, educazione rituale', 1896: Diana as instrument of providence, p. 684. Denying having fallen for the hoax and the Pope's 'great serenity', 'Cronaca', 8 May 1897, pp. 30ff.

C. Clark and W. Kaiser (eds), *Culture Wars: Secular-Catholic Conflict in Nineteenth-Century Europe*, Cambridge, 2004.

F. Conti, *Storia della massoneria italiana: dal Risorgimento al fascismo*, Bologna, 2003. 'Priestly pox', Adriano Lemmi quoted, p. 143.

F. Conti, 'Massoneria e sfera pubblica nell'Italia liberale, 1859–1914', in Cazzaniga (ed.), *Storia d'Italia. Annali, 21. La Massoneria*, Turin, 2006.

J. Dickie, 'Antonio Bresciani and the Sects: Conspiracy Myths in an Intransigent Catholic Response to the Risorgimento', *Modern Italy*, 22 (1), 2017.

R. Gildea, *Children of the Revolution: The French, 1799–1914*, London, 2008.

The Glasgow Herald, 26 July 1870, 'The storm, to many a superstitious mind'.

Humanum genus. Text consulted on 25 November 2019 at http://www.vatican.va/content/leo-xiii/en/encyclicals/documents/hf_l-xiii_enc_18840420_humanum-genus.html.

A. Halpern, 'Freemasonry and Party Building in Late Nineteenth-Century France', *Modern & Contemporary France*,' 10 (2), 2002.

D. Harvey, 'Lucifer in the City of Light: The Palladium Hoax and "Diabolical Causality" in Fin de Siècle France'. *Magic, Ritual, and Witchcraft*, 1, 2008.

M. Jarrige, *L'Église et les Francs-maçons dans la tourmente. Croisade de la revue La Franc-maçonnerie démasquée*, Paris, 1999.

W.R.A. Jones, 'Palladism and the Papacy: an Episode of French Anticlericalism in the Nineteenth Century', *Journal of Church and State*, 12 (3), 1970.

D. Kertzer, 'Religion and society, 1789–1892', in J.A. Davis (ed.), *Italy in the Nineteenth Century*, Oxford, 2000.

D. Kertzer, *Prisoner of the Vatican: The Popes' Secret Plot to Capture Rome from the New Italian State*, Boston, MA, 2004.

H.-C. Lea, *Léo Taxil, Diana Vaughan et L'église romaine. Histoire d'une mystification*, Paris, 1901.

O. Logan, 'A journal. *La Civiltà Cattolica* from Pius IX to Pius XII (1850–1958)', in R.N. Swanson (ed.), *The Church and the Book*, Woodbridge, 2004 (Studies in Church History 38).

G. Miccoli, 'Leo XIII e la massoneria', in G.M. Cazzaniga (ed.), *Storia d'Italia. Annali, 21. La Massoneria*, Turin, 2006. On Taxil and Vaughan supposedly being murdered before press conference, p. 236.

A. Mola, 'Muratori del Belpaese', in *Storia e Dossier*, August 1994. Numbers of Italian Lodges, p. 94.

P. Nord, *The Republican Moment: Struggles for Democracy in 19th-Century France*, Cambridge, MA, 1995. Some 40 per cent of civilian ministers of the Third Republic were on the Square, pp. 15–30.

A. Pike, *A Reply for the Ancient and Accepted Scottish Rite of Free-Masonry to the Letter 'Humanum Genus' of Pope Leo XIII*, Charleston, SC, 1884. 'A declaration of war against the human race', p. 28.

J.F. Pollard, *Money and the Rise of the Modern Papacy: Financing the Vatican, 1850–1950*, Cambridge, 2005.

J.F. Pollard, *Catholicism in Modern Italy: Religion, Society and Politics since 1861*, London, 2008.

T. Rouault, *Léo Taxil et la Franc Maçonnerie satanique: analyse d'une mystification littéraire*, Rosières-en-Haye, 2011. Reproduces newspaper reports of final press conference in Taxil story, which I have drawn on for my account.

La Semaine religieuse du diocèse de Rouen, 15 March 1887.

Syllabus of Errors, text consulted on 25 November 2019 at http://www.papalencyclicals.net/pius09/p9syll.htm.

L. Taxil, *La chasse aux corbeaux*, Paris, 1879. A collection of his journalism.

L. Taxil, *Les soutanes grotesques*, Paris, 1879.

L. Taxil, *Le Fils du Jésuite, précédé de Pensées Anti-Cléricales*, 2 vols, with an introduction by G. Garibaldi, Paris, 1879.

L. Taxil, *Les amours secrètes de Pie IX*, Paris, 1881.

L. Taxil, *La Bible amusante. Pour les grands et les petits enfants*, Paris, 1881.

L. Taxil, *La vie de Jésus*, Paris, 1882.

L. Taxil, *Un Pape femelle (Roman historique)*, Paris, 1882.

L. Taxil, *Calotte et Calotins. Histoire illustrée du clergé et des congregations*, vol. 1, Paris, 1885.

L. Taxil, *Révélations complètes sur la Franc-Maçonnerie*, vol. 1, *Les Frères Trois-Points*, Paris, 1885. 'Grotesque and hateful rituals', p. 4. For the figure of 1,060,005 Brothers in total, see p. 119. 'Do not laugh. Do not believe that Freemasonry is joking', p. 254.

L. Taxil, *Les soeurs maçonnes*, Paris, 1886.

L. Taxil, *Confessions d'un ex-libre penseur*, Paris, 1887. 'Inextricable labyrinth of evil', p. 8.

L. Taxil, *Les Assassinats maçonniques*, Paris, 1890.

L. Taxil, *Y a-t-il des femmes dans la Franc-Maçonnerie?*, Paris, 1891. 'The incarnation of Satanism, as if Lucifer's blood was flowing in her veins', p. 390.

L. Taxil, *Révélations complètes sur la Franc-Maçonnerie*, vol. 3, *Les Sœurs maçonnes*, Paris, 1895. 'French mothers! Lock up your daughters!', p. 9. 'Now that we have grasped the secret meaning in Masonic jargon', p. 110.

L. Taxil (writing as 'Dr Bataille'), *Le diable au XIXe siècle ou les mystères su spiritisme*, 2 vols, Paris, 1896. 'The devil has now turned himself into a bacteriologist', vol. 1, p. 543. 'The Arcula Mystica is nothing other than a diabolic telephone', vol. 1, p. 392. 'Stupefying credulity', vol. 1, p. 710.

L. Taxil (writing as 'Miss Diana Vaughan'), *Le 33e Crispi. Un Palladiste Homme d'État Démasqué*, Paris, 1896.

L. Taxil (writing as 'Miss Diana Vaughan'), *Mémoires d'une ex-Palladiste, parfaite Initiée, Indépendante*, Paris, 1895–97. 'The Great-Grandmother of the Antichrist', p. 284.

L. Taxil and K. Milo, *Les débauches d'un confesseur*, Paris, 1883.

L. Taxil and K. Milo, *Les Maîtresses du Pape. Roman historique anti-clérical*, Paris, 1884.

R. Tombs, *The Paris Commune 1871*, Harlow, 1999.

L'Univers, 'Léo Taxil', 14 July 1885 and 25 July 1885.

Vatican Council of 1870 on Infallibility, consulted on 25 November 2019 at http://traditionalcatholic.net/Tradition/Council/Vatican/Fourth_Session,_Chapter_4.html; 'Is possessed of that infallibility'.

E. Weber, *Satan Franc maçon. La mystification de Leo Taxil*, Paris, 1964. The classic account on which I have drawn heavily. It reproduces many key documents from the case, notably the speech in which Taxil exposed his hoax that gives a narrative of events.

E. Weber, 'Religion and Superstition in Nineteenth-Century France', *The Historical Journal*, 31 (2), 1988.

Chapter 10: Allahabad: Mother Lodges of the Empire

(With reference to Rudyard Kipling titles, note that in most cases I have consulted the Kipling Society's online edition of many of his works, which contains very useful notes. For example, 'The Mother Lodge' (http://www.kiplingsociety.co.uk/poems_

motherlodge.htm) and 'Cities and Thrones and Powers', http://www.kiplingsociety.co.uk/poems_cities.htm.)

Anon., *Resumé of the History of the District Grand Lodge of Barbados 1740–1936*, Bridgetown, Barbados, 1937.

Anon., 'Chronicle'. Brief account of Lodge Rising Star meeting in Bloemfontein, *AQC*, 14, 1901. 'We are pleased to note that not only were there many Boer Brothers', pp. 95–6.

S.R. Bakshi, *Indian Freedom Fighters: Struggle for Independence – Vol. 10: Motilal Nehru*, New Delhi, 1990.

S. Basu, *For King and Another Country: Indian Soldiers on the Western Front, 1914–18*, New Delhi, 2015.

C.A. Bayly, *The Local Roots of Indian Politics: Allahabad 1880–1920* (1975), in *The C.A. Bayly Omnibus*, Oxford, 2009. Three per cent of the population, p. 52. On the Masonic Lodge as one of the few integrated institutions, p. 56.

J. Beamish Saul, *Historical Sketch of the Lodge of Antiquity*, Montreal, 1912.

Lord Birkenhead, *Rudyard Kipling*, London, 1980. Such was Kipling's love of things Masonic and clubby that, while in Bloemfontein, he tried to get his fellow journalists to create a brotherhood with a rite rather like the Masons, pp. 209–10.

J.M. Brown, 'India', in in J. Brown and W.R. Louis (eds), *The Oxford History of the British Empire – Volume IV: The Twentieth Century*, Oxford, 1999.

Caribbean Disaster Emergency Response Agency (2005), 'NEMO remembers the great hurricane of 1780', consulted 1 August 2018 at https://web.archive.org/web/20131004223823/http://www.cdera.org/cunews/news/saint_lucia/article_1314.php.

G. Chakravarty, *The Indian Mutiny and the British Imagination*, Cambridge, 2005.

A. Conan Doyle, *Memories and Adventures* (1924), Oxford, 1989.

K.R. Cramp and G. Mackaness, *A History of the United Grand Lodge of Ancient, Free and Accepted Masons of New South Wales*, vol. 1, Sydney, NSW, 1938.

G.H. Cumming, *The Foundations of Freemasonry in Australia*, Sydney, NSW, 1992.

G.H. Cumming, *Freemasonry and the Emancipists in New South Wales*, Sydney, NSW, 2015.

S. Deschamps, *Franc-maconnerie et pouvoir colonial dans l'Inde britannique (1730–1921)*, PhD thesis, Université Bordeaux Montaigne, 2014. Umdat-ul-Umrah Bahadur, pp. 178–81. 'Our race differ[s] in every essential point from that of the Asiatic', quoted p. 374.

S. Deschamps, 'Freemasonry and the Indian Parsi Community: A Late Meeting on the Level', *Journal for Research into Freemasonry and Fraternalism*, 3 (1), 2012.

S. Deschamps, 'Looking to the East: Freemasonry and British Orientalism', *Journal for Research into Freemasonry and Fraternalism*, 5 (2), 2014.

S. Deschamps, 'From Britain to India: Freemasonry as a Connective Force of Empire', *E-rea*, 14 February 2017, consulted online 12 July 2018.

J. Fingard, 'Race and Respectability in Victorian Halifax', *The Journal of Imperial and Commonwealth History*, 20 (2), 1992.

J. Fingard, J. Guildford and D. Sutherland, *Halifax: The First 250 Years*, Halifax, NS, 1999.

W.K. Firminger, *The Early History of Freemasonry in Bengal and the Punjab*, Calcutta, 1906.

V.J. Fozdar, 'Constructing the "Brother": Freemasonry, Empire and Nationalism in India, 1840–1925', PhD thesis, University of California, Berkeley, 2001. Important work on Masonry in India, particularly Bombay. '*Jadughar*, or "magic-house" ... *bhutkhana*, or "demon-house"', p. 332. 'A Parsi, a Moslem draughtsman, a Sikh', p. 285. Between 1885 and 1907, 43 per cent of Congress presidents were Masons, p. 450.

V.J. Fozdar, 'Imperial brothers, imperial partners: Indian Freemasons, race, kinship, and networking in the British empire and beyond', in D. Ghosh and D. Kennedy (eds), *Decentring Empire: Britain, India, and the transcolonial world*, London, 2006.

V.J. Fozdar, '"That Grand Primeval and Fundamental Religion": The Transformation of Freemasonry into a British Imperial Cult', *Journal of World History*, 22 (3), 2011.

The Freemasons' Quarterly Review, 'Nova Scotia', 31 March 1854, p. 171.

P. Fussell, Jr, 'Irony, Freemasonry, and Humane Ethics in Kipling's "The Man Who Would be King"', *ELH*, 25 (3), 1958.

D. Gilmour, *The Long Recessional: The Imperial Life of Rudyard Kipling*, London, 2002. 'The dark places of the earth', quoted p. 126. For Kipling's various hates, see p. 212 and *passim*. Kipling on babus, p. 64. On the Andrew Hearsey episode, p. 73. Kipling as Laureate of Empire, pp. 119–24. 'Great War' and 'the Hun', p. 117.

D. Griffiths, *Fleet Street: Five Hundred Years of the Press*, London, 2006. On *Daily Mail* circulation, pp. 132–3.

I.H. Haarburger, '*Charity*': A Masonic Analysis. An address delivered in the Lodge Rising Star, no. 1022, at Bloemfontein, by W. Bro ... Ivan H. Haarburger and read in the Lodge 'Star of Africa', Jagersfontein, by W. Bro ... Chas. Palmer, on 18th April, 1900*, Jagersfontein, 1900.

I.H. Haarburger, *A Mourning Lodge Convened by the Rising Star Lodge no. 1,022, Bloemfontein*, Bloemfontein, 1901.

J.L. Harland-Jacobs, 'All in the Family: Freemasonry and the British Empire in the Mid-Nineteenth Century', *Journal of British Studies*, 2 (4), 2003.

J.L. Harland-Jacobs, *Builders of Empire: Freemasons and British Imperialism, 1717–1927*, Chapel Hill, NC, 2007. A ground-breaking survey of its subject. My section on Masonic events from Barbados, Sydney, etc. is meant to summarise her findings and draws partly on her work. 'Passport in all parts of the globe', quoted p. 246. 'The Society of Freemasons increases in numbers and prosperity' Proceedings of United Grand Lodge of England 7 September 1887, quoted p. 254. 'That unite the Dominions with the Mother Country', quoted p. 11.

J.B. Harrison, 'Allahabad: a sanitary history', in K. Ballhatchet and J. Harrison (eds), *The City in South Asia: Pre-modern and Modern*, London, 1980. 'A noisome ditch, with crawling fetid contents', sanitary report 1879, quoted p. 186. 'If the natives chose to live amidst such insanitary surroundings', p. 167.

W. Henley, *History of Lodge Australian Social Mother no. 1, 1820–1920*, Sydney, 1920.

R. Holland, 'The British Empire and the Great War, 1914–1918', in J. Brown and

W.R. Louis (eds), *The Oxford History of the British Empire – Volume IV: The Twentieth Century*, Oxford, 1999.

T. Hunt, *Ten Cities that Made an Empire*, London, 2014. See the chapter on Bridgetown for its colonial economy and society.

B.L. Huskins, *Public Celebrations in Victorian Saint John and Halifax*, PhD thesis, Dalhousie University, Halifax, NS, 1991.

A. Jackson, *The British Empire: A Very Short History*, Oxford, 2013. For figures on the extent of the British Empire, p. 5.

R. Jaffa, *Man and Mason: Rudyard Kipling*, Milton Keynes, 2011.

D. Judd and K. Surridge, *The Boer War: A History*, London, 2013.

H.G. Keene, *A hand-book for visitors to Lucknow: with preliminary notes on Allahabad and Cawnpore*, London, 1875.

G. Kendall, 'Freemasonry during the Anglo-Boer War 1899–2002', AQC, 97, 1984. Contains a misleading account of Masonic events in Bloemfontein during the war.

R. Kipling [writing as Anon.], 'A Study of the Congress', *The Pioneer*, 1 January 1889. In Sussex University Kipling Papers collection, Printed Material, 1. Press-Cuttings, a. Bound Volumes, 28/4, *Stories, Poems, Articles*, 1887–91.

R. Kipling, *Something of Myself: An Autobiography* (1937), London, 2007. 'Large-boned, mountainous, wooded', p. 75. 'Here I met Muslims, Hindus, Sikhs', p. 38.

R. Kipling, *The Complete Barrack-Room Ballads of Rudyard Kipling*, ed. C. Carrington, London, 1974.

R. Kumar and D.N. Panigrahi, *Selected Works of Motilal Nehru, vol. 1 (1899–1918)*, New Delhi, 1982.

R. Lethbridge, *The Golden Book of India*, London, 1893. On the Maharaja of Kapurthala, p. 233.

Library and Museum of Freemasonry, London, *English Freemasonry and the First World War*, Hersham, 2014. For numbers of English Constitution Lodges in 1914, pp. 10–11. For growth in membership after the war, and lifting of the ban on the disabled, pp. 93–4.

The London Gazette, 28 May 1886. For Sir John Edge's transfer, p. 2572.

R.S. Longley, *A Short History of Freemasonry in Nova Scotia*, Halifax, NS, 1966.

P. Longworth, *The Unending Vigil: A History of the Commonwealth War Graves Commission*, Barnsley, 2010. Canadian units digging own graves, p. 22. 'To keep alive the ideals for the maintenance and defence', quoted p. 28.

A. Lycett, *Rudyard Kipling*, London, 2015.

P. Mason, *Kipling: The Glass, the Shadow and the Fire*, London, 1975. 'Soul-cleansing routine', p. 25. 'To belong to an inner circle, with secret passwords', p. 84.

The Masonic Illustrated, July 1901. 'Thrill[s] the heart of every Craftsman', p. 214.

J. McBratney, 'India and Empire', in H.J. Booth (ed.), *The Cambridge Companion to Rudyard Kipling*, Cambridge, 2011.

B. Metcalf and T. Metcalf, *A Concise History of Modern India*, Cambridge, 2002. On Allahabad in this period, pp. 108–9.

R.J. Moore, 'Imperial India, 1858–1914', in A. Porter (ed.), *The Oxford History of the British Empire: Volume III: The Nineteenth Century*, Oxford, 1999.

M. Mukherjee, *India in the Shadows of Empire: A Legal and Political History, 1774–1950*, New Delhi, 2010. On vakils and lawyers in Congress, pp. 105–49.

B.R. Nanda, *The Nehrus: Motilal and Jawaharlal*, Bombay, 1962.

B.R. Nanda, *Motilal Nehru*, New Delhi, 1964.

T. Pakenham, *The Boer War*, London, 1979.

A. Pershad and P. Suri, *Motilal Nehru: A Short Political Biography*, Delhi, 1961. 'A people ripening into nationhood', quoted p. 17.

B. Phillips, 'Rudyard Kipling's war, Freemasonry and misogyny' in D. Owen and M.C. Pividori (eds), *Writings of Persuasion and Dissonance in the Great War: That Better Whiles May Follow Worse*, DQR Studies in Literature, vol. 61, 2016.

T. Pinney (ed), *The Letters of Rudyard Kipling*, vol. 2, *1890–99*, London, 1990. 'My affection for England', pp. 155–6. 'Naturally I believe there has been no civilizing experiment', p. 235.

T.H. Raddall, *Halifax: Warden of the North*, Toronto, 1948.

J. Ralph, *War's Brighter Side: The story of The Friend newspaper edited by the correspondents with Lord Roberts's Forces, March–April 1900*, London, 1901. Date Kipling left Bloemfontein, p. 258.

J. Ranston, *Masonic Jamaica and the Cayman Islands*, Kingston, Jamaica, 2017. The only possible objection to the conclusion that the Lodge of 'In the Interests of the Brethren' is all-white is that Kipling mentions that one of the Masons came from Jamaica. Ranston's research, and a conversation with the author, leads me to conclude that the picture in his mind is of a Jamaican Brother from among the white planters.

Rising Star Lodge no. 1,022, *Minutes of a Mourning Lodge held 31st January 1901 in Memory of her Late Most Gracious Majesty Queen Victoria*, Bloemfontein, 1901.

M. Roberts, *British Poets and Secret Societies*, London, 1986. On Kipling, pp. 102–25.

B. Russell, *Unpopular Essays*, Oxford 2009 (1950). 'The most refined religions are concerned', p. 105.

R. Sohrabji Sidhwa, *District Grand Lodge of Pakistan (1869–1969)*, Lahore, 1969.

'Solving the mystery of Rudyard Kipling's son', 18 January 2016, https://www.bbc.co.uk/news/magazine-35321716.

Statistical, Descriptive and Historical Account of the North-Western Provinces of India, vol. VIII, part II, *Allahabad*, Allahabad, 1884.

J. Summers, *Remembered: The History of the Commonwealth War Graves Commission*, London, 2007.

Thacker's Indian Directory, Calcutta, 1890, Part 1. For Lodge meeting days in Allahabad, p. 227.

United Indian Patriotic Association, *Pamphlets issued by the United Indian Patriotic Association no. 2, Showing the Seditious Character of the Indian National Congress*, Allahabad, 1888. Esp. 'The *Pioneer* on sedition', pp. 79–91.

G.E. Walker, '250 Years of Masonry in India', AQC, 92, 1979. 'They were not obligated to be present at the Initiation of a Turk', quoted p. 177.

F. Ware, *The Immortal Heritage: An Account of the Work and Policy of the Imperial War Graves Commission during Twenty Years, 1917–1937*, Cambridge, 1937.

K. Watson, *The Civilized Island: Barbados – A Social History 1750–1816*, Barbados, 1979.

L.H. Wienand, *The First Eighty-One Years: A Brief History of the Rising Star Lodge from 1864 to 1945*, Bloemfontein, 1955. Reproduces press reports and other documents I have drawn on for Bloemfontein Lodge meetings. 'They are eternal. In our day and generation', p. 50.

C.G. Wyndham Parker, *Thirty-Five Masters: The Story of the Builders of the Silent Cities Lodge*, London, 1962.

C. Wynne, *The Colonial Conan Doyle: British Imperialism, Irish Nationalism, and the Gothic*, London, 2002.

A.M. Zaidi and S. Zaidi (eds), *The Encyclopedia of Indian National Congress, vol. 1, 1885–1890, The Founding Fathers*, New Delhi, 1976. On Allahabad Congress, pp. 233ff.

Archival sources from the Museum and Library of Freemasonry, London

Letter of John Seed, Secretary of the Union Lodge, No. 362 [erased], Bridgetown, Barbados, 28 December 1795, GBR 1991 AR/1273/3. 'Labour in all brotherly love, for the future Welfare and Support'.

Copy of the minutes of the St John's Day Celebrations at the Union Lodge, No. 362, Bridgetown, Barbados, 28 December 1795, GBR 1991 AR/1273/4.

Freemason Membership Registers, 1751–1921, available on Ancestry.com. Analysed for various Indian Lodges, especially those of Kipling and Nehru.

Loyal Address from several Lodges in Bengal, India to Queen Victoria, 1887. GBR 1991 LA 1/2/179.

Chapter 11: Hamburg: *De Profundis*

F.J. Böttner, *Aus der Geschichte der Großen Loge von Hamburg 1914–1935: Cäsar Wolf zum Gedächtnis*, Bayreuth, 1988.

N. Cohn, *Warrant for Genocide*, London, 1996 (1967).

A. Di Fant, 'Stampa cattolica italiana e antisemitismo alla fine dell'Ottocento', in C. Brice and G. Miccoli (eds), *Le racines chrétiennes de l'antisémitisme politique (fin XIXe–XXe siècle)*, Collection de l'Ecole française de Rome, vol. 306, 2003.

R. Esposito, *Chiesa e Massoneria*, Fiesole, 1999. Repeats the Hamburg Grand Lodge story on p. 148.

R. Freke Gould, *A Concise History of Freemasonry*, London, 1904. For origins of German Masonry, pp. 455ff.

B. Hamann, *Hitler's Vienna: A Portrait of the Tyrant as a Young Man*, London, 2010. On Hitler as a reader of von List, pp. 206–16.

J. Holtorf, *Die verschwiegene Bruderschaft: Freimaurer-Logen: Legende und Wirklichkeit*, Munich, 1984.

J. Katz, *Jews and Freemasons in Europe, 1723–1939*, Cambridge, MA, 1970.

E. Levi, *Mozart and the Nazis: How the Third Reich Abused a Cultural Icon*, New Haven, CT, 2010.

J. MacPherson, 'The Magic Flute and Freemasonry', *University of Toronto Quarterly*, 76 (4), 2007.

G. Miccoli, 'Santa Sede, questione ebraica e antisemitismo fra Otto e Novecento', in C. Vivanti (ed.), *Gli ebrei in Italia*. vol. II. *Dall'emancipazione a oggi*, Turin, 1997.

G.L. Mosse, *The Crisis of German Ideology: Intellectual Origins of the Third Reich*, London, 1964. On von List, pp. 72–5.

G.L. Mosse, *Germans and Jews: The Right, the Left, and the Search for a 'Third Force' in Pre-Nazi Germany*, London, 1970. On *völkisch* ideology, pp. 8–26.

J. Rogalla von Bieberstein, 'The Story of the Jewish-Masonic Conspiracy, 1776–1945', *Patterns of Prejudice*, 11 (6), 1977.

K. Thomson, 'Mozart and Freemasonry', *Music & Letters*, 57 (1), 1976.

F. Venzi, *Massoneria e Fascismo*, Rome, 2008. Contains a version of the Hamburg Grand Lodge closure story on p. 23.

Chapter 12: Rome: Roasting the Bedraggled Chicken

Avanti!, 28 April 1914. Reproduces Mussolini's speech at Ancona.

C. Baldoli, 'L'ossimoro cremonese. Storia e memoria di una comunità fra Bissolati e Farinacci', *Italia Contemporanea*, June 1997. On Farinacci as Freemason.

R.J.B. Bosworth, *Mussolini's Italy: Life under the Dictatorship, 1915–1945*, London, 2005. For the battering in the parliamentary toilets, p. 173.

Camera dei Deputati, *Atti Parlamentari*, XXVII Legislatura del Regno d'Italia, 16 May 1925. 'Camorra', from a speech by Gioacchino Volpe, p. 3645. 'Parasitic intoxication', from a speech by Egilberto Martire, p. 3655. Gramsci's speech, pp. 3658–61.

F. Conti, 'Massoneria e sfera pubblica nell'Italia liberale, 1859–1914', in Cazzaniga (ed.), *Storia d'Italia. Annali, 21. La Massoneria*, Turin, 2006, esp. pp. 606–10.

F. Conti, *Storia della massoneria italiana. Dal Risorgimento al fascismo*, Bologna, 2006. On Lemmi's Grand Mastership, pp. 115–47. For an evaluation of the evidence about Masonic funding for the March on Rome, pp. 289–90. Destruction of Torrigiani's villa, p. 317.

F. Conti, 'From Universalism to Nationalism: Italian Freemasonry and the Great War', *Journal of Modern Italian Studies*, 20 (5), 2015.

Corriere della Sera, 17 May 1925; for the description of Gramsci as 'a little hunch-back'.

R. De Felice, *Mussolini il rivoluzionario 1883–1920*, Turin, 1965. For the context of the Ancona speech, see pp. 177–95.

M. Di Figlia, *Farinacci. Il radicalismo fascista al potere*, Rome, 2007; for Farinacci's career. On Farinacci as a Mason, pp. 98–9.

Fascio e compasso. RAI3 documentary, first shown in 2018, which cites Domizio Torrigiani's congratulatory telegram.

M.A. Finocchiaro, *Beyond Right and Left: Democratic Elitism in Mosca and Gramsci*, New Haven, CT, 1999. For an analysis of Gramsci's speech, pp. 179–200.

D. Forgacs, 'Gramsci Undisabled', *Modern Italy*, 21 (4), 2016.

A.M. Isastia, 'Massoneria e fascismo: la grande repressione', in Z. Ciuffoletti and S. Moravia (eds), *La Massoneria. La storia, gli uomini, le idee*, 2nd edn, 2004. On *squadrista* violence against Masons from 1923, pp. 202–3. On episodes where Masons loyal to one Grand Lodge used the violence as cover to get one over on their Brothers from a rival branch, see p. 235.

A. Lyttelton, *The Seizure of Power: Fascism in Italy, 1919–1929*, London, 1973. On the anti-Masonry campaign as an instrument against the bureaucracy, p. 177. Farinacci and Masonry, p. 281. On the violence in Florence, p. 282.

P. Mattera, *Storia del PSI, 1892–1994*, Rome, 2010. Reports of Mussolini's speech at Ancona cited on pp. 56–9.

A.A. Mola, *Storia della Massoneria dall'Unità alla Repubblica*, Milan, 1976. On Masons absenting themselves from the Chamber to make it inquorate, pp. 476ff. Farinacci, Masons should be 'shot *en masse*', quoted p. 503. On the reaction against Masons following the Zaniboni assassination attempt, pp. 509–10. 'Bedraggled chicken', quoted p. 513.

C. Palmieri, *Mussolini e la Massoneria*, Milan, 2017.

Rivista Massonica. The following issues document Fascist raids on Lodges: January 1924; September 1924; December 1924. The issue of September to October 1925 contains Torrigiani's order closing down all Lodges in Florence.

G. Salvemini, 'Il <<Non Mollare>>', in G. Salvemini, E. Rossi and P. Calamandrei, *Non Mollare (1925)*, Florence, 1955, for an account of the violence in Florence. 'Masonry must be destroyed', quoted p. 23.

G. Sircana, 'Farinacci, Roberto', in *Dizionario Biografico degli Italiani*, Rome, 1995.

La Stampa. The Turin newspaper looks back over its coverage of Freemasonry, and in particular of its 'electoral choreography', in the issue of 21 June 1896. For a report on the Freemasonry debate, which mentions Fascists listening attentively to Gramsci, and Gramsci leaning on a Fascist (Italo Balbo) to finish his speech, 17 May 1925.

G. Vannoni, *Massoneria, fascismo e Chiesa Cattolica*, Rome/Bari, 1979. On Farinacci supposedly being part of Masonic plot to replace Mussolini, pp. 234–41.

Chapter 13: Munich: The Beer-Hall strategy

I. Abrams, 'The multinational campaign for Carl von Ossietzky'. A paper presented at the International Conference on Peace Movements in National Societies, 1919–39, held in Stadtschlaining, Austria, 25–9 September 1991, consulted at http://www.irwinabrams.com/articles/ossietzky.html on 16/1/20: 'a trembling, deadly pale something …'

H. Arendt, *Eichmann in Jerusalem*, London, 1963. Arendt (pp. 28–9) mentions that Eichmann tried to join 'the Freemasons' Lodge Schlaraffia' in Austria early in 1932 before he joined the SS. However, Schlaraffia is not a Masonic organisation, and has more frivolous aims.

M. Berenbaum (ed.), *A Mosaic of Victims, Non-Jews Persecuted and Murdered by the Nazis*, New York, 1990.

D.L. Bergen, *War and Genocide: A Concise History of the Holocaust*, New York, 2003.

C. Campbell Thomas, *Compass, Square and Swastika: Freemasonry in the Third Reich*, PhD thesis, Texas A&M University, 2011. On Masonic informers, p. 76. On the 2,000 membership of Leopold Müffelmann's strand of Masonry, p. 48. 'Poster child of Masonic victimization and courageous resistance', p. 17.

R.J. Evans, *The Coming of the Third Reich*, London, 2003. Most writing by Freemasons on the Nazi repression lacks even a minimum understanding of the context. I have drawn mainly on Evans and Kershaw (below) to provide that context.

R.J. Evans, *The Third Reich in Power, 1933–1939: How the Nazis Won Over the Hearts and Minds of a Nation*, London, 2006. On Carl von Ossietzky, *passim*.

R.J. Evans, *The Third Reich at War: How the Nazis Led Germany from Conquest to Disaster*, London, 2008.

A. Hitler, *Mein Kampf*, translated by R. Manheim, London, 1992 (1943). On Freemasonry, p. 285.

A. Hitler, 'Rede Hitlers zur Neugründung der NSDAP am 27. Februar 1925 in München', downloaded 31 January 2019 from: http://www.kurt-bauer-geschichte. at/lehrveranstaltung_ws_08_09.htm. 'Either the enemy walks over our corpse', p. 6. On the importance of a single enemy, p. 7.

C. Hodapp, *Freemasons for Dummies*, Hoboken, NJ, 2013. The implausible claim of 200,000 Masons killed by the Nazis is on p. 85. It should be said that Hodapp is an engaging and fair-minded Masonic writer, and this introduction is recommended.

E. Howe, 'The Collapse of Freemasonry in Nazi Germany, 1933–5', *AQC*, 95, 1982. On sales of Ludendorff's book, p. 26. On the attacks on Lodges in Düsseldorf and Landsberg an der Warthe, pp. 29 and 32. Suicide of Walter Plessing, p. 33.

J. Katz, *Jews and Freemasons in Europe, 1723–1939*, Cambridge, MA, 1970. On *The Protocols*, pp. 180–94. On the proportion of Jews in German Lodges, pp. 189–90.

I. Kershaw, *Hitler: 1889–1936: Hubris*, London, 1998. On Hitler's speech at the Bürgerbräukeller in 1925, pp. 266–7. Hitler accuses Ludendorff of being a Mason, p. 269. On Hjalmar Schacht, p. 356 and *passim*.

I. Kershaw, *Hitler 1936–45: Nemesis*, London, 2000.

R.S. Levy (ed.), *Antisemitism: A Historical Encyclopedia of Prejudice and Persecution*, Santa Barbara, CA, 2005, vol. 2. Entry on *The Protocols of the Elders of Zion*, pp. 567–70.

E. Ludendorff, *Destruction of Freemasonry Through Revelation of Their Secrets* (trans. J. Elisabeth Koester), Los Angeles, 1977.

Masonic Encyclopedia, 'Österreich 1938–1945: 692 Freimaurer wurden Opfer des Nazi-Terrors', which summarises research on the Nazi repression of Masonry in Austria. https://freimaurer-wiki.de/index.php/%C3%96sterreich_1938-1945:_692_ Freimaurer_wurden_Opfer_des_Nazi-Terrors, consulted 12 February 2019.

R. Melzer, 'In the Eye of a Hurricane: German Freemasonry in the Weimar Republic and the Third Reich', *Totalitarian Movements and Political Religions*, 4 (2), 2003. For the number of Masons and Lodges in 1925, p. 114.

R. Melzer, *Between Conflict and Conformity: Freemasonry during the Weimar Republic and Third Reich*, Washington DC, 2014. By far the most systematic and authoritative study, which I have drawn on heavily for my interpretative framework and on many points of detail. May 1923, an Old Prussian Lodge invited Ludendorff, p. 85. Old Prussian Lodge in Regensburg adopted the Nazi swastika as its badge, p. 157. In 1926, two of the three Old Prussian Grand Lodges considered introducing 'Aryan' symbols, p. 81. Göring snubbed the Masons' emissary, pp. 99–100. 'Our German Order is *völkisch*', quoted pp. 95–6. In Hamelin Lodge, a Master appears in SS uniform, p. 177. Letter to Hitler offers assurance that the

Lodges would stay true to their 'national and Christian tradition', quoted p. 151. 'You damned pigs, I need to throw you and this Jew-band in a pot!', quoted p. 153. Lodges adopt swastika as symbol, p. 159. 'Grand National Lodge of Freemasons of Germany' becomes 'German Christian Order', p. 154. 'We are no longer Freemasons', quoted p. 156. Humanitarian Lodges Aryanised, pp. 162–72. Confusion and hesitancy in Nazi policy, pp. 188–91. On Adolf Eichmann, p. 188. Hamburg Grand Lodge only open to 'German men of Aryan descent', quoted p. 170. On Leopold Müffelmann, pp. 173–5.

S. Naftzger, '"Heil Ludendorff": Erich Ludendorff and Nazism, 1925–1937', PhD thesis, City University New York, 2002. On von Kemnitz, pp. 23–30 and *passim*.

R.M. Piazza, 'Ludendorff: The Totalitarian and *Völkisch* Politics of a Military Specialist', PhD thesis, Northwestern University, 1969.

L.L. Snyder, *Encyclopedia of the Third Reich*, London, 1976. For the SA and its numbers, p. 304.

R. Steigmann-Gall, *The Holy Reich: Nazi Conceptions of Christianity, 1919–1945*, Cambridge, 2003. On Ludendorff, pp. 87–91.

C. Thomas, 'Defining "Freemason": Compromise, Pragmatism, and German Lodge Members in the NSDAP', *German Studies Review*, 35 (3), 2012.

P. Viereck, *Metapolitics: The Roots of the Nazi Mind*, New York, 1961 (1941). On Mathilde von Kemnitz, p. 297.

Chapter 14: Salamanca: Hyenas and Concubines

G. Álvarez Chillida, *El Antisemitismo en España*, Madrid, 2002. 'One race's hatred, as transmitted through a skilfully managed organisation', quoted p. 320.

V.M Arbeloa Muru, 'La masonería y la legislación de la II República', *Revista Española de Derecho Canónico*, 37 (108), 1981. For Masons involved in drawing up the Republican constitution, p. 369. 'There has been no more perfectly Masonic political revolution', quoted from *Boletín Oficial del Supremo Consejo del Grado 33 para España y sus dependencias*, p. 374. 'The spectre of the Lodges', quoted p. 380.

J. Blazquez Miguel, *Introduccion a la historia de la Masonería española*, Madrid, 1989. Particularly for the late nineteenth-century membership figures and newspapers, pp. 92–105.

R. Carr, *Spain: 1808–1975*, 2nd edn, Oxford, 1982. On Masonry and the origins of 'culture war' in Spain, pp. 127–8.

J. de la Cueva, 'The assault on the city of Levites: Spain', in C. Clark and W. Kaiser (eds), *Culture Wars: Secular-Catholic Conflict in Nineteenth-Century Europe*, Cambridge, 2004.

J. Domínguez Arribas, *L'ennemi judéo-maçonnique dans la propagande franquiste (1936–1945)*, Paris, 2016. On the origins of Franco's anti-Masonry, pp. 93–118. See the brilliant pages on APIS, from which my account is drawn, pp. 119–45. On Tusquets, pp. 221–73.

J. Dronda Martínez, *Con Cristo o contra Cristo. Religión e movilización antir-republicana en Navarra (1931–1936)*, Villatuerta, 2013. 'We are governed by a small number of Freemasons', quoted p. 285.

J.A. Ferrer Benimeli, *Masonería española contemporánea. Vol. 2. Desde 1868 has nuestros días*, Madrid, 1980. The key starting point for this topic. For the widely cited early estimates for the number of Masonic victims of the Nationalist repression, pp. 144–50. 'The country is writhing in the anguish of a tragic agony', quoted p. 122. CEDA's leader as Minister of War moved to ban Masons in the military, pp. 287ff. 'Freemasonry shall not pass!', quoted p. 278. 'All of Spain is calling for exemplary and rapid punishment', quoted p. 143. Málaga, October 1937, eighty prisoners executed for being Masons, p. 146. On Franco's supposed attempts to become a Mason, pp. 169–70. Franco outlaws the Craft under his command in September 1936, 'crime of rebellion', 'could be judged offensive to the Church', pp. 140–1. 'Lucky Hitler!', Mauricio Karl, quoted p. 141. Card index system in Salamanca contains 80,000 suspected Brothers, estimate p. 157.

J.A. Ferrer Benimeli, *El contubernio judeo-masónico-comunista*, Madrid, 1982. Catholic youth movement manifesto 'declaring war' on Masonry, p. 274.

J.A. Ferrer Benimeli (ed.), *Masoneria, politica y sociedad*, vol. II, Zaragoza, 1989. In particular the following important essays: J.-C. Usó i Arnal, 'Nuoevas aportaciones sobre la repression de la masoncría Española tras la Guerra Civil'; J. Ortiz Villalba, 'La persecución contra la Masonería durante la Guerra Civil y la Post-guerra'; R. Gil Bracero and M.N. López Martínez, 'La repression anti-masónica en Granada durante la guerra civil y la postguerra'; F. Espinosa Maestre, 'La represión de la Masonería en la Provincia de Huelva (1936–1941)'.

N. Folch-Serra, 'Propaganda in Franco's time', *Bulletin of Spanish Studies*, 89 (7–8), 2012. Judges on the Special Tribunal nominated by the regime, p. 235. Continued use of Salamanca archive after 1964, pp. 234–7.

R.G. Jensen, 'Jose Millan-Astray and the Nationalist "Crusade" in Spain', *Journal of Contemporary History*, 27 (3), 1992.

F. Lannon, 'The Church's crusade against the Republic', in P. Preston (ed.), *Revolution and War in Spain 1931–1939*, London, 1984.

F. Lannon, *Privilege, Persecution, and Prophecy: The Catholic Church in Spain, 1875–1975*, Oxford, 1987. For figures of the number of clergy killed in the Civil War, p. 201.

F. Lannon, *The Spanish Civil War*, Oxford, 2002.

D. Manuel Palacio, 'Early Spanish Television and the Paradoxes of a Dictator General', *Historical Journal of Film, Radio and Television*, 25 (4), 2005; on the background to Franco's last speech.

P. Preston, 'Juan Tusquets: a Catalan contribution to the myth of the Jewish–Bolshevik–Masonic conspiracy', in A. Quiroga and M. Ángel del Arco (eds), *Right-Wing Spain in the Civil War Era*, London, 2012. 'Tusquets saw Freemasons everywhere', quoted p. 183.

P. Preston, *The Spanish Holocaust: Inquisition and Extermination in Twentieth-Century Spain*, London, 2012. 'Eliminate leftist elements', quoted on p. 133 from Mohammad Ibn Azzuz Hakim, *La Actitud de los moros ante el alzamiento: Marruecos 1936*, Málaga, 1997. Tusquets starts a fire to cause a distraction, pp. 35–7. On the birth of the Salamanca archive, pp. 487–90.

P. Preston, *Franco: A Biography*, London, 1993. On Franco's anti-Masonry, p. 4 and *passim*.

J. Ruiz, 'A Spanish Genocide? Reflections on the Francoist Repression after the Spanish

Civil War', *Contemporary European History*, 14 (2), 2005. All of Ruiz's writing on this topic is fundamental, and I have drawn on him heavily throughout this chapter, such as for the workings of the anti-Masonic tribunal.

J. Ruiz, *Franco's Justice: Repression in Madrid after the Spanish Civil War*, Oxford, 2005. Those found to have taken part in the 'red rebellion' were singled out for execution if they were suspected of being Masons, p. 200. Rotary Club and League for the Rights of Man as Masonic front organisations, p. 202.

J. Ruiz, 'Fighting the International Conspiracy: The Francoist Persecution of Freemasonry, 1936–1945', *Politics, Religion & Ideology*, 12 (2), 2011. This essay also contains a useful short history of Spanish Masonry. On the supposed Judeo-Masonic conspiracy in the school curriculum, 1939, p. 181. Seventy-six per cent of those brought before the Special Tribunal receive the minimum sentence, p. 191. 'Fusion within the Presidency of the United States of supreme executive power and the supreme Masonic powers', quoted p. 194. 'Daughter of evil', quoted p. 195.

H. Thomas, *The Spanish Civil War*, London, 2003 (1961). On Unamuno's speech, pp. 486–9. On the stripping and flogging of the parish priest in Torrijos, near Toledo, p. 260.

J. Treglown, *Franco's Crypt: Spanish Culture and Memory since 1936*, London, 2013. On the archive in Salamanca, pp. 57–84.

M. De Unamuno, *Epistolario inédito II (1915–1936)*, Madrid, 1991. 'Lately they've killed the Protestant pastor', pp. 353–5.

The archival documentation on the posthumous trials of Atilano Coco Martin are in the records of the Tribunal Especial para la Represión de la Masonería y el Comunismo in Ministerio de Educación, Cultura y Deporte – Centro Documental de la Memoria Histórica, Salamanca.

The images of Franco's final speech can be viewed at https://www.youtube.com/watch?v=qCpQocHBRFk, consulted 11 March 2019.

The video in the Salamanca museum explaining its context can be viewed at http://www.culturaydeporte.gob.es/cultura/areas/archivos/mc/archivos/cdmh/exposiciones-y-actividades/audiovisuales.html, consulted 16 May 2019.

Chapter 15: New York: A Golden American Century Closes

Anon., *Freemasonry among Men of Color in New York State*, New York, 1954.

J.L. Belton, 'The missing Master Mason', http://www.themasonictrowel.com/leadership/management/membership_files/the_missing_master_mason_by_belton.htm, consulted 30 May 2019. A useful analysis of the decline of American Masonry.

B.C. Cooper, '"They are nevertheless our Brethren": The Order of the Eastern Star and the Battle for Women's Leadership, 1874–1926', in P.P. Hinks and S. Kantrowitz (eds), *All Men Free and Brethren: Essays on the History of African American Freemasonry*, London, 2013.

M.A. Clawson, 'Masculinity, Consumption and the Transformation of Scottish Rite

Freemasonry in the Turn-of-the-century United States', *Gender & History*, 19 (1), 2007.

S. Cordery, 'Fraternal orders in the United States: a quest for protection and identity', in M. van der Linden (ed.), *Social Security Mutualism: The Comparative History of Mutual Benefit Societies*, Bern, 1996. Especially on the importance of fraternalism for new immigrants. On the need to band together to buy a burial ground as a prompt for African Americans, pp. 87–8.

V. Danacu, *Partial Study about 'the Occult': The Oppression of Freemasonry by the Security of the Communist Regime in Romania*, Bucharest, 2010.

R.V. Denslow, *Freemasonry in the Eastern Hemisphere*, Trenton, MO, 1954. On the double suicide of Masons in Hungary, p. 193. 'Meeting places of the enemies of the people's Communist republic', quoted p. 195. On Masonry in Communist China, pp. 312–23.

B. Elkin, 'Attempts to Revive Freemasonry in Russia', *The Slavonic and East European Review*, 44 (103), 1966.

The Empire State Mason, September–October 1964, 'Reports of our Masonic Center at the World's Fair'; November–December 1964, 'Our Masonic Brotherhood Center'; see January–February 1966, 'Our Masonic Brotherhood Center: It's gone … But is it?', for total number of visitors.

B. Friedan, *The Feminine Mystique*, New York, 1963. Drop in marriage age and education of women, p. 16.

Grand Lodge of F. & A. M. of Alabama, *Proceedings of the Grand Lodge of F. & A. M. of Alabama at the 147th Annual Communication*, 21–2 November 1967, Montgomery, Alabama. 'I feel that there is something very valuable in preserving the racial integrity', pp. 131–5.

C. Haffner, *The Craft in the East*, Hong Kong, 1977.

W.S. Harwood, 'Secret Societies in America', *The North American Review*, 164 (486), 1897.

C. Hodapp, *Solomon's Builders: Freemasons, Founding Fathers, and the Secrets of Washington DC*, Berkeley, CA, 2007. For an admirably patient take-down of the various conspiracy theories surrounding Masonic symbols on the Great Seal, in Washington DC, etc. etc., see chapter 8.

R.L. Huish, 'Made of Paper and Stone: The Place of José Martí in Cuban National Identity', MA thesis, Queen's University, Kingston, Ontario, 2003.

J. Huyghebaert and W.F. Parker, 'History of Freemasonry in the Czech Republic', 2010, available at https://u3h.webnode.cz/news/history-of-freemasonry-in-the-czech-republic/, consulted 29 May 2019.

R. Khambatta, 'The District Grand Lodge of the Punjab', *AQC*, 103, 1990.

L. Koppel, *The Astronaut Wives Club*, London, 2013. Gordon 'Gordo' Cooper and his wife, pp. 18–21. Cape Cookies, pp. 47–9.

J.M. Landau, 'Muslim Opposition to Freemasonry', *Die Welt des Islams*, 36 (2), 1996.

Life Magazine, 'The US Masons', 8 October 1956; 4 February 1957, 'Masons enjoy each other's company, sometimes find it useful in business', p. 25.

M. Mazzucato, *The Value of Everything: Making and Taking in the Global Economy*, London, 2018. On growth in the financial security industry, p. 143.

D. McCullough, *Truman*, New York, 1992. On his Masonry, see p. 78 and *passim*.

S.B. Morris, 'The Public Image of Freemasonry: A Survey of the Literature Describing

American Freemasonry', paper presented to The August Scene, 7 August 1982, Deep Creek Lake, Maryland. Kindly provided by the author.

S.B. Morris, 'Boom to Bust in the Twentieth Century: Freemasonry and American Fraternities', Anson Jones Lecture, Texas Lodge of Research, 19 March 1988. An insightful study of Masonry's declining numbers.

S.B. Morris, 'Masonic Membership Myths', *The Scottish Rite Journal*, 97 (11), 1990.

G. Moshinsky, *Behind the Masonic Curtain: The Soviet Attack on Masonry*, Denver, CO, 1986.

W.A. Muraskin, *Middle-Class Blacks in a White Society: Prince Hall Freemasonry in America*, Berkeley, CA, 1975. 'Is he a clean, right-living man, sober and industrious?', quoted p. 44. Prince Hall Brothers in *Who's Who in Colored America*, p. 56. On Prince Hall Masonry and Civil Rights, see chapters 10 and 11. Medgar Evers Memorial Award, pp. 234–5.

W.H. Murphy, 'A History of Freemasonry in Cuba', *Walter F. Meier Lodge of Research no. 281 Masonic Papers*, vol. 4, 1974.

The New Age Magazine, April 1964, LXXII, 4, 'Masonry only fraternity at 1964 World's Fair'; July 1964, LXXIII, 7, 'A Masonic image at the New York World's Fair'.

M. Novarino, 'Dalle "scominiche" dell'Internazionale Comunista alle repressioni in Unione Sovietica e nelle Repubbliche democratiche popolari', in M. Cuzzi et al. (eds), *Massoneria e totalitarismi nell'Europa tra le due guerre*, Milan, 2018.

M.J. O'Brien, *We Shall Not Be Moved: The Jackson Woolworth's Sit-In and the Movement it Inspired*, Jackson, MS, 2013; on Medgar Evers. 'Freedom has never been free', quoted p. 189. Evers' funeral, pp. 214–15.

J.T. Patterson, *Grand Expectations: The United States, 1945–1974*, Oxford, 1996. Important for the context of this whole period. For figures of those with origins in countries with a Catholic tradition of anti-Masonry, p. 15. Of the US population, 10.6 per cent (in 1960) is African American, p. 380; 95 per cent of African Americans were denied the vote in Mississippi, p. 413. For the Surgeon General's report on the dangers of smokng, see p. 445. 'Chocolate cities and vanilla suburbs', quoted by Patterson from Parliament, *Chocolate City*, title track of the 1975 album.

R.S Patterson and R. Dougall, *The Eagle and the Shield: A History of the Great Seal of the United States*, Washington DC, 1976. For the pyramid design on the Great Seal and then on the dollar bill, see pp. 402–7 and pp. 529–32.

N.V. Peale, 'What Masonry Means to Me', *The Short Talk Bulletin*, February 1973. (Text of a lecture given in 1970.) The quote is from p. 8.

Prince Hall Sentinel, 16 (3), 1963, 'Martyr to Freedom', with Evers' photo on front cover.

Prince Hall Grand Lodge, Jurisdiction of the State of Alabama, *97th Annual Communication*, Mobile, Alabama, 25–7 July 1967. 'Let me impress upon you my brothers', p. 46.

D. Richter, 'Fidel Castro & the Curious Case of Freemasonry in Cuba', http://www.thebohemianblog.com/2016/12/fidel-castro-the-curious-case-of-freemasonry-in-cuba.html, consulted 30 May 2019.

J.L. Romeu, 'Characteristics and Challenges of Cuban Freemasons in the Twentieth Century: A Demographic Approach', *Revista de Estudios Históricos de la Masonería*, 2015.

L.R. Samuel, *The End of the Innocence: The 1964–1965 New York World's Fair*, New York, 2007. 'The final gasp of American innocence', p. xviii. I have drawn heavily on this book for my account of the World's Fair and its troubles. 'A promotional orgy for American business', quoted p. 95. 'Whoosh and voom' and figures for visitors to the most popular attractions, p. 83.

T. Skocpol, A. Liazos, M. Ganz, *What a Mighty Power We Can Be: African American Fraternal Groups and the Struggle for Racial Equality*, Princeton, NJ, 2006. 'Next to the Negro church in importance, as affecting the social life of the people, are the secret orders', quoted p. 8.

A.C. Stevens, *The Cyclopaedia of Fraternities*, New York, 1899. 'Few who are well informed on the subject will deny', pp. v–vii, xv.

M.A. Tabbert, *American Freemasons: Three Centuries of Building Communities*, NY, 2005. One of the best examples of Masonic history written by a Mason, which is notable also for embracing both Prince Hall and mainstream traditions. I have drawn on it extensively for my account of the 'Golden Age' of fraternalism and the early twentieth century. Like Tabbert, historians generally use 'Golden Age of Fraternalism' to refer to the second half of the nineteenth century, but I have extended its use here for reasons set out in my narrative. Between 1865 and 1900, 235 brotherhoods founded, with six million members, p. 87. The Independent Order of Odd Fellows, pp. 87, 112. Knights of Columbus, p. 100. Shriners, pp. 127–31. Rotary Club, pp. 162–4. On the scale of new Grand Lodge buildings in the late nineteenth century, including the Philadelphia Masonic Temple, p. 135. On the importance of Masonry to an increasingly mobile population, p. 124. And on its importance for the growing business class, p. 166. Figures for the scale of Masonic Temples in St Louis and Detroit, p. 172.

N. Thompson, *Light this Candle: The Life and Times of Alan Shepard – America's First Spaceman*, New York, 2004. 'Man's greatest adventure', quoted p. 175. Marital break-ups among astronauts, p. 370.

Time Magazine, 'The World's Fair', 5 June 1964, 'A tacky, plastic, here-today-blown-tomorrow look', p. 46.

C.D.B. Walker, *A Noble Fight: African American Freemasonry and the Struggle for Democracy in America*, Chicago, IL, 2008.

J. Williams, *Eyes on the Prize: America's Civil Rights Years, 1954–1965*, New York, 1987. For Evers' Oldsmobile, p. 209.

T. Zarcone, *Le Croissant et le Compas. Islam et franc-maçonnerie de la fascination à la détestation*, Paris, 2015. For French reluctance to spread Masonry to the colonies, p. 64. Young Ottomans and Young Turks, pp. 71–81. President Sukarno banned Freemasonry in 1961, p. 112.

My figures for Masonic membership in the USA are from https://www.msana.com/msastats.asp, consulted 28 May 2019.

The permanent exhibition 'The Golden Age of Masonic Architecture' at the George Washington Masonic National Memorial, Alexandria, VA, is an invaluable resource on America's great Masonic temples. Visited 14 April 2019.

The documentation from the creation, building and running of the Masonic

Brotherhood Center, including its brochure, is all held in the archive of The Chancellor Robert R Livingston Masonic Library, 71 West 23rd Street, 14th floor, New York.

I have also consulted a great deal of documentation about the Masonic Brotherhood Center in the Museum of Freemasonry in London.

'Testimonial Dinner' in Washington DC, 1966, to mark Thurgood Marshall's appointment as a Thirty-third Degree Prince Hall Freemason. Programme for the evening kindly supplied to the author by Ken Collins.

Rosa Parks' Eastern Star documentation can be accessed online via the Library of Congress site: https://www.loc.gov/resource/mss85943.001520/?sp=1, viewed 24 May 2019. I would like to thank James R. Morgan III, a relative of Rosa Parks', for the information about her Masonic father in a personal communication.

Information on the Prince Hall Temple in Jackson: https://issuu.com/visitjacksonms/docs/2014_civilrightsdrivingtourweb, consulted 24 May 2019.

For the trials of Medgar Evers' assassin, https://caselaw.findlaw.com/ms-supreme-court/1046038.html, consulted 20 August 2019.

Chapter 16: Arezzo: The Man Who Would Be Puppet-Master

Camera dei Deputati / Senato della Repubblica, VIII Legislatura, *Commissione parlamentare d'inchiesta sul caso Sindona e sulle responsabilità politiche ad amministrative ad esso eventualmente connesse, Relazione conclusiva* (relatore G. Azzaro), 24 March 1982. Esp. pp. 60–75 and 161–78.

Camera dei Deputati / Senato della Repubblica, VIII Legislatura, *Commissione parlamentare d'inchiesta sulla Loggia massonica P2*. The vast and unwieldy documentation from the P2 Inquiry can be consulted here: http://www.fonti taliarepubblicana.it/DocTrace/. I consulted the following in particular from the above: *Relazione Anselmi*: http://www.fontitaliarepubblicana.it/documents/121-000-relazione-anselmi.html: '[The P2 story] is uniquely rich in ambivalence and in facts with a double meaning', p. 145. 'The threat of the Communist Party, in agreement with clericalism, which is close to conquering power', quoted pp. 16–17. The 'double pyramid', p. 154. On Gelli's past and the secret services, pp. 60ff. 'The threat of the Communist Party, in agreement with clericalism', quoted pp. 16–17. 'We can formulate all kinds of abstract hypotheses, and no conclusion is obviously absurd', p. 76. 'Injustices (if any) suffered during your career', quoted p. 53; Piano di Rinascita democratica: 09-leg-doc-xxiii-n-2-4quater-3-tomo-7-bis-ocr.pdf; A. Corona, 'Libro bianco sulla Loggia Massonica P2', in Allegati alla relazione, Serie II: Documentazione raccolta dalla Commissione, vol. VI Loggia P2 e Massoneria, Tomo XV, Rome, 1987; Audizione Rosseti: 09-leg-doc-xxiii-n-2-3ter-03-ocr.pdf; Auduzione Bozzo: http://www.fontitaliarepubblicana.it/documents/257-09-leg-doc-xxiii-n-2-4quater-3-tomo-3-ocr.html; Audizione Tassan: Din 09-leg-doc-xxiii-n-2-3ter-01-ocr.pdf p. 294.

G. Colombo, *Il vizio della memoria*, Milan. First-hand account by one of the magistrates who discovered the P2 documentation. 'He tried to say something to us, but for a good couple of minutes he couldn't articulate a single word', p. 58.

A. Comba, 'I volti della Massoneria nel secondo dopoguerra', in Z. Ciuffoletti and S. Moravia (eds), *La Massoneria. La storia, gli uomini, le idee*, 2nd edn, Milan, 2004.

F. Cordova, 'Ricostituzione della massoneria italiana e riconoscimenti internazionali (1943–48)', in Cazzaniga (ed.), *Storia d'Italia. Annali, 21. La Massoneria*, Turin, 2006.

Corriere della Sera, 5 October 1980, 'Il fascino discreto del potere nascosto. Parla, per la prima volta, il signor P2'. Maurizio Costanzo's famous interview of Licio Gelli.

Costituzione della Repubblica Italiana, articolo 18; https://www.mondadorieducation.it/media/contenuti/pagine/campus_economico_giuridico/02_discipl_giuridiche/2_biennio/10_costituzione_commentata/articoli/art18.html, consulted 19 June 2019.

M. della Campa, 'Da Garibaldi al dopo Gelli', in M. della Campa and G. Galli, *La Massoneria Italiana. Grande Oriente: più luce. Due opinioni a confronto*, Milan, 1998.

N.M. Di Luca, *La Massoneria. Storia, miti e riti*, Rome, 2000.

R. Fabiani, *I Massoni in Italia*, Rome, 1978. For details of Gelli's biography, pp. 8–12.

S. Flamigni, *Trame atlantiche. Storia della Loggia massonica segreta P2*, Milan, 1996.

G. Galli, *La venerabile trama. La vera storia di Licio Gelli e della P2*, Turin, 2007. The most convincing of the many scholars to devote their attention to P2: my conclusions follow his. The figures for money confiscated from Gelli are from loc. 1791 Kindle edition. 'For fifty years, in the shelter furnished by the struggle against Communism, people built dazzling political and economic careers', loc. 1228.

G. Gamberini, *Attualità della Massoneria. Contenti gli operai*, Ravenna, 1978. 'A political force, a power-centre, an ideological school', p. 11. 'False Brothers', p. 189. On women's 'different road'. On feminism, pp. 138–9. 'Masonic teaching exclusively addresses the individual', p. 182. For the disingenuous claim that P2 was now just a normal Masonic Lodge, see p. 252.

L. Magnolfi, *Networks di potere e mercati illeciti. Il caso della loggia massonica P2*, Soveria Mannelli, 1996. This is an extremely interesting account of P2's structure under Gelli, which I have drawn on here. For an analysis of P2 *raccomandazioni*, pp. 61–6. 'Only by turning to P2, that is to Mr Gelli, could he satisfy the numerous requests for solidarity', quoted p. 25. Gelli browbeats members into joining the Lodge, p. 54. '[Gelli] made me realize that he was able to acquire knowledge of anything', quoted p. 54. On P2 and the tax-dodging oil importation scheme, pp. 110–13. On Anna Bonomi, pp. 92–4. On Rizzoli, pp. 89ff.

F. Martelli, 'La Massoneria italiana nel periodo repubblicano (1948–2005)', in Cazzaniga (ed.), *Storia d'Italia. Annali, 21. La Massoneria*, Turin, 2006.

A.A. Mola, *Storia della Massoneria italiana. Dalle origini ai nostri giorni*, Milan, 2001. On Gelli thought to have circulated compromising documents on the Grand Master, pp. 749–51.

A.A. Mola, *Gelli e la P2. Fra cronaca e storia*, Foggia, 2008.

La Repubblica, 'Licio Gelli, al centro di innumerevoli casi giudiziari', 16 December

2015 (for a summary of the legal actions against Gelli); 'La P2 non cospirò contro lo Stato', 28 March 1996; 'Gelli e la P2, capitolo chiuso', 22 November 1996.

D. Speroni, *L'intrigo saudita. La strana storia della maxitangente Eni-Petromin*, Rome, 2015.

La Stampa, 'Gelli riacciuffato a due passi dalla Croisette', 11 September 1998 (on his escape and recapture in disguise); 'Gelli e la P2. Assoluzione definitiva', 22 November 1996 (on legal costs); '"Diffamò Montanelli" Gelli è condannato', 14 November 1992.

G. Turone, *Italia Occulta*, Milan, 2019. An important account of the P2 affair, which draws on documents such as first-hand accounts by *Finanzieri* of the search of Gelli's properties, by one of the magistrates who led the investigation; loc. 4027 Kindle edition.

'Pots of gold', BBC News online, 14 September 1998. http://news.bbc.co.uk/1/hi/world/europe/170679.stm, consulted 8/8/2019. On the gold discovered in Gelli's garden.

My calculations of Gelli's riches in today's values come from https://inflationhistory.com/, consulted 15 August 2019.

17 Legacies

G. Baldessarro, '"Affiliazioni irregolari e inquinamento malavitoso". E il Grande Oriente d'Italia sospende la loggia', *La Repubblica*, 17 November 2013.

C. Blank, 'For Freemasons, Is Banning Gays or Being Gay un-Masonic?', NPR, 22 March 2016, https://www.npr.org/2016/03/22/471414979/for-freemasons-is-banning-gays-or-being-gay-un-masonic?t=1580893580748, consulted 14 August 2019.

D. Brown, *The Lost Symbol*, New York, 2010. 'For the record, ma'am, the entire Masonic philosophy', p. 99.

A. Brown-Peroy, 'La franc-maçonnerie et la notion de secret dans l'Angleterre du XXe siècle', PhD thesis, University of Bordeaux Montaigne, 2016; for the whole Knight-Brotherhood affair in the UK. Number of expulsions rocketed from twelve, between 1934 and 1986, to 277, between 1987 and 1996, p. 289.

P. Calderwood, *Freemasonry and the Press in the Twentieth Century: A National Newspaper Study of England and Wales*, London, 2013.

M.W. Chapman, 'Pope Francis: "Masonic Lobbies ... This Is the Most Serious Problem for Me"', CNS News, 2 August 2013, https://www.cnsnews.com/news/article/pope-francis-masonic-lobbies-most-serious-problem-me, consulted 20 January 2020.

O. Chaumont, *D'un corps à l'autre*, Paris, 2013.

O. Chaumont and A. Pink, 'A Sister with Fifty Thousand Brothers', *Journal for Research into Freemasonry and Fraternalism*, 4 (1–2; single issue), 2013.

J.T. Chick, *The Curse of Baphomet*, Dubuque, IA, 1990.

Commissione parlamentare d'inchiesta sul fenomeno delle mafie e sulle altre associazioni criminali, anche straniere, 'Relazione sulle infiltrazioni di Cosa Nostra e della 'ndrangheta nella Massoneria in Sicilia e Calabria', relatore R. Bindi, 27 December 2017.

Congregation for the Doctrine of the Faith (J.A. Ratzinger), 'Declaration on Masonic Associations', 26 November 1983. Can be consulted at http://www.vatican.va/roman_curia/congregations/cfaith/documents/rc_con_cfaith_doc_19831126_declaration-masonic_en.html.

C. Cordova, *Gotha. Il legame indicibile tra 'ndrangheta, massoneria e servizi deviati*, Rome, 2019. An invaluable overview of the charges in the vast Gotha trial.

Il Dispaccio, 'Masso-'ndrangheta, parla l'ex Maestro Di Bernardo: "La situazione in Calabria mi spinse a dimettermi dal GOI"', http://ildispaccio.it/reggio-calabria/216683-masso-ndrangheta-parla-l-ex-maestro-di-bernardo-la-situazione-in-calabria-mi-spinse-a-dimettermi-dal-goi, consulted 12 September 2019.

F. Forgione, *Oltre la cupola, massoneria, mafia e politica*, Milan, 1994.

A. Heidle and J.A.M. Snoek (eds), *Women's Agency and Rituals in Mixed and Female Masonic Orders*, Leiden, 2008.

C. Hodapp, 'The Moon, the Masons, and Tranquility Lodge', 16 July 2019, http://freemasonsfordummies.blogspot.com/2019/07/the-moon-masons-and-tranquility-lodge.html, consulted 26 August 2019.

S. Knight, *The Brotherhood: The Secret World of the Freemasons*, with a new foreword by M. Short, London, 2007. Short's foreword contains biographical information on Knight.

G. Leazer, *Fundamentalism and Freemasonry: The Southern Baptist Investigation of the Fraternal Order*, New York, 1995.

L. Mahmud, 'The Name of Transparency: Gender, Terrorism, and Masonic Conspiracies in Italy', *Anthropological Quarterly*, 85 (4), 2012.

L. Mahmud, '"The world is a forest of symbols": Italian Freemasonry and the Practice of Discretion', *American Ethnologist*, 39 (2), 2012.

M. Maqdsi, 'Charter of the Islamic Resistance Movement (Hamas) of Palestine', *Journal of Palestine Studies*, 22 (4), 1993.

R. Mckeown, 'Mystery 200-year-old letter revealed World War 3 plans – and final battle against Islam', *Daily Star*, 7 March 2016.

R. McWilliams, 'Resting Places: A History of Australian Indigenous Ancestral Remains at Museum Victoria', downloaded from https://museumsvictoria.com.au/about-us/staff/robert-mcwilliams/, consulted 5 February 2020.

A.A. Mola, *Storia della massoneria in Italia. Dal 1717 al 2018: tre secoli di un ordine iniziatico*, Milano, 2018. For a review of recent Church positions on Masonry, pp. 643–50.

L. Musolino, 'Calabria, Grande Oriente chiude 3 logge massoniche: "Infiltrate dalla 'ndrangheta"', *Il Fatto Quotidiano*, 18 March 2015, https://www.ilfattoquotidiano.it/2015/03/18/musolino-logge-massoniche/1508927/, consulted 2 August 2019.

H. Richardson, 'Chilling letter written almost 150 years ago predicted both world wars and a THIRD battle against Islamic leaders', the *Sun*, 7 March 2016.

R.S. Sidhwa, *District Grand Lodge of Pakistan (1869–1969)*, Lahore, 1969.

M.A. Tabbert, *American Freemasons*, New York, 2005. On fundamentalist Christianity and Masonry, pp. 213–14.

Tribunale Ordinario di Roma, Sezione dei giudici per le indagini preliminari Ufficio 22, Decreto di archiviazione, 3 July 2000. (On the Cordova investigation into Freemasonry.)

Tribunale di Reggio Calabria, Sezione G.I.P.–G.U.P., Ordinanza su richiesta di applicazione di misure cautelari, De Stefano, Giorgio + 7, 12 July 2016 ('Inchiesta Mammasantissima').

Tribunale di Reggio Calabria, Processo Gotha. Rito abbreviato. Motivazioni della sentenza, 1 March 2018.

United Grand Lodge of England, 'Gender reassignment policy', https://www.ugle.org.uk/gender-reassignment-policy, consulted 25 August 2019.

T. Zarcone, *Le Croissant et le Compas. Islam et franc-maçonnerie de la fascination à la detestation*, Paris, 2015. On the fate of Masonry, and of Kipling's Mother Lodge, in Pakistan, p. 113. On Iran, p. 115.

I owe the phrase 'the mafia of the mediocre' to the BBC series *Line of Duty*, series 4 episode 4. Interestingly, the character who uses the phrase (Thandie Newton as Detective Chief Inspector Roz Huntley) is trying to defend herself against charges of corruption by hurling accusations back at her accusers. She turns out to be guilty. Transcript available here: https://subsaga.com/bbc/drama/line-of-duty/series-4/episode-4.html, consulted 20 January 2020.

TEXT PERMISSIONS

Every reasonable effort has been made to acknowledge the ownership of the copy-righted material included in this volume. Any errors that may have occurred are inadvertent, and will be corrected in subsequent editions provided notification is sent to the author. The author would like to thank the following for granting permission to quote from published sources, as follows:

Quatuor Coronati Lodge no. 2076 / QC Correspondence Circle Ltd for permission to use various quotes from S. Vatcher, 'John Coustos and the Portuguese Inquisition', *AQC*, 81, 1968.

Taylor & Francis for permission to quote from J.M. Burke, 'Freemasonry, Friendship and Noblewomen: The Role of the Secret Society in Bringing Enlightenment Thought to Pre-revolutionary Women Elites', *History of European Ideas*, 10 (3), pp. 283–93, (p. 289).

The National Trust for Places of Historic Interest or Natural Beauty for permission to quote from T. Pinney (ed.), *The Letters of Rudyard Kipling*, vol. 2, 1890–99, London, Cape, 1990.

Most Worshipful Prince Hall Grand Lodge F & AM of Alabama for permission to quote from Prince Hall Grand Lodge, Jurisdiction of the State of Alabama, 97th Annual Communication, Mobile, Alabama, 25–7 July 1967.

The Masonic Service Association for permission to quote from N.V. Peale, 'What Masonry Means to Me', *The Short Talk Bulletin*, February 1973.

Avv. Giorgio Assumma, in his capacity as legal representative of Dr Maurizio Costanzo, for permission to quote several passages from the interview with Licio Gelli in the *Corriere della Sera*, 5 October 1980.

© Giangiacomo Feltrinelli Editore, Milano, for permission to quote from G. Colombo, *Il vizio della memoria*, Milan, Feltrinelli, 1991. Prima edizione in 'Serie Bianca', novembre 1996. Prima edizione in 'Universale Economica', ottobre 1998.

Angelo Longo Editore for permission to quote from Giordano Gamberini, *Attualità della Massoneria. Contenti gli operai*, Ravenna, Longo, 1978.

Parliamentary information licensed under the Open Parliament Licence v3.0 for Jeremy Corbyn's speech in Parliament in June 1988, https://www.parliament.uk/site-information/copyright-parliament/open-parliament-licence/.

The Koori Mail for permission to quote from an interview with a member of the Victoria Museum's Indigenous Advisory Committee, in the article 'Remains "are not trophies"', *Koori Mail*, 13 November 2002.

For the speech about 'racial integrity' by the Grand Orator of the Grand Lodge of Alabama at the 1967 Annual Communication, I requested permission to quote some sentences from the speech verbatim, but the Grand Lodge of Alabama refused. The speech can be found on pp. 131–5 of Proceedings of the Grand Lodge of F. & A. M. of Alabama at the 147th Annual Communication, 21–2 November 1967, Montgomery, Alabama.

PICTURE PERMISSIONS

479

Index

481

Poppy Berry

John Dickie is professor of Italian Studies at University College, London. His book, *Cosa Nostra: A History of the Sicilian Mafia*, is an international bestseller, with over 20 translations, and won the CWA Dagger Award for nonfiction. Since then he has published *Delizia! The Epic History of the Italians and their Food* (2007)—now a six-part TV series for History Channel Italia and other networks worldwide. In 2005 the president of the Italian Republic appointed him a Commendatore dell'Ordine della Stella della Solidarietà Italiana. He lives in London.

PublicAffairs is a publishing house founded in 1997. It is a tribute to the standards, values, and flair of three persons who have served as mentors to countless reporters, writers, editors, and book people of all kinds, including me.

I. F. STONE, proprietor of *I. F. Stone's Weekly*, combined a commitment to the First Amendment with entrepreneurial zeal and reporting skill and became one of the great independent journalists in American history. At the age of eighty, Izzy published *The Trial of Socrates*, which was a national bestseller. He wrote the book after he taught himself ancient Greek.

BENJAMIN C. BRADLEE was for nearly thirty years the charismatic editorial leader of *The Washington Post*. It was Ben who gave the *Post* the range and courage to pursue such historic issues as Watergate. He supported his reporters with a tenacity that made them fearless and it is no accident that so many became authors of influential, best-selling books.

ROBERT L. BERNSTEIN, the chief executive of Random House for more than a quarter century, guided one of the nation's premier publishing houses. Bob was personally responsible for many books of political dissent and argument that challenged tyranny around the globe. He is also the founder and longtime chair of Human Rights Watch, one of the most respected human rights organizations in the world.

·   ·   ·

For fifty years, the banner of Public Affairs Press was carried by its owner Morris B. Schnapper, who published Gandhi, Nasser, Toynbee, Truman, and about 1,500 other authors. In 1983, Schnapper was described by *The Washington Post* as "a redoubtable gadfly." His legacy will endure in the books to come.

Peter Osnos, *Founder*